ART
in a
BOX

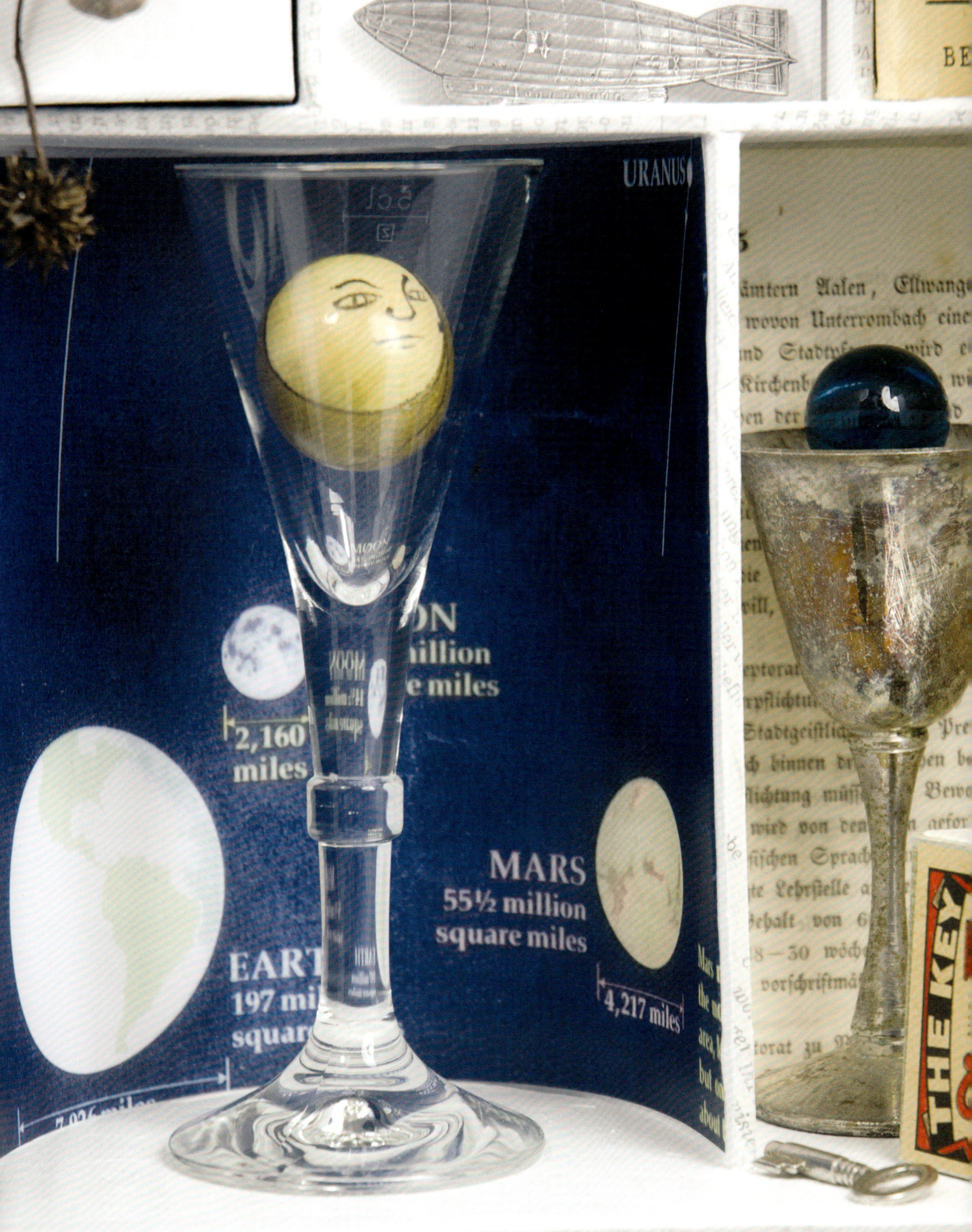
URANUS
2,160 miles
MARS
55½ million
square miles
4,217 miles
THE KEY

Marlis Maehrle

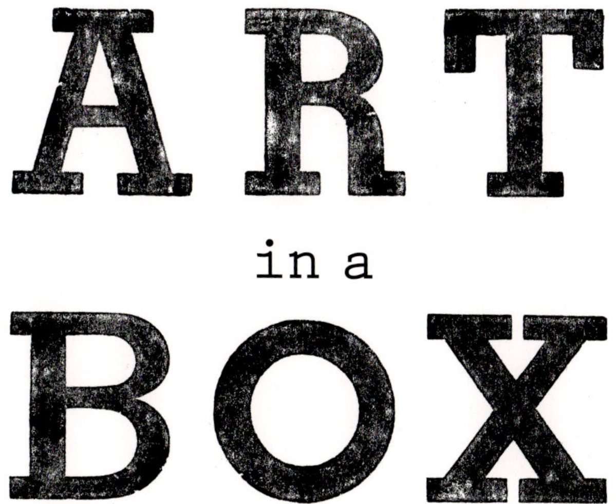

ART in a BOX

30 Creative Projects in Mixed-Media Assemblage

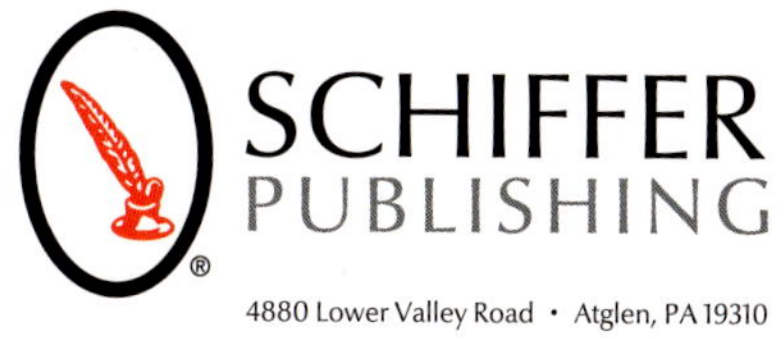

SCHIFFER PUBLISHING
4880 Lower Valley Road • Atglen, PA 19310

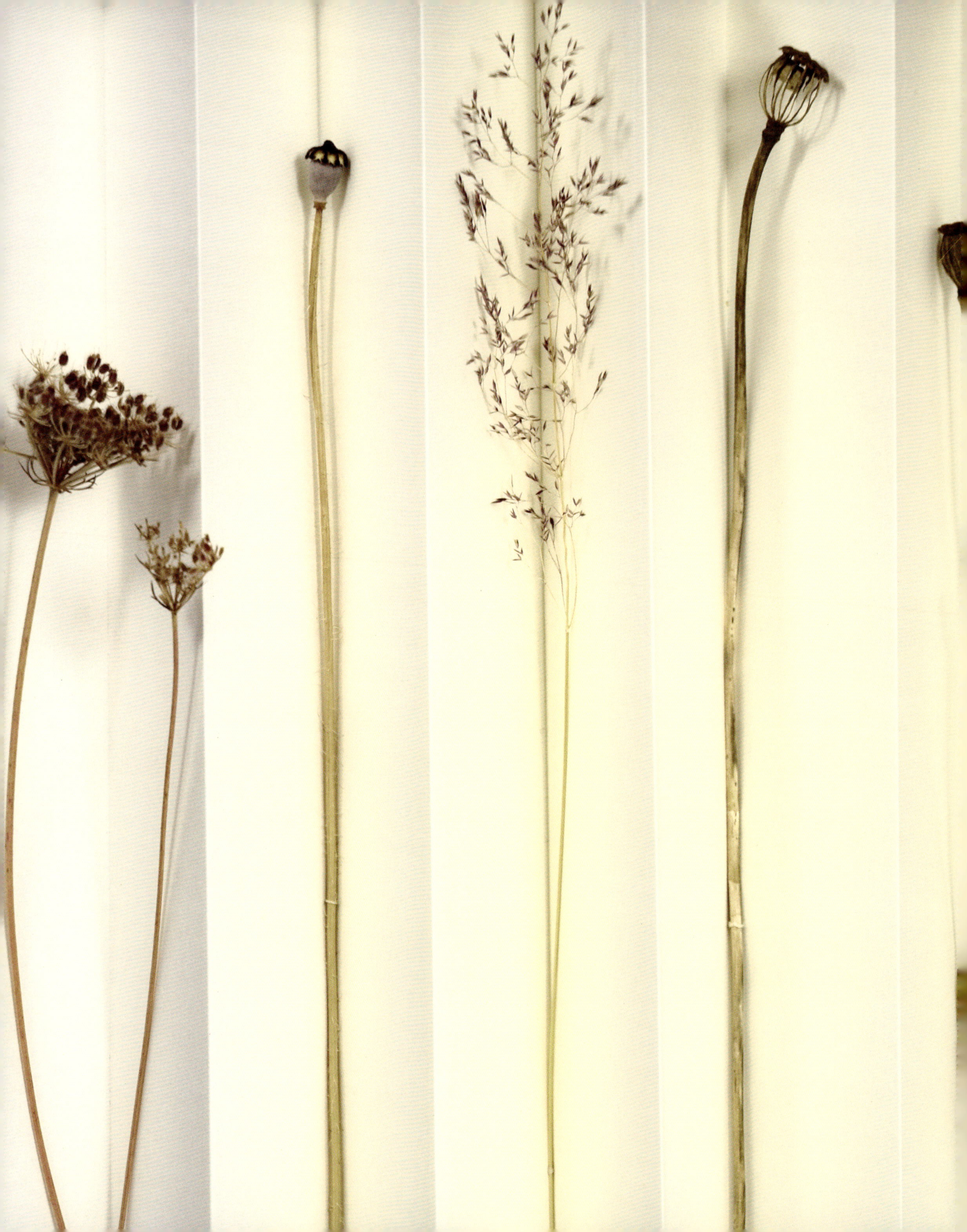

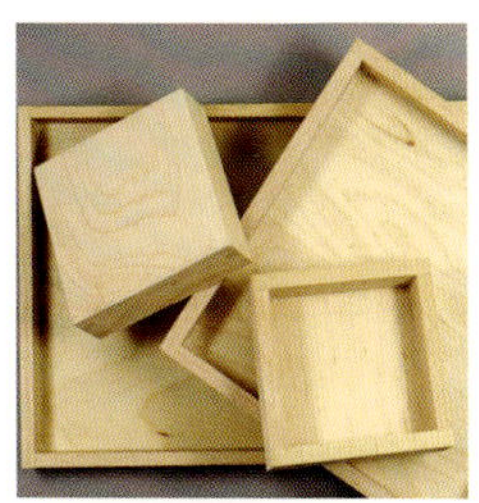

Contents

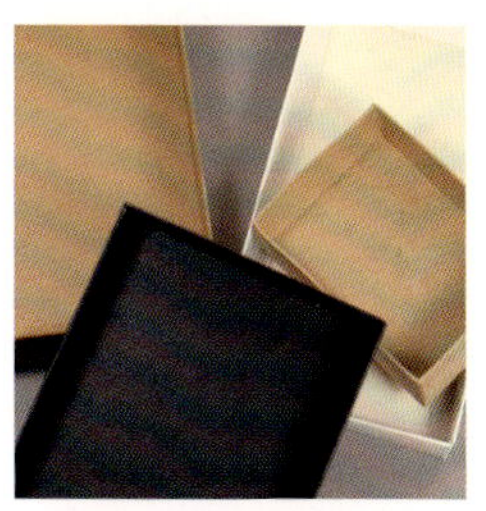

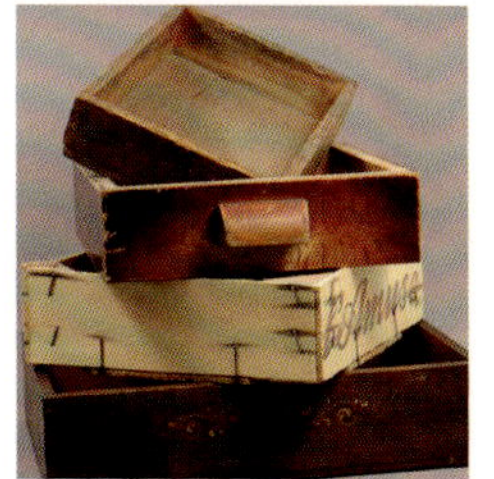

Instructions & Suggestions

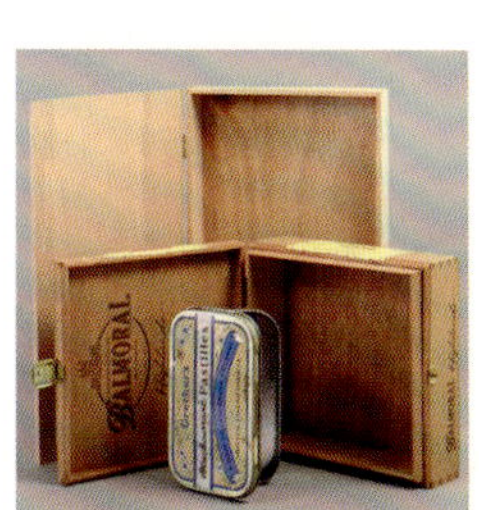

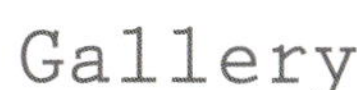

Gallery

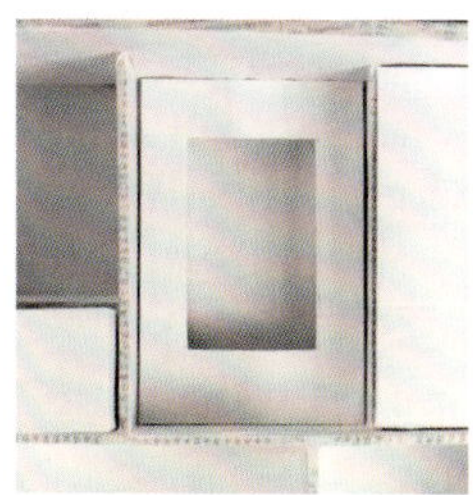

Welcome to the World of Small Things

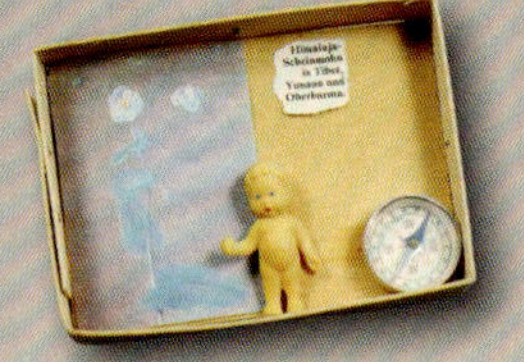

Early works

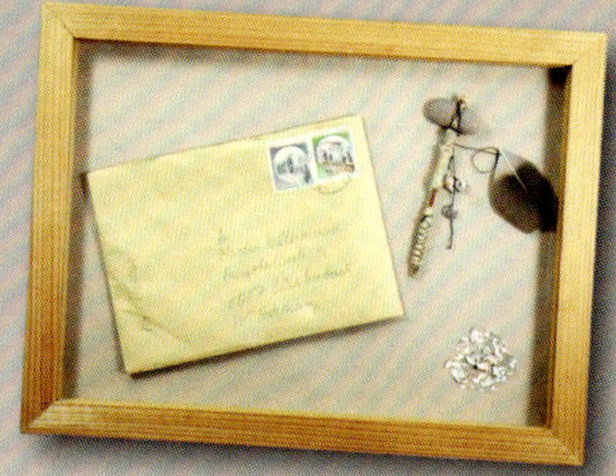

and the discovery of magic.

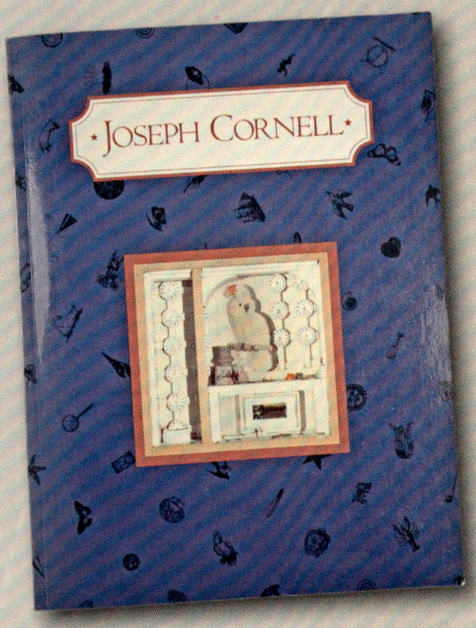

Shadow box, 3-D collage, miniature installation, memento house, peep box, assemblage, collector's box, cabinet of curiosities, rarities cabinet . . . all these terms are used to describe a fascinating world and a wide variety of expressions—a variety that the phrase "art in a box" only inadequately encapsulates. That's because this world includes so much that is unexpected, beginning with the containing drawer, carton, or memory corner itself. The overall "art in a box" image is fascinating because of the arrangement of things and the stories they tell.

That can also be said of the "cabinet of curiosities," or Wunderkammer, which originated in the 16th century in Europe. Not only do the things that were collected and displayed there tell a story, but so do the selection and arrangement, which give you a sense of mixed curiosity, longing, and romantic illusions, thus expressing very human needs. That's the core reason that the "art in a box" theme still remains contemporary and very much alive.

Even as a teenager, I built (and mostly gave away) boxes that gathered together small things about specific themes or occasions. During the 1980s, a Joseph Cornell exhibition catalog from the Museum of Modern Art in New York fell into my hands in an antique shop. Stunned and delighted, I carried the book home—and found a (small box) world strangely familiar to me, of magic and surreal romanticism, for which Cornell, who was relatively unknown in Europe at the time, has now received much more recognition. He was the pioneer for many, master of the philosophical game of poetic quotations, of longing for distant places and other times—an independent explorer of mysterious, invisible connections beyond the artistic conventions.

Encouragement from Joseph Cornell's work still supports me today. The way in which he pursued his own very personal themes over decades—from astronomy to ballet, birds, Medici portraits, opera, and Hollywood starlets to natural history—and transformed them into mysterious worlds is an invitation for you to likewise venture beyond the decorative in your own unique way. Antique boxes with antique contents are always effective eye-catchers, of course. But anyone who doesn't have the New York junk shops of the 1930s available instead focuses on his or her own collections and sharpens his or her eye for poetic objects—or the oddity value of everyday things, once they've been taken out of their usual context.

The main point of this book of instructions isn't to invite you to merely rework any of the projects. Instead, it's to inspire you to discover personal finds and individual design themes.

The techniques and design patterns presented here serve as suggestions for transforming whatever may be available into your own box designs. Likewise, it goes without saying that the personal memorabilia you see in these projects can't be used as materials for your work. However, you'll notice that the objects shown in the sample designs are included in the materials lists for the purpose of illustration.

The voyage of discovery next leads you to a wide assortment of projects, from simple examples for arranging, organizing, and mounting, through designs with sophisticated paper structures, to constructing the housing boxes yourself.

For further inspiration, a whole range of very different works are collected into an extensive gallery. That I have found so many box enthusiasts just in my network alone, whom I was able to invite to take part, already shows how widespread this joy in collecting and in small, sheltered spaces is. Also, the statements from artists on personal box philosophy will certainly seem relevant to many.

I hope that all who work with this book will get as much enjoyment from it as I've had in creating it, and I hope the gallery will offer you suggestions that express the definition of the poet Octavio Paz, who described the boxes by his wife, Marie José Paz, in the following words:

"Marie José's structures and boxes are three-dimensional objects, transformed by virtue of her fantasy and sensitivity into visual ideas, mental puzzles that sometimes transport bizarre, disturbing images; sometimes ironic reflections. These are less objects to look at as wings for traveling, sails for roaming and wandering away, mirrors to step through."

Marlis Maehrle

"Unintentional boxes"

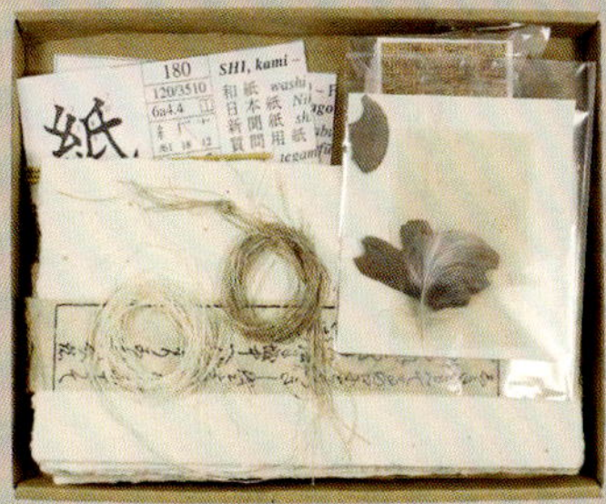

that fell into my hands

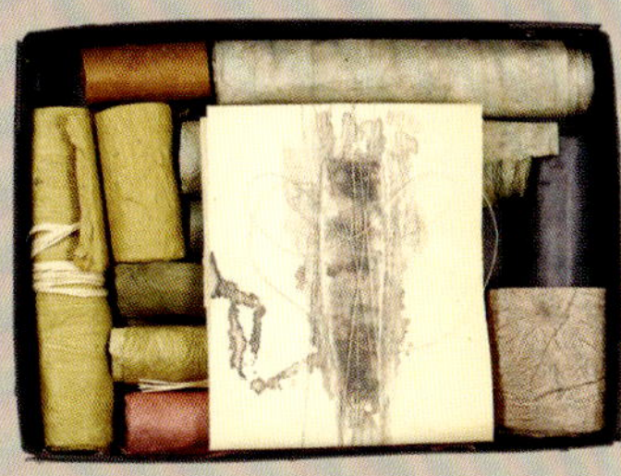

when moving my studio.

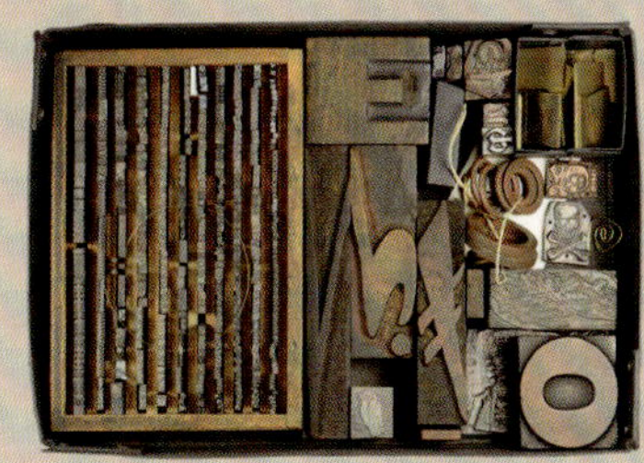

Tools

Pricking awl from a hardware store
Cutting ruler with metal edge
Drawing triangle for drawing 90° angles and parallel lines
Felt for underlay
Graphic cutter or scalpel for finer cutting
Fine bookbinder's awl with exchangeable tip
Large cutter for paperboard, cutting mat
Scissors
Needles in various sizes and strengths
Hole puncher from a bookbinding supplier with interchangeable inserts for various hole sizes
Small hammer
Small hacksaw
Small wire cutters (side cutters) for trimming ends and a pair of bending pliers
Simple punching tool from the hardware store

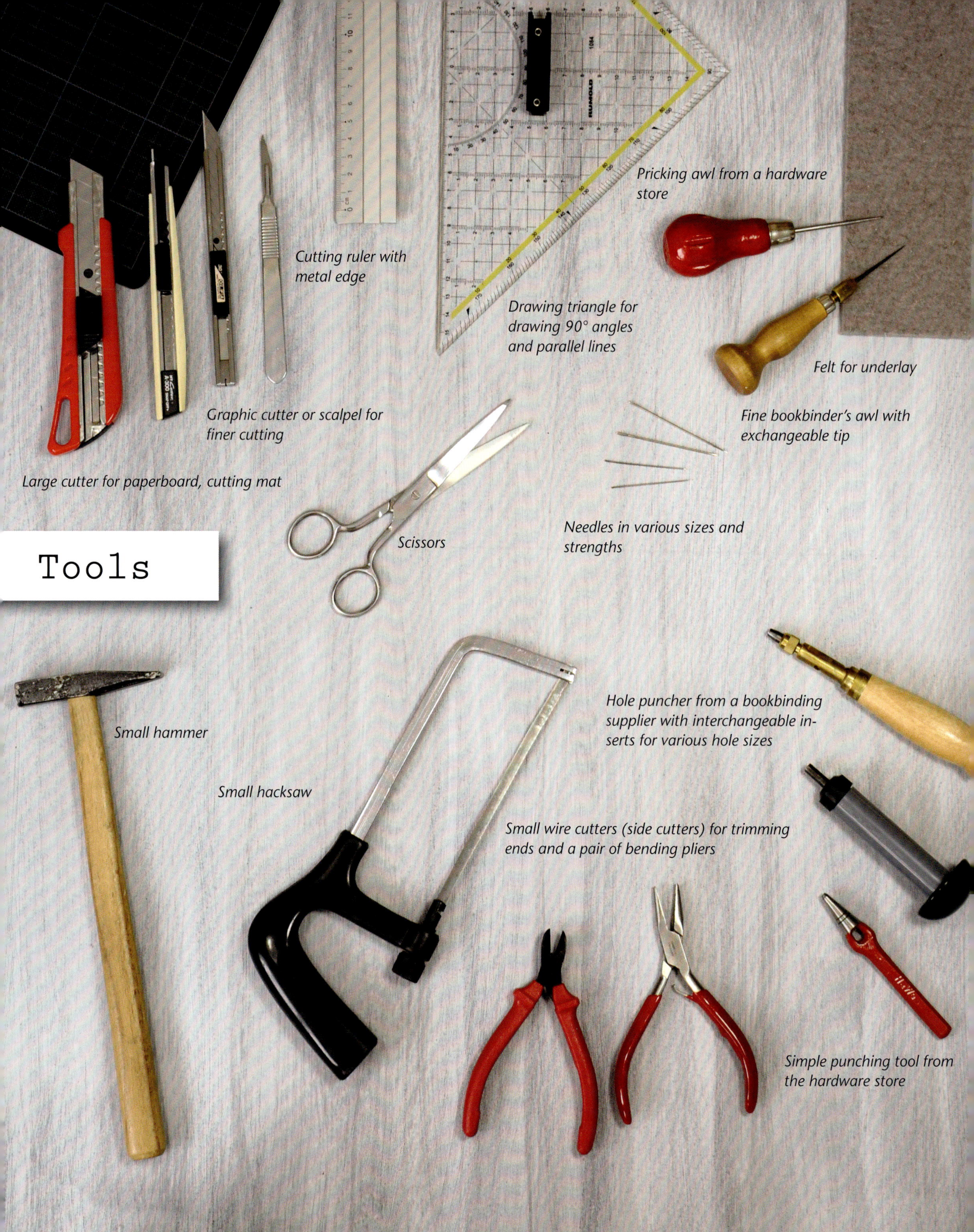

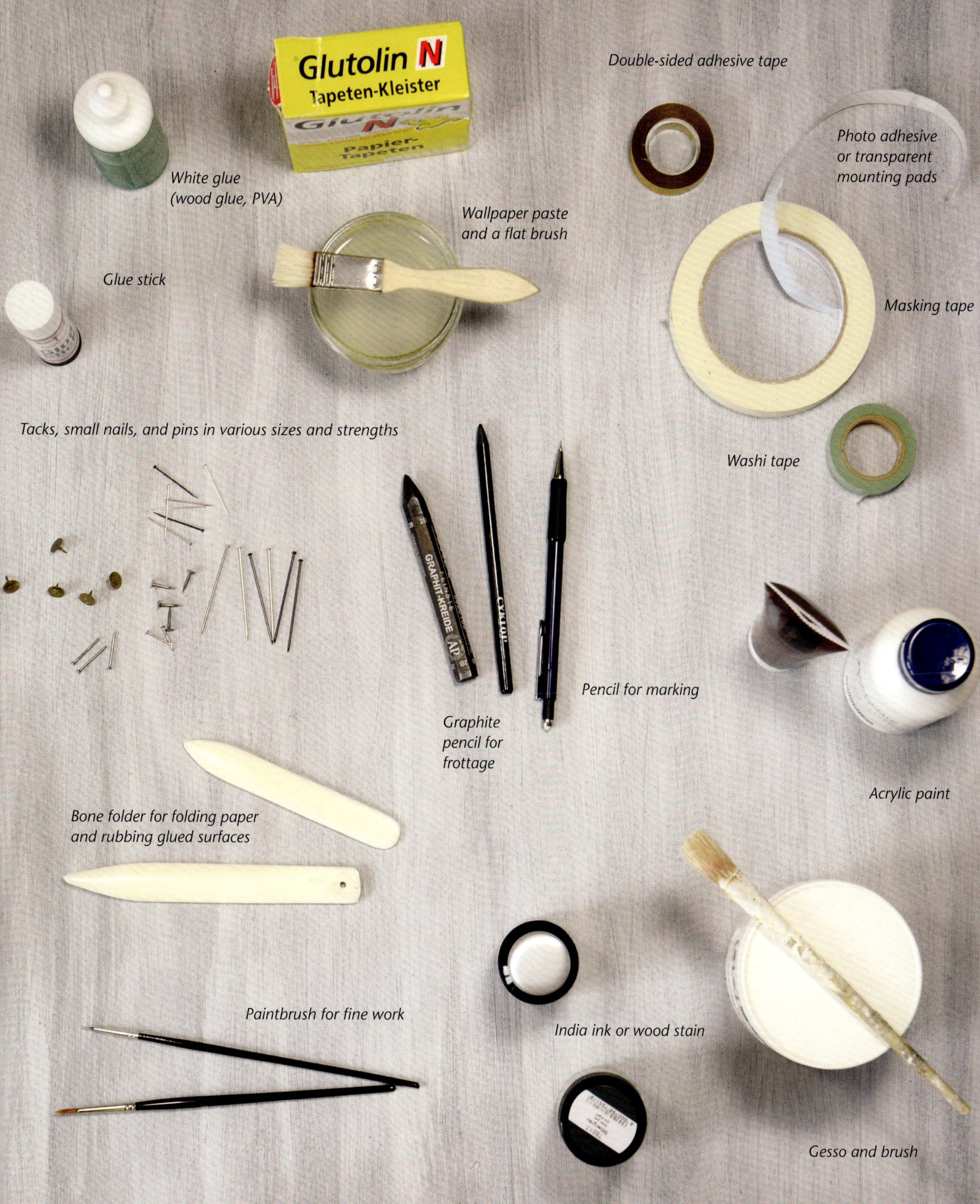
Glutolin N
Tapeten-Kleister
Papier-Tapeten
White glue
(wood glue, PVA)
Double-sided adhesive tape
Photo adhesive
or transparent
mounting pads
Wallpaper paste
and a flat brush
Glue stick
Masking tape
Tacks, small nails, and pins in various sizes and strengths
Washi tape
GRAPHIT-KREIDE
Pencil for marking
Graphite
pencil for
frottage
Acrylic paint
Bone folder for folding paper
and rubbing glued surfaces
Paintbrush for fine work
India ink or wood stain
Gesso and brush

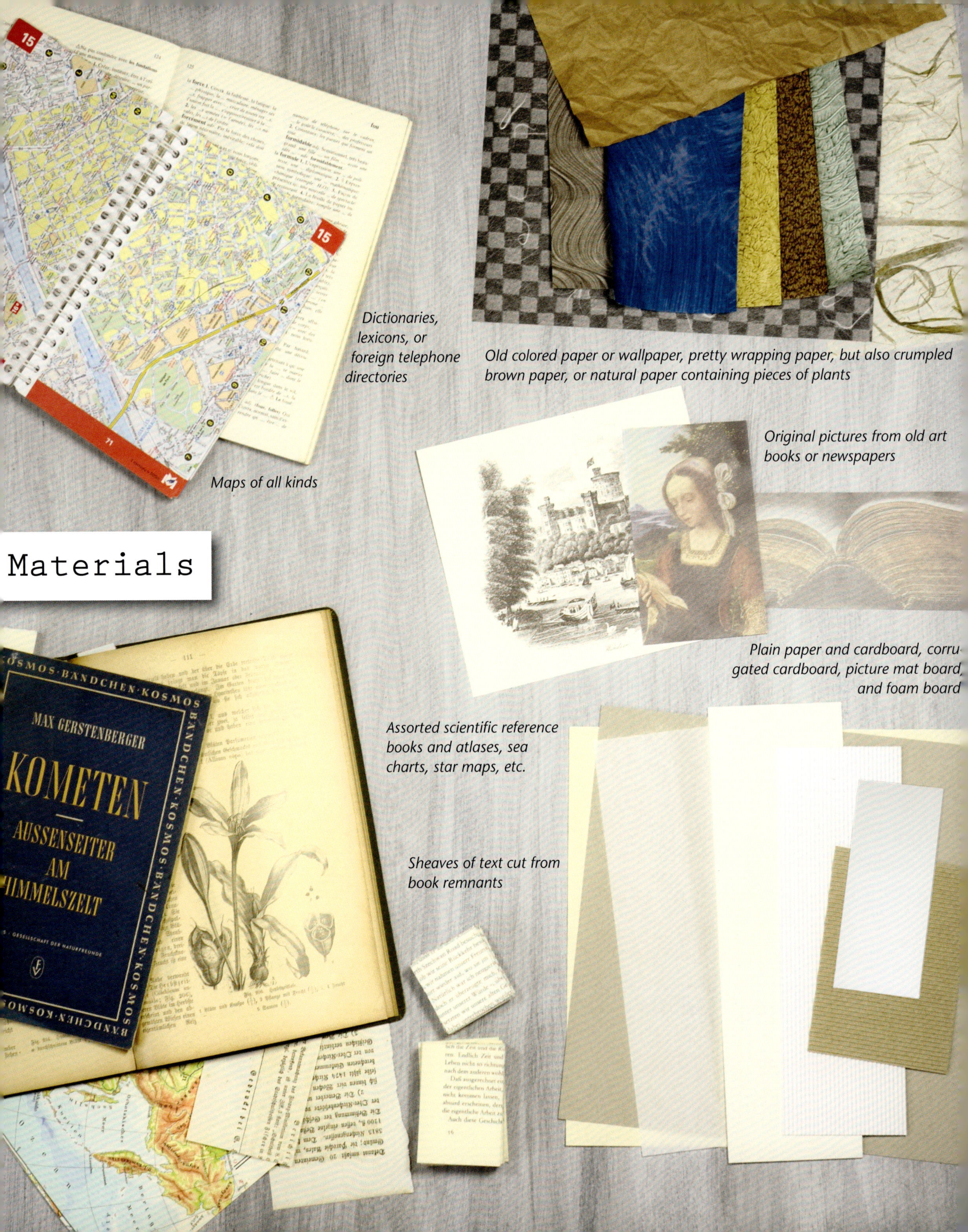

Materials

Maps of all kinds

Dictionaries, lexicons, or foreign telephone directories

Old colored paper or wallpaper, pretty wrapping paper, but also crumpled brown paper, or natural paper containing pieces of plants

Original pictures from old art books or newspapers

Plain paper and cardboard, corrugated cardboard, picture mat board, and foam board

Assorted scientific reference books and atlases, sea charts, star maps, etc.

Sheaves of text cut from book remnants

Old photos from the flea market or (historical) family photos

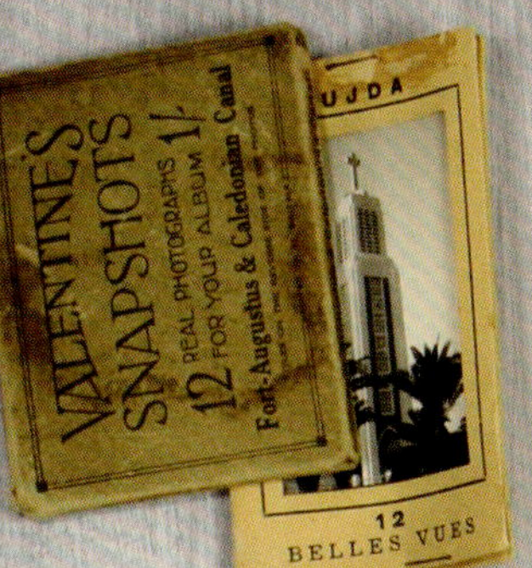

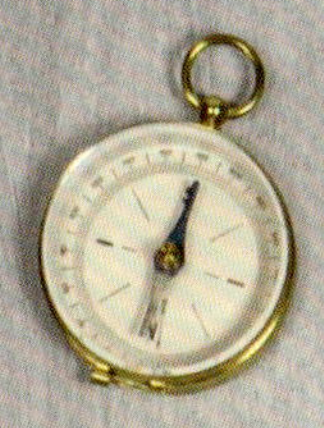

Toy compass or old watch

Model figures

Building blocks and other pieces of wood for miniature pedestals

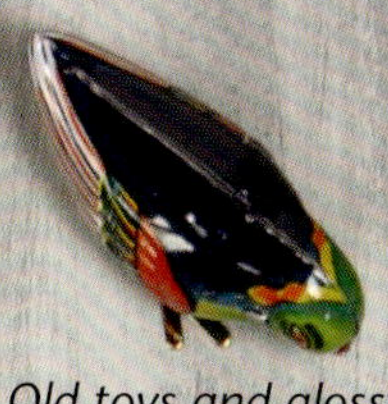

Old toys and glossy prints

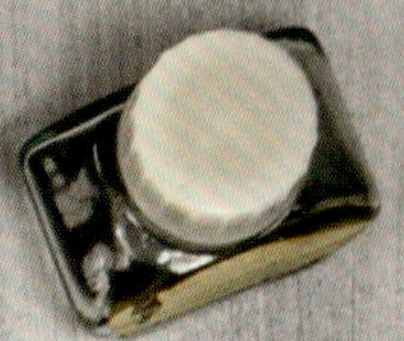

Old ink bottles, small containers, etc.

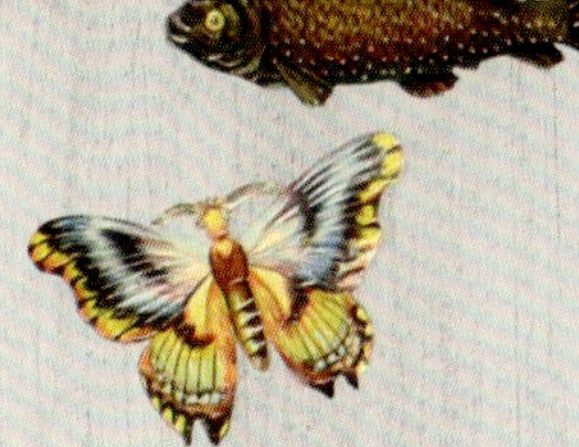

Glass marbles

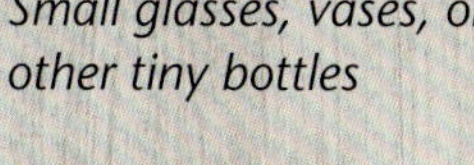

Small glasses, vases, or other tiny bottles

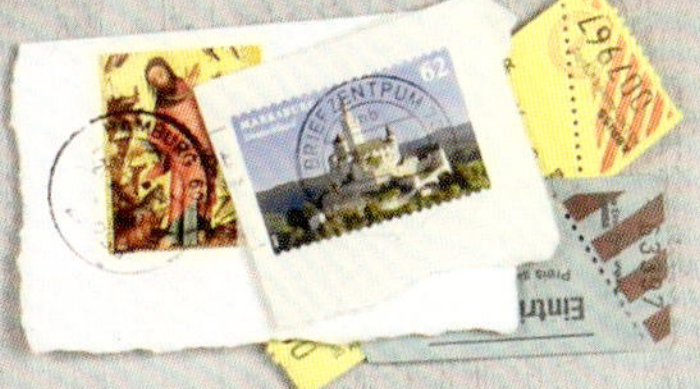

Stamps, tickets, and movie tickets

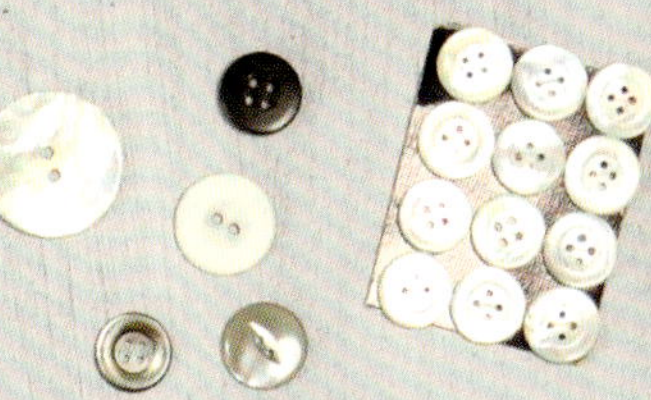

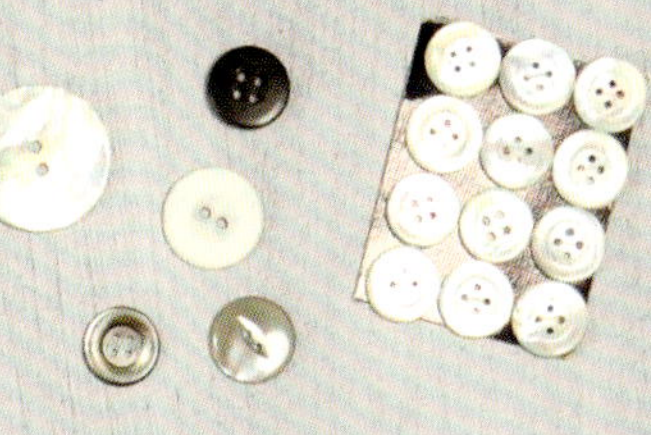

Everything from your sewing box: buttons, spools, thimbles, measuring tapes, etc.

Feathers

Modern plastic containers for cosmetic samples or travel-size

All kinds of sticks: twigs, iron wire, small paper rolls . . .

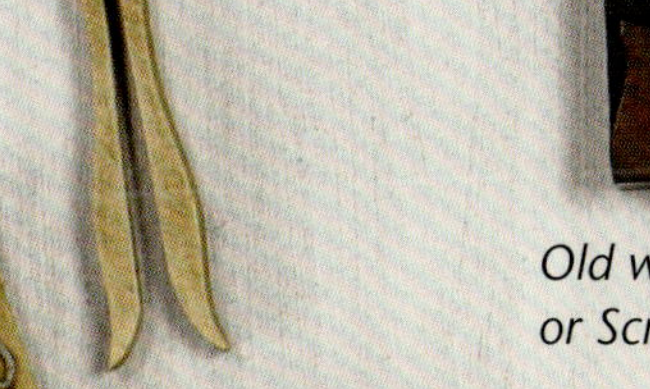

Old wooden letters or Scrabble letters

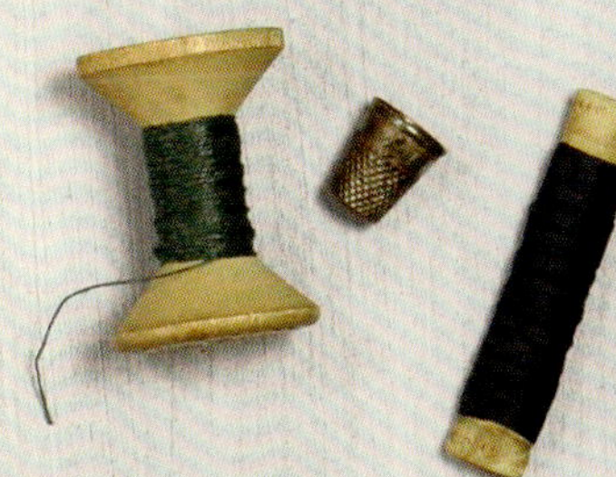

Beach finds: stones, shells, driftwood, and sea glass

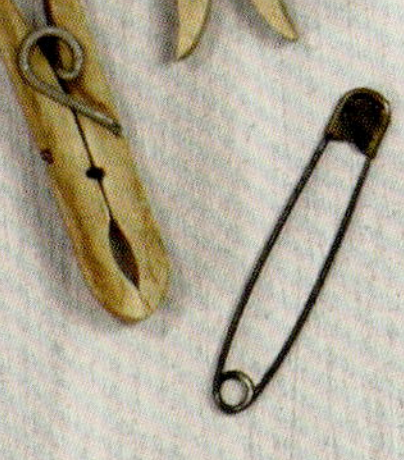

Old clothespins, safety pins

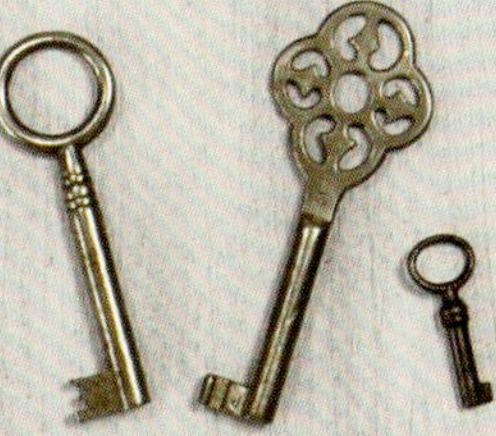

Old keys; small spoons are also interesting

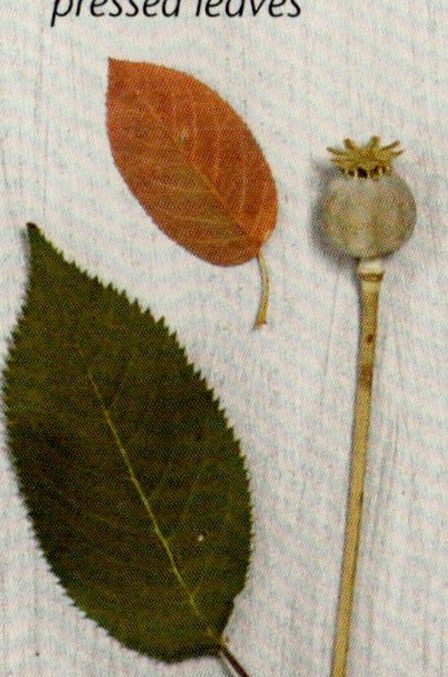

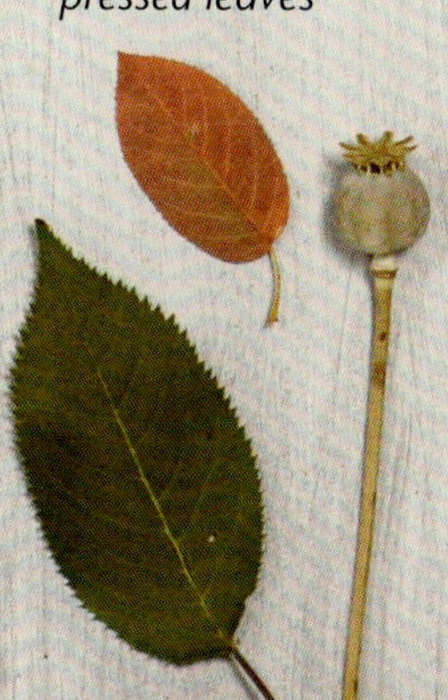

Dried plant parts and pressed leaves

Matchboxes or other small (old) containers

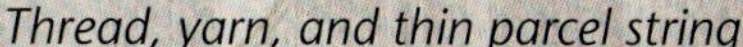

Thread, yarn, and thin parcel string

A Few Small Tips before Getting Started

Individual techniques will be introduced in the chapters. But to allow you to get started right away, here are the most-important tips:

Images

Images of all kinds—often nostalgic, but also surreally distorted, or very personal, such as family photos—are an effective design tool in the boxes. It's important to make sure they're not glossy, and they should be printed on the most highly absorbent paper possible. You may be reluctant to use or cut up beautiful old script fragments, maps, or original photos. But often you won't have to make that decision, because it's rare that the original piece is of the ideal size for the planned design. In most cases you can work with a color copy or a color printout (appropriately enlarged or reduced). Ink jet prints on standard paper have a softer appearance compared to laser prints, and the images sink nicely into the paper. I recommend using prints only from printers with (more expensive) lightfast ink cartridges.

Interesting images from newspapers provide for a unique, often slightly shabby flair. Plus, you can use paste on the absorbent newsprint paper in such a way that it adheres nicely to the substrate. However, when you're working with bright motifs you may find the letters show through from the back. Such an effect sometimes works well. If you don't want this, you should prepare the substrate by using dark acrylic paint or black gesso. To prevent getting a wild hodgepodge of shades when using family photos, you can photocopy colored and black-and-white photos together on a color copier, using the black-and-white setting, and thus harmonize them—and at the same time historicize a bit. In principle, all black-and-white photos can be reproduced better as color copies.

Back Panel

The back panel can often be wallpapered directly using paper and water-based paste (in bookbinding terms this is called "laminating," but for me, the boxes are miniature rooms). When working with raw wood, though, you should be careful to prime it with gesso beforehand. Otherwise the paste could cause discoloration of the wood, and that might eventually penetrate to the front. Lacquered wood, and even metal or glass, can also be wallpapered using paste. Since the inner sides of the boxes aren't subjected to any stress, even if

Templates

Because it isn't possible to define the dimensions of most of the boxes in this book, there are no special pages with design templates. However, all of the paper cuttings are photographed so that they can be traced or copied from the photo of the sample box and then scaled up or down on a copier in proportion to the size of your project.

they're made of a nonabsorbent material, the wallpapered surface approach usually works for them.The back panels of some boxes are made of hard materials, such as MDF or beechwood, which makes it difficult to poke or drill holes into or through the back panel to attach objects. In those cases it's helpful to use inserts, cut to fit, made of 5 mm thick foam board or soft paperboard (see page 63). You can glue these inserts to the back panel and then easily thread through them, insert pins, and so on. Paperboard or foam board inserts can also be wallpapered, but both tend to warp when paste is used, so the piece must therefore be counterlaminated from the back so that it doesn't buckle. Instead, since the insert in the box is visible only from the front side, you can either attach the paper covering in a way that's as dry as possible using spray adhesive or double-sided adhesive tape, or simply turn the wallpaper over the edges, smooth it onto the back, and fasten it on with adhesive tape (see chapter 3).

Gluing

There are many ways to decoratively fasten on objects by using nails or knots. Sometimes, though, a neutral, invisible type of attachment works best, and in those cases you need glue. It is important to understand how to distinguish which type of glue you should use for each situation.

You should use water-based paste only to glue something flat. To do so, apply it to the back of the paper, using a brush, working from the center outward and beyond the edges. Simple wallpaper paste (methylcellulose) can be mixed in small quantities; when using it, apply it a little thicker than the package directs for heavy wallpaper. If stored in a cool and dark place, the paste can be kept in a tightly closed container for several weeks to months. For small surfaces you can also use a glue stick, which has an adhesive power similar to that of the paste.

To attach objects, you need the much-stronger adhesive power of white glue (wood glue, PVA), a dispersion adhesive that bonds quickly and (in contrast to paste) dries water resistant. Use the small bottles with an applicator tip instead of larger containers that make it necessary to use a brush to apply it.

Background

Selecting the background is an essential design element for the box's interior. This can simply be the back panel itself—but as on a theater stage, very different effects are created depending on how you arrange the areas.

In addition to painting, these all work well to create a background: paper samples of all kinds, pieces of text from dictionaries or foreign-language newspapers, maps, or images that lend a three-dimensional appearance by showing subjects such as open books, archways, or landscapes.

Dimensions

Except for chapters 1 and 5, in which it was possible to provide some of the box dimensions, the original project's size is shown next to its full-page photo for orientation purposes.

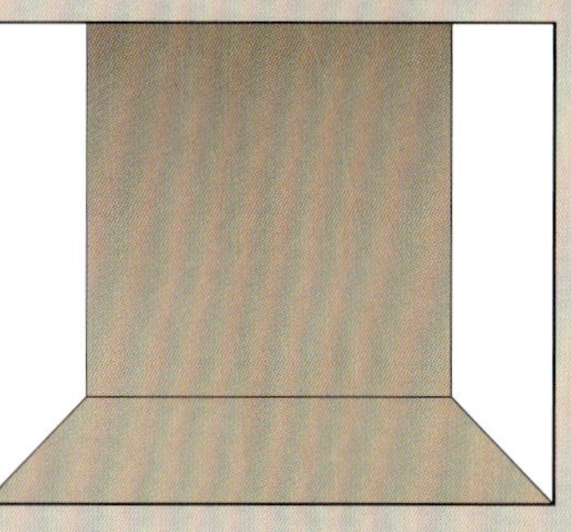

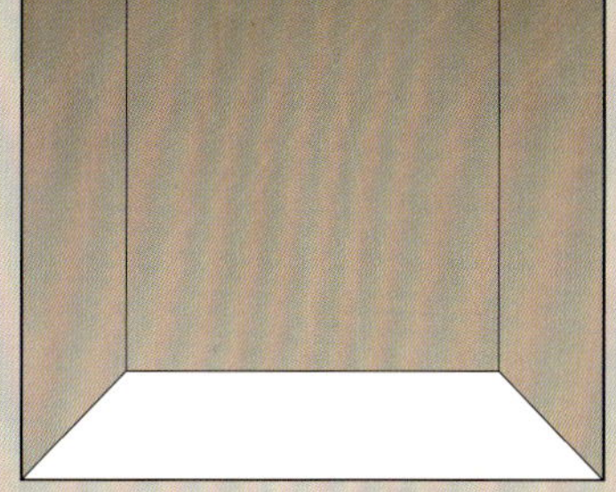

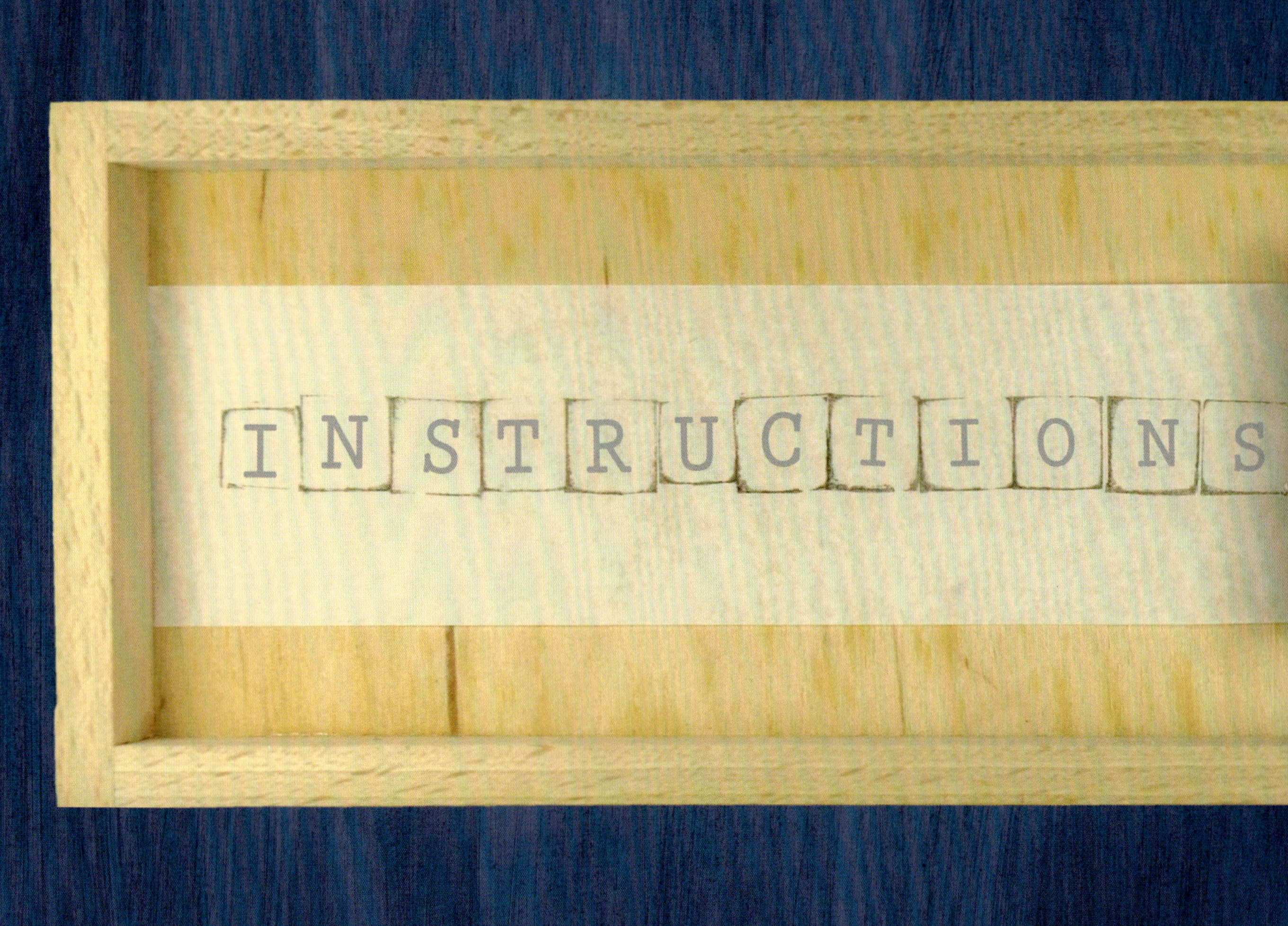
INSTRUCTIONS

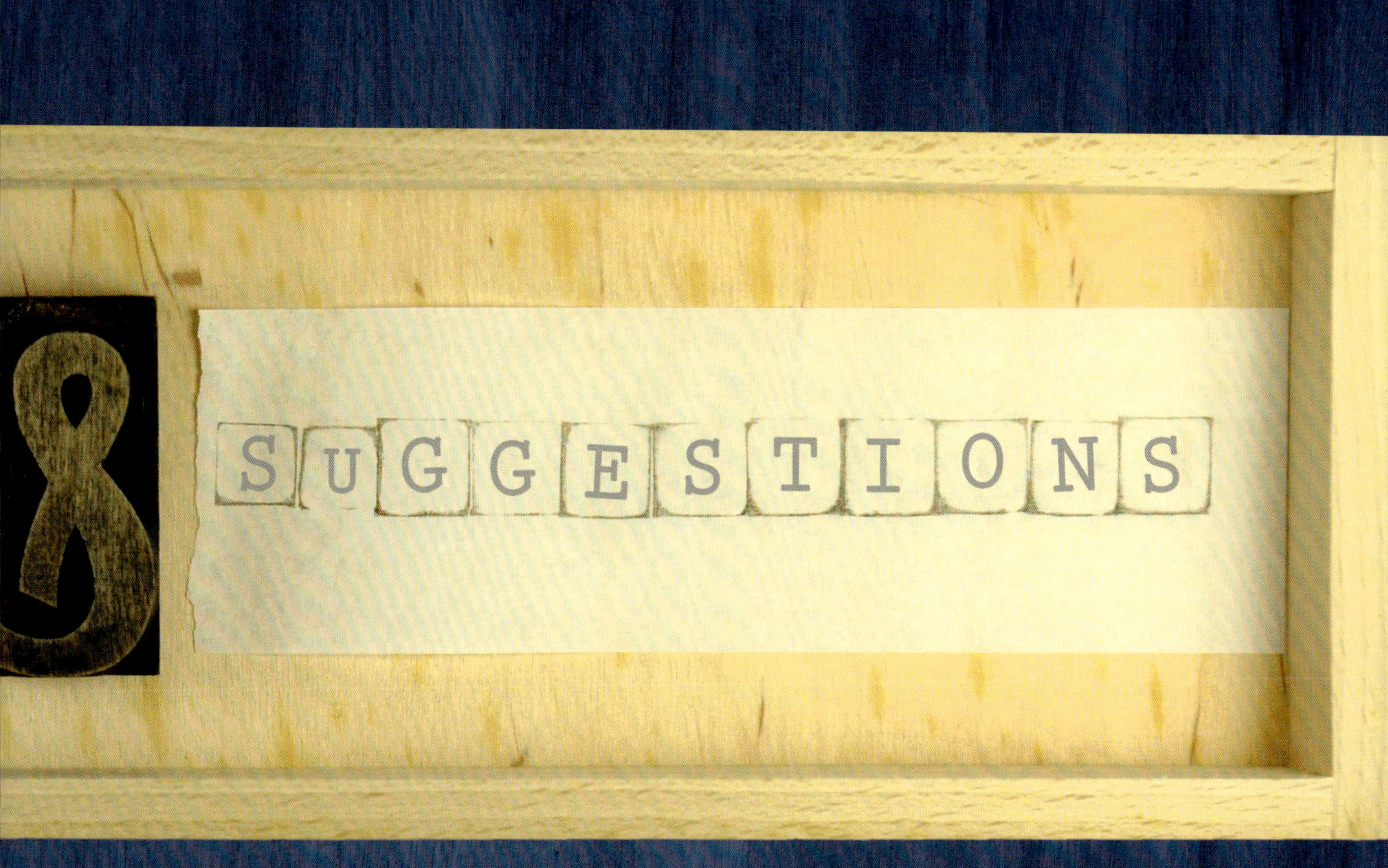
8
SUGGESTIONS

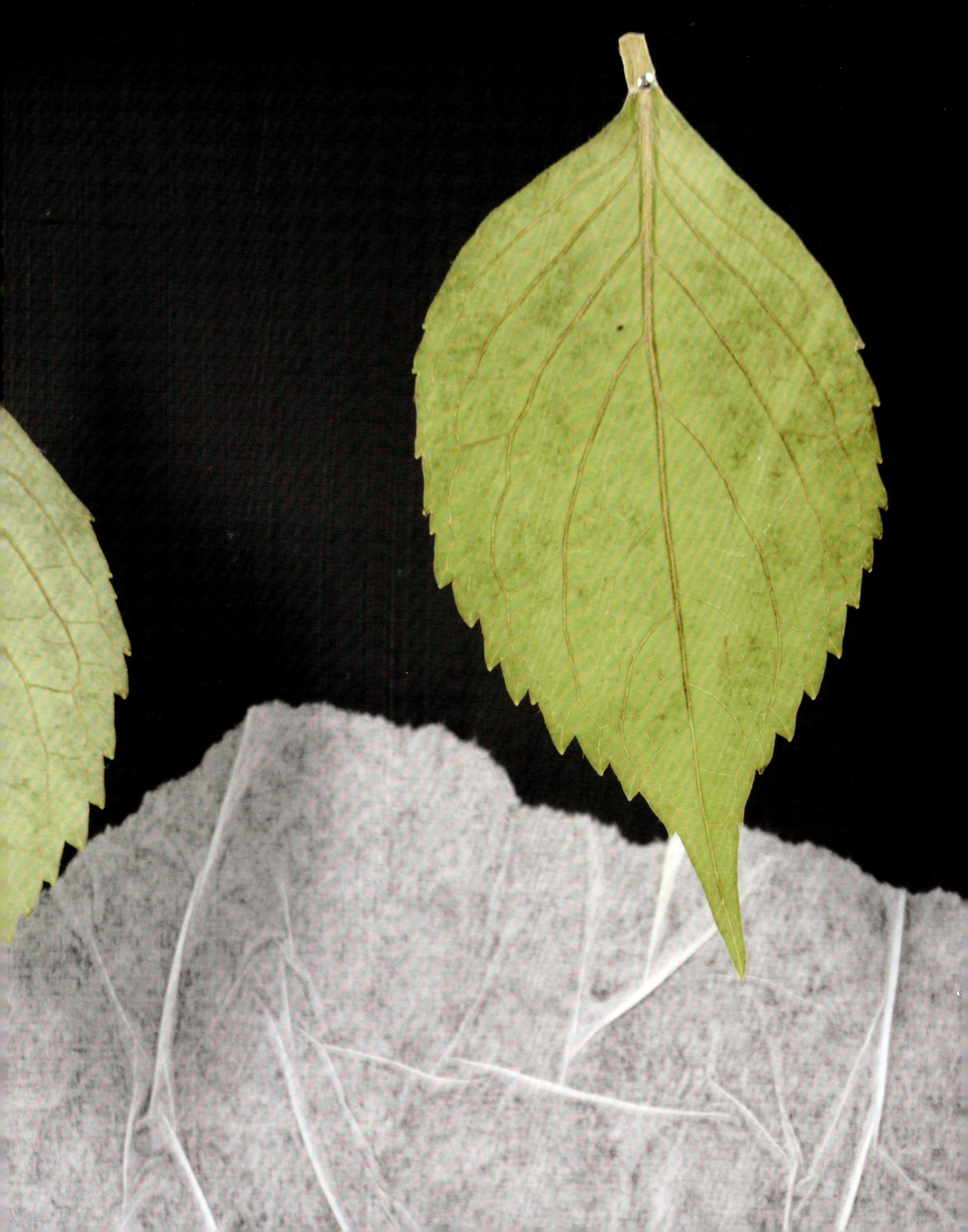

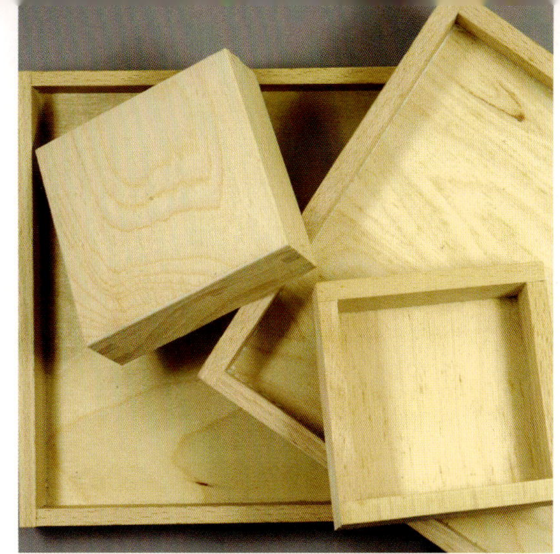

1

Ready-Made Boxes

Wooden or hardboard painting panels, with the back side turned to the front, can be used as boxes and are available in many sizes. Since the outer frame—called a cradle—is usually about 1″ wide, they aren't very deep, which lets you illuminate the contents well. Ready-made shadow boxes—also known as "object boxes"—are already fitted with a glass pane and have more depth but are available only in a few formats.

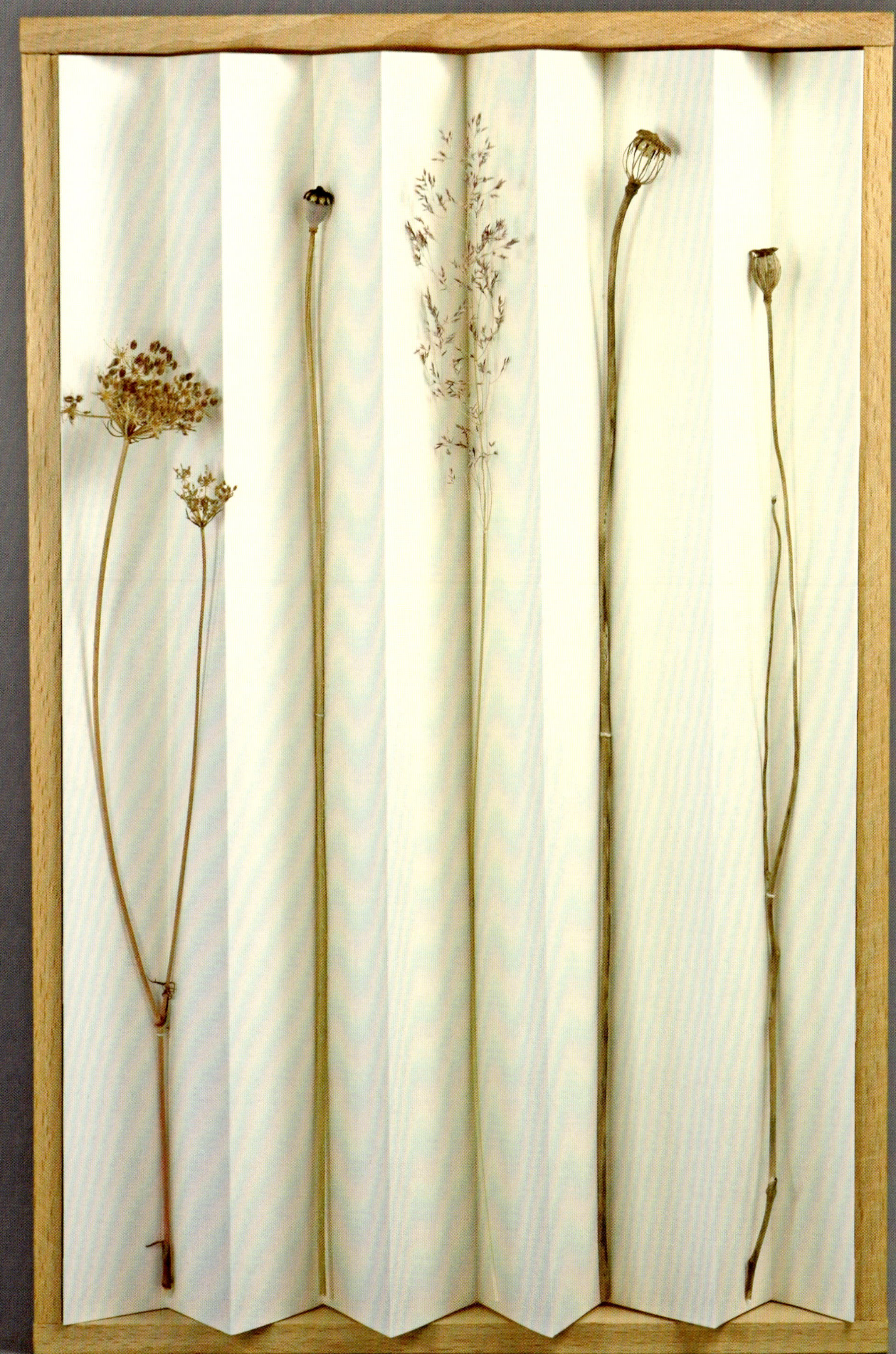

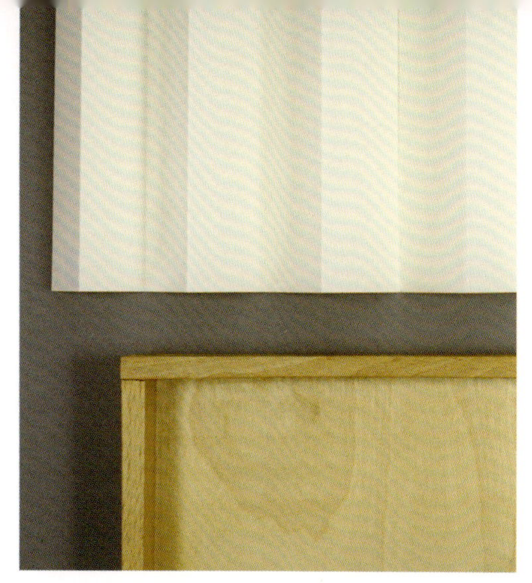

Creating Partitioning and Structure with a Zigzag Fold

Materials + Tools

Wooden or hardboard painting panel, 12" × 8"

Sturdy paper or thin cardboard, about 150–200 gsm, 12" high, at least 16" wide, with the grain direction (also called the machine direction) parallel to the shorter side

Ruler, cutter, and cutting mat

Bone folder

Awl for pricking holes

Needle and thread

Double-sided adhesive tape or white glue

Dried plants

I love herbariums, but not all plants will tolerate being pressed while drying. It is possible to carefully dry seed pods and plants with curved stems by hanging them upside down so that they retain their three-dimensional shape. Merely gluing these "plant sculptures" into a box wouldn't do them justice. Using paper folded in a zigzag as a "back panel with divisions" is much more beautiful; this shows each plant to best advantage in its own space and still binds them all together. In addition, the white paper creates a nice contrast to the natural wood of the frame.

The material for the zigzag fold should be reasonably stable according to the size of the box, but not hard to fold (for example, photo-mounting board is not suitable for this size of box). Check the grain direction of the paper (see page 20), then cut the sheet so that its height is a little less (max. 1/16") than the inner dimension of the box so that the fold will not get stuck later.

You may make the fold irregular, depending on your whim, and you may also like to have it extend forward outside the frame. The only necessary thing is to have the width of the two side parts correspond as much as possible to the depth of the box (here, for example, the inner dimension is approximately 1").

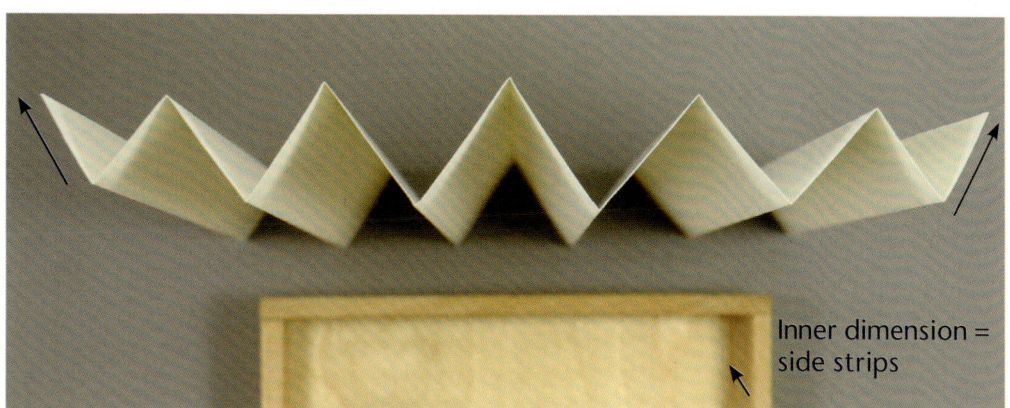

◀ *12" × 8" × 1½"*

Folding paper:

Working with the grain direction of the paper or cardboard (*see arrow*) makes it much easier to use some pressure to bend the sheet in one direction [1], rather than to bend it to the other side [2]. The fold should also run in this direction, [1] = along the grain direction.

One way to make folds all of the same width without measuring is to trim the paper strip to four or eight times the planned fold width before you fold it. Then fold exactly at the center [3] and align both open ends along the edge of the middle fold and fold [4]. This creates a four-fold zigzag [5].

To make an eight-fold zigzag, again align the open edges along the next folded edge [5]. Then turn the middle fold over in the opposite direction [6] and align it along the next folded edge [7]. After that, the last folded edge—and your eight-fold zigzag is finished.

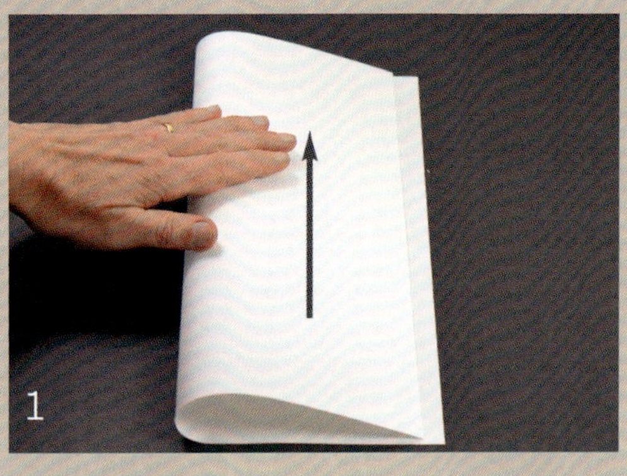
1

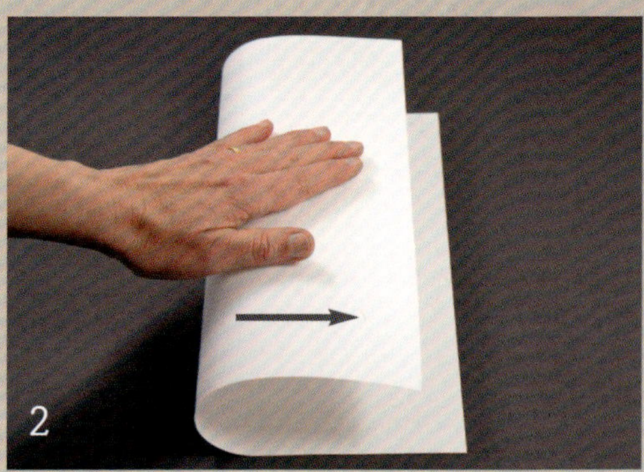
2

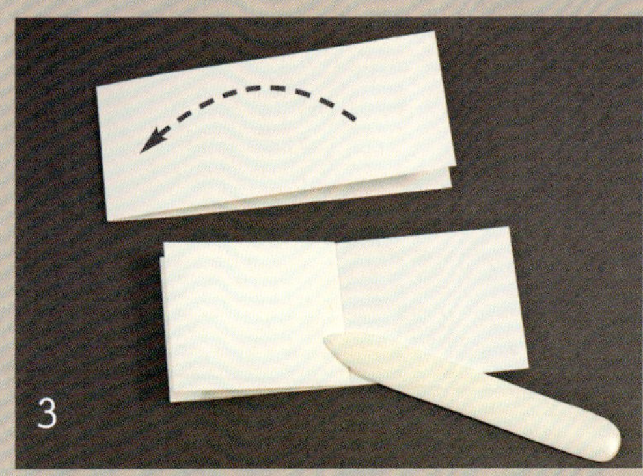
3

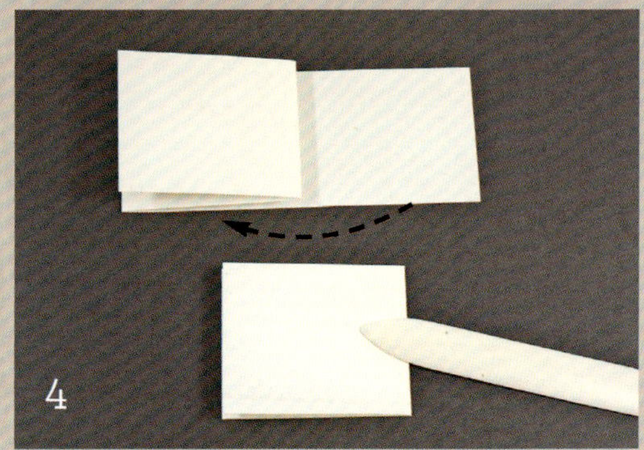
4

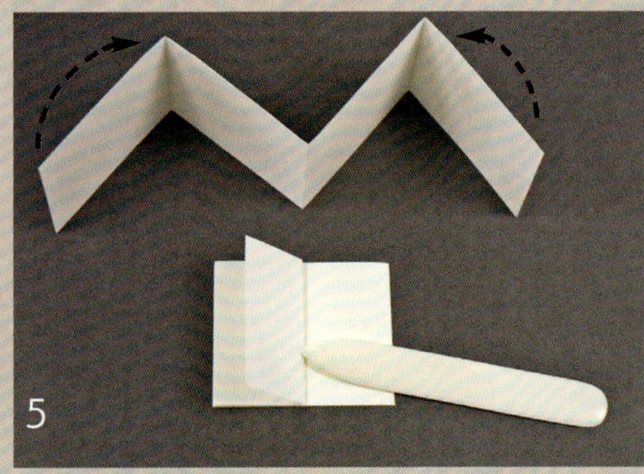
5

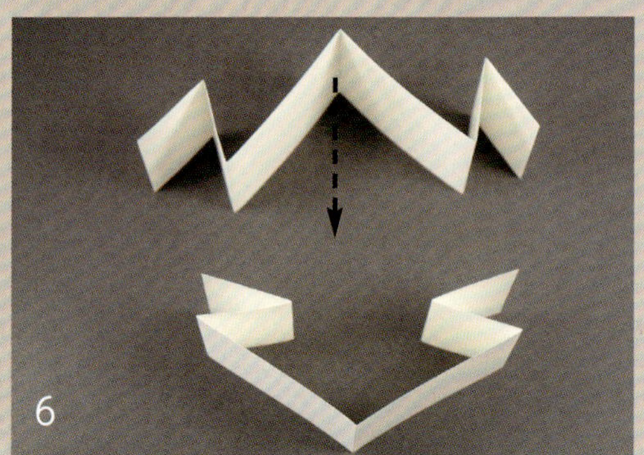
6

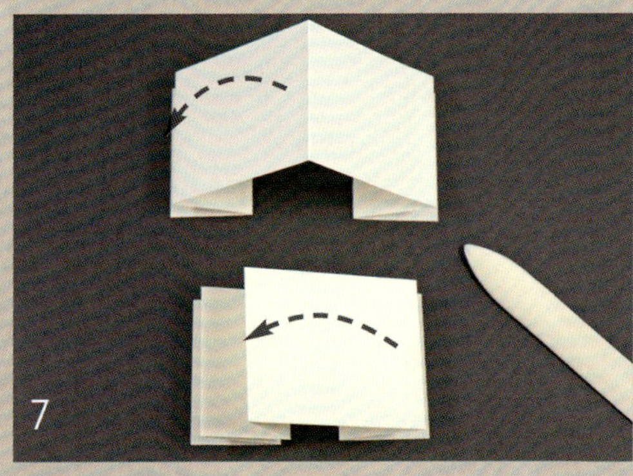
7

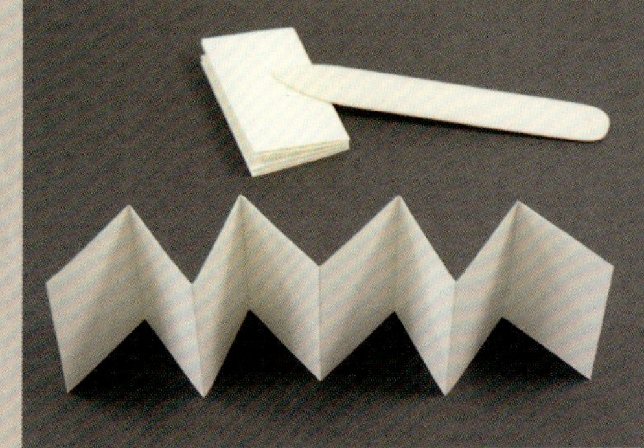

Using a fine awl or a thick needle, prick one or two attachment points each exactly in the valley fold under the plant stems.

Then use the needle to pierce through from the back, pass the thread over the stem, and pull it through to the back again through the same hole. Knot it on the back side.

Finally, attach the outermost edges to the inside of the box, using white glue or double-sided adhesive tape. If the paper is not that stable and threatens to unfold in the middle, you can also apply adhesive to the back sides of the valley folds and fasten them to the back panel that way.

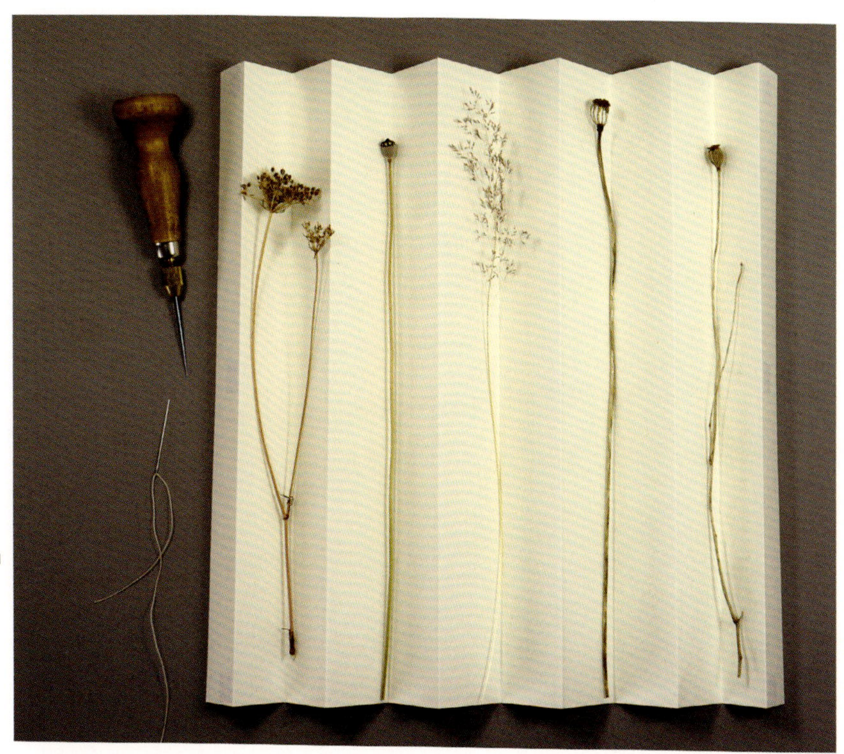

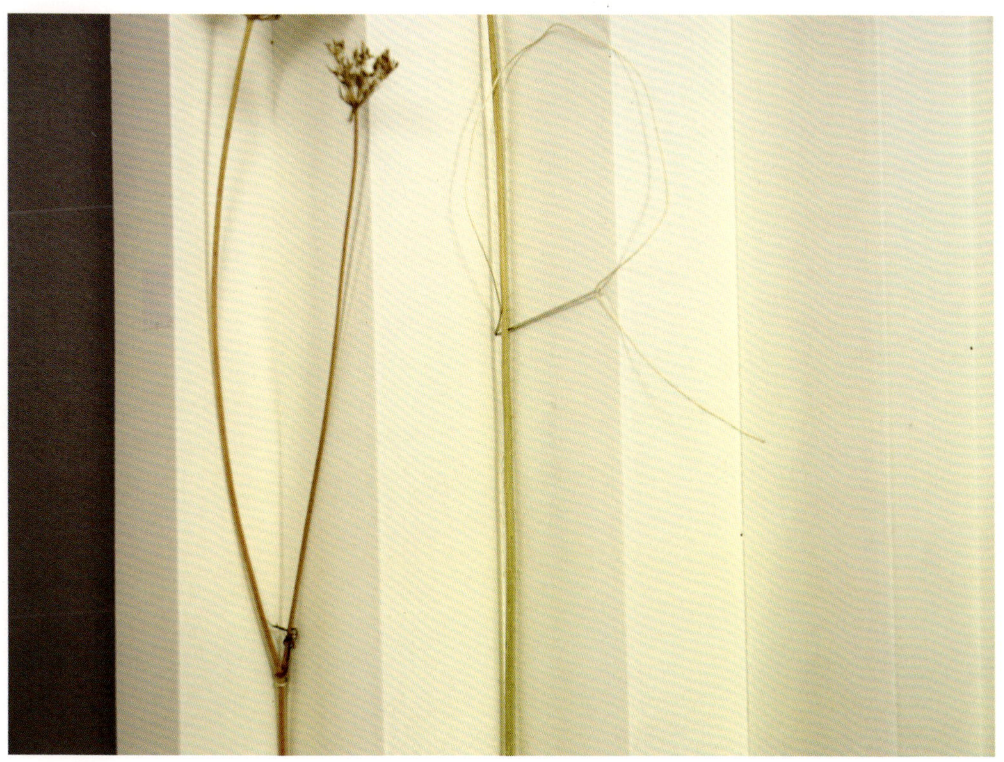

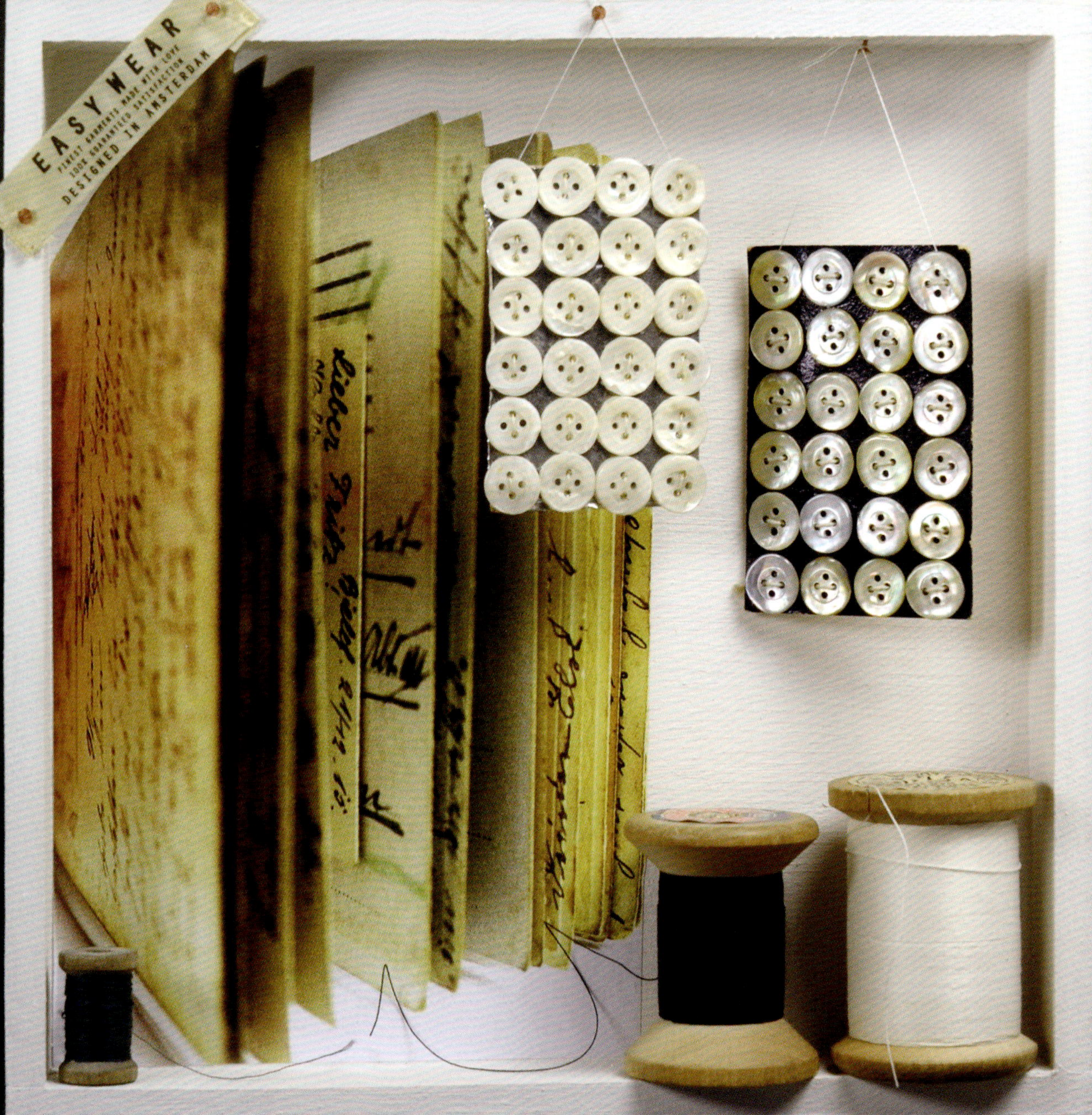
EASYWEAR
FINEST GARMENTS MADE WITH LOVE
100% GUARANTEED SATISFACTION
DESIGNED IN AMSTERDAM

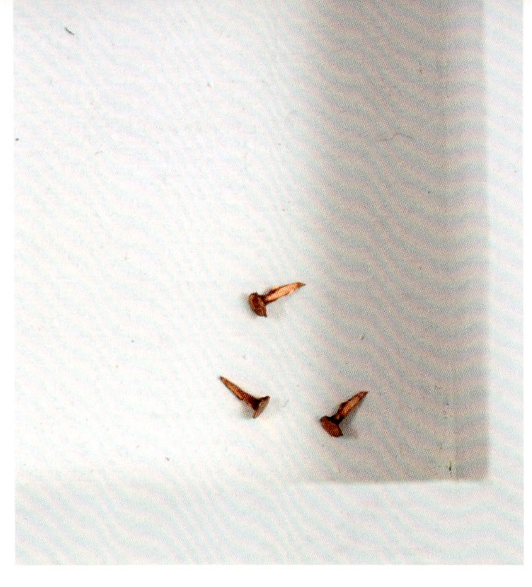

Neutral Background Using White Primer

The first change that you can make to a ready-made natural-colored box is adding a coat of paint. Gesso works particularly well for this because this chalky primer has some body and vividly shows the brushstrokes. The chalky white is very beautiful, but dust and dirt will coat gessoed surfaces after the piece is displayed for a length of time. To avoid this, apply a top layer of white acrylic paint.

Instead of using glue, you can fasten the objects on by using small nails, or hang them up by using thread. Only the background image—on absorbent, nonglossy paper—was wallpapered to the back panel, using paste.

Materials + Tools

Wooden or hardboard painting panel, 8″ × 8″

White gesso and brush

Paste and brush

A colored image that fits with the theme, for the background

Thread for hanging things

Small nails with heads (such as shaker nails)

Awl for pricking holes (the beech strips are hard, so otherwise small nails easily slip sideways)

Small pliers to hold the nails

Small hammer

Collected things, such as old button cards, spools of thread, textile labels . . .

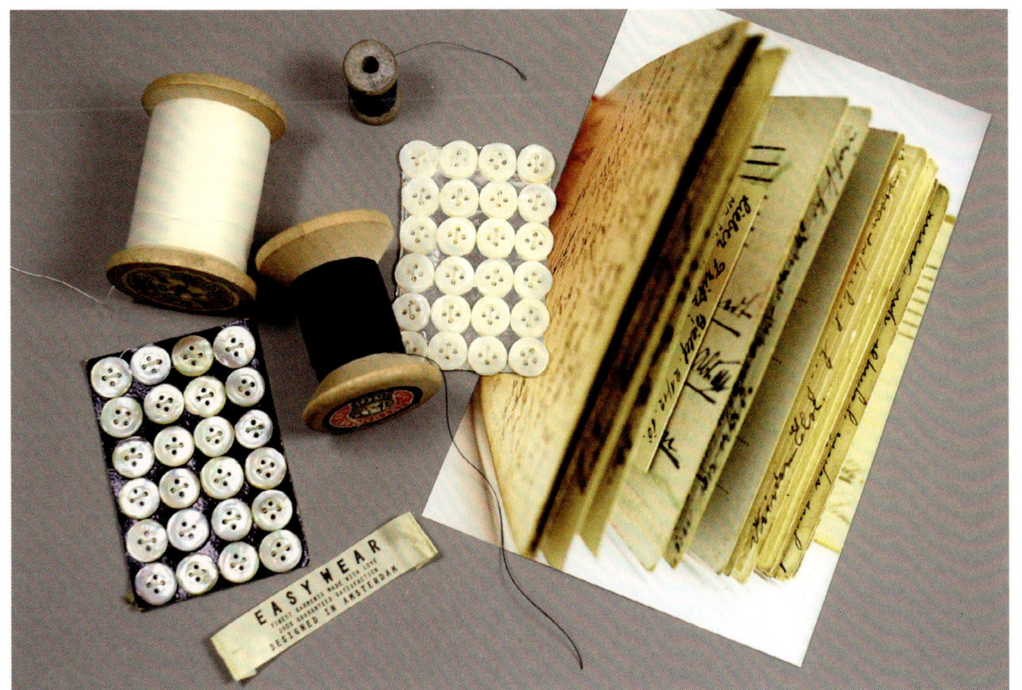

◀ *8″ × 8″ × 1½″*

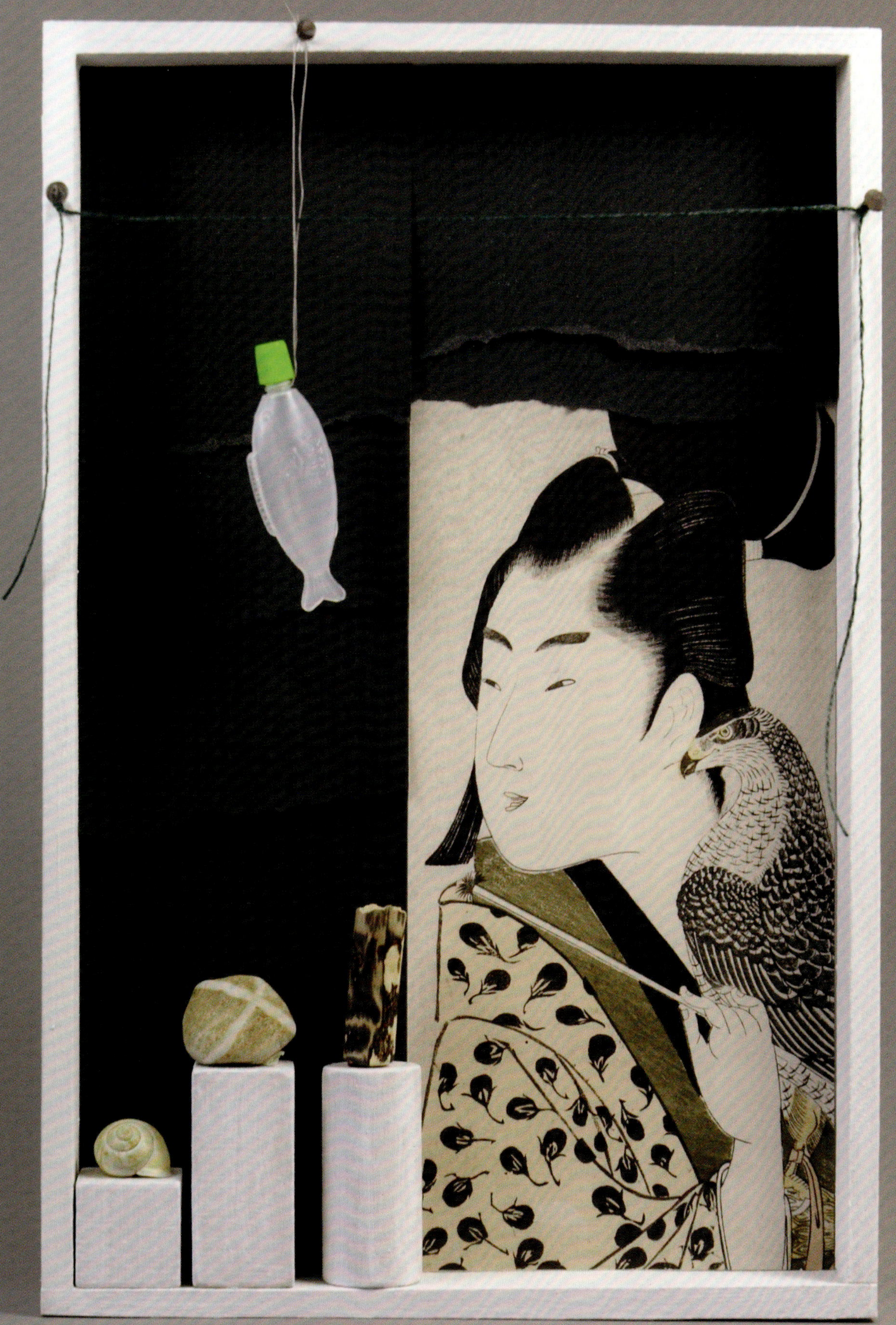

Background Partly Wallpapered, Partly Shingled

Using gesso as a primer not only works well on the box as a whole, but also for its "furnishings," such as on miniature pedestals you can use to display small objects. Simple wooden blocks, pieces of plastic packaging, or toy building blocks as shown here are given the appearance of a traditional gallery by using gesso and will adapt to any background.

The background here is partly wallpapered with a page from an exhibition flyer printed on natural paper. The remainder is covered with torn, shingle-like overlapping strips of paper. Here you should work from the bottom upward; the strips are always glued on only from the top edge, and it's necessary only to trim the top two sheets even at the top. Pieces of thread and objects can be attached to the frame using small nails.

Materials + Tools

Wooden or hardboard painting panel, 12" × 8"

White gesso and brush

Paste and brush

Image for the background

Matching color paper for the background

Building blocks

Thin thread and thicker yarn

Small nails with heads (such as tacks)

Awl for pricking holes

Small pliers to hold the nails

Small hammer

Collection of little things that match the atmosphere of the image

◀ *12" × 8" × 1½"*

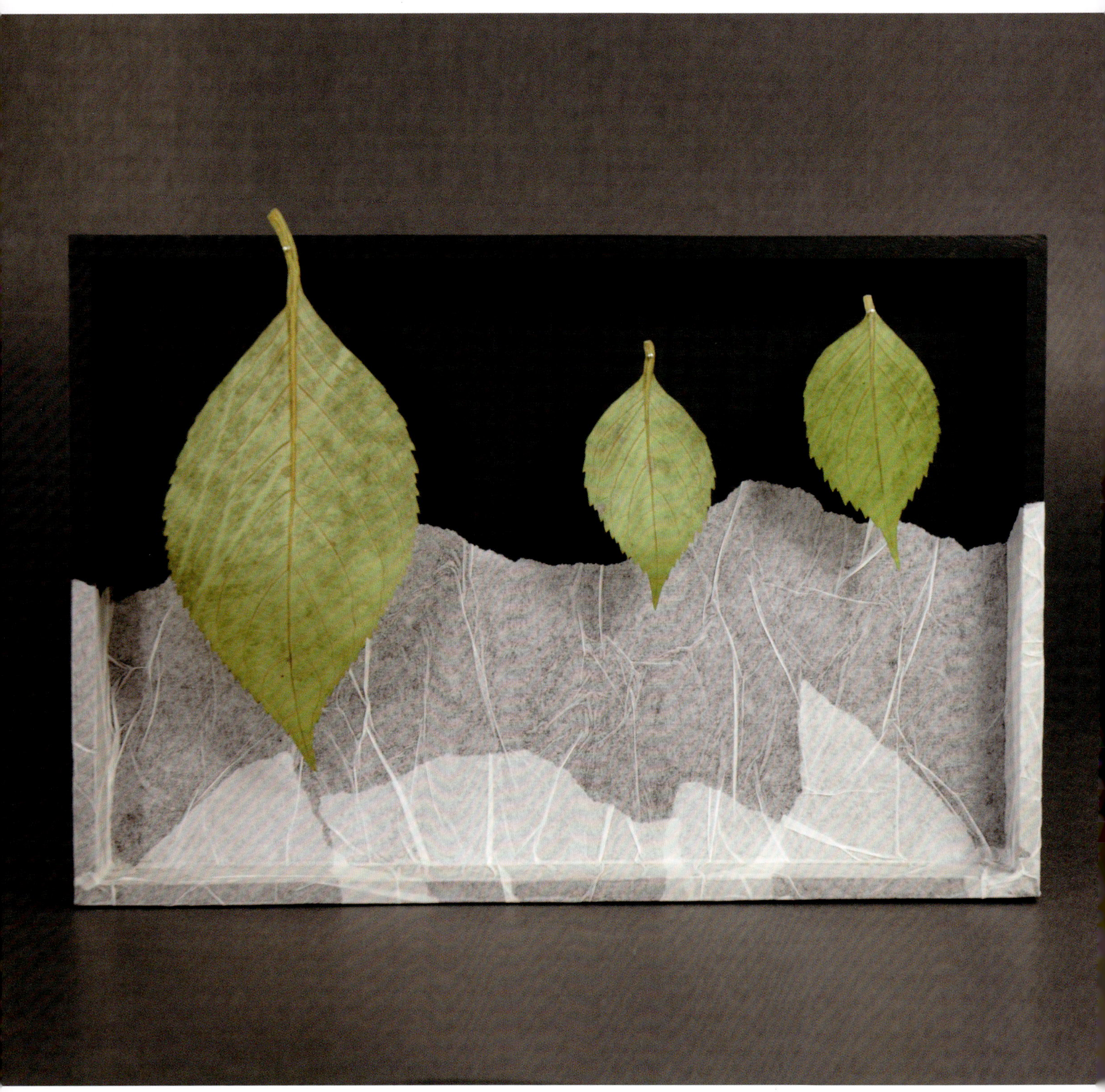

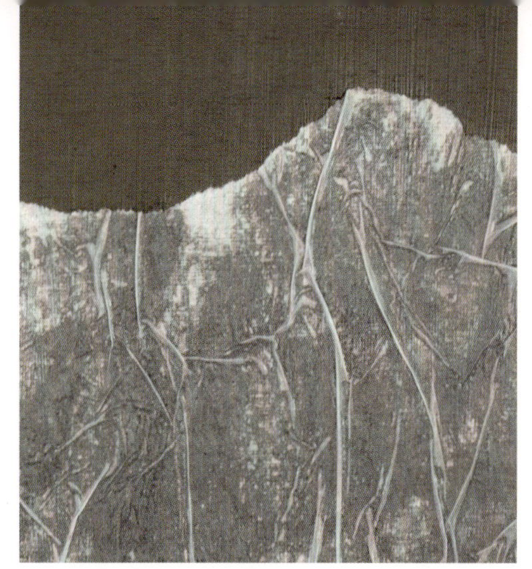

Black Primer, Wall-papered with Folded Tissue Paper

Gesso is not available only in classic chalky white, but also in black. This primer doesn't quite have the interesting consistency of the white but nevertheless has enough body to show some brushwork.

You can then create a special effect by applying folded thin tissue paper. Coat it with paste. Spread a large, roughly torn piece on the lower part of the box and cover the edges with smaller torn pieces. After they've dried, the overlapping pieces of tissue paper yield interesting gradations in the translucent areas. Finally, stick pressed leaves on long needles to also conjure shadows on the back panel.

Materials + Tools

Wooden or hardboard painting panel, 8" × 12"

Black gesso and brush

Paste and brush

Torn pieces of white tissue paper

Long, thin nails or strong pins

Awl for pricking holes

Small hammer

Pressed leaves of different sizes

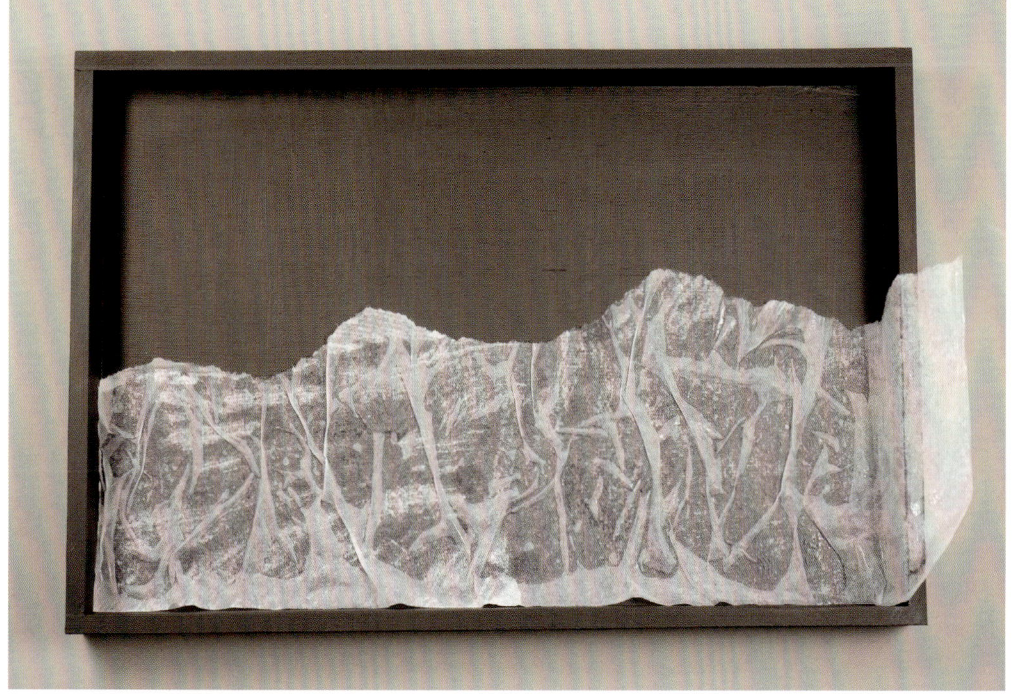

◀ *8" × 12" × 1½"*

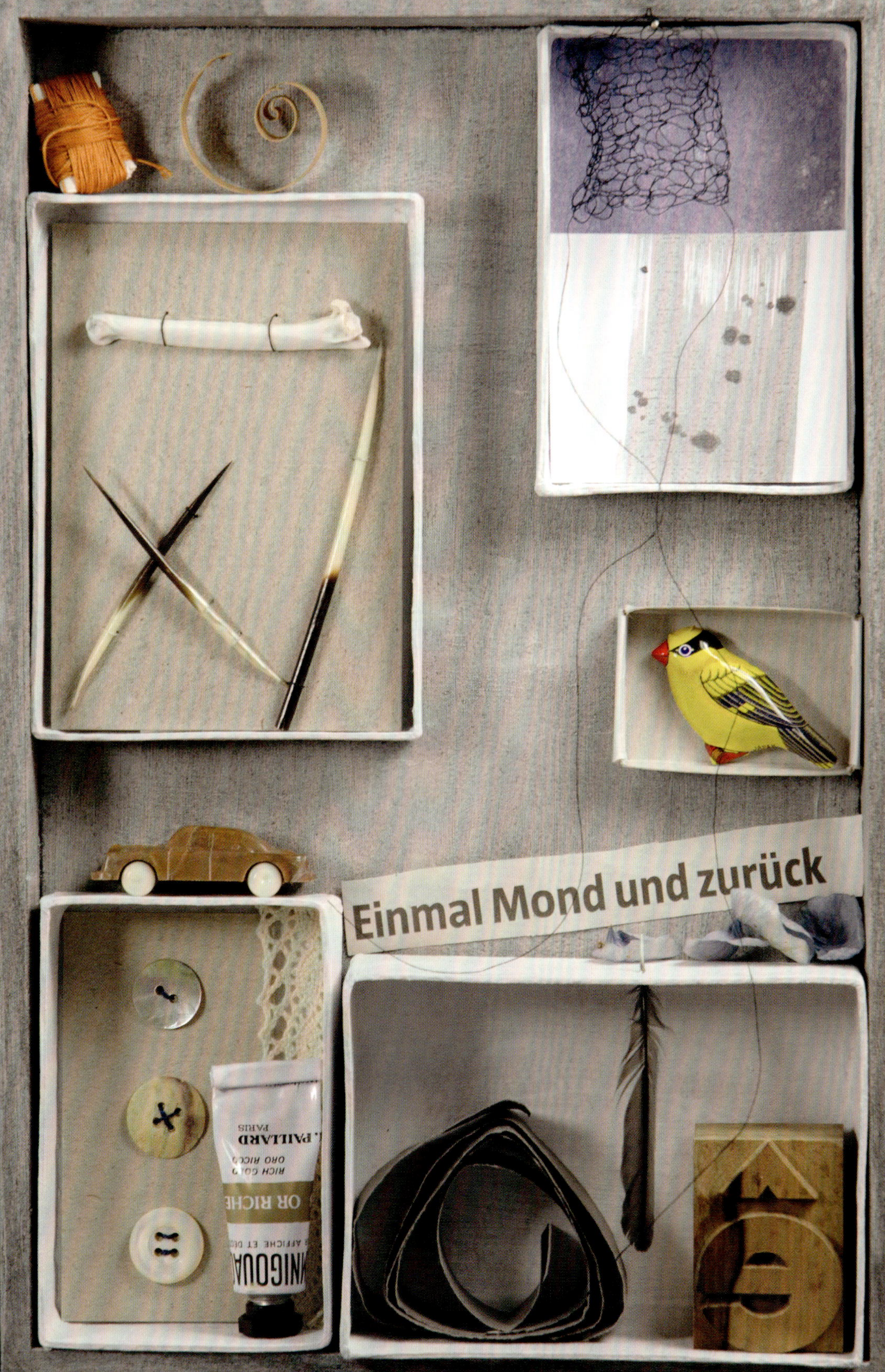
Einmal Mond und zurück

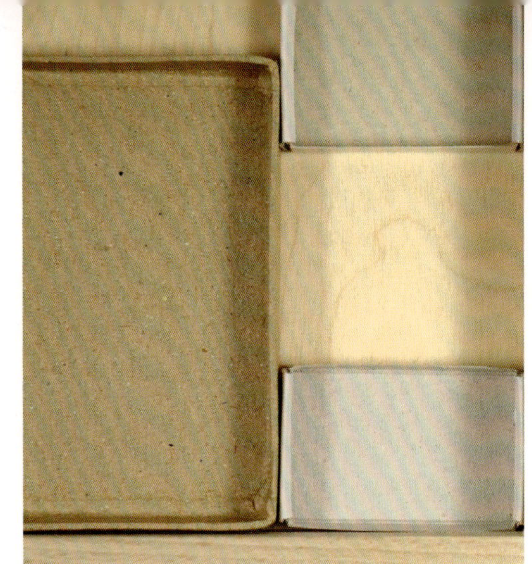

Organizing Space by Using Small Boxes

Materials + Tools

Wooden or hardboard painting panel, 12″ × 8″

White gesso and brush

Acrylic paint and brush

White glue

Small boxes or box lids of different sizes

Finds

Priming the painting panel with gesso, in combination with heavily diluted acrylic paint applied as a glaze, creates a delicately animated background surface thanks to the structure of the brushstrokes.

To be able to fill the relatively flat box well, using an arrangement of flat little boxes or box lids glued on with white glue is definitely nicer than gluing on the objects by themselves. This way, it's easy to arrange the objects and take them out again. And, in addition, the space between the boxes offers display space or room for images and lettering. These "boxes in a box" create their own small, protected worlds to design. Prime the boxes uniformly with gesso paint. Leave only the small drawers of matchboxes as they are; they're neutral enough and painting could warp them badly. Instead of painting or covering the box back panel, you can also insert a piece of cardboard (possibly even at an angle) for the background. In this way, you allow for interchangeable "images" using knotted-on finds without having to prick a hole through the back panel of the box.

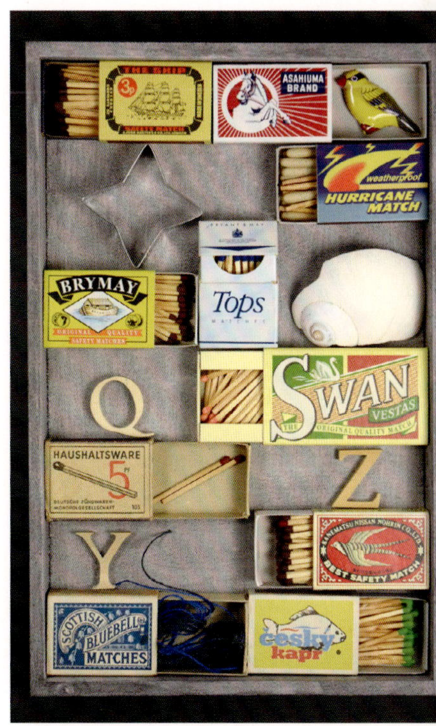

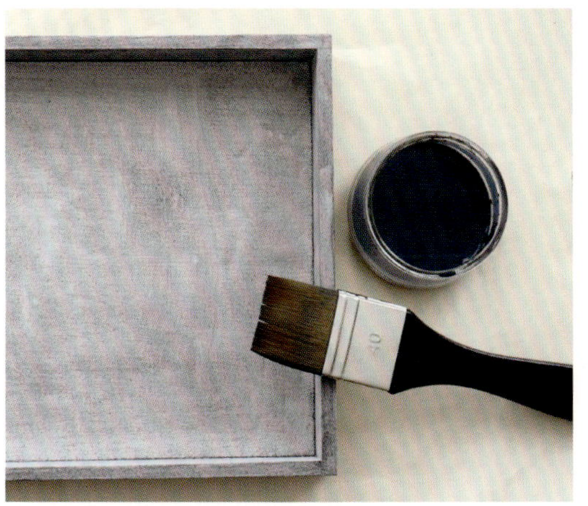

Alternative design:

A completely different overall image is created when you use only matchboxes for the arrangement and also install them half open.

◀ *12″ × 8″ × 1½″*

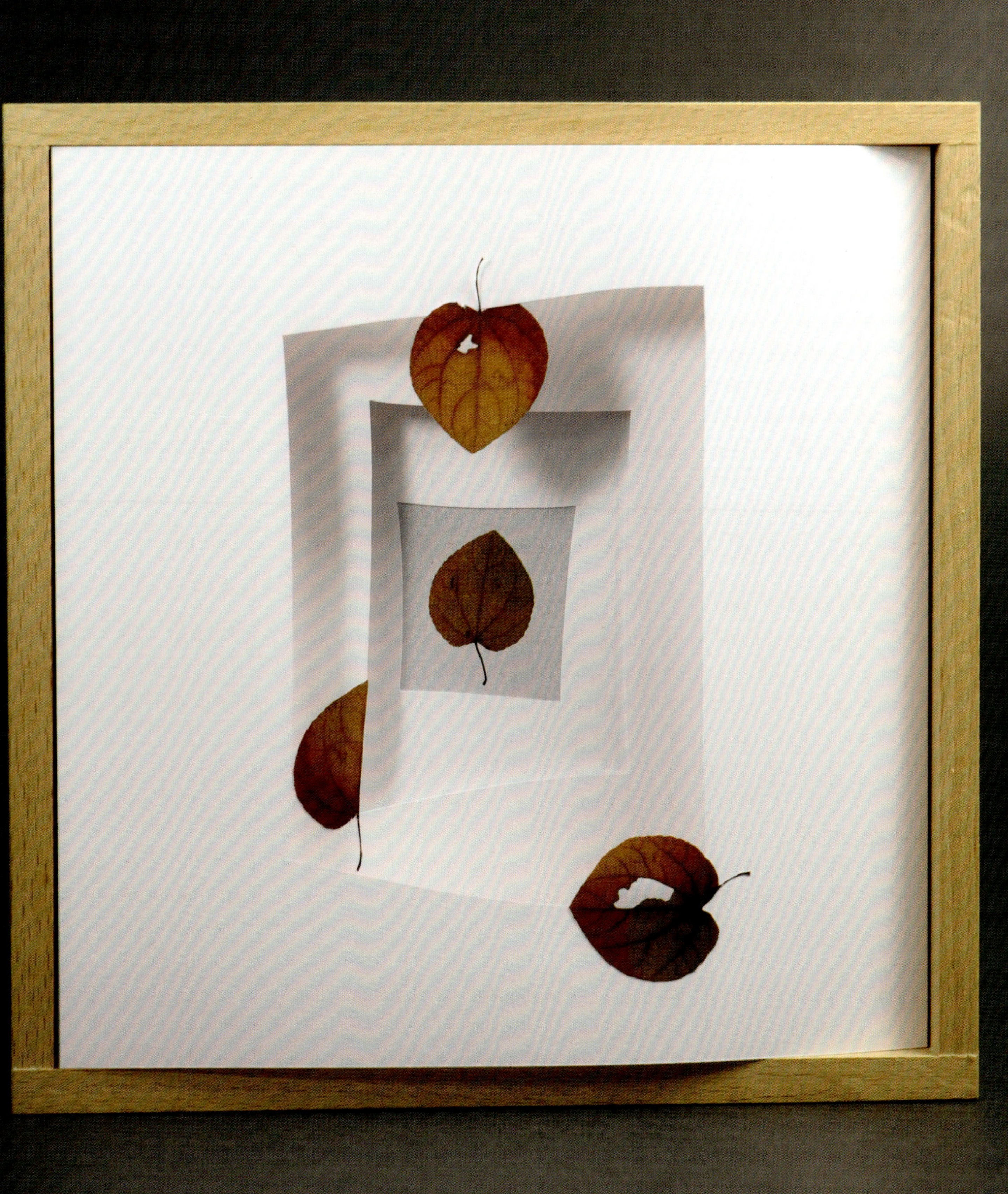

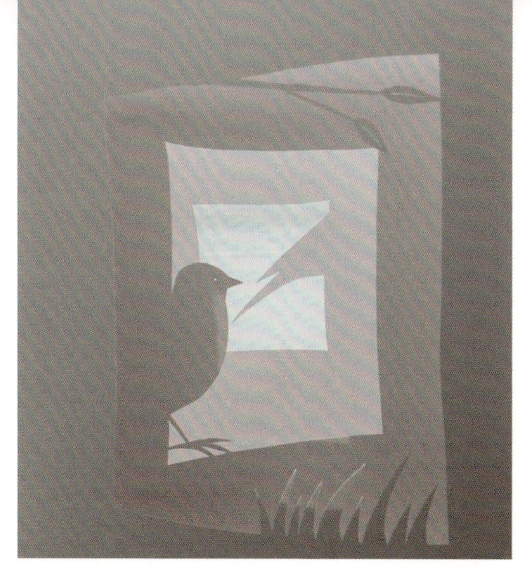

Making a Tunnel Backdrop by using Zigzag Folds

A "tunnel" that draws you into the box is a particularly fine type of design; it's created by folding a piece of paper or cardboard. As we saw for the 3-D herbarium, the stability of the paper depends on the size of the box. For a 7½" wide panel, a thickness of 150–180 gsm is sufficient; photo mounting board would be too coarse.

First, determine the grain direction of the sheet (see page 20) and then cut the paper strip to the correct height—once again, it should be a little bit (max. 1/16") smaller than the inner dimension of the box. Then fold the left edge of the strip over so it is approx. 15/16" wide (for a 1" box depth). Make the second fold (right) at 7 7/16" (for a box width of 7½"), the third and fourth folds each at 7 3/8" (to allow more air), and finally make the fifth fold at the center of the last piece of the strip.

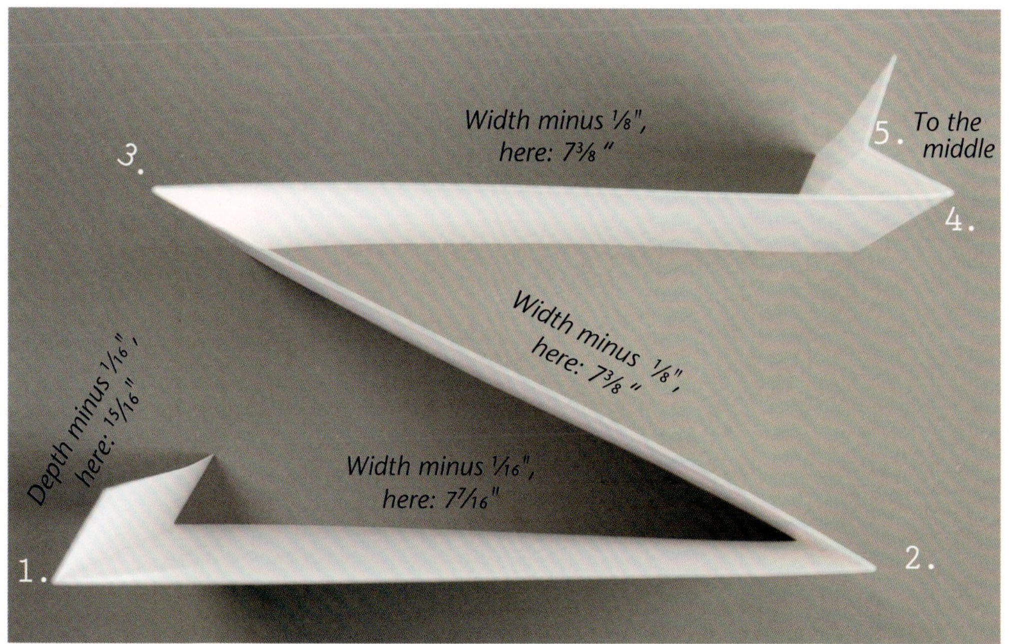

Materials + Tools

Wooden or hardboard painting panel, 8" × 8"

Sturdy paper or thin cardboard 7½" high and about 26" wide, with the grain direction running parallel to the shorter side

Bone folder

Ruler, graphic cutter, scalpel, and cutting mat

Awl for pricking holes

Tracing paper

Wood sticks or paperboard as spacer

White glue and double-sided adhesive tape

◀ *8" × 8" × 1½"*

Cutting Out a Tunnel:

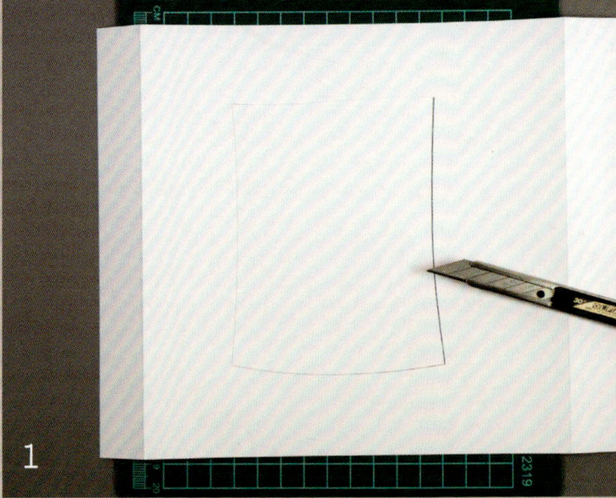
1

If you don't want to have a "well-behaved" right-angle tunnel, it's a good idea to cut it freehand with panache. Just be brave! Simply try it out with a piece of scrap paper; this is really fun and the cutter is much easier to handle. As an aid, you can use the awl to prick holes so you can align the desired corner points.

It is important to cut from the front to the back, so that you can see where you have to aim in relation to the front cutout. To do this, unfold the folded strip and place the first side (with the narrow piece folded to the left) on the cutting mat. Lay the other two sides (out of range of the cutter) unfolded to the right. Now make the front, largest tunnel cutout [1]. Lift this side and fold the second side over it to the left. The third side is to the left. After cutting the second, middle-sized cutout [2], finally fold the third side back to the right and make the last small cutout [3].

Now you have the tunnel in front of you as a zigzag—with the narrow fastening strip, which will be glued to the edge of the box, to the left and the small double fold to the right, creating a little volume so that the sheets don't just lie flat on top of each other.

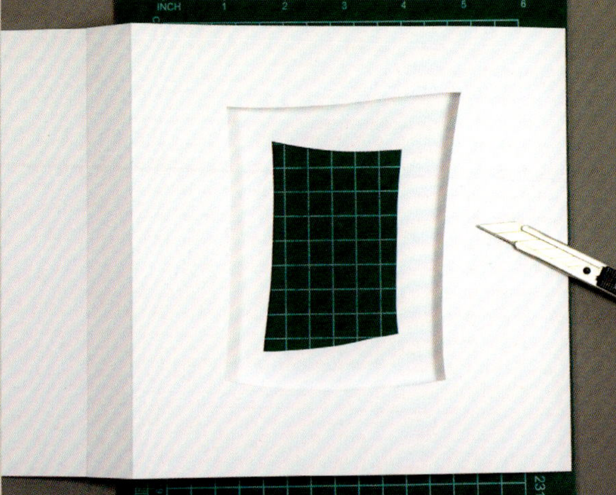

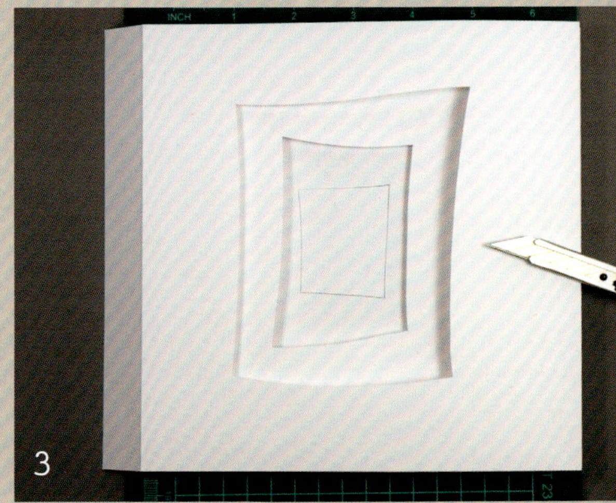
3

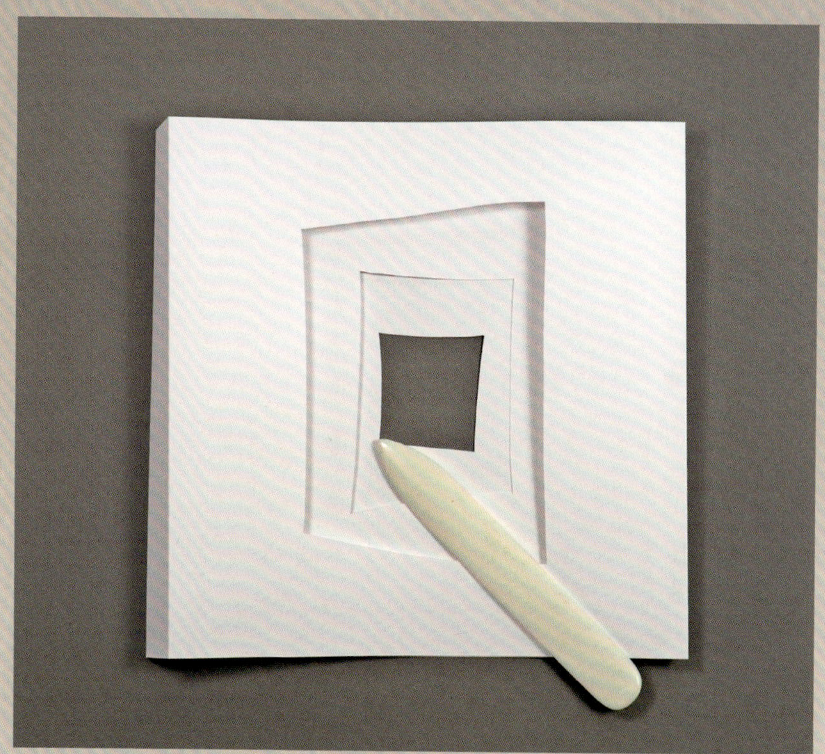

You can smooth out any possible rough cutting edges nicely by using the bone folder.

If you prefer to be on the safe side, you can draw a cutting template. To do this, cut a piece of tracing paper to the width of the side and mark the upper left corner as a limit. Align this edge along the top of the side when making all three cuts.

When working with a preliminary drawing, it is essential to pay attention so that you make the cutouts for the tunnel in reverse order. The ratio of the cutouts to each other has already been determined, so you don't have to see the previous cuts. And when you are cutting the front, largest cutout, the preliminary drawings for all further cuts will be cut out of the template. Thus, this time you should start with the third side (*right*). Then turn this side over to the left and pull the second side to the right on the cutting mat. Finally, make the cutout in the first side from above again.

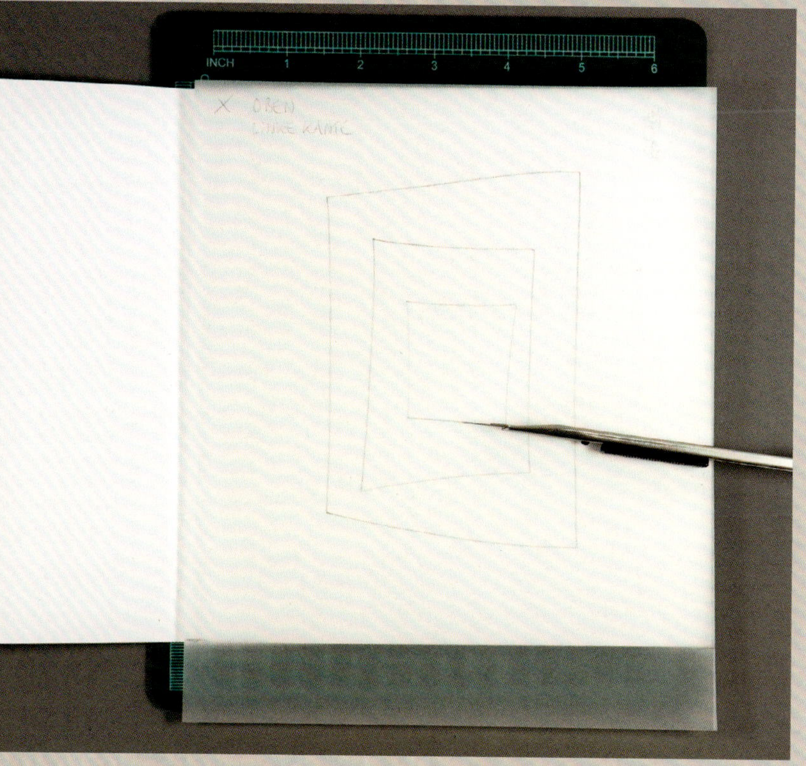

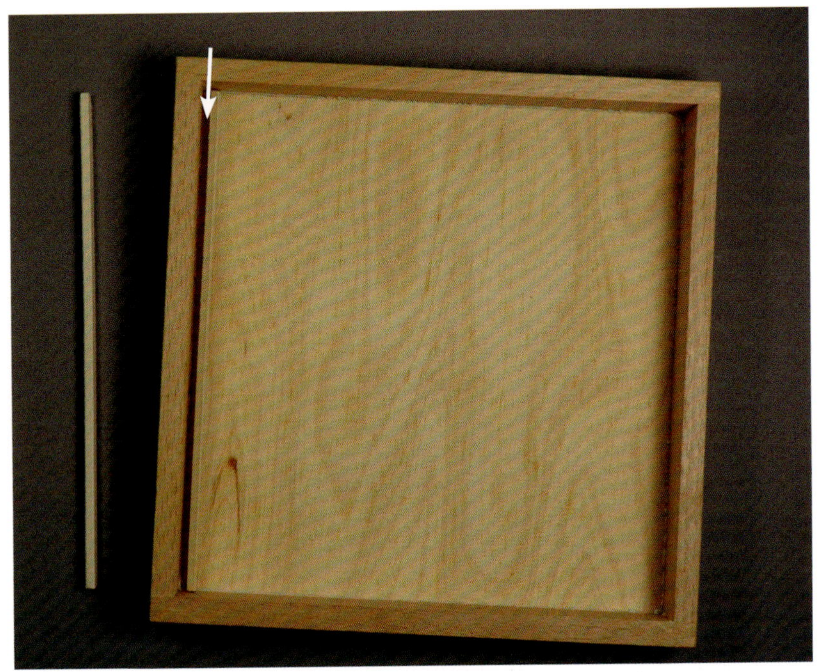

To make sure that there is enough space for a zigzag tunnel and the sides are not too close together, it helps to use some kind of spacer. Trim a wooden stick with a diameter of 3 to 5 mm or a narrow strip of paperboard about 3 mm thick to the inner height of the box and use white glue to fasten it about 5 mm away from the left-side edge.

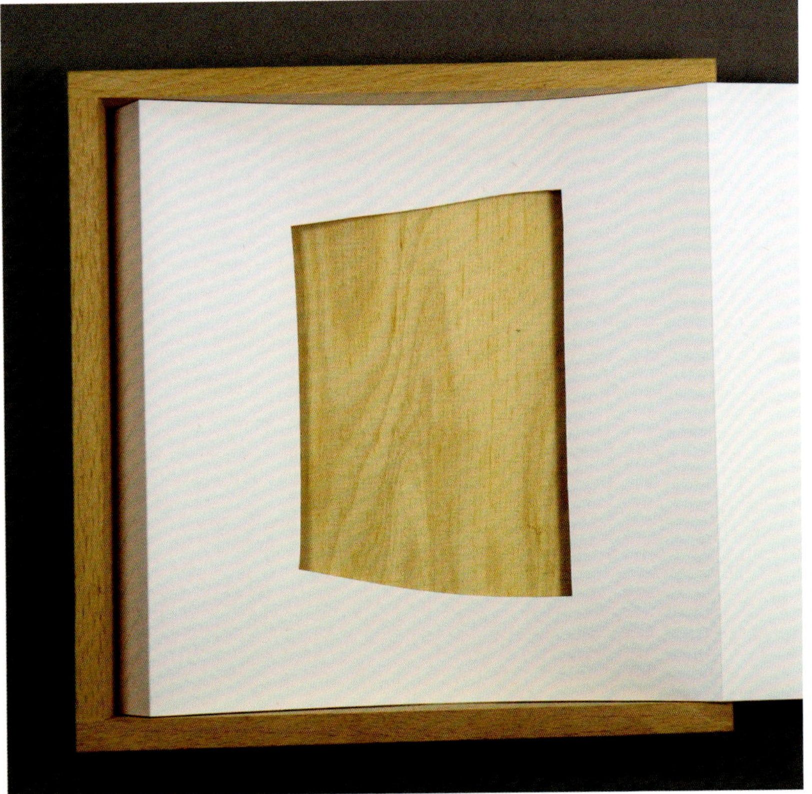

Now you should test beforehand to see if everything fits. Place the left-folded edge between the spacer and the side panel, to which it is later glued fast. Then fold the whole thing from right to left (to the back).

At the very end, glue the rear side of the v-shaped folded edge on the right to the back panel of the box, using white glue.

Before doing this, when turning the zig-zag tunnel to the right, make sure that the edge of the third fold rests on the left side of the spacer. If, after gluing in the finished tunnel, the right front fold is in danger of slipping out, you can glue a small tab underneath and attach it to the inner side of the box with double-sided adhesive tape.

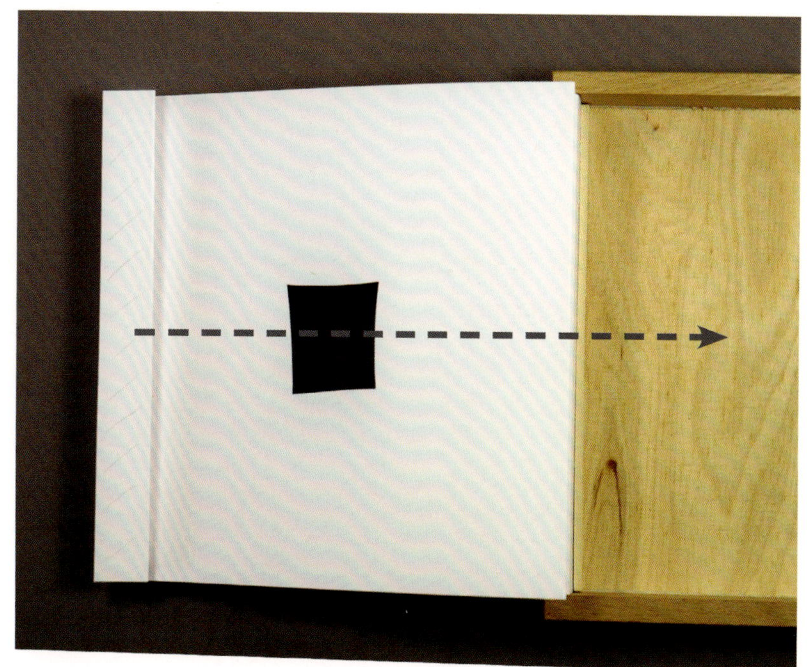

This way everything will sit in the box well, nothing gets stuck, and the shadows of the finished tunnel brought out by the spacing are beautiful to see.

Now you can design the tunnel. The pattern box on page 30 shows a very simple arrangement using pressed, interestingly nibbled leaves of a katsura tree that I photographed against the light. Reduced copies of this, cut out with a scalpel and glued along the edges of the tunnel, were sufficient to create a delicate impression.

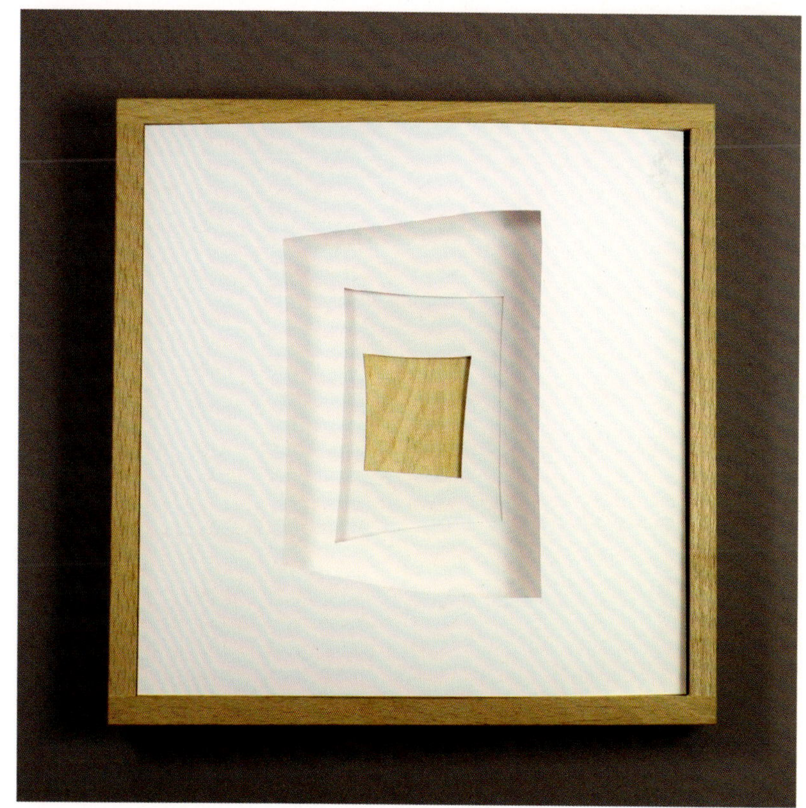

For further suggestions see the following page.

Alternative design:

A monochrome white paper cutout creates a classy effect in the natural wood box, and the shadows come into their own in an especially beautiful way. The last cutout can also be highlighted using a color surface, which, when glued directly to the box back panel, creates another small shadow line.

If the motifs and tunnel edges partially overlap, as here in the sample, it makes sense to make a separate preliminary drawing for each side.

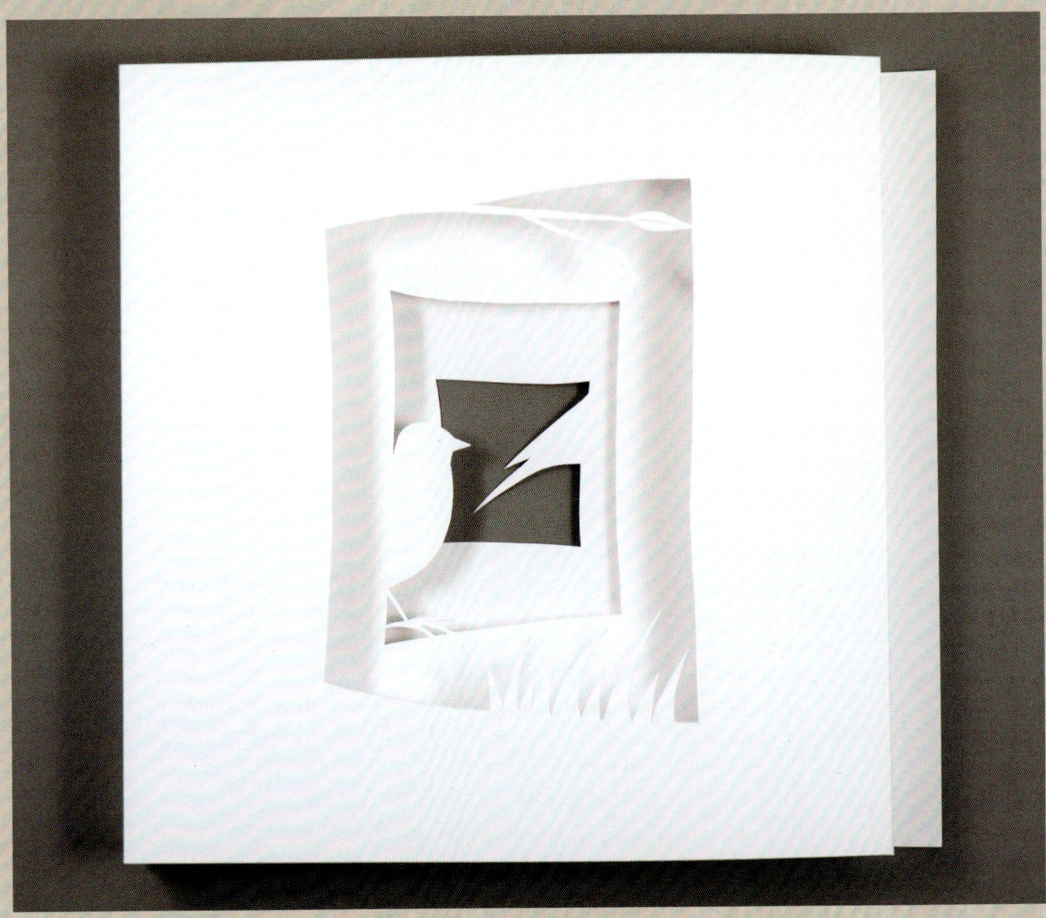

Alternative design:

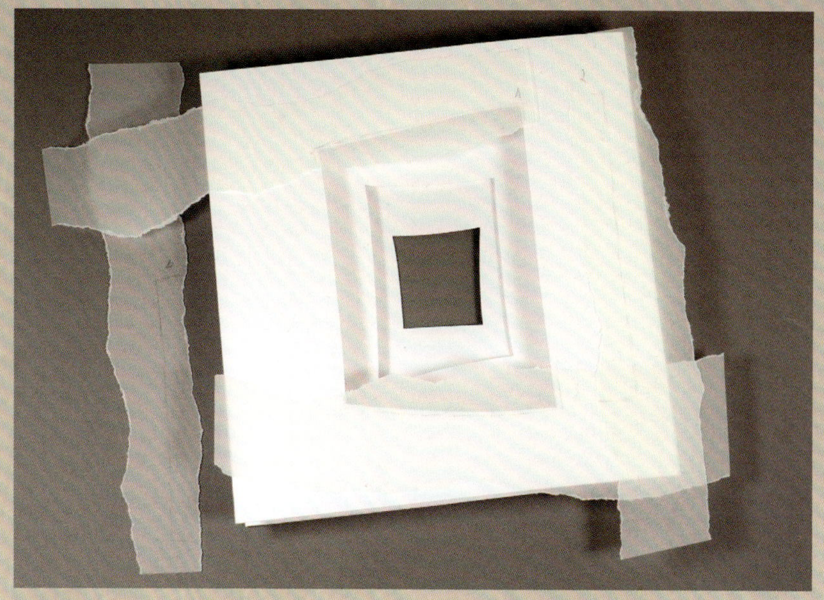

A tunnel decorated with texts on tracing paper also creates a beautiful play of shadow and the fall of light. To do this, tear strips of tracing paper and lay them on the edges of the tunnel cutouts. Arrange them so that the tear lines and tunnel edges fit together in the best way, and mark the corners in pencil.

You can now write on the tracing paper strips in the areas between the marks and then paste them from the back side (overlapping at the corners) to the edges of the tunnel. Glue a section for the back panel here directly from behind to the last side of the zigzag tunnel.

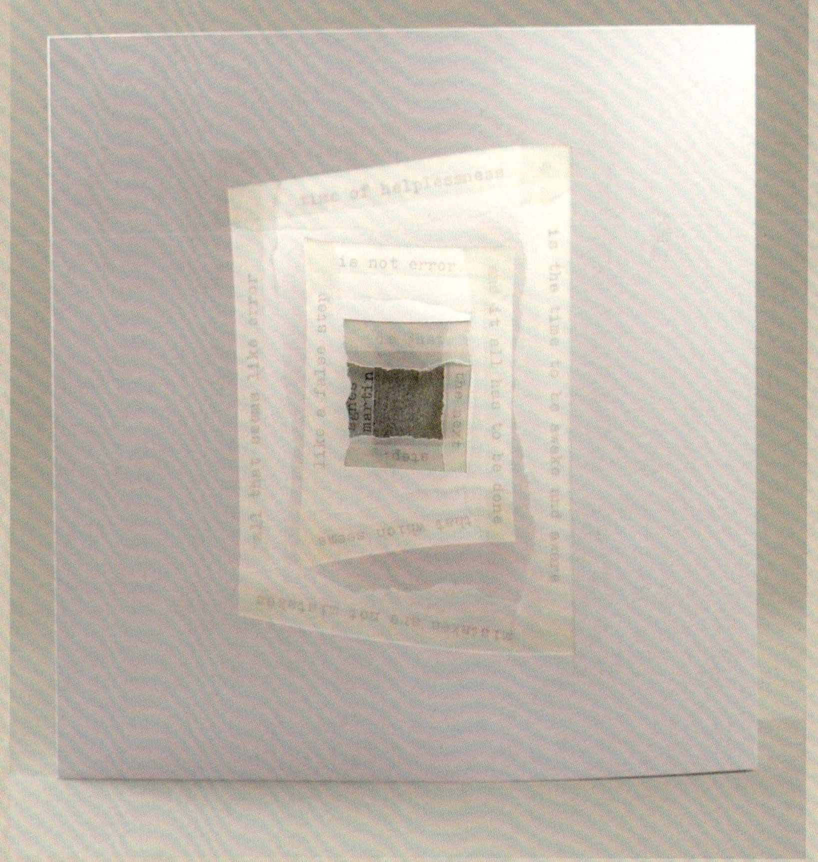

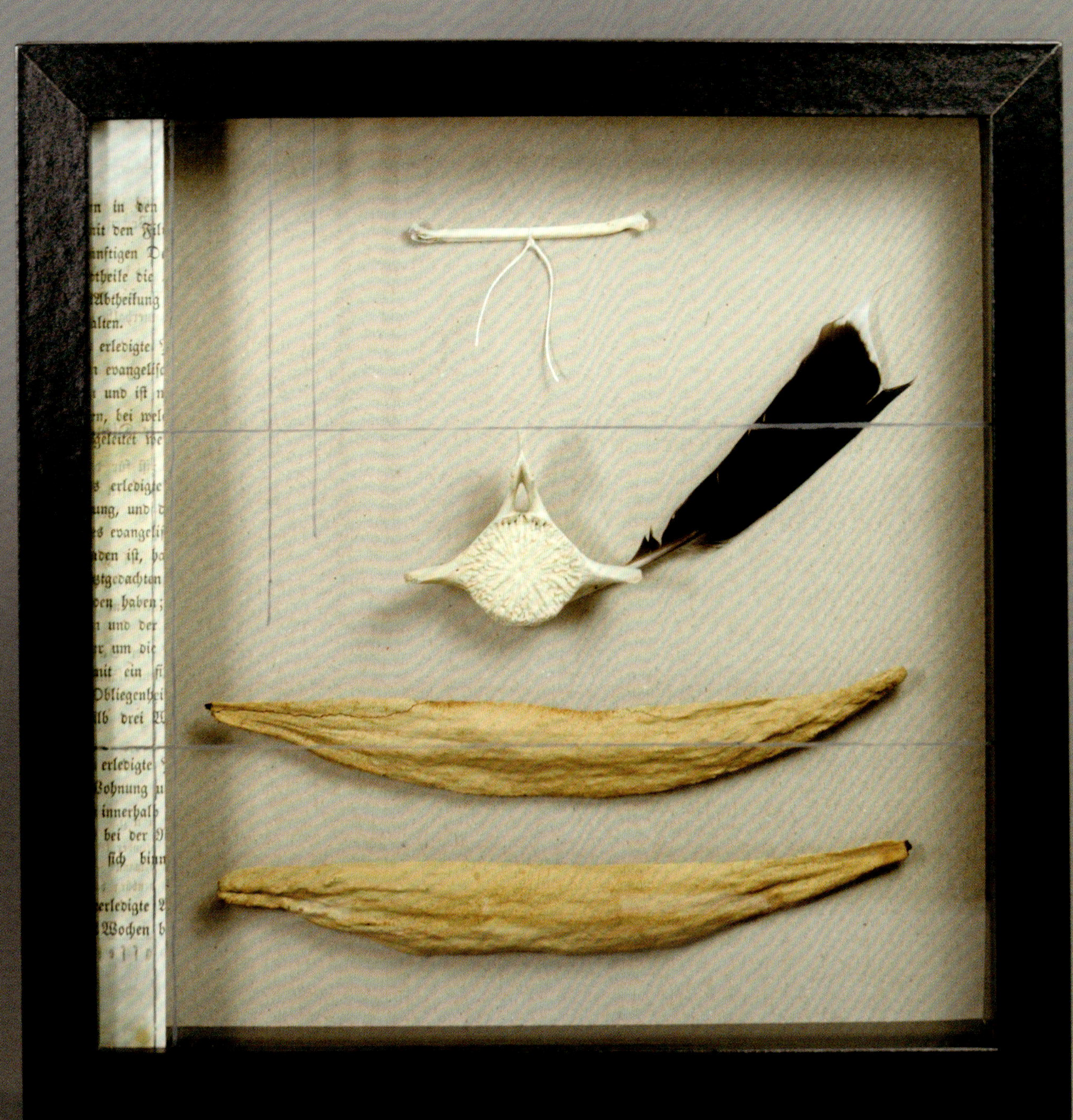
n in den
mit den Fil
nftigen D
theile die
Abtheilung
alten.
erledigte
evangelisch
n und ist
n, bei wel
geleitet we
erledigte
ung, und
s evangeli
den ist, b
stgedachten
en haben;
n und der
r um die
mit ein
Obliegenh
lb drei
erledigte
Wohnung
innerhalb
bei der
sich binn
erledigte
Wochen

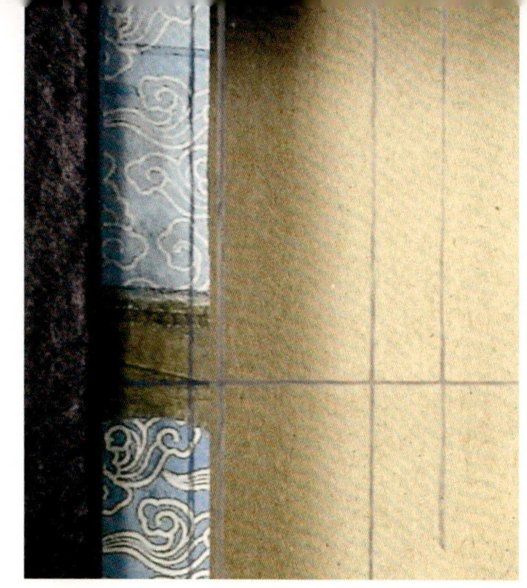

Shadow Box with Glass Pane and Lines

Ready-made shadow boxes with a glass pane are usually 1¼" to 2¾" deep. The glass pane is an important component; it contributes a great deal to the character of the finished box. Therefore, it should also be deliberately included in the design.

The sample box includes vertical and horizontal lines that are drawn directly onto the glass from the inside, using a drawing triangle. You can do this with a thin brush and acrylic paint, an oil-based glass marker pen, or simply with a kohl pencil (then wipe the edge of the triangle well). Then use paste to attach a narrow strip of text to the glass sideways along the lines, working from the inside. The text strip already creates a three-dimensional effect behind the lines that is enhanced by the shadows of the lines on the background.

The back panel is made of very hard material, and therefore it is not easy to pierce it. If the finds to be fastened on are relatively light, you can use a thread drawn through the background cardboard. Then fasten the cardboard to the back panel with dots of glue and knot the small bone on the thread. Because they are quite light, you can attach all the other elements by using white glue or double-sided adhesive tape directly onto the background cardboard and thus fasten them on invisibly.

The loose way the thread ends fall livens up this otherwise rather austere composition.

Materials + Tools

Shadow box with a glass pane, about 10" × 10"

Cardboard for the background

Needle and thread

Glass marker pen, acrylic paint, or eyeliner pencil

Set square

Paste and brush

White glue and double-sided adhesive tape

Strips of text or image from a newspaper

Finds such as bone, feather, boat-shaped kapok tree pods . . .

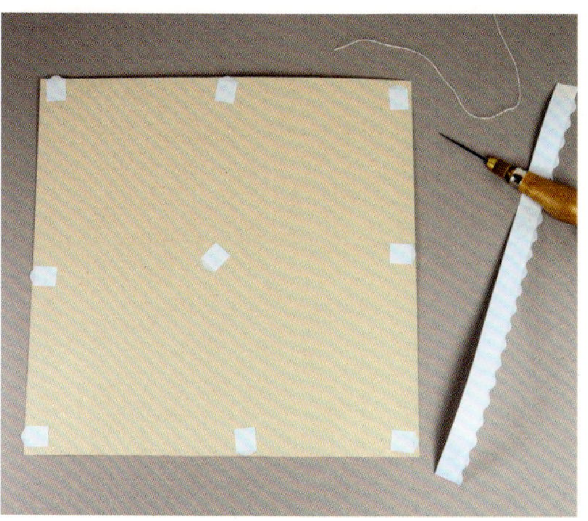

If you replace the text strip with a newspaper clipping of a fragment of an image that has a blue tone that corresponds to the blue behind the feather, this changes the overall character of the box.

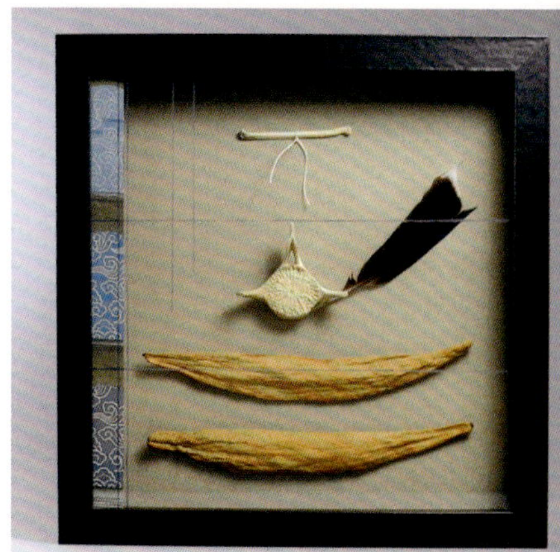

◀ *10" × 10" × 2"*

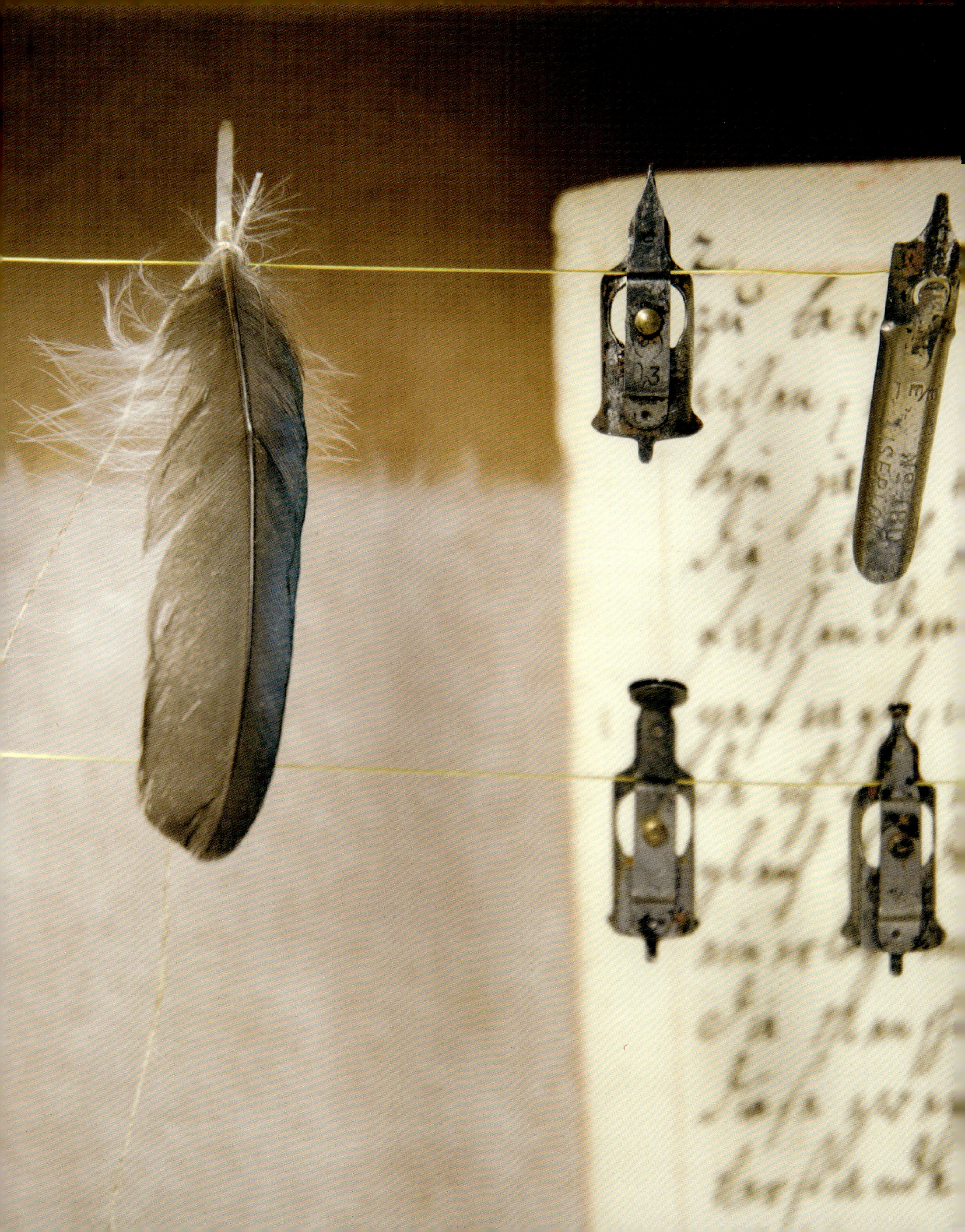

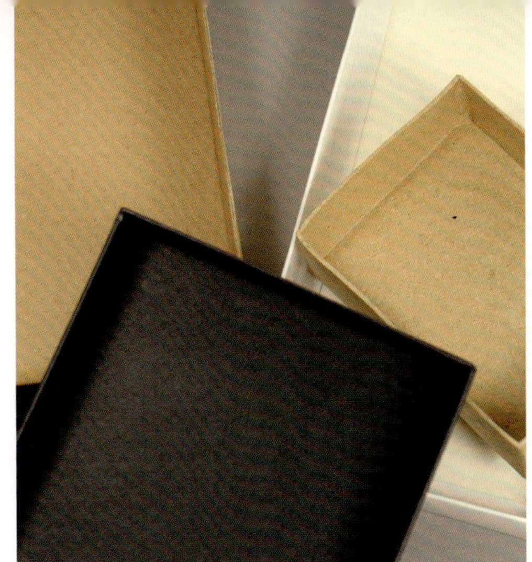

2 Sturdy Cartons and Carton Lids

Simple packing cartons that have a separate lid and are made of strong cardboard or corrugated cardboard can also be used as shadow boxes. Above all, if you need a personal gift in a hurry, you can improvise wonderfully using such simple boxes as these.

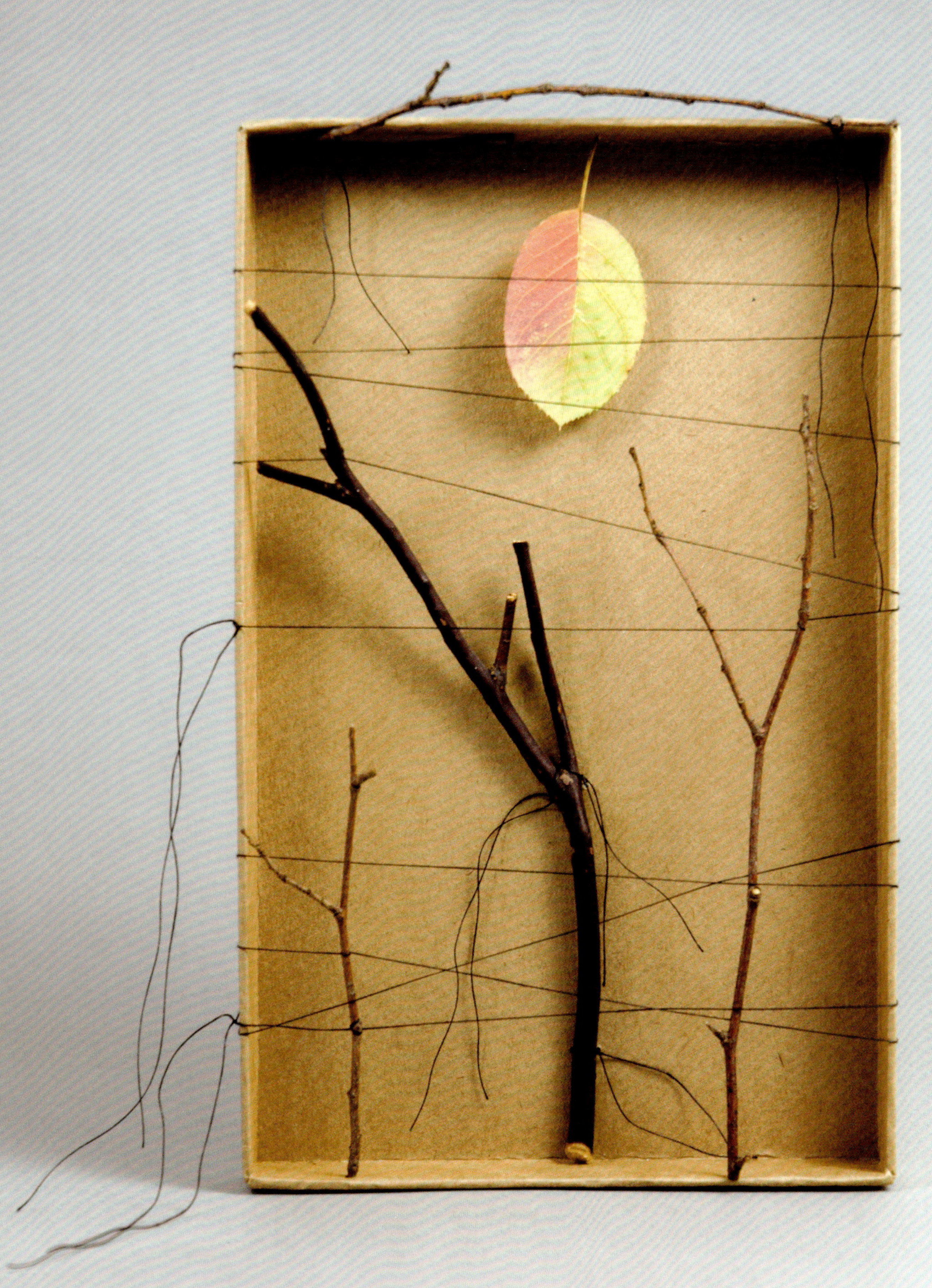

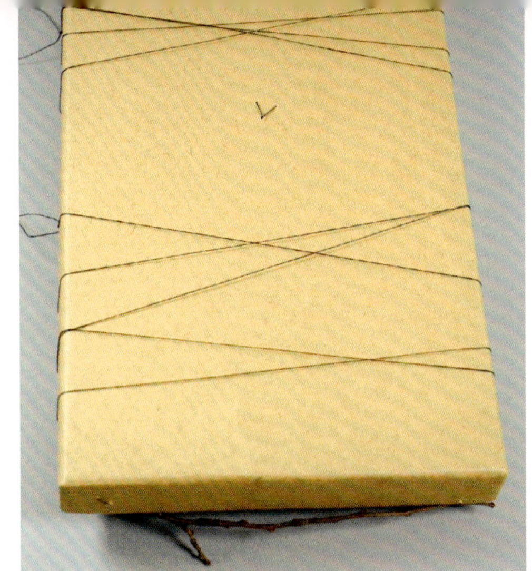

Thread for Fastening and Wrapping

Materials + Tools

Carton lid, at least ¾" deep

Strong twine in a contrasting color

Awl and needle

Small forked twigs

Pressed leaf

Some white glue

Sturdy, natural brown cartons are available in your artist's supply store or a stationery shop. The neutral packing paper cover works very well for presenting natural materials without any painting or varnishing.

A fundamental advantage of using these cartons for shadow boxes is that, unlike wood, it is easy to pierce the material with an awl. This creates inspiring attachment and design options with thread, without any need for using a noisy drill.

Y-shaped twigs have a "magical" shape and can be arranged nicely in a flat carton lid. They can be knotted to the back panel, drawn upward and outward, or anchored free-standing in a hole pierced beforehand into the bottom. Fasten the stem of the pressed leaf with a drop of white glue into a predrilled hole in the lid and wrap the entire carton in thread, which then forms a graphic pattern—including on the back panel.

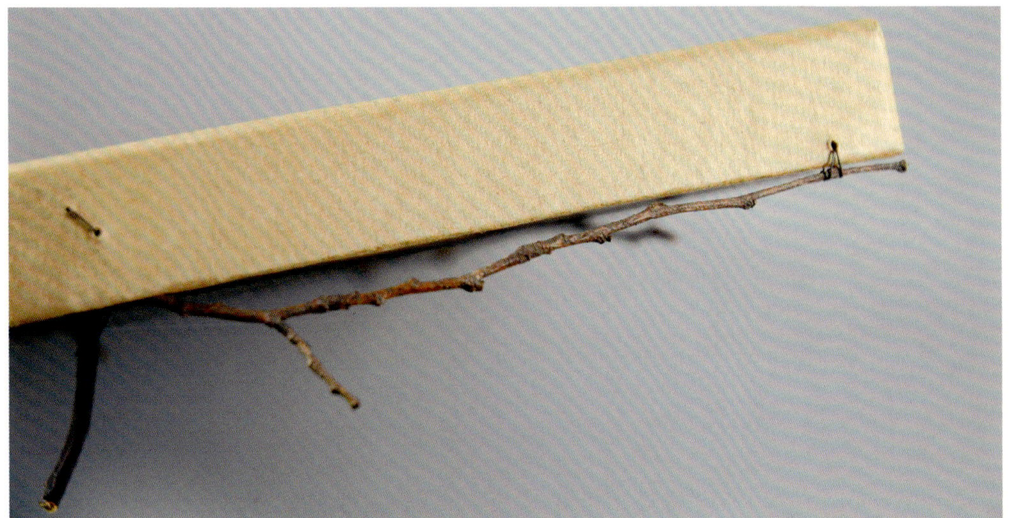

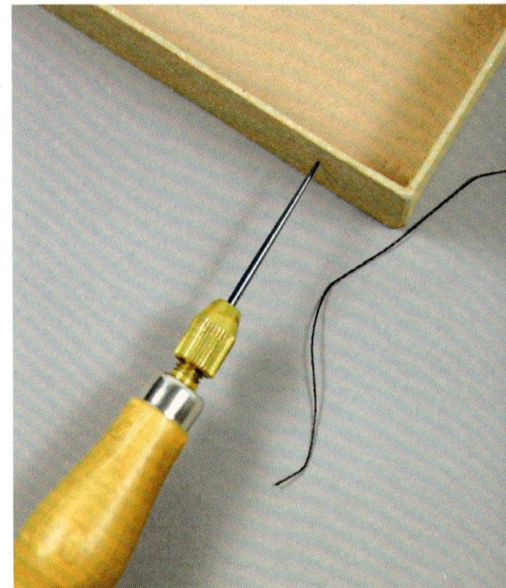

◀ *8½" × 5½" × ¾"*

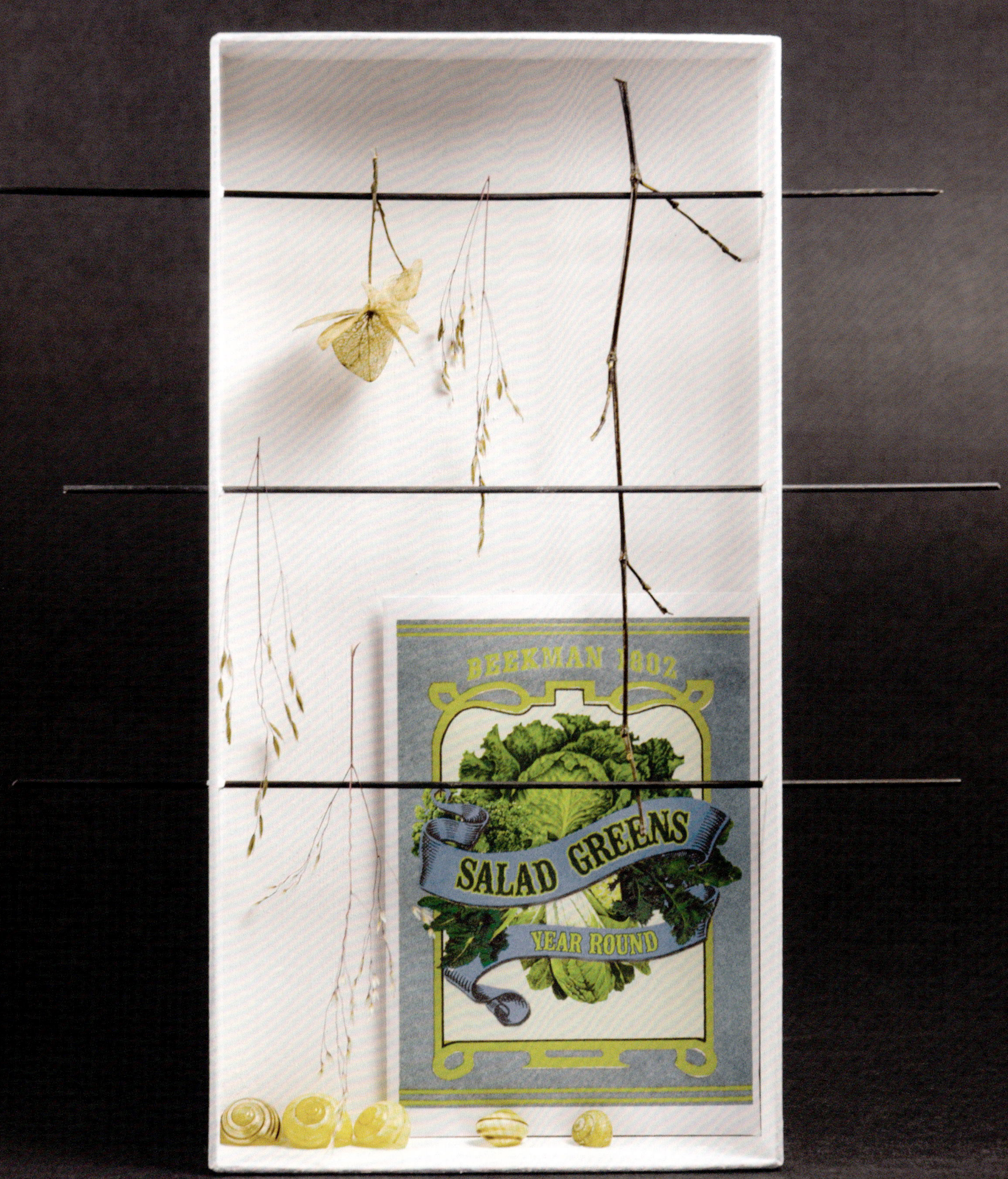
BEEKMAN 1802
SALAD GREENS
YEAR ROUND

Suspending Objects on Horizontally Inserted Thin Wire Stems

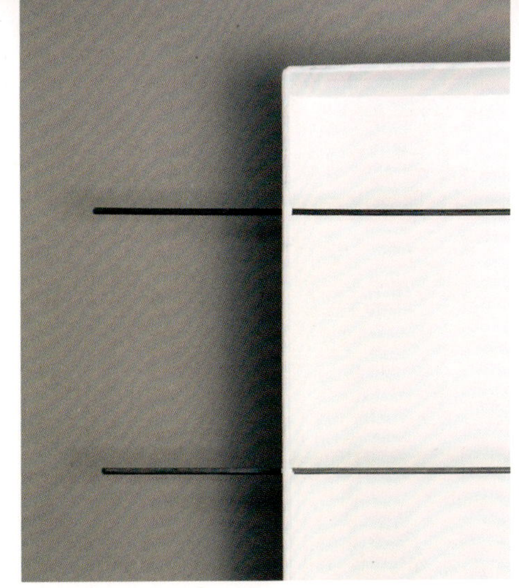

Materials + Tools

Carton bottom, at least 1¼" deep

White gesso and brush

Ruler

Awl

Wire cutter (side cutter)

Wire flower stems (annealed), about 1–1.5 mm thick, or very thin bamboo sticks

Finds on a garden theme, such as special seed pods, small twigs, grass seeds, dried flowers, snail shells . . .

With a white gesso coating, the dark-green bottom of a sturdy chocolates box becomes an ideal background for small, delicate things.

To be able to fill the narrow vertical format upward without gluing anything fast, insert thin wire stems horizontally to serve as hangers. Thin wire stems from a florist supplier make an interesting contrast to the white box. You can also use bamboo or wood sticks—as thin as possible.

First put the exhibits temporarily in the box to work out the arrangement. Then measure the intended height for the sticks on the two long side panels of the box with a ruler and mark the drill holes in pencil. Pierce through the side panels from outside to inside. If the exit points from the awl fray in an unsightly way on the inside, you can smooth them out again using a bone folder. You can place or insert the objects on the bottom of the box. Then hang them over the sticks higher up, creating an airy, mobile effect. Another advantage of this type of presentation is that you can exchange the objects at any time.

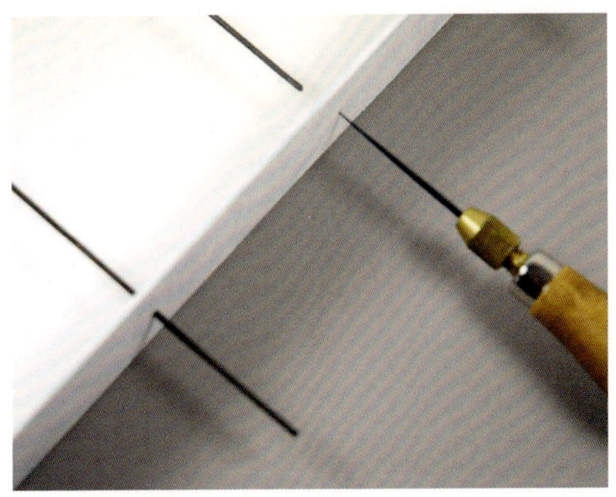

Please note: A shadow box of this kind is intended as a wall object for adults and should be kept out of the hands of children, since the tips protruding from the sides could be dangerous.

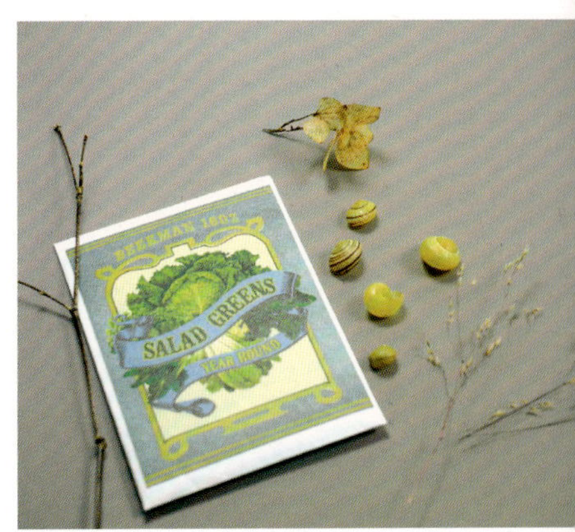

◀ *9" × 5" × 1½"*

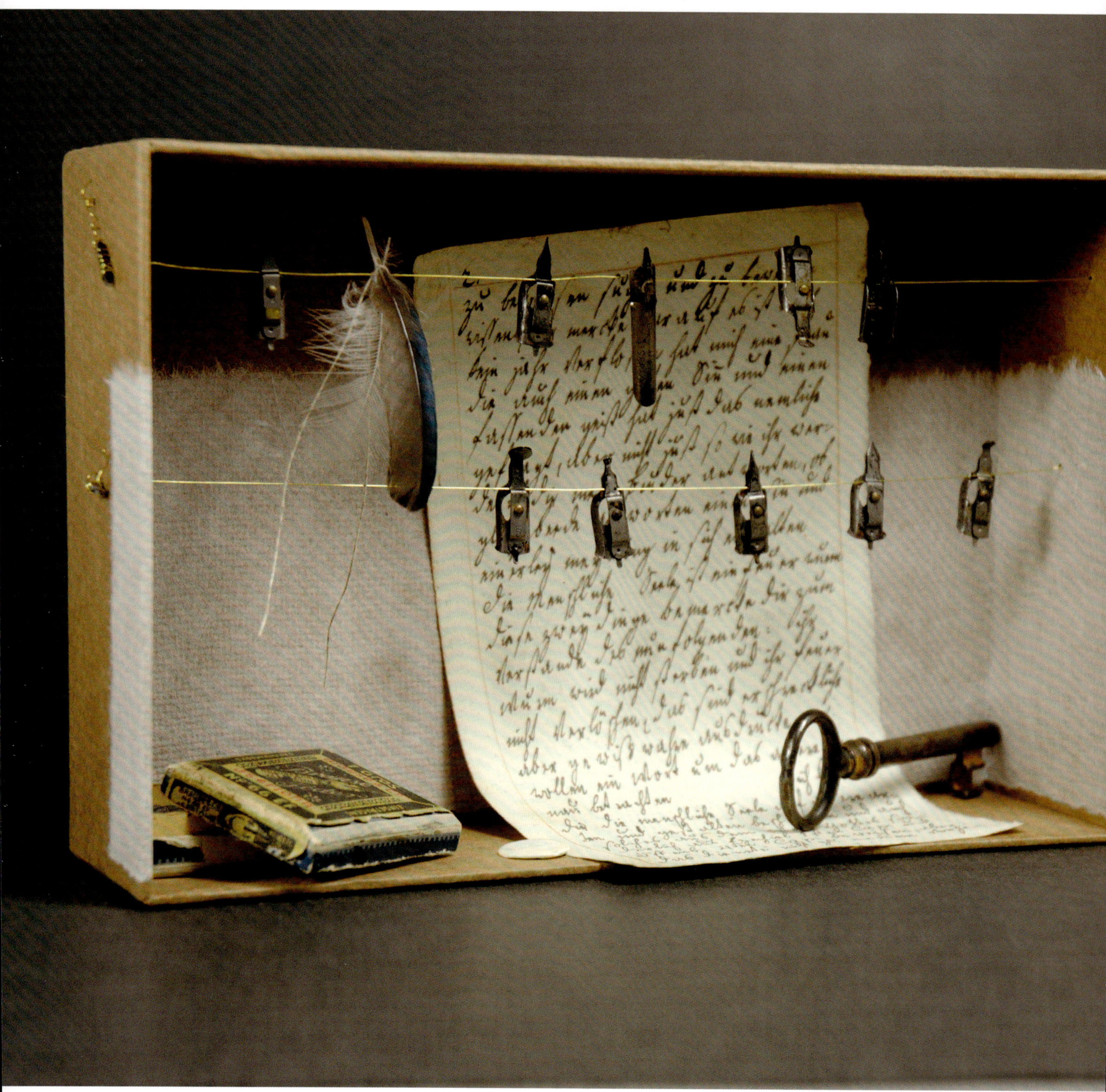

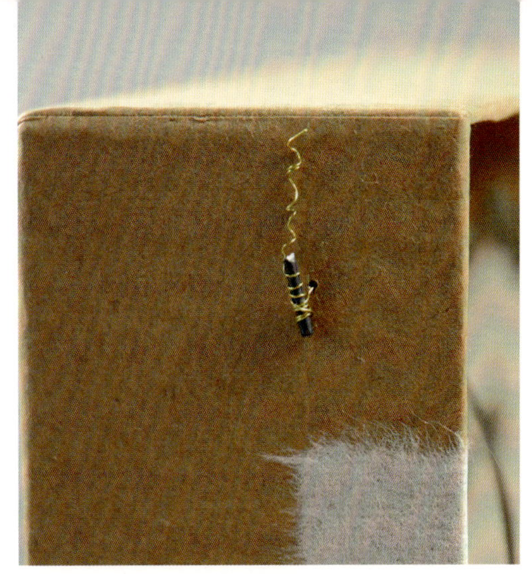

Suspending Objects on Wire Stretched Sideways

The deep bottom of the natural brown carton whose cover you used for the Y-shaped twigs houses a diorama on the theme of old pen nibs, set in landscape format. To lighten up the background, the inside panels are wallpapered with light natural paper about two-thirds high. At the same time, let some of the paper run over to the outside of the box.

To fill the space and be able to hang up the pen nibs, stretch thin brass wire horizontally. To do this, wind the wire around small leftover pieces of wire rods (or toothpicks) outside the drilled holes and then tighten it. Insert the sheet of writing loosely and fasten it to the back panel with a piece of double-sided adhesive tape.

Materials + Tools

Carton bottom, at least 2" deep

Paste and brush

Thin brass wire

Wire pliers and awl

Leftover pieces of wire or small pieces of toothpick

Natural paper with a torn edge

Collected things and finds, such as here on the theme of old pen nibs

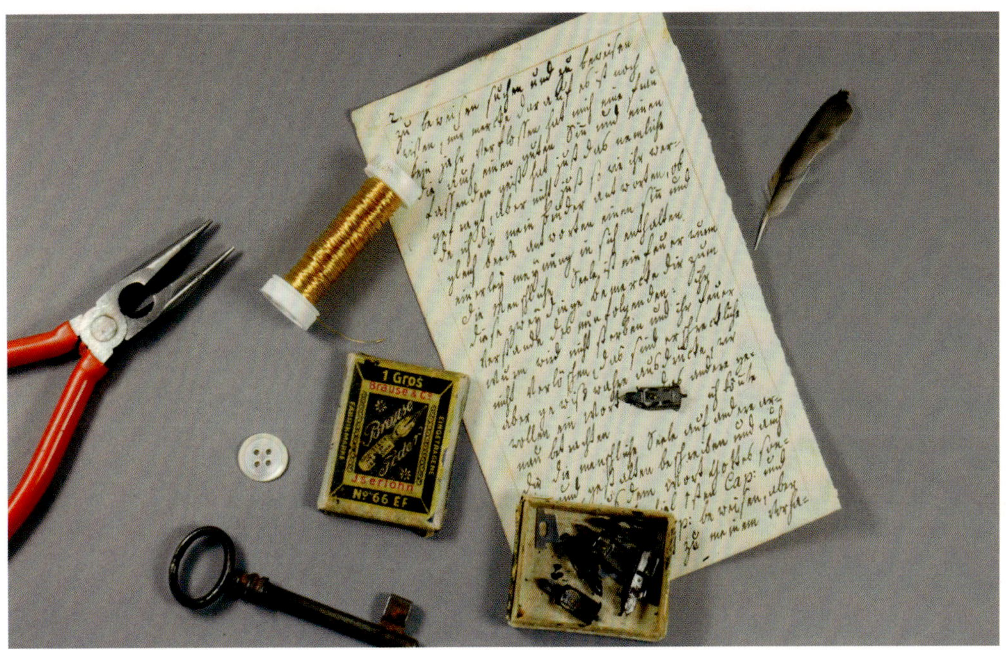

◀ *5" × 9" × 2½"*

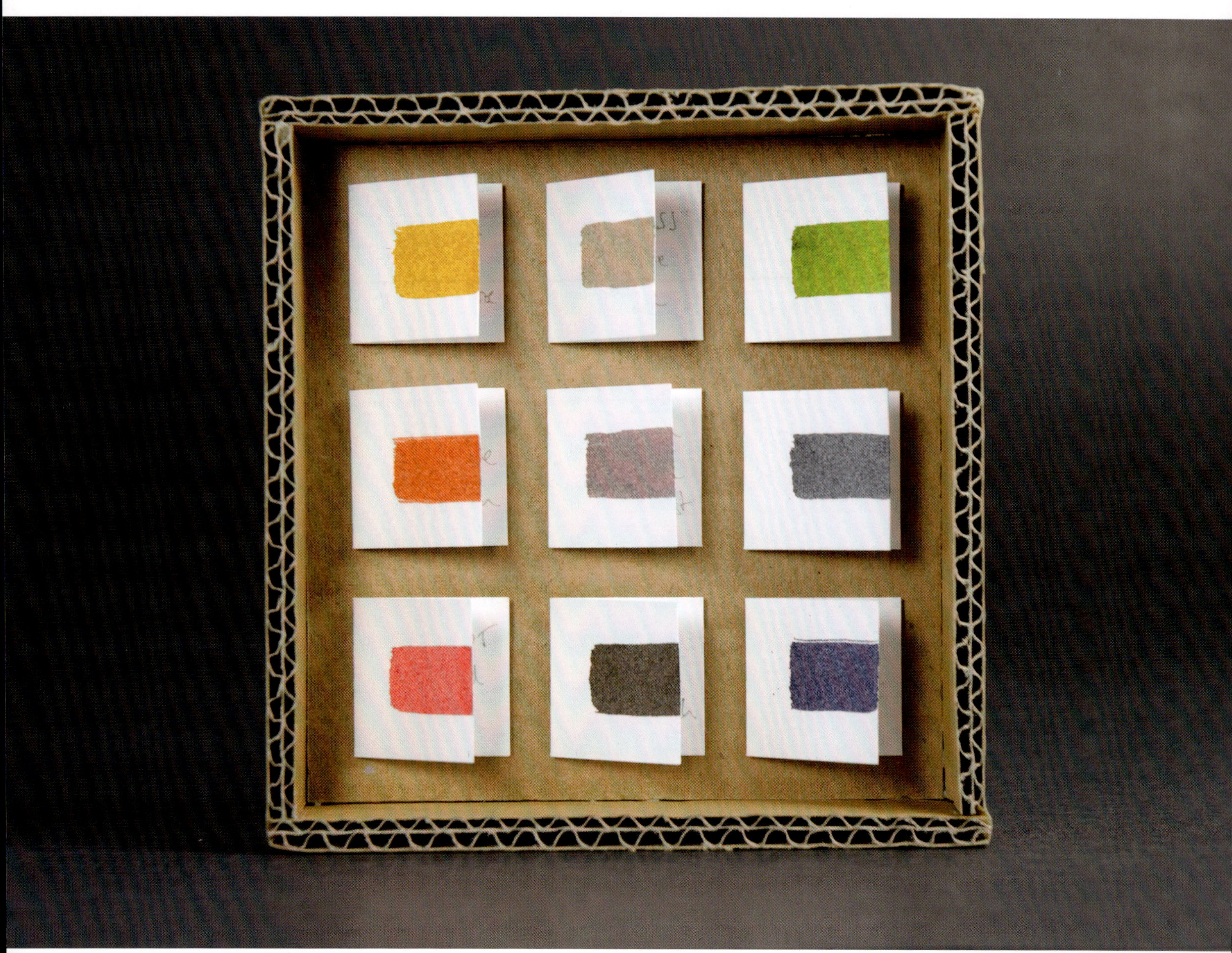

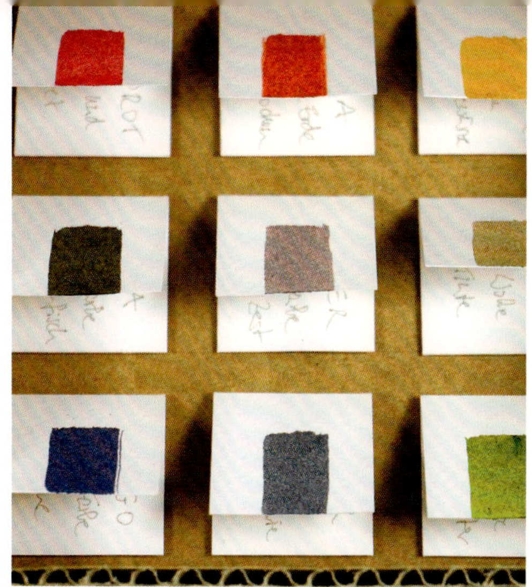

Sequences—Such as Color Swatches

A packing carton made of corrugated cardboard offers an edge that is graphically interesting when you use a sharp cutter to trim the height of the carton neatly all around. The neutral tone of the packing paper provides a warm background for a collection or sequence of similar things.

Color swatches become something wonderful when they are presented in sequence. You can put together a composition of your favorite colors or create a color theme for travel or other memories in this box. The inner sides of the folded cardboard pieces can be inscribed according to the theme. The texts, slightly obscured from the front, remain discreetly in the background. To prevent them from adhering flat to the back panel, the color swatches are mounted on an in-between layer of cardboard remnants and fastened to the back panel, using white glue. This small spacing creates a subtle shadow.

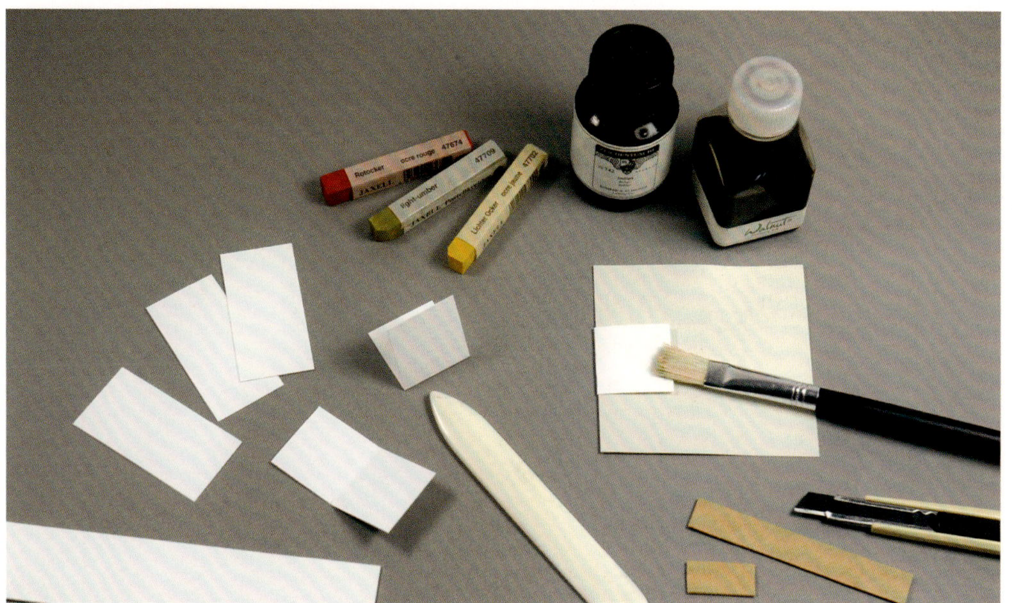

Materials + Tools

Corrugated cardboard carton

Lengthwise pieces of watercolor board with the grain direction parallel to the short side

Bone folder

Ruler, graphic cutter, and a cutting mat

Waste pieces of cardboard or pasteboard, about 1 mm thick

White glue

Flat brush for applying colors such as India ink, watercolors, and diluted acrylic paint applied as a glaze

Or pastel crayons, crayons, paper samples, yarn samples . . .

◀ *5½" × 5½" × 1½"*

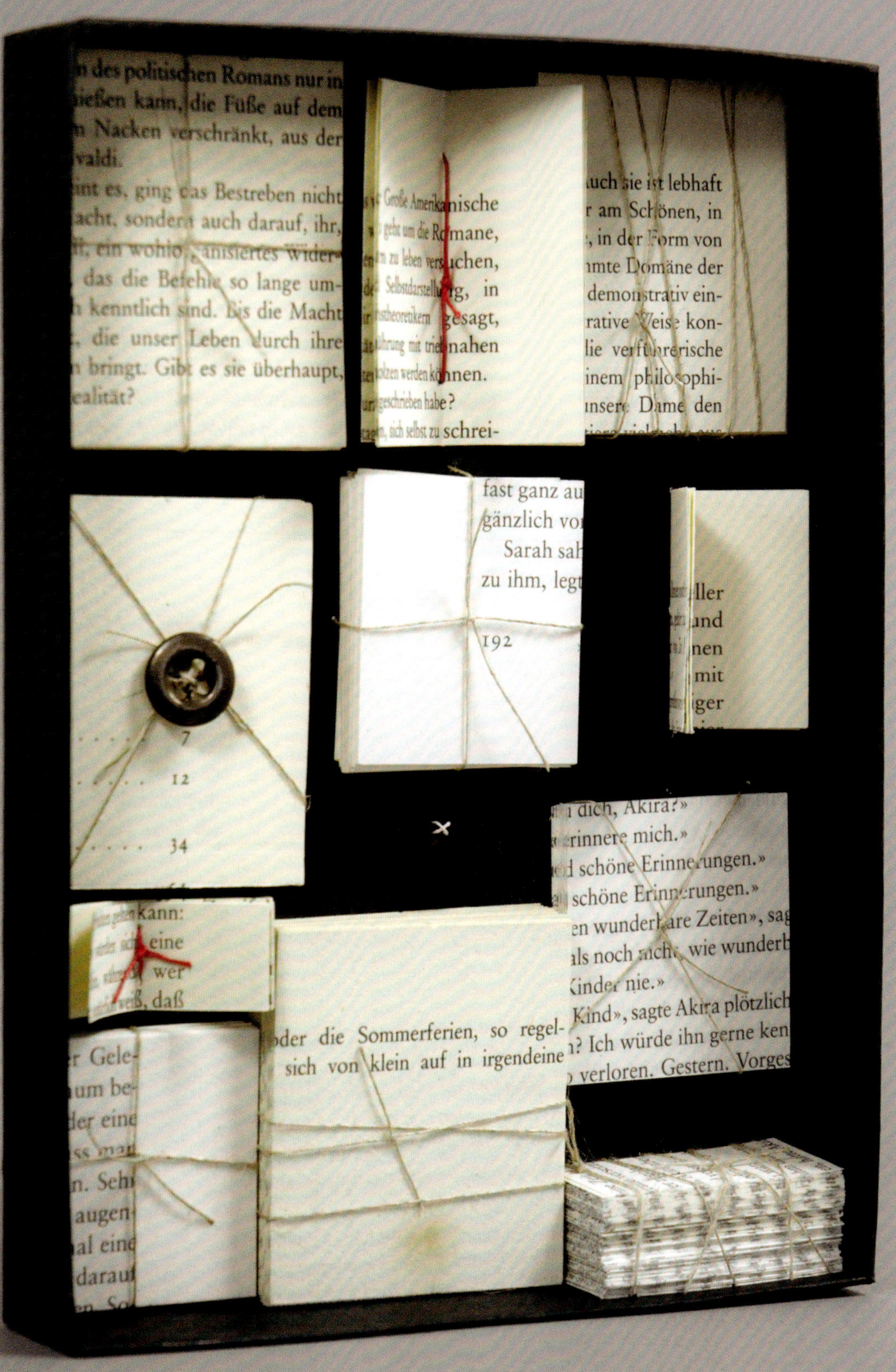
n des politischen Romans nur in
ießen kann, die Füße auf dem
n Nacken verschränkt, aus der
valdi.
int es, ging das Bestreben nicht
acht, sondern auch darauf, ihr,
das die Befehle so lange um-
h kenntlich sind. Bis die Macht
, die unser Leben durch ihre
n bringt. Gibt es sie überhaupt,
ealität?
Große Amerikanische
geht um die Romane,
zu leben versuchen,
Selbstdarstellung, in
gesagt,
nahen
können.
geschrieben habe?
ich selbst zu schrei-
auch sie ist lebhaft
r am Schönen, in
, in der Form von
mte Domäne der
demonstrativ ein-
rative Weise kon-
lie verführerische
inem philosophi-
unsere Dame den
fast ganz au
gänzlich vo
Sarah sah
zu ihm, legt
192
ller
und
nen
mit
ger
7
12
34
kann:
eine
wer
weiß, daß
dich, Akira?»
erinnere mich.»
schöne Erinnerungen.»
schöne Erinnerungen.»
en wunderbare Zeiten», sag
als noch nicht, wie wunderb
Kinder nie.»
Kind», sagte Akira plötzlich
? Ich würde ihn gerne ken
verloren. Gestern. Vorges
oder die Sommerferien, so regel-
sich von klein auf in irgendeine
r Gele-
aum be-
der eine
n. Seh
augen-
al eine
darauf

Firmly Knotted Bundles of Text

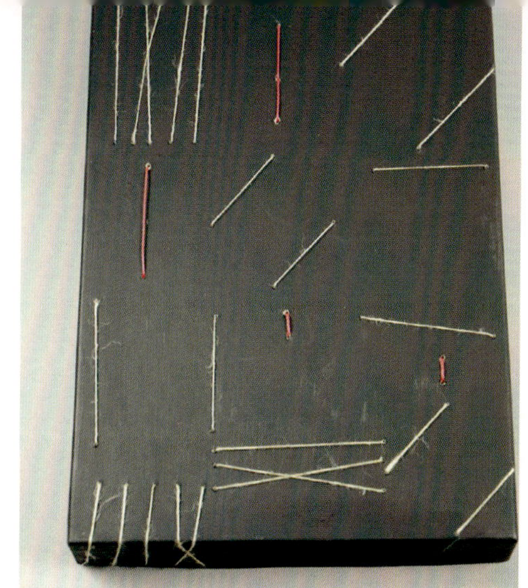

Materials + Tools

Small carton lid, at least 3/4" deep

Black acrylic paint and brush

Old book to cut up

Bone folder

Ruler, graphic cutter, and cutting mat

Awl and needle

Red thread and natural linen thread

Small, decorative elements, such as buttons . . .

Here, the fact that it is easy to bore through the carton back panel is used purposely to fasten on a number of bundles of text. As a contrast to the white of the paper, the carton was painted black.

First, separate the book block of an old book into stacks of pages almost 5/8" thick. Extend the cutter blade so that it matches the height of the stack, and patiently cut the pages into several different (small) rectangular stacks. Either use the cut stacks directly as a bundle or fold the individual leaves in the middle, stitch through the center fold as in a book, and firmly knot the leaves to the back panel. Small additions, such as buttons or other finds, will loosen up the field of text a bit.

You can also make the bundles of text out of old letters or diaries, which—cut into pieces—are turned into an object with a very personal meaning. You can then even turn the box around, so that only the back panel with the intentionally created thread artwork is visible and the private content remains concealed.

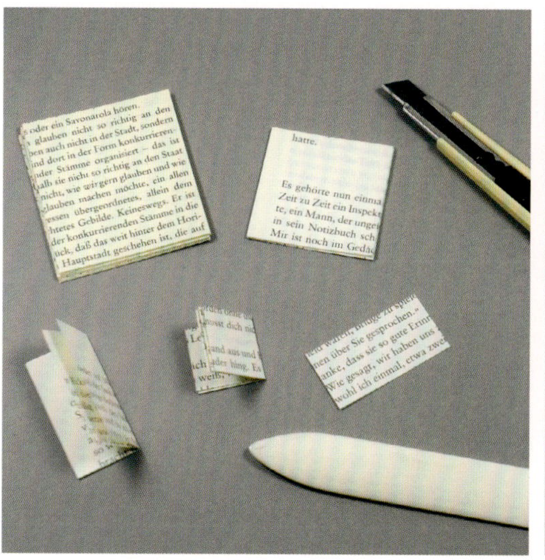

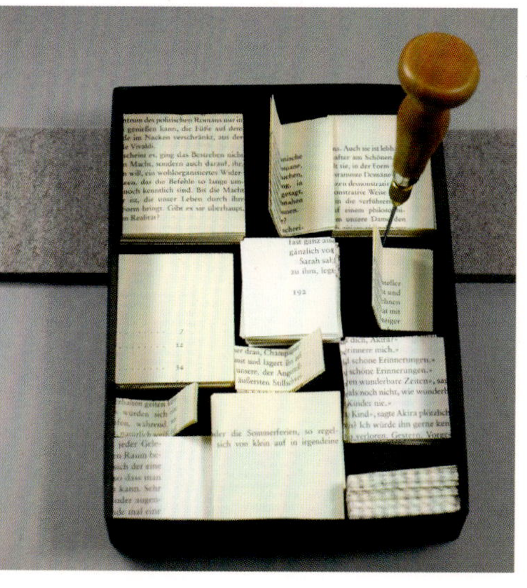

◀ *7½" × 5½" × 1¼"*

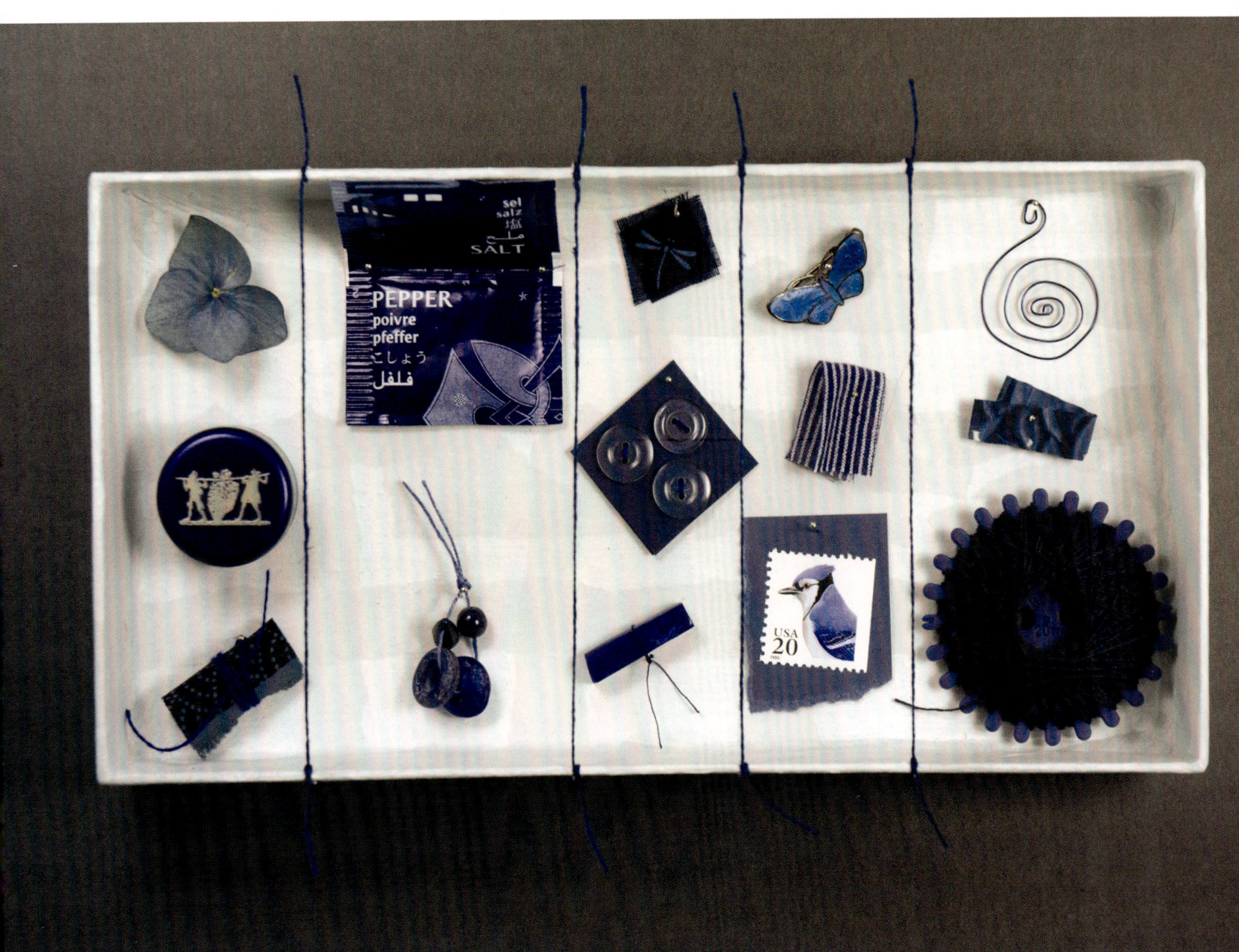
sel
salz
塩
ملح
SALT
PEPPER
poivre
pfeffer
こしょう
فلفل
USA
20

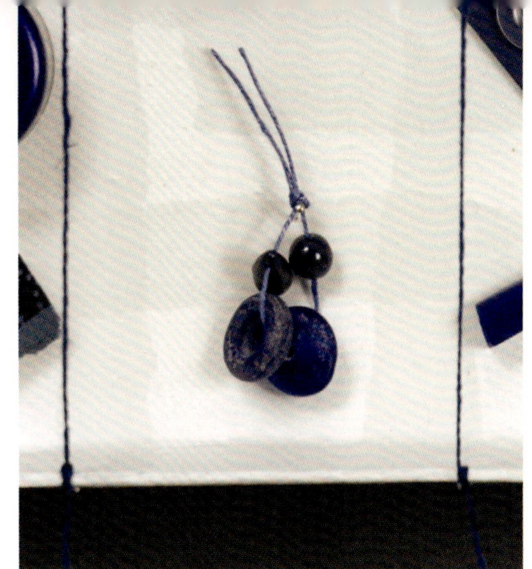

Thread Lines to Create Graphic Divisions

A sequence can consist of identical or very similar objects, such as the color swatches on page 48. You can also arrange completely different objects in a sequence, if you set a feature in the foreground that binds all of the objects together. Here, this is the color blue.

The carton lid on page 44 is now used in landscape format and is first primed with white gesso. Then tear light-gray tissue paper into irregular pieces, paste them in, and scatter them over the entire carton so that they overlap unevenly. Smooth gently, using a flat brush. The various shades of blue of the collected objects stand out beautifully against this delicately structured, not-sterile-white background.

The objects are fastened to the back of the carton so that they are clearly visible, using tiny nails —a somewhat tricky task that is easier to do if you hold the nails with a small pair of pliers. If the back panel is not thick enough to support the little nails, you can also glue some soft paperboard to the back of the carton. When arranging the objects, you should already have in mind how you are going to divide them into columns. Finally, prick the holes for the stretched threads a small space from the front edge at the same height above and below and tie on the vertical "thread lines."

Materials + Tools

Carton lid, at least 1¼" deep

White gesso and brush

Light gray tissue paper

Paste and brush

Tiny nails

Small pliers to hold the nails

Ruler and pencil

Awl and needle

Strong yarn and thin thread that match the color theme

Things that are connected (only) by their color

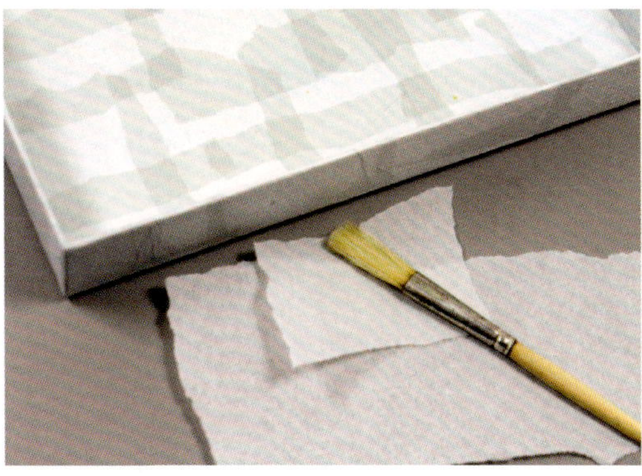

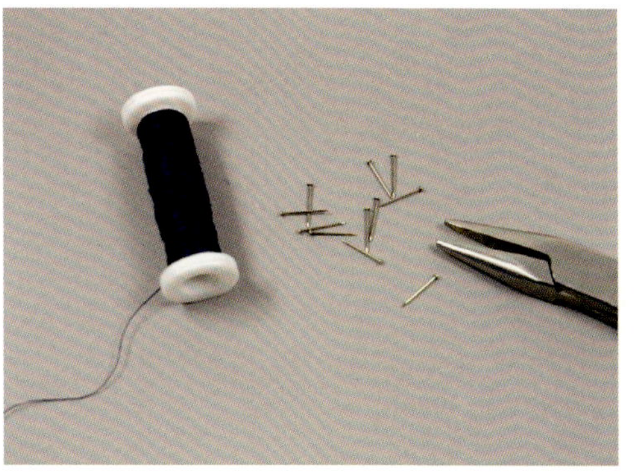

◀ ***5" × 9" × 1¼"***

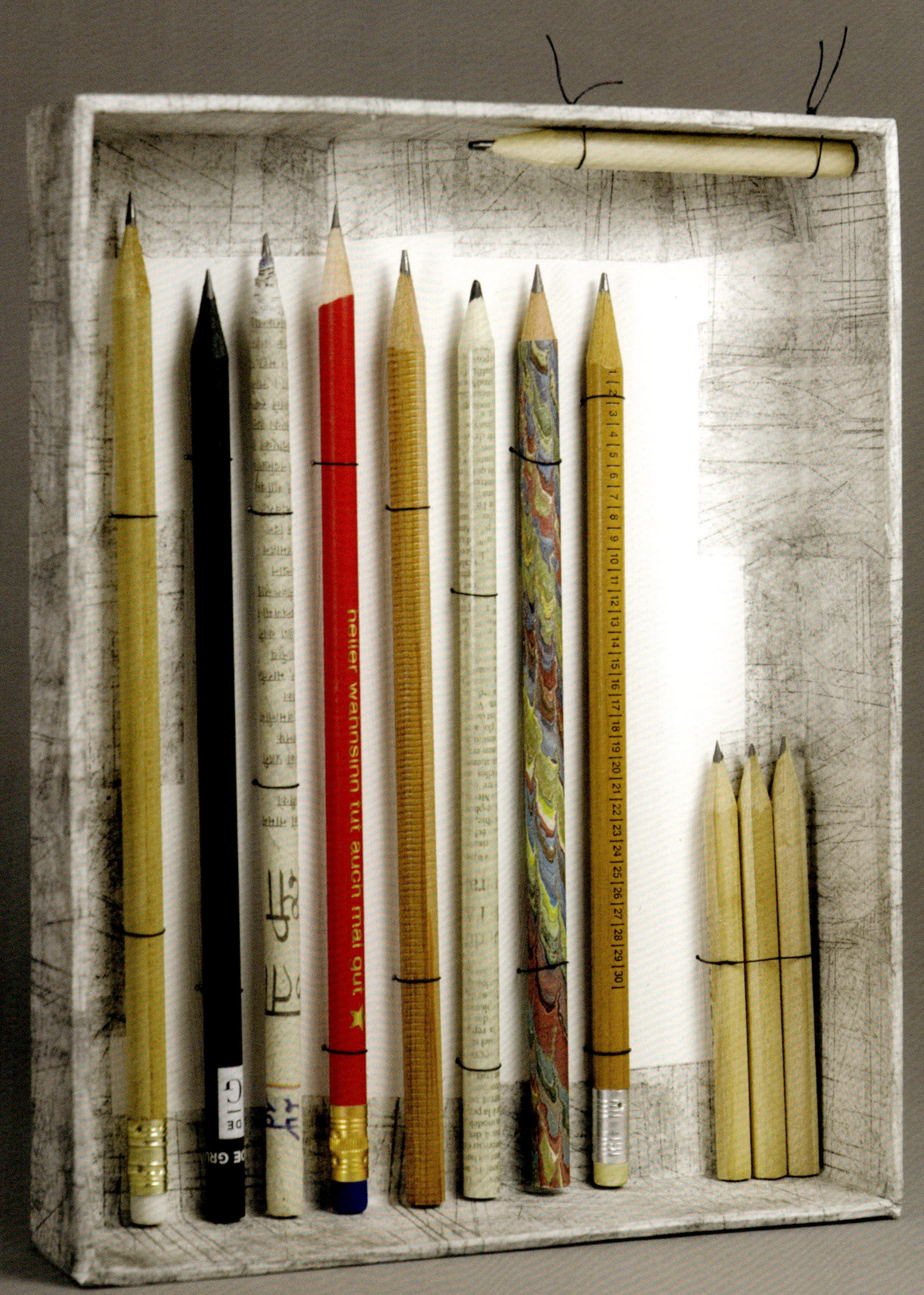
heiter wahnsinn tut auch mal gut

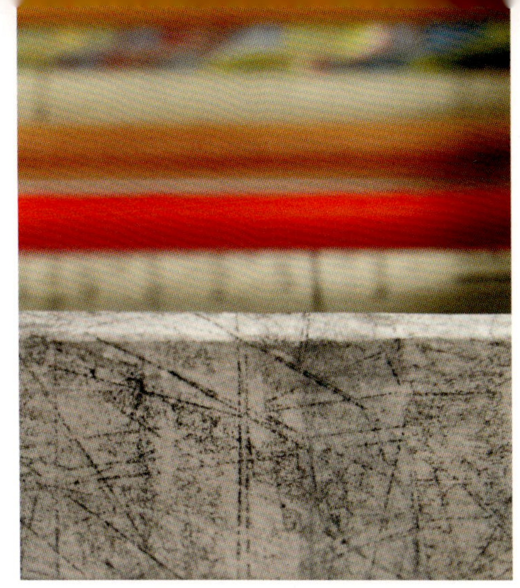

Cover Made of Frottage-Decorated Paper

Materials + Tools

Sturdy carton slightly higher than the length of a pencil

White gesso and brush

Graphite pencil (not water-soluble)

Ruler, graphic cutter, scissors, and a cutting mat

Translucent paper, such as sandwich wrap paper or hard-to-tear tissue paper

Paste and brush

Awl and needle

Strong black or gray thread (linen yarn)

Several pencils or other suitable collector's objects (see alternative design on page 57)

A box cover created using graphic frottage on translucent paper fits this pencil collection theme perfectly.

The box should first be primed inside and outside with white gesso, which also gives a little extra stability to thinner boxes and prevents the water-containing paste from damaging them.

Frottage is done in the same way as when you rub over a coin with a pencil—something most people tried when they were children. Graphite pencils (without the wooden casing) work much better for rubbing surfaces than a pencil you hold flat. Water-soluble graphite pencils are also available, but you should not use them for this because you will work on the frottage further, using paste. You cannot use paper that is soft or thick to do frottage. For this project, where the transparency of the paper plays an important role, thin sandwich wrap paper or thick tissue paper is best. You can find surfaces to rub everywhere. Whether wood floors, place mats, surfaces of folders, etc.—it is worth it to experiment! Every fine unevenness yields unimaginable results.

For dense areas of frottage, keep turning the sheet a bit to create an abstract structure and so the underlying surface is no longer recognizable. Then use the cutter to cut the paper into long, slightly slanted strips and use scissors to cut off irregular rectangles (also slightly slanted).

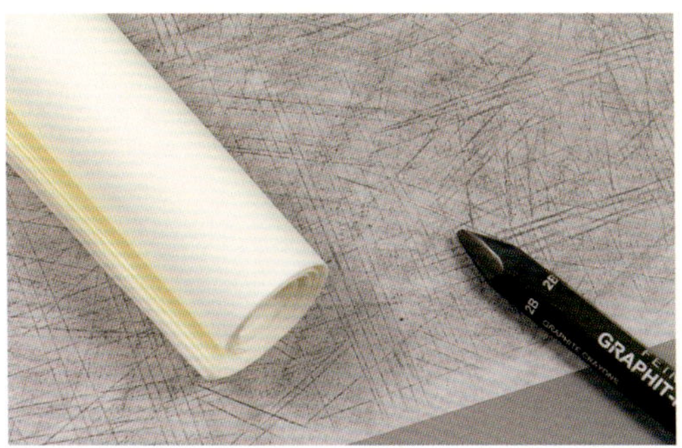

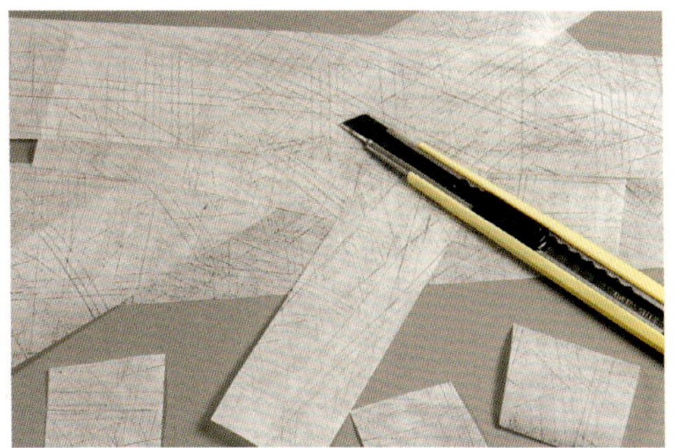

◀ *8″ × 6½″ × 1¼″*

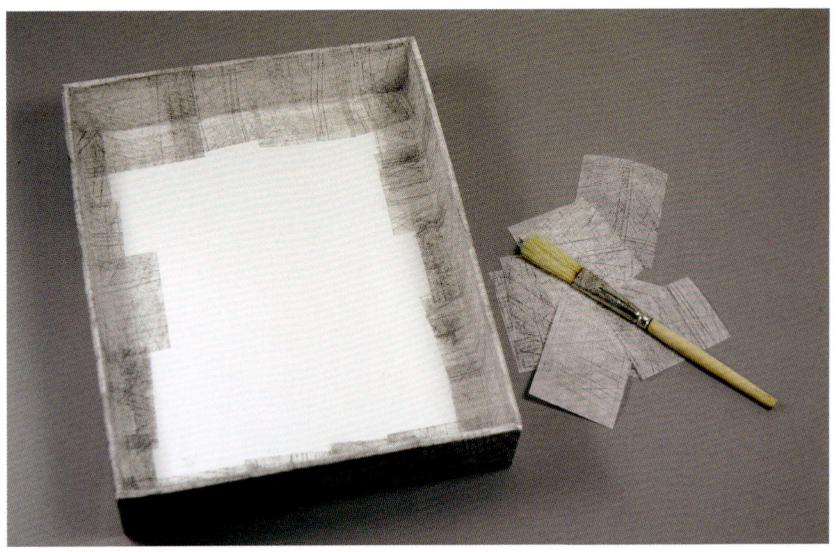

Apply the paste to the graphite side of the frottage and overlap the irregular pieces from the outside to the inside to laminate the box. Even if you didn't use a water-soluble graphite pencil, you should nevertheless take care not to spoil the frottage and not to damage other areas if your fingers are damp from the paste. The pieces applied to the inside of the side panels are here laminated to a kind of irregular rim that runs over onto the back panel.

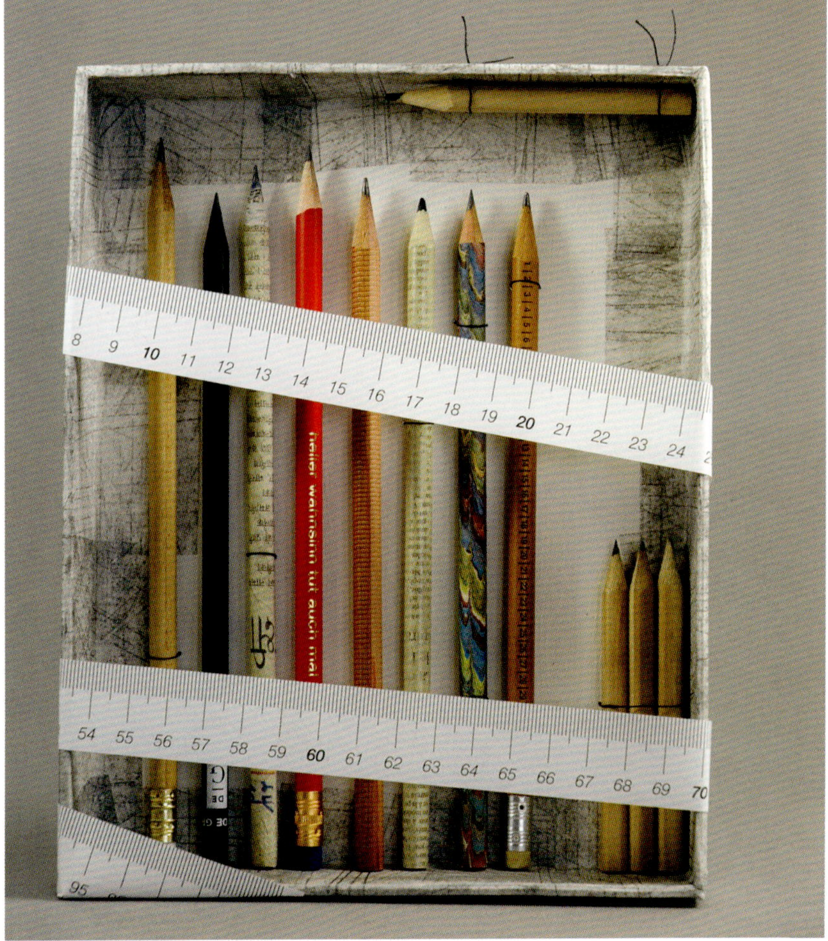

Arrange the collected pencils in the laminated box and use an awl to prick two holes each to the right and left of each pencil. Then use needle and thread to draw the thread from the back through the first hole inward, wind the thread around the pencil, pull it out through the second hole, and knot on the back.

You can often get small pencils for free in home improvement stores or large furniture stores. Paper-measuring tapes are also often available. To carry the collection forward thematically, you can wind a measuring tape diagonally around the box (*see figure at left*).

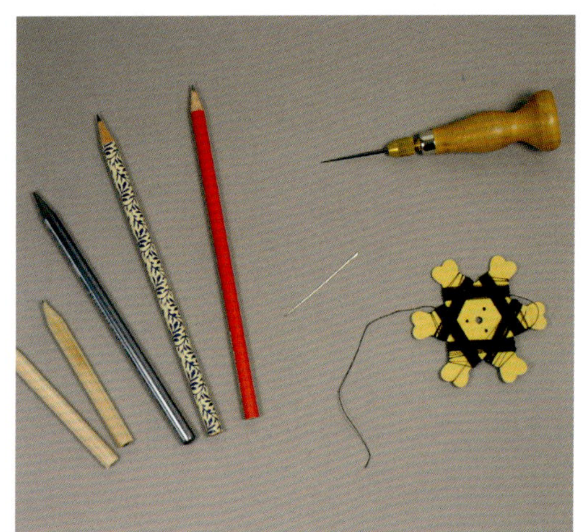

At the same time, be sure to fold the tape at a slight diagonal in the opposite direction on the back panel and use masking tape or washi tape to tape it so that it lies flat along the front edge.

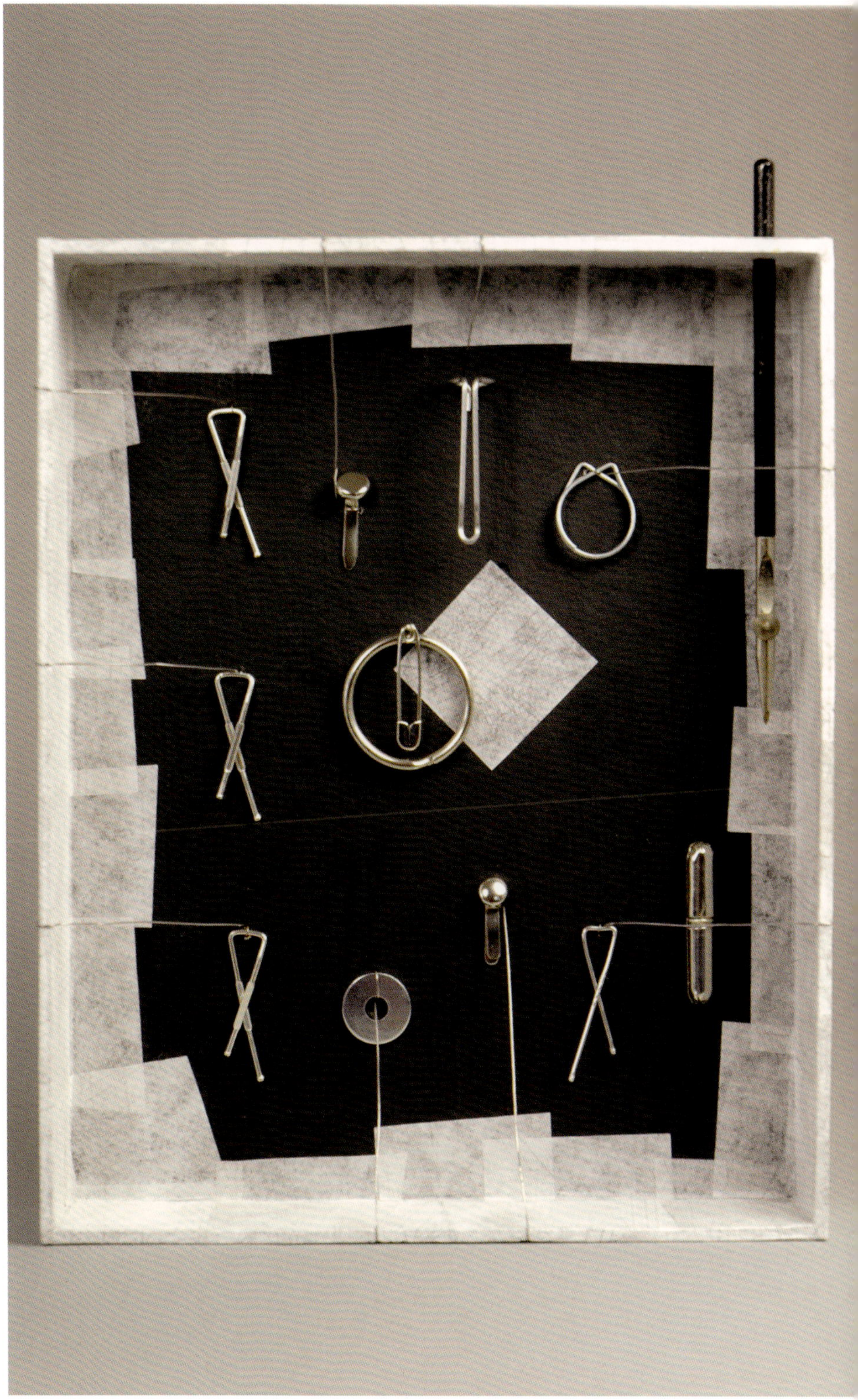

Alternative design:

Cover the carton by using the same technique, but after priming it with white gesso; here the back panel was painted with black acrylic paint. Fasten on some office supplies and small silver-colored metal objects, but rather than using thread, match the theme by winding thin wire (a long piece) around the edges of the carton each time, creating an interesting graphic effect. An opening for the drawing pen was bored in the top of the box with a hole punch.

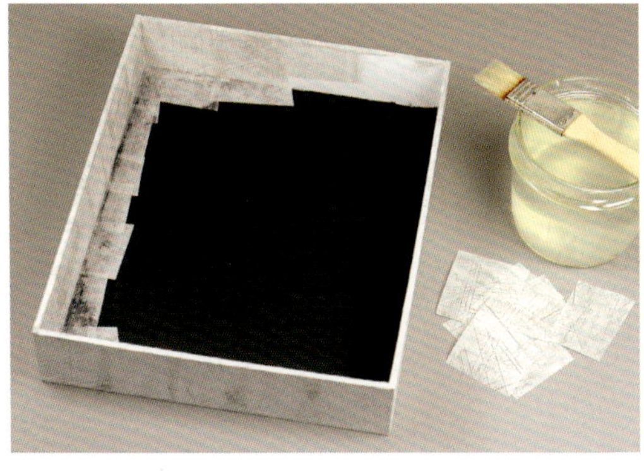

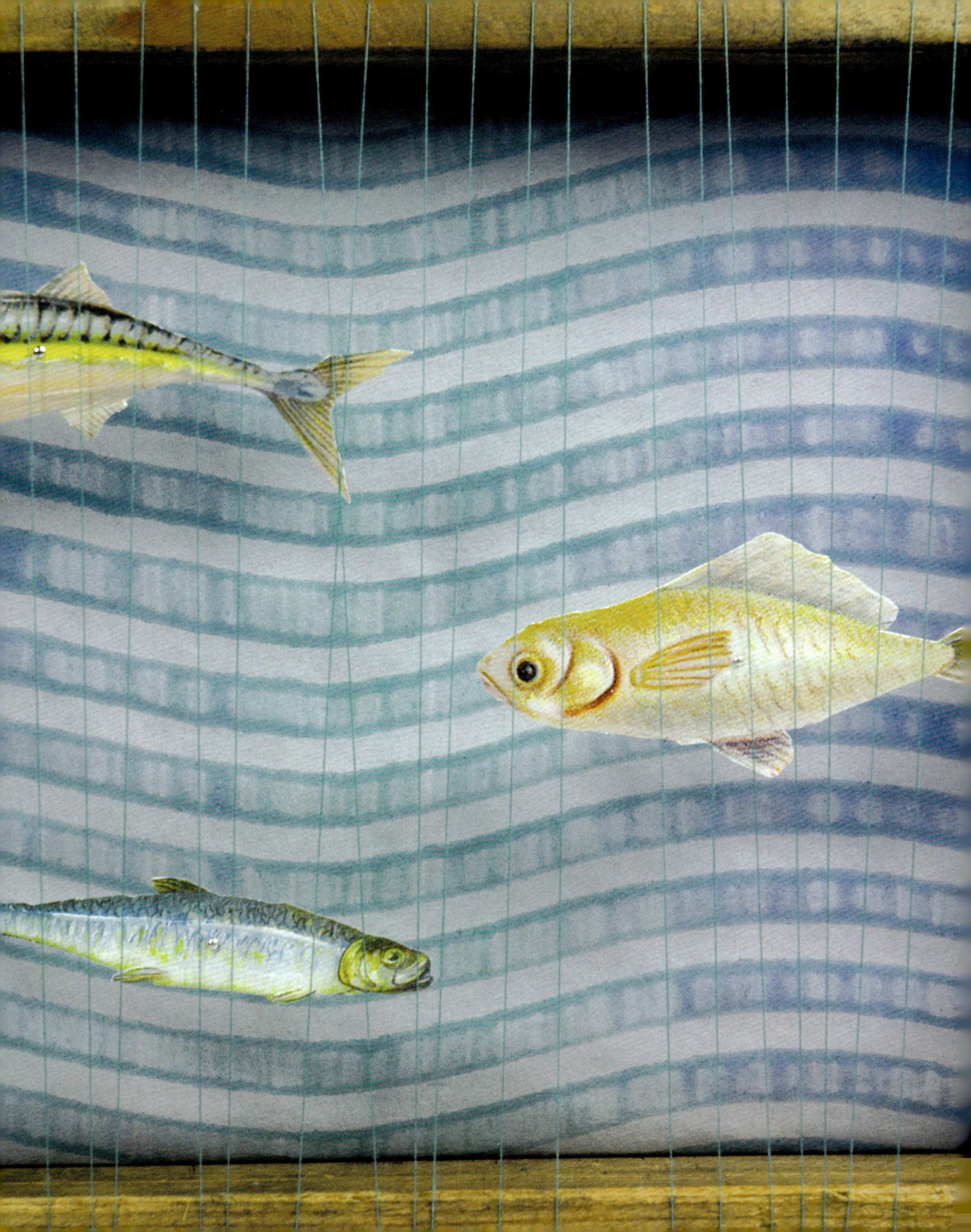

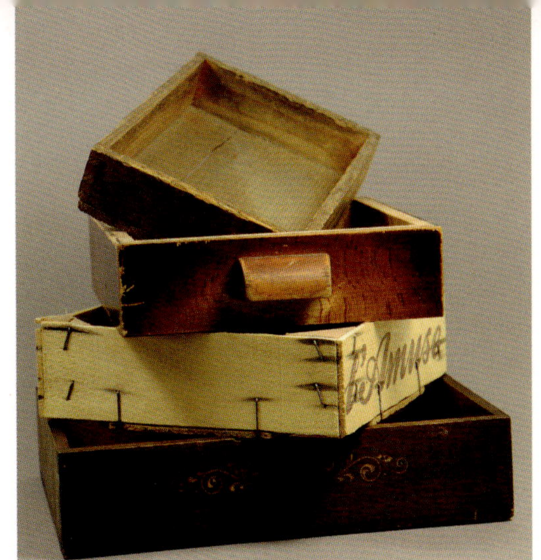

3

Old and New Wooden Boxes

Antique boxes, recycling boxes—even crates you converted yourself, drawers, or picture frames are the real classics in the world of boxes. Their character, predefined by their original function, thus becomes an invitation to "accommodate" them into fitting themes, or to alienate them ironically.
In addition, their dimensions do not match today's standards and thus offer an idiosyncratic variety.

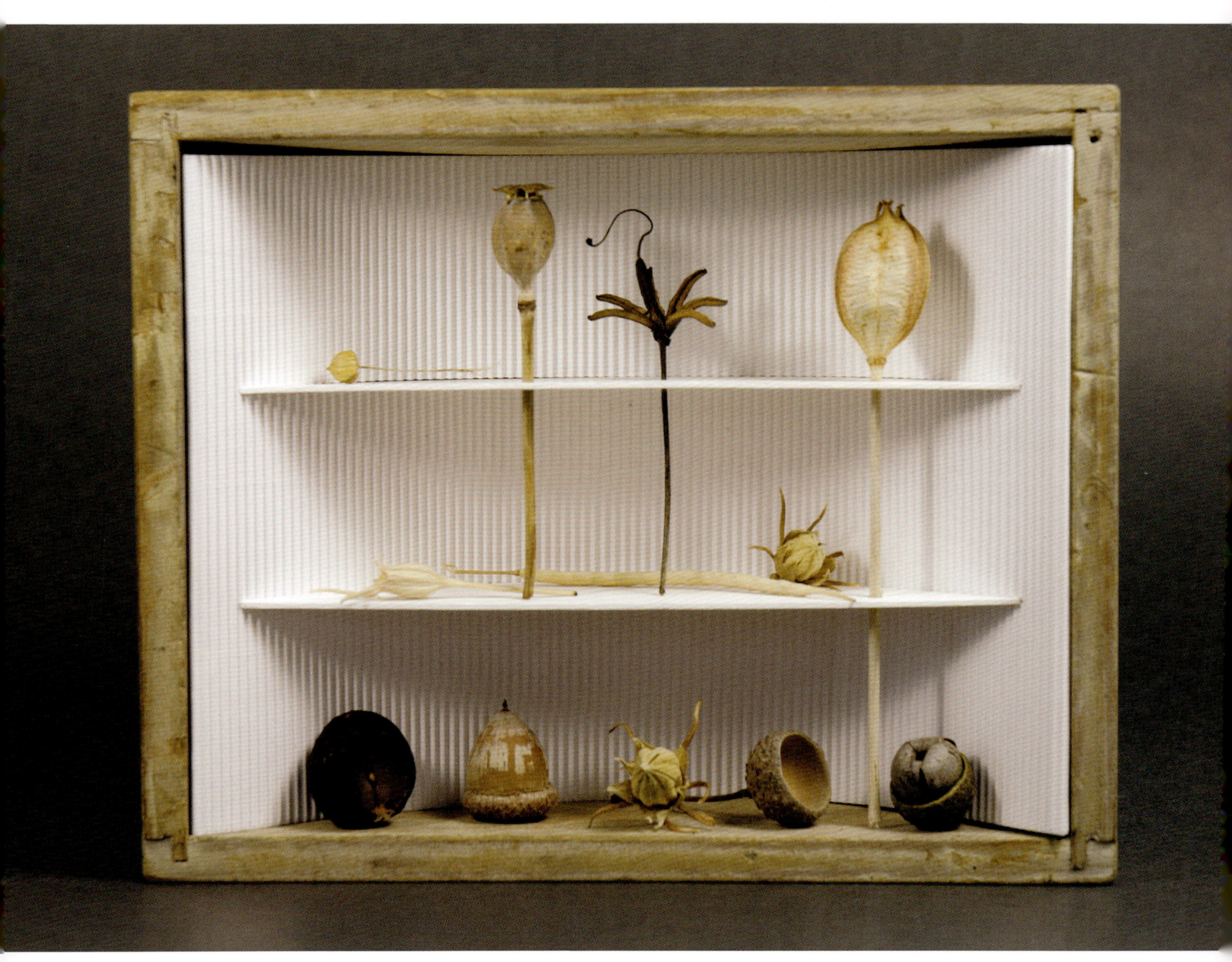

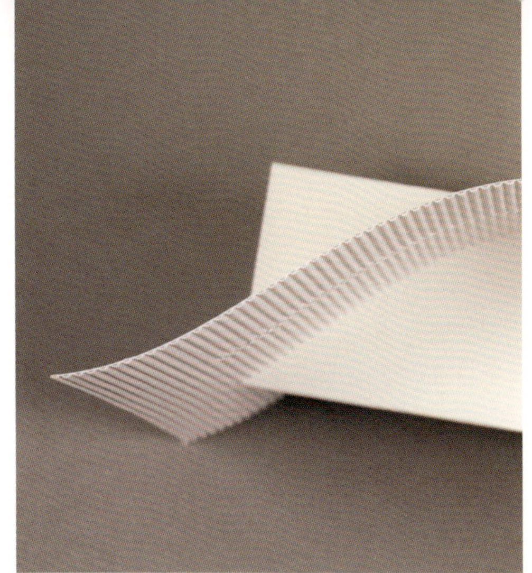

Inserted "Shelves"

Besides herbariums, seed collections are among my favorite themes. Thus, this amazingly simple solution for presenting very different seeds was born. You need a piece of finely corrugated cardboard, cut to the height (inner dimension) of the box. Trim it to 1 mm lower than the measured height, so that the piece fits in well. Place the corrugated cardboard in the box so that it curves in the middle, up to the back panel. Mark the box edge on both sides and fold the corrugated cardboard backward from there. Cut off the excess length on both side pieces back to about 3/4".

Cut the shelves out of 1–2 mm thick paperboard remnants with a cutter. They should be about 1/4" shallower than the box interior and about 3/4" narrower. Mark where the shelves should sit on the corrugated cardboard. Then bore the endpoints with the awl about 1/2" from the folded edges.

Use the cutter to make horizontal cuts into the smooth back of the corrugated cardboard. They should only just match the thickness of the paperboard pieces, so that the shelves sit tightly and hold the curvature in place. Depending on the type of seed, make a hole in the little shelves to pass the stems through. If necessary, you can glue the folded edges firmly to the inside of the box.

Materials + Tools

Small, sturdy wooden box

Ruler, cutter, and cutting mat

Awl or paper drill

Double-sided adhesive tape or white glue if needed

Finely corrugated cardboard (here: white)

Paperboard remnants of a matching color 1–2 mm thick (remnants of white matte board create an especially beautiful effect)

Collected seeds, pods, nuts, etc.

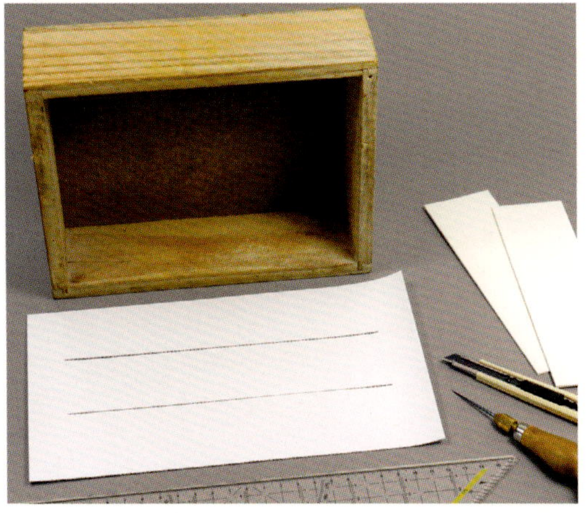

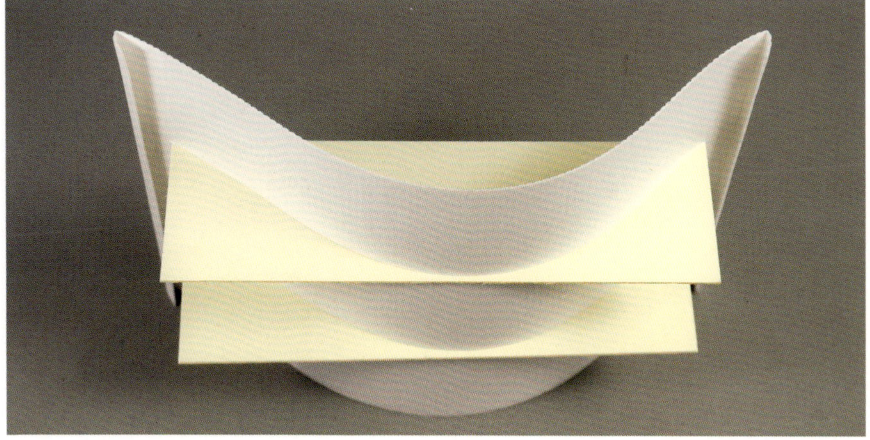

◀ *About 6½" × 8" × 2½"*

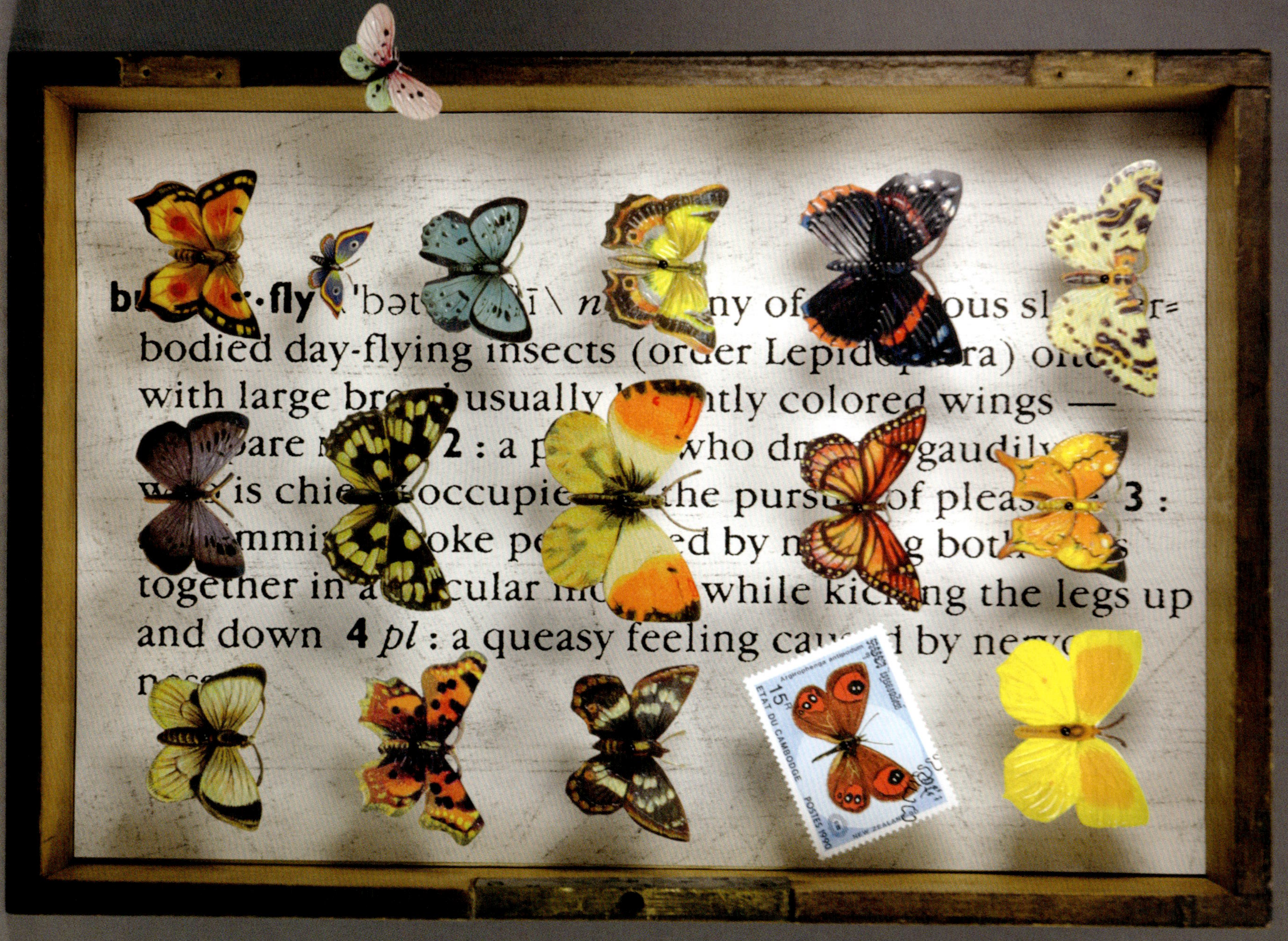
bodied day-flying insects (order Lepido
with large br usually ntly colored wings —
2 : a p who d gaudily
is chie occupie the purs of pleas 3 :
oke p ed by n g both
together in a cular while ki ng the legs up
and down 4 pl : a queasy feeling ca d by ne
15R
ETAT DU CAMBODGE
POSTES 1990

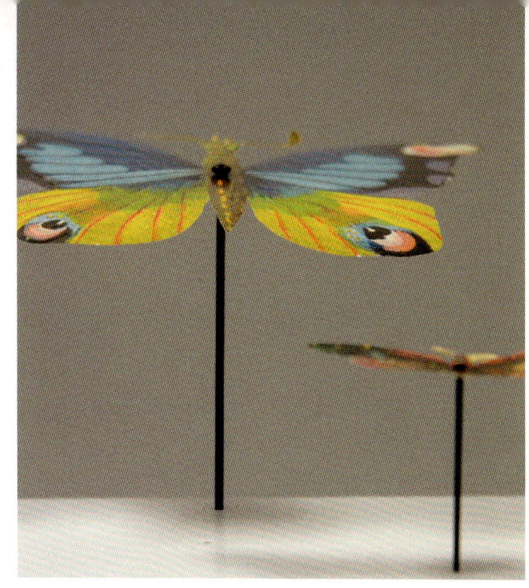

Collections Mounted on Pins

A butterfly display case is a symbol of historical scientific collections. Fortunately, in the mid-19th century, glossy relief image prints were invented, which even the tender-hearted (like myself) can pierce with a pin.

Since sticking pins into the back panel of a wooden box is tedious work, it is best to resort to using an aid: so-called foam board is a several-millimeter-thick, feather-light mat made of plastic foam that is laminated on both sides with cardboard. Used as a back panel, foam board allows you to insert pins neatly and effortlessly, and the firm cardboard lamination holds the pins securely and in the right place.

Test how to cut out the back panel so that it fits by inserting the piece of foam board halfway into the box, once lengthwise and once crosswise. If it does not stick when you do this, the back panel is the right size. Please do not fully insert the foam board, because it can be very difficult to get it out again once it has been inserted properly. You can paint or cover the white foam board. The easiest way to do this is to have the cover paper overlap a good deal on the long sides, but on the other hand trim it close to the edge on the short sides. Then fold the long sides tightly over the edges and fasten to the back panel with adhesive tape.

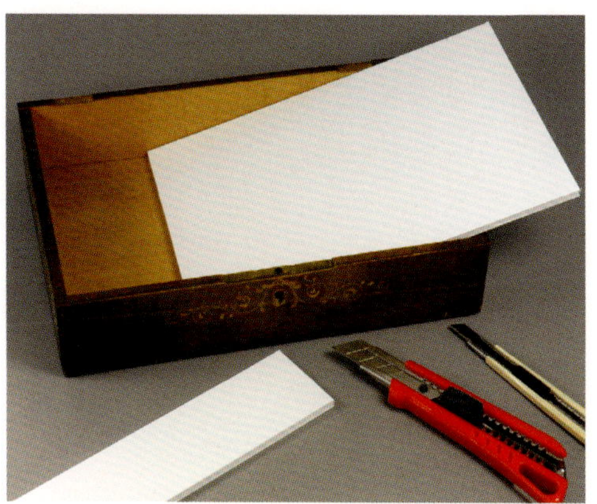

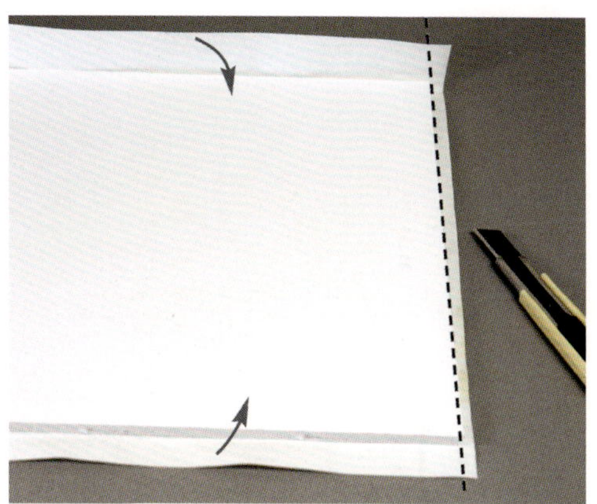

Materials + Tools

Large and small old wooden boxes

Ruler, cutter, scalpel, and cutting mat

Small scissors

Awl, and felt for underlay

Decorative nails, 40–50 mm long

Foam board, 5 mm thick

India ink and brush or tea bags (black tea)

Pastel crayons and cotton balls or a graphite pencil

Colored thread

Book pages that match the background, glossy prints, stamps, old envelopes, etc.

Masking tape, double-sided adhesive tape

◀ *10″ × 7½″ × 2½″*

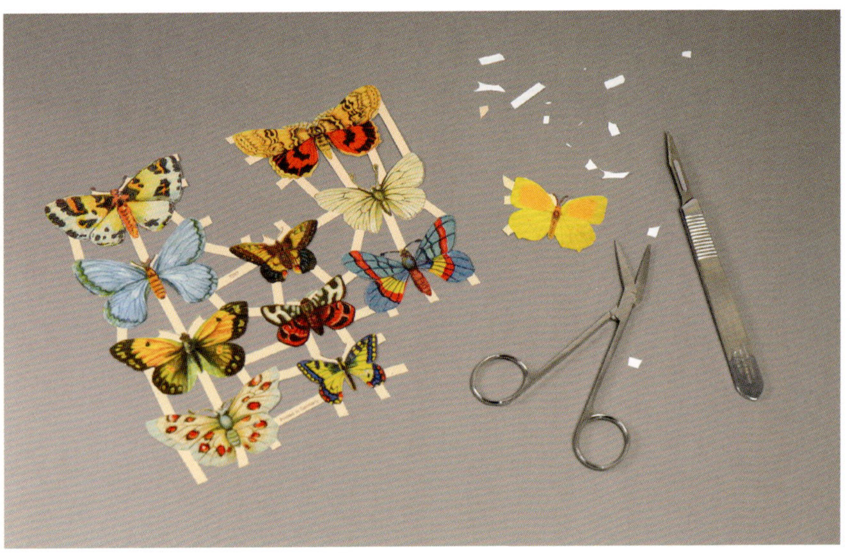

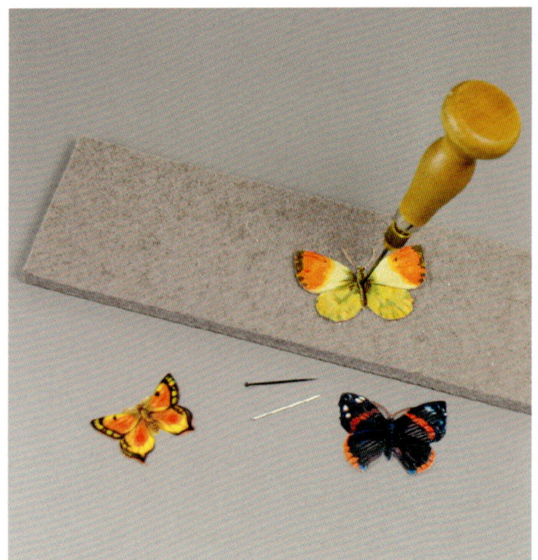

Use a small pair of scissors to cut the butterflies out from the sheet of glossy prints. Use a scalpel to cut out the tiny spaces between the antennae, which may not be stamped out. Then, on top of a piece of felt, prick a hole (not too deep) in the middle of the body.

If you want to give the box a nostalgic appearance and make it reminiscent of an old natural-history collection, you can photocopy pages from old biology books enlarged to the box size to use on the back panel. To "age" them, coat the copy with diluted India ink or use a squeezed-out black teabag, or rub the copy with pastel chalk, which you then smudge with a cotton ball.

On the other hand, you can alienate the historical impression a bit by photocopying a greatly enlarged modern dictionary entry (such as on page 62) and giving it a two-dimensional design with graphite frottage (see page 55).

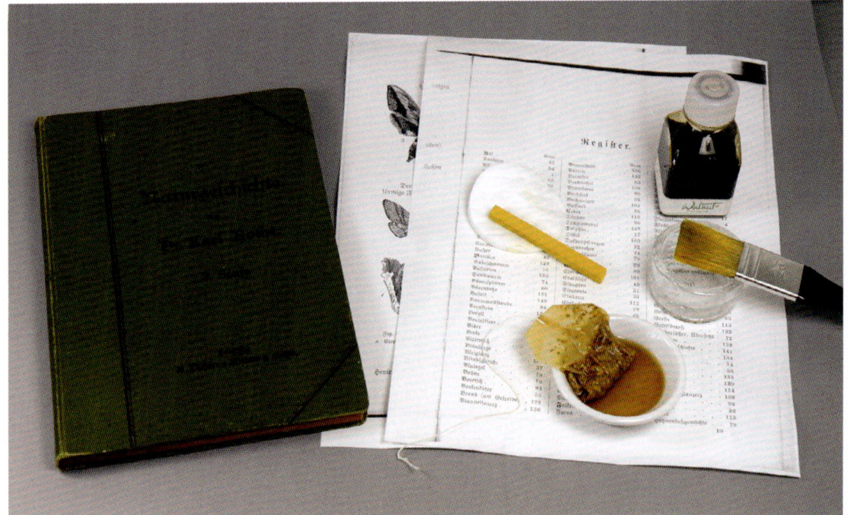

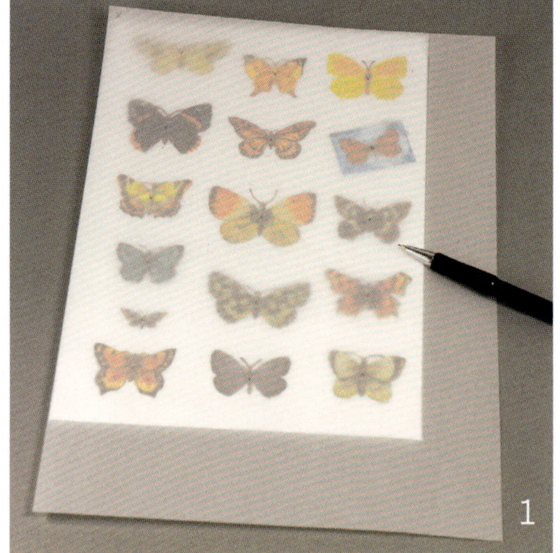

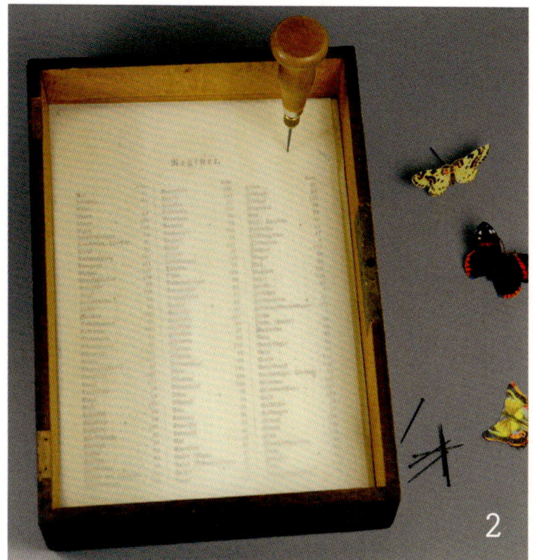

The "historical" version of the back panel: The enlarged photocopy of the index from a 19th-century biology book dyed with a black teabag.

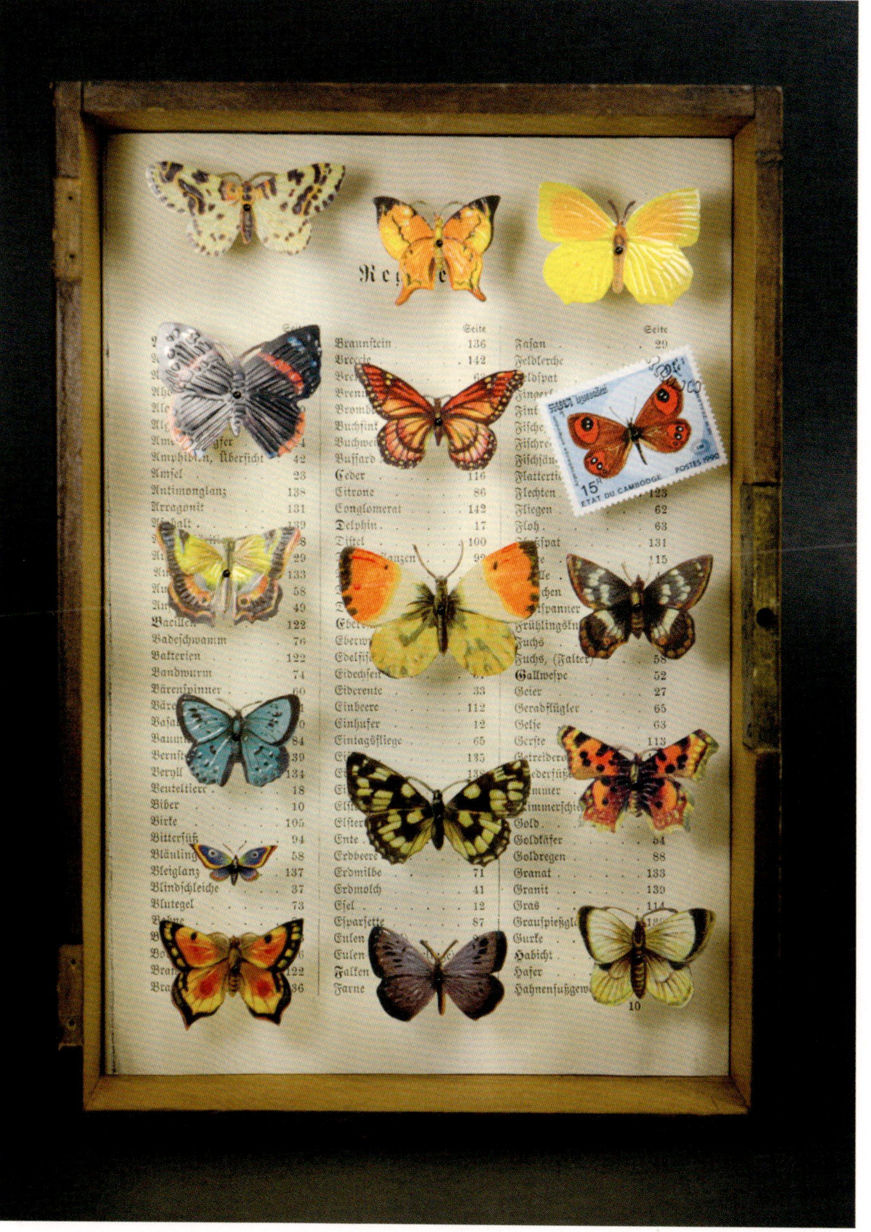

It is difficult to mount a full set of butterflies onto a back panel without damaging them. Therefore, arrange the butterflies on the back panel before mounting them in the box. Then lay a piece of tracing paper on top and make a small cross on the tracing paper to mark where the holes were pierced into the butterfly's body [1].

Trim the tracing paper to the size of the back panel, then stick a piece of double-sided adhesive tape on the back of the panel and insert it firmly. Now put the marked tracing paper into the box and use the awl to bore very lightly and not too deeply through the marks into the covered foam board [2]. The marks should not be too big for the pins you are using or the butterflies will wiggle. After removing the tracing paper, push the butterfly pins in really deep to hold them firmly.

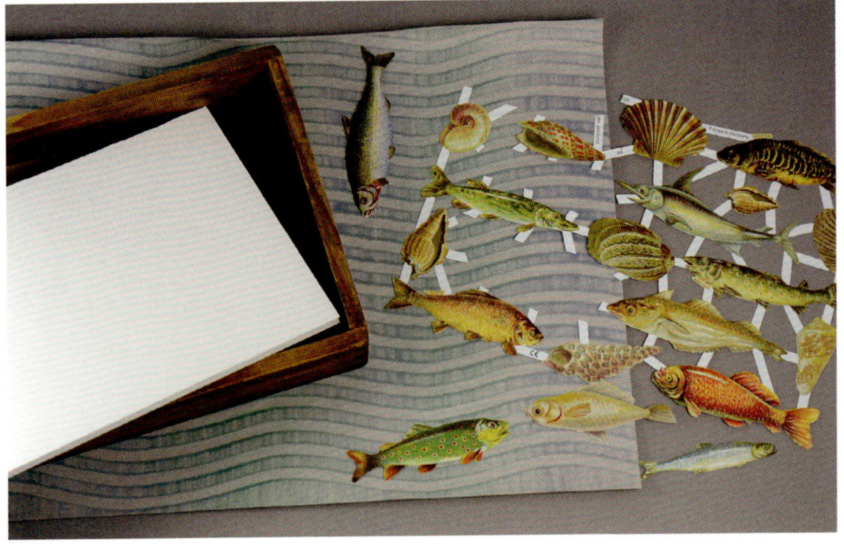

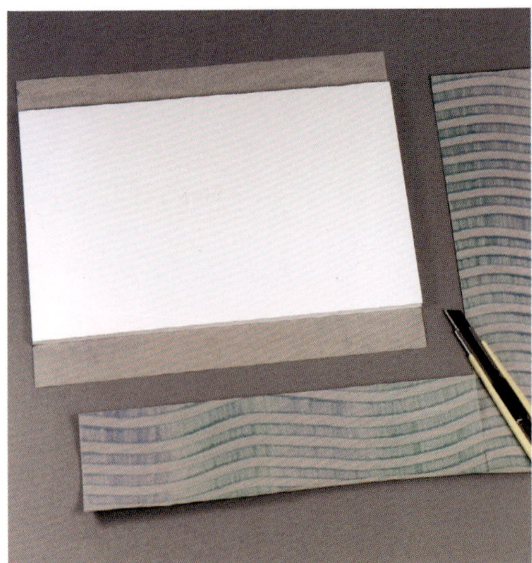

Glossy print sheets are available not only of butterflies, but also of many other animals, flowers, etc. You can use them to present a wide variety of themes in totally different dioramas. Here, for example, a small, old wooden crate on the theme of fish.

This time a piece of handmade paste paper is applied around the back panel. Stick the fish on pins of different lengths to enhance the three-dimensional effect. Wrapping with sea-green sewing thread also contributes to this and carries the underwater world farther outside the box, where the fish glued to the outside of the frame mark another level.

As with all elements mounted on pins, the shadows contribute a great deal to the spatial impression.

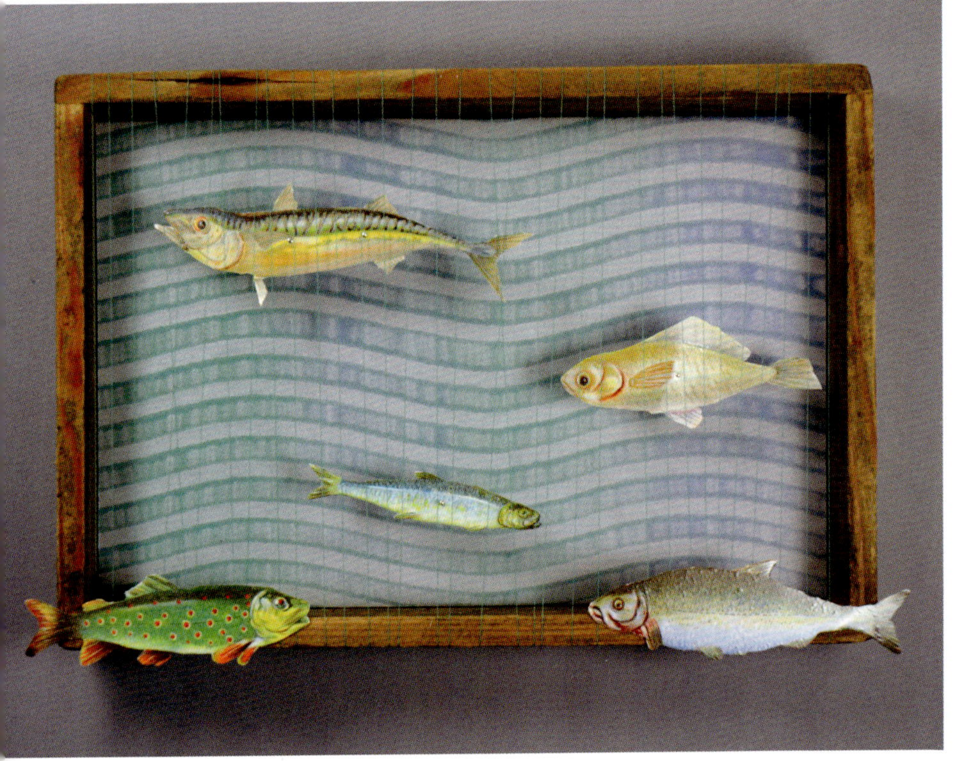

◀ *6½" × 10" × 1½"*

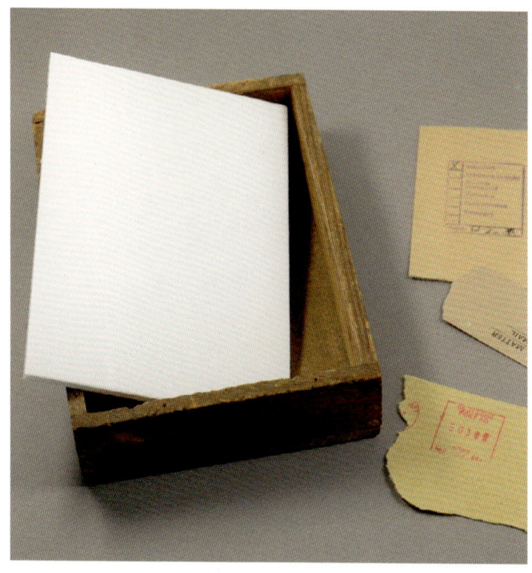

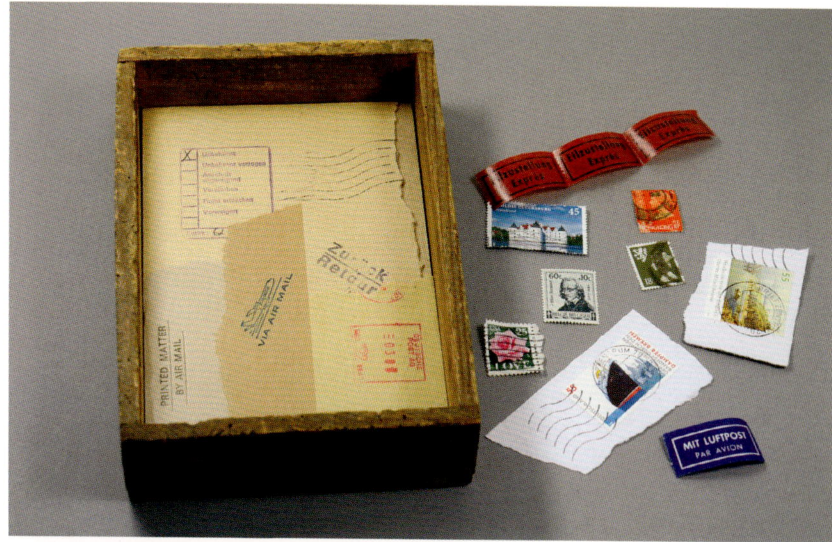

Alternative design:
Using the same technique—but with a distinctly different result—an old wooden box is designed with a collection on the theme of letter mail.

Here, the foam board is collaged as a back panel with fragments of envelopes made of brown paper. Stamps and mailing labels are mounted on the pins, and an old office stamp "grounds" the bits of official paper, which at first glance seem to be floating.

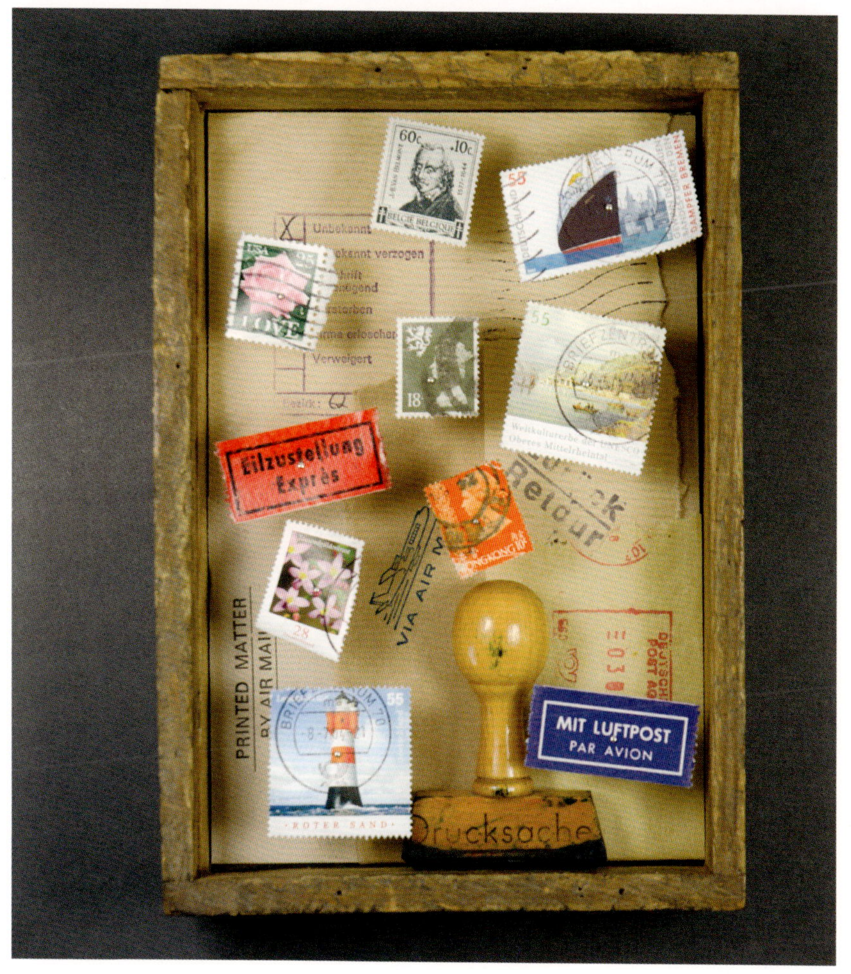

8″ × 5½″ × 1½″ ▶

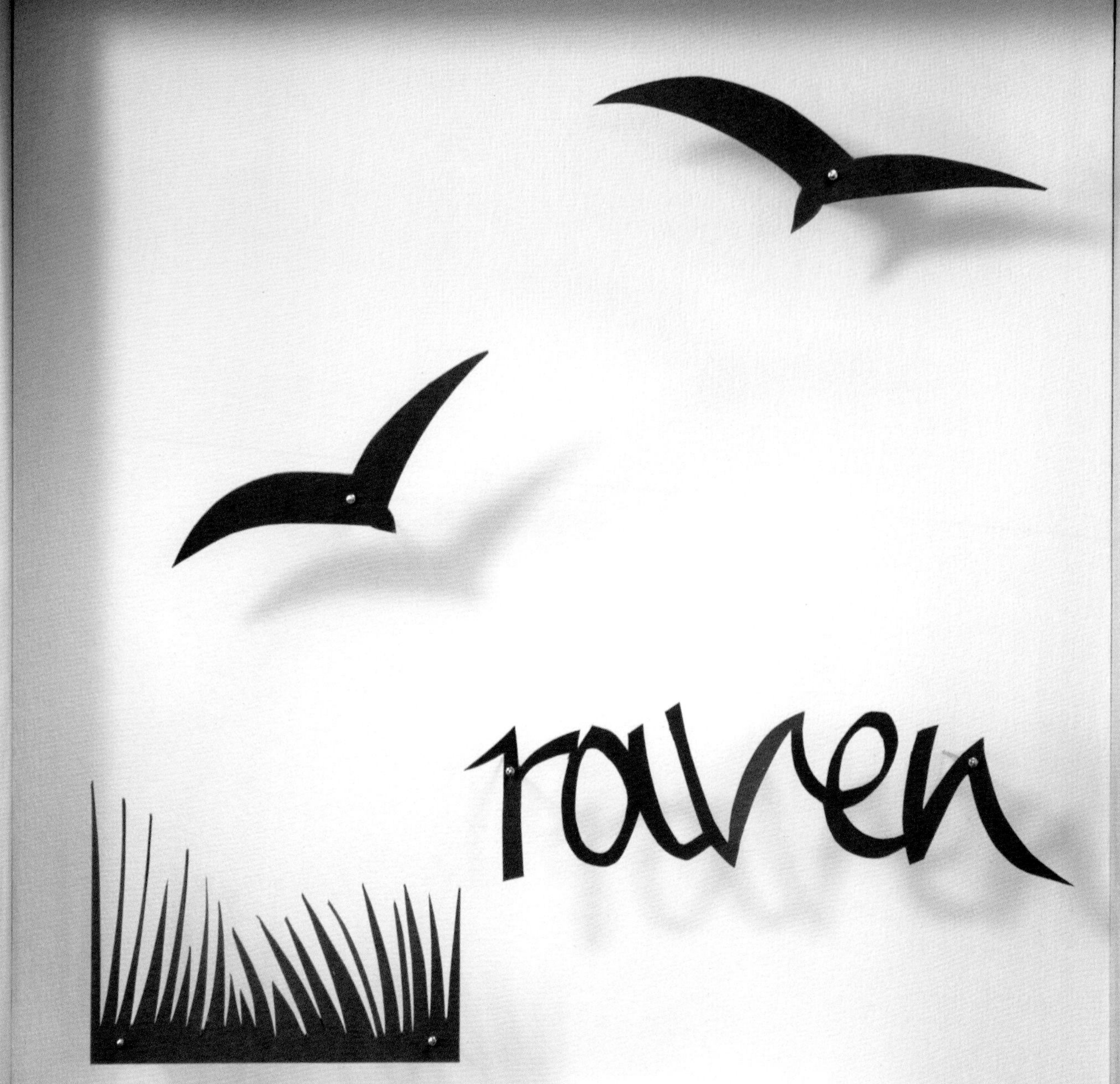
raven

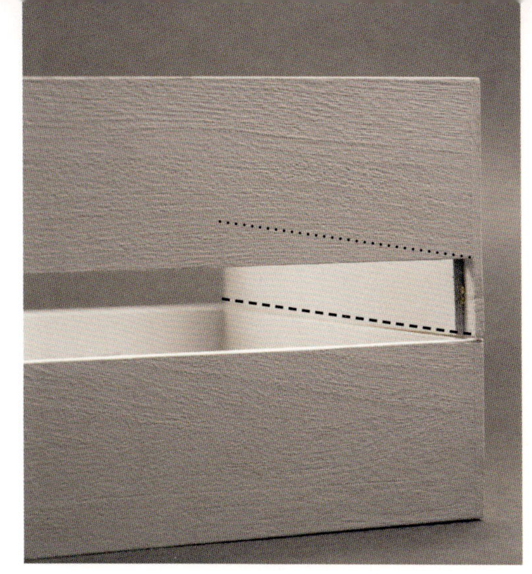

Paper Cuttings Can Also Become Butterflies

The beauty of the shadows created by a presentation on pins is particularly effective when paper cuttings are used.

A light-gray garden box from your decorations supplier provides an unobtrusive background. If you saw the box apart between the two side slats, you make it into two boxes. You then have to add a base to the upper frame (see page 83), and here the upper edge of the just-sawn-off lower frame will be painted white. Watercolor paper attached to the front of the foam board with photo adhesive gives the shadows a delicate structure. Solid, dark paper or thin, fine cardboard work well to make the paper cuttings. The most beautiful are free-cut motifs, where you can let the momentum of your knife guide you. Script is the easiest to sketch out, where you write the word in normal writing on tracing paper and then trace over it using a broad marker to give it volume. The small number of paper elements are pinned directly to the inserted rear panel, which has been fastened on with double-sided adhesive tape.

Abstract pieces of cut paper can be given yet another (shadow) dimension by connecting the inserted pins with a piece of thin black thread.

Materials + Tools

Decorative box

Small hacksaw

Ruler, cutter, graphic cutter, and cutting mat

Decorative nails, 40–50 mm long

Foam board, 5 mm thick

Watercolor paper for the back panel, tracing paper, and dark construction paper

Masking tape, double-sided adhesive tape

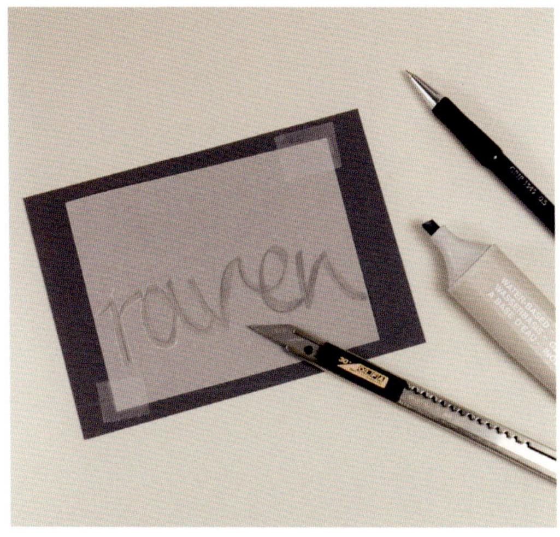

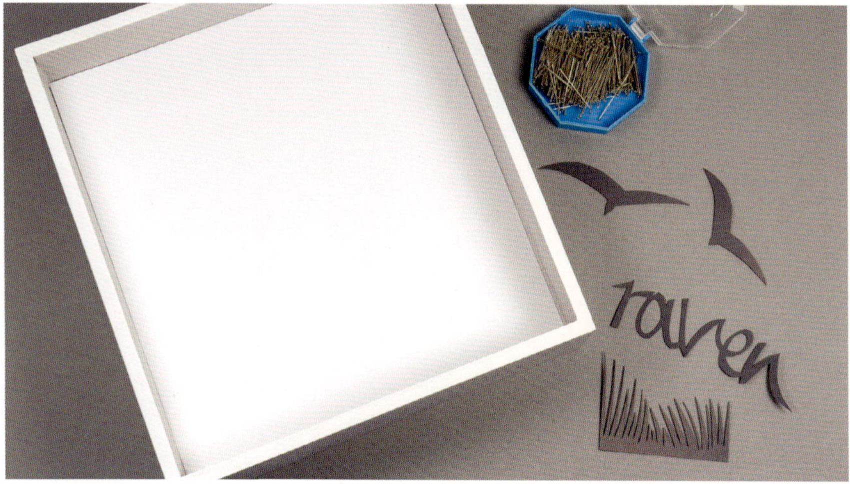

◀ *9½" × 9" × 2½"*

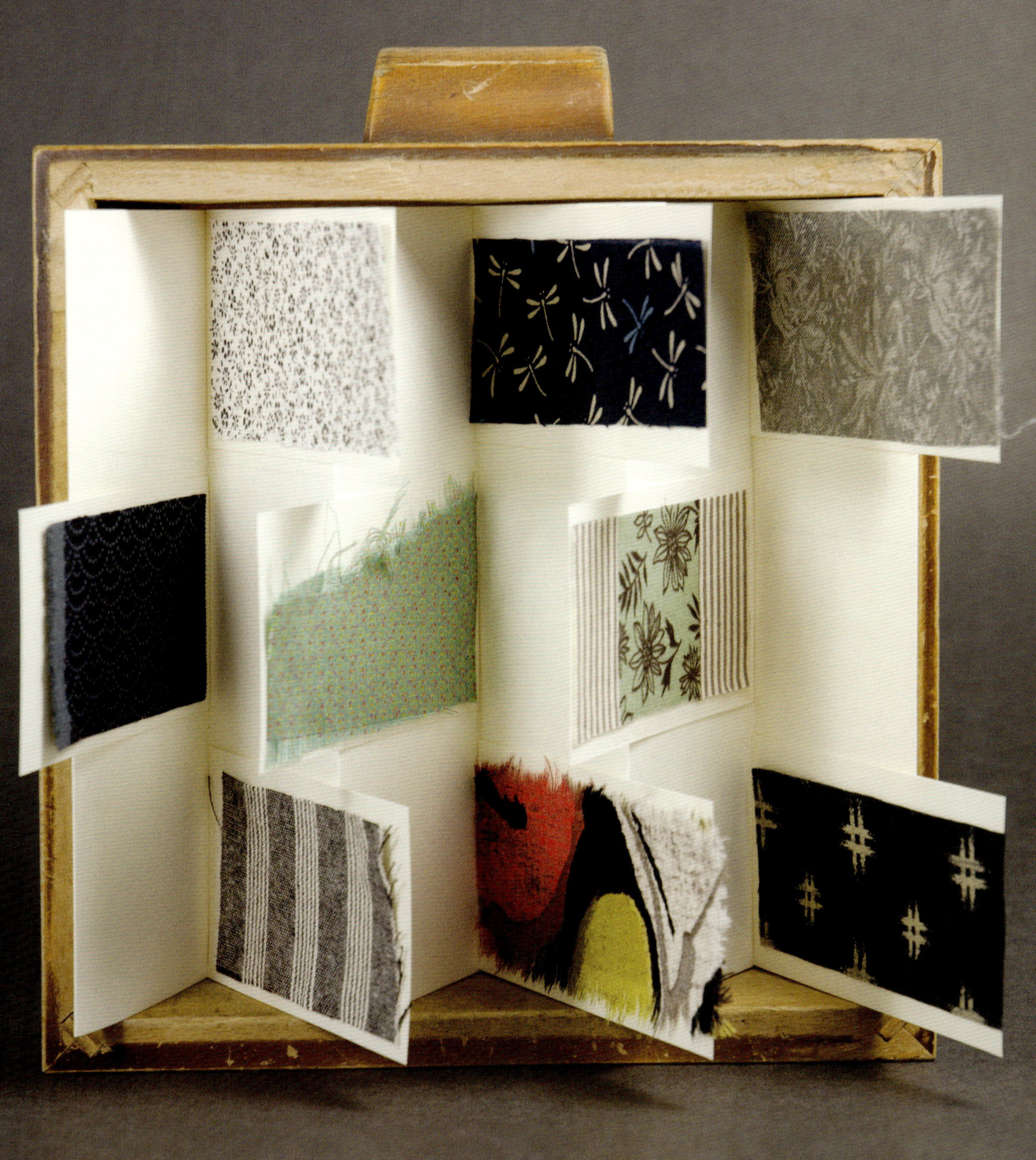

Collection of Cloth Swatches in an Old Sewing-Box Drawer

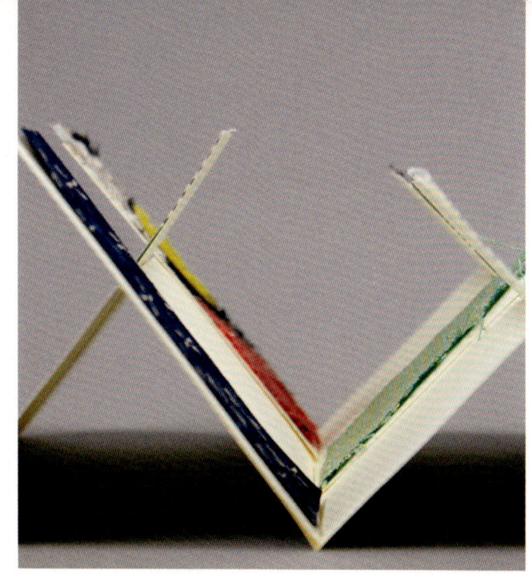

Materials + Tools

Small, sturdy wooden box or sewing box drawer

Ruler, cutter, and cutting mat

Bone folder

A strip of sturdy paper or thin cardboard (150–200 gsm) with the grain direction parallel to the short side

Small pieces of cardboard (here: 2″ × 4″) with the grain direction parallel to the long side

Awl for pricking holes

Needle and thread

Double-sided adhesive tape or white glue if needed

Small swatches of fabric or other things on the theme of textiles, such as yarn, buttons, or ribbons

Small swatches of fabric, yarn samples, and other textile gems can be beautifully presented in a paper construction that was developed by book artist Hedi Kyle and is known worldwide as a "flag book."

For this you will need a zigzag fold as was made for the herbarium in chapter 1. As always, first check the grain direction of the paper (see page 20). Trim the paper strips to a size about 1 mm smaller than the inner dimensions of the box, so that nothing will get stuck later. They should be about three times as wide as the box width (inner dimension). Make an eight-sided zigzag fold (see page 20). There is no fixed width for the folded sides; it is fine if they extend beyond the edges of the box instead of disappearing into it, but all should be the same width.

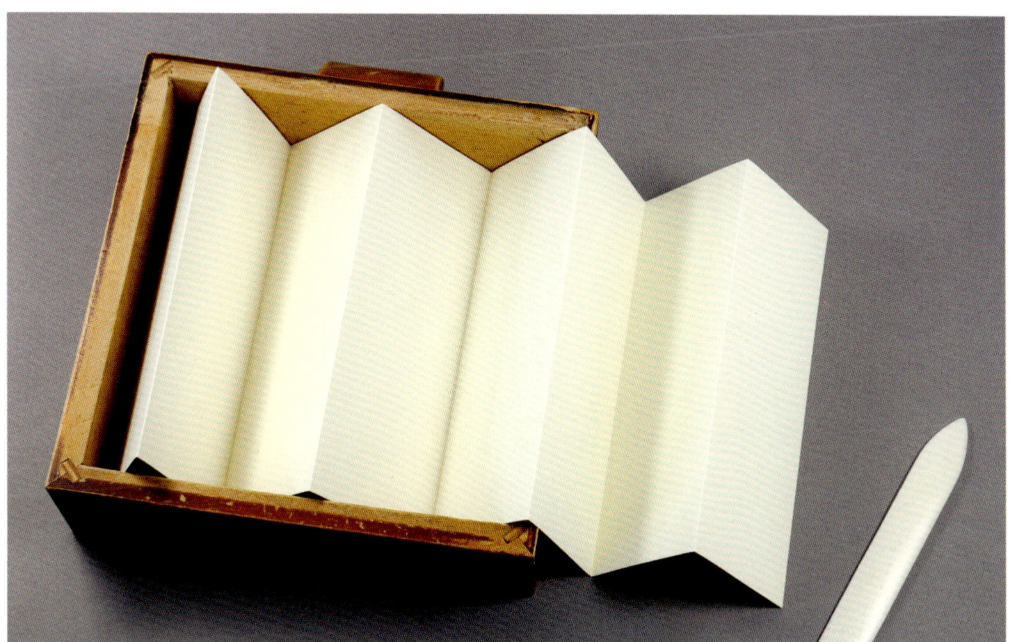

◀ *7½″ × 7½″ × 2″*

The two outer sides of the zigzag fold are left free. Distribute the cards of swatches along horizontal lines on the sides; this creates three "rows of swatches."

For each "row," the cards can be affixed only in one direction (either to the left or right in the valley fold). The distance to the next card above or below should be about 2 mm each time. At the outer edges, finish fixing on the cards so they are flush with the top and bottom edges of the zigzag fold.

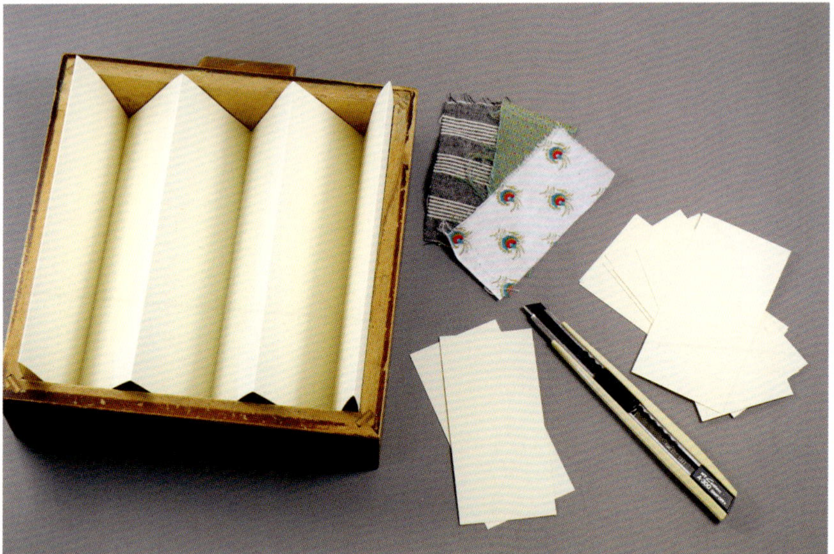

A glue stick works well to firmly glue thinner cloth swatches to the little cards—this way nothing can show through. The cards should be glued to the zigzag fold with white glue or double-sided adhesive tape, depending on the material thickness.

When you have fitted the zigzag fold into the box well, then use glue or double-sided adhesive tape to fasten the backs of mountain folds to the back panel of the box. If necessary, the side sections can also be attached to the side panels.

Alternative design:

Collection of feathers:

A completely different effect is created if the objects extend beyond the cards, which also run in only one direction.

▶

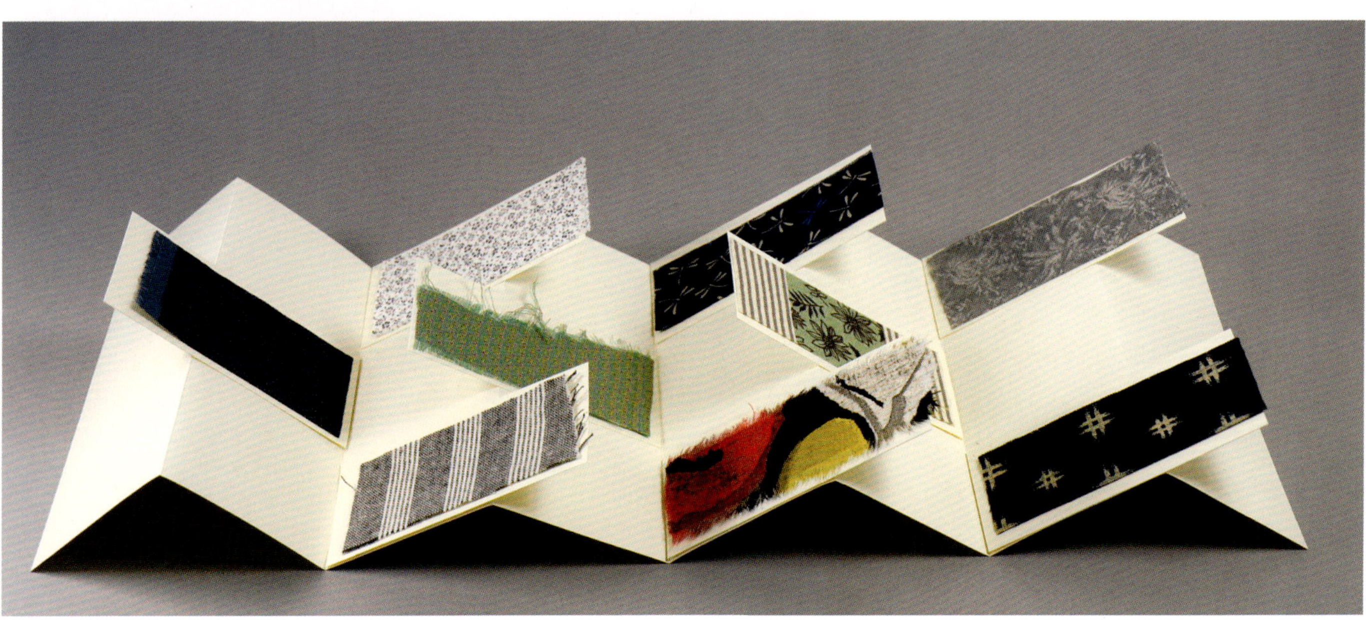

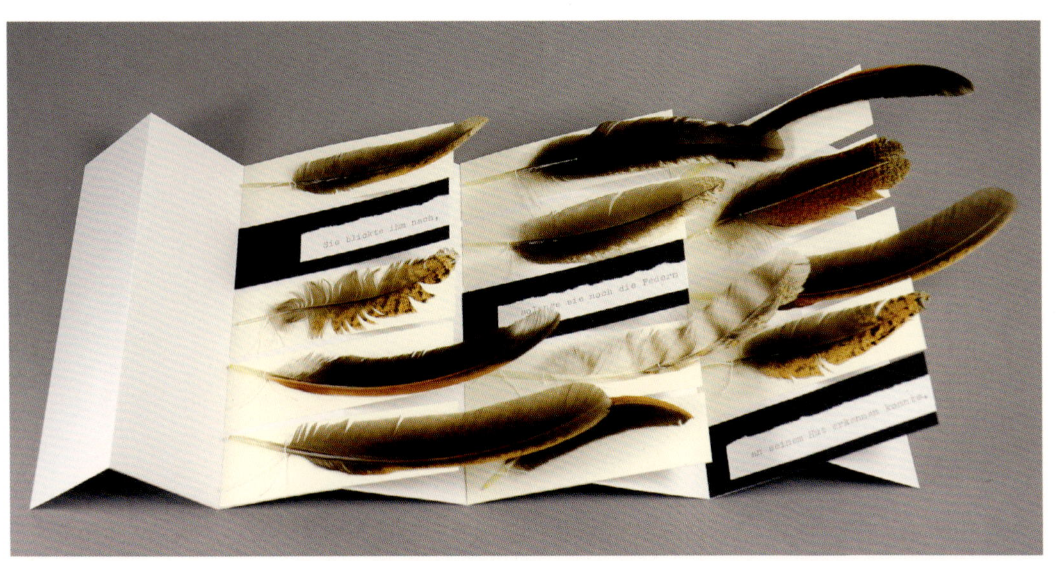

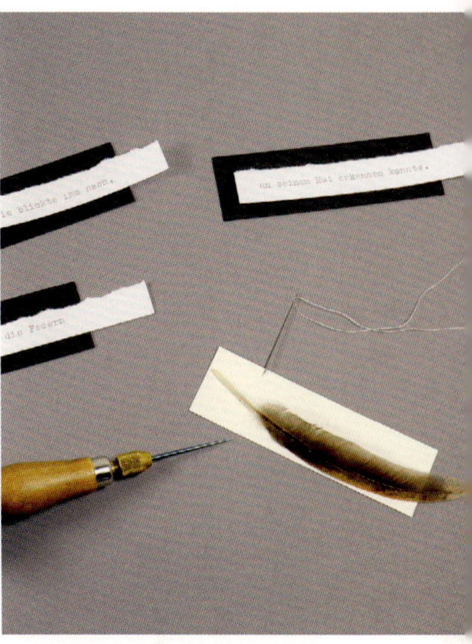

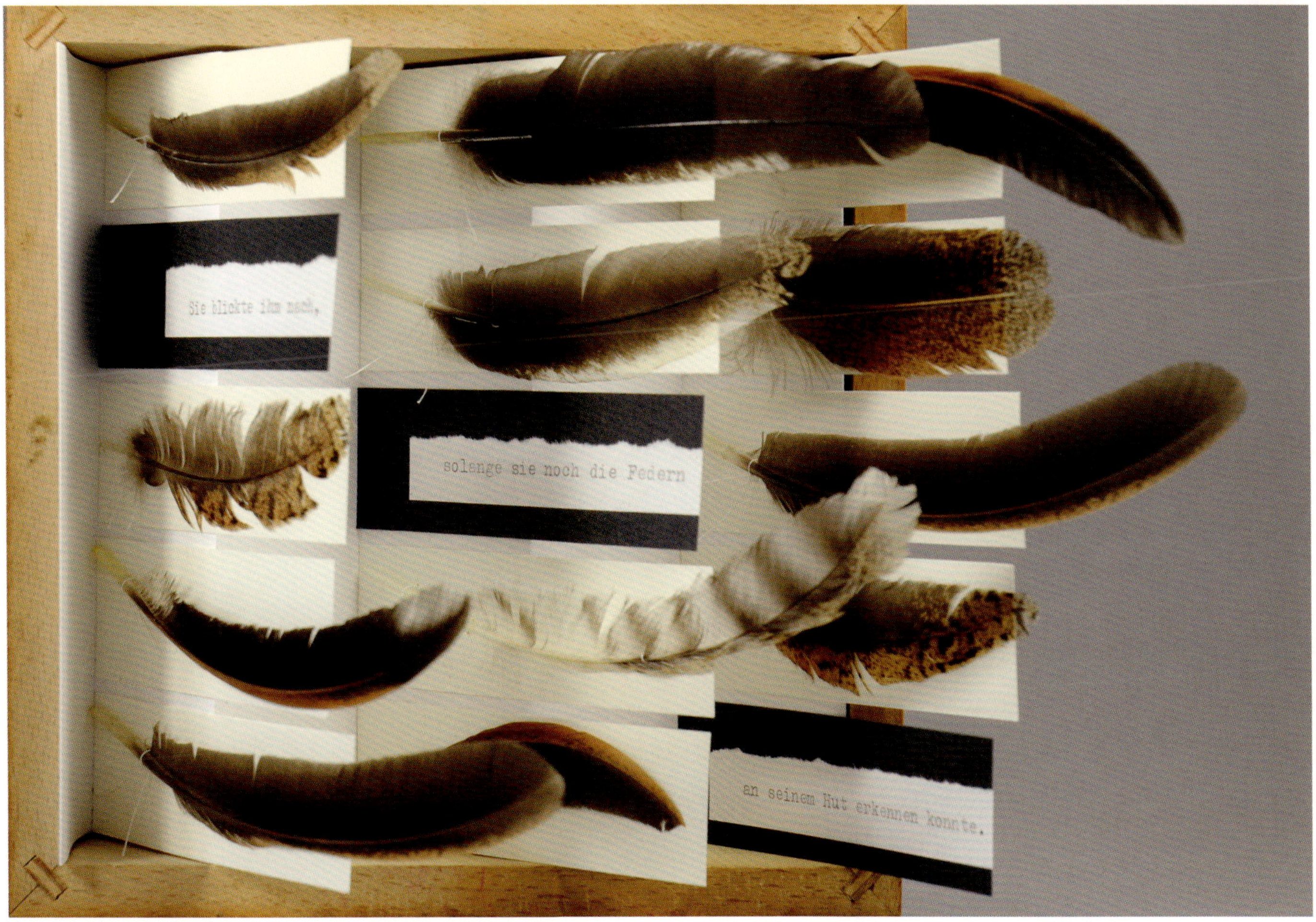

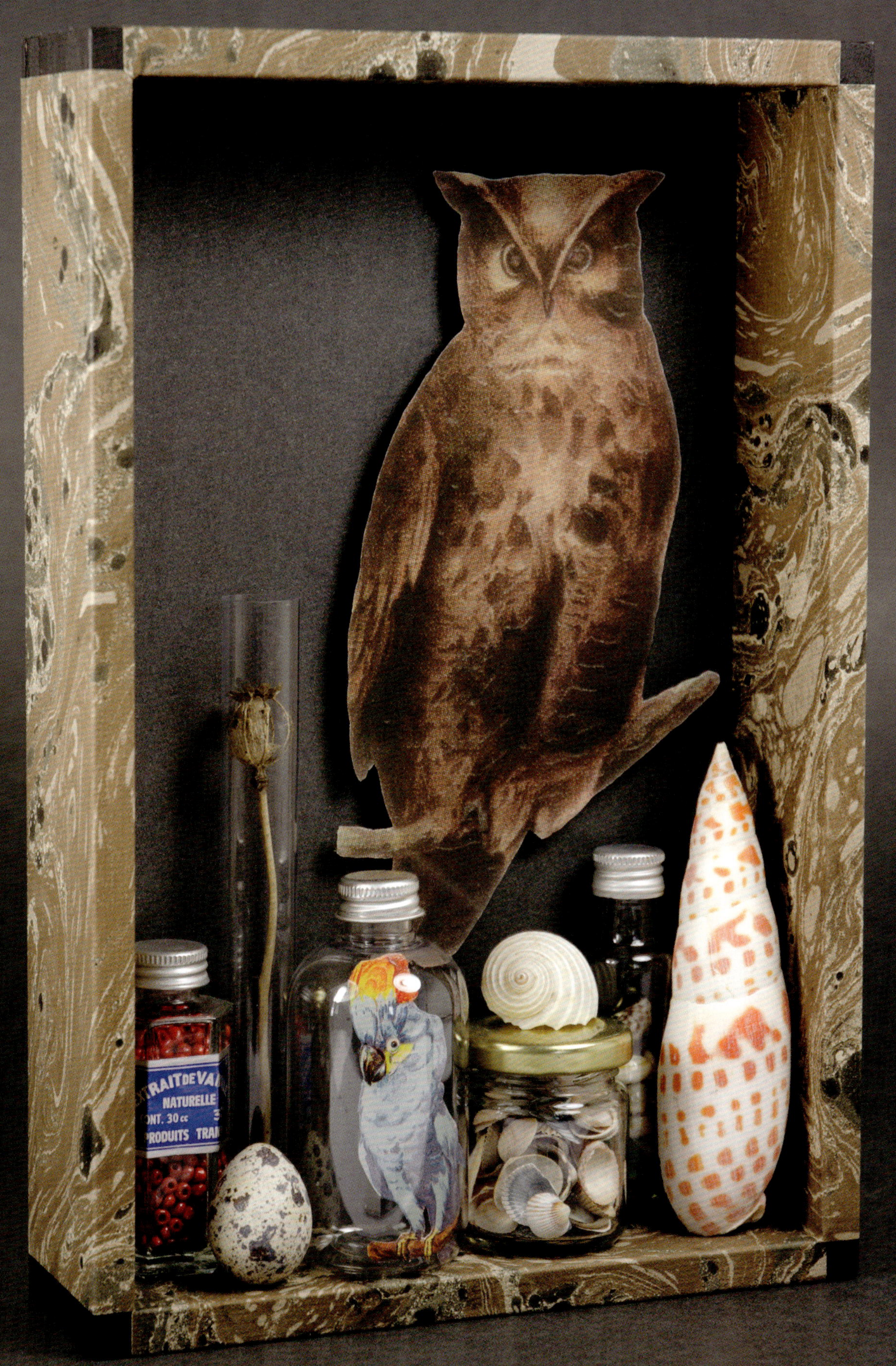
NATURELLE

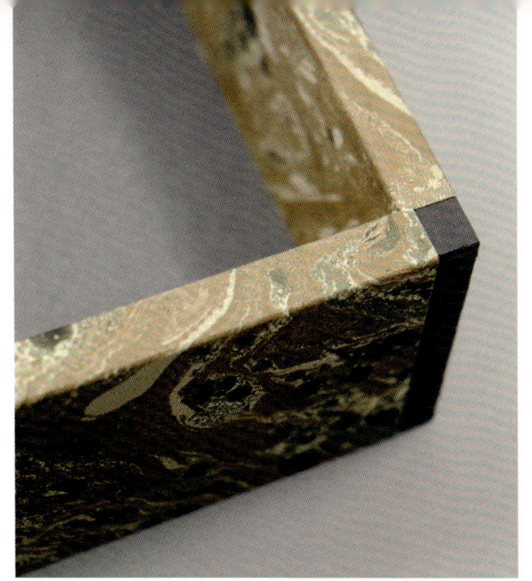

In the Style of Victorian Natural-History Collections

Cases containing natural-history contents that are covered with classic colored paper (marbled paper, paste paper, etc.) instinctively recall Victorian interiors—or Harry Potter films. You can—like Joseph Cornell did—play with these in a wonderful way and alienate them in a surreal way, or simply re-create a whimsical, old-fashioned flair.

Without prior knowledge of bookbinding, it is somewhat tedious to make a cover for a wooden box. Therefore, here is a simple version that spares you having to cover the corners: To do this, paint the inside and outside of the box with acrylic paint that matches the cover paper, at the same time going at least twice the thickness of the panel beyond the side edges. Now you just have to trim the four side sections of the cover paper so that the height is three times the depth and the width corresponds exactly to the inner dimensions of the box, and coat them with paste. Then apply the paper to the back of the box about 3/4" wide, fold it over to the front, and smooth it well over the edges inward. Carefully press the excess length on the bottom of the box into the inner edge by using the bone folder and smooth it firmly onto the back panel.

The paper for the rear panel can likewise be fastened on using glue or double-sided adhesive tape.

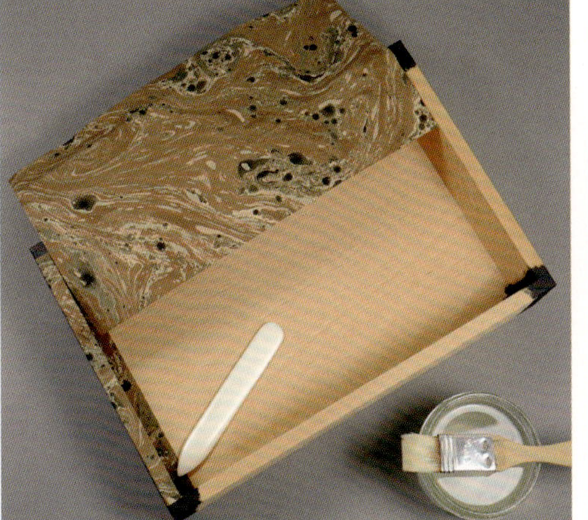

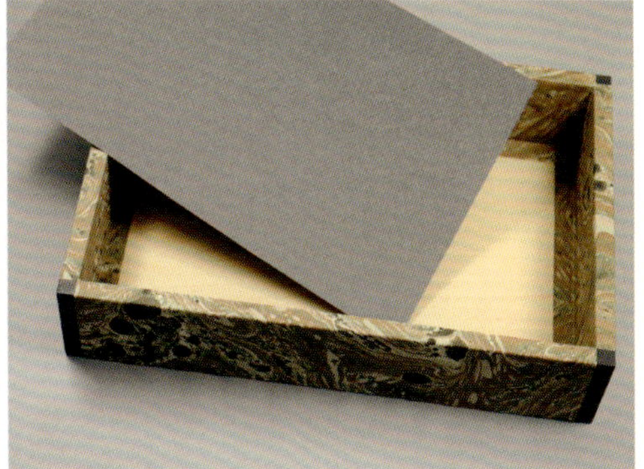

Materials + Tools

Large, sturdy wooden box

Ruler, cutter, and cutting mat

Scissors

Acrylic paint and brush

Paste and brush

Marbled paper, paste paper, or matte wrapping paper with a similar pattern

Paper or cardboard suitable for the back panel

Remnant piece of cardboard

Remnant piece of foam board

Double-sided adhesive tape, white glue

Collections . . .

◀ *11½" × 8" × 2½"*

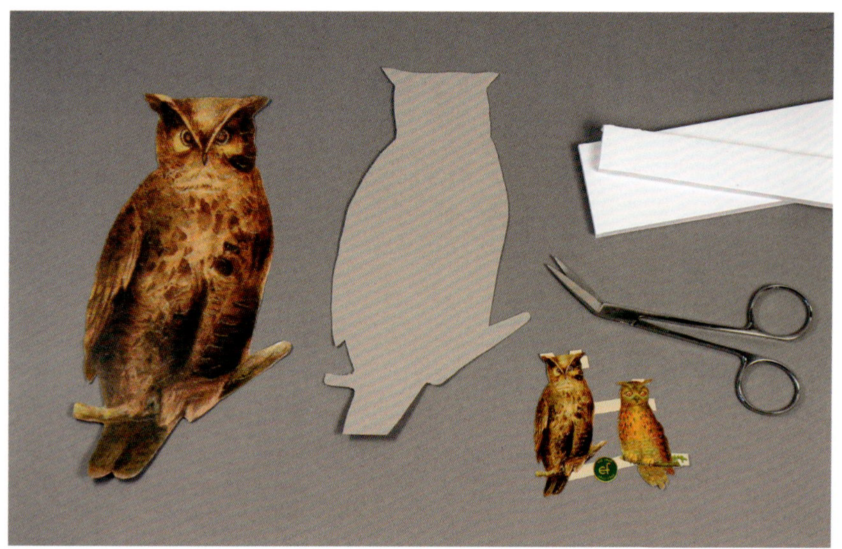

Here the collections are presented mainly in small glass containers. If necessary, the freestanding things can be held in place with double-sided adhesive tape.

The owl in the background is a color copy from a glossy print—extremely enlarged—which lends it an additional peculiar aura. To not stick it flat on the back panel, reinforce the back with a piece of cardboard (cut out the cardboard owl 1 mm smaller) and use remnants of foam board as a spacer, ensuring that it creates a dignified shadow.

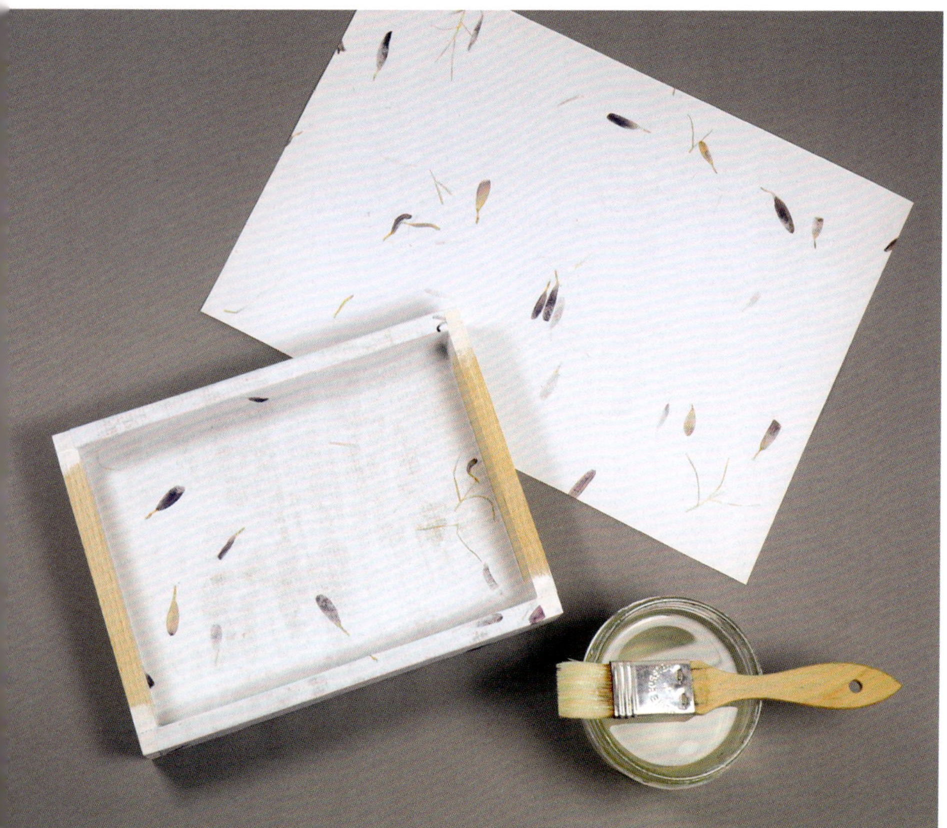

`Alternative design:`
A small wooden box is given a completely different character by using the same technique. The corners were glazed with white acrylic paint. Since the cover paper is not as dark and determining as the marbled paper, you can also laminate the back panel with it (in one piece with the long sides) throughout.

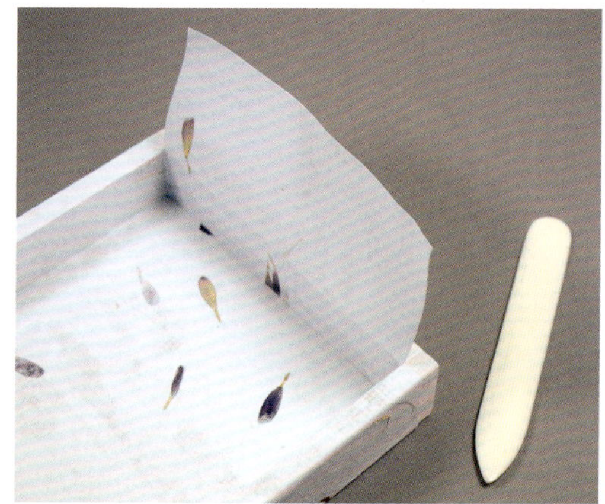

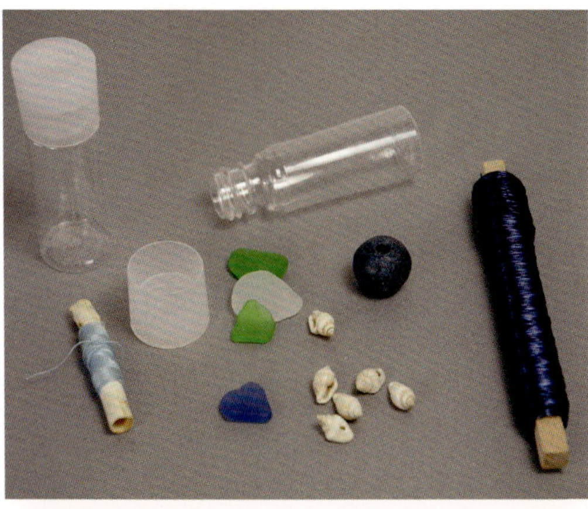

This creates a brighter, more playful "place to live" for finds.

Here, modern cosmetic sample vials work well as containers, as well as airy decorative objects made of wire in a matching color.

▼ *6″ × 8″ × 1½″*

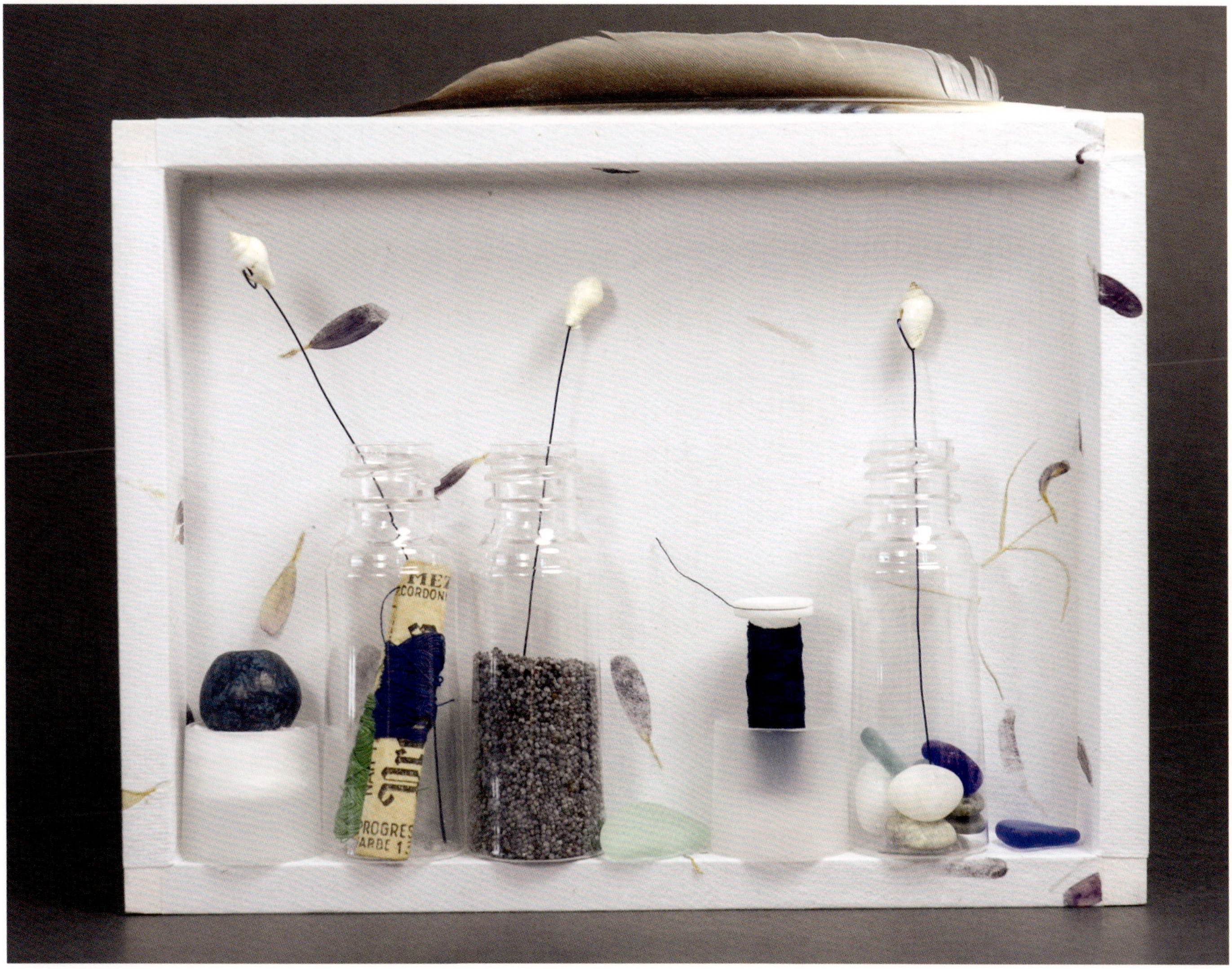

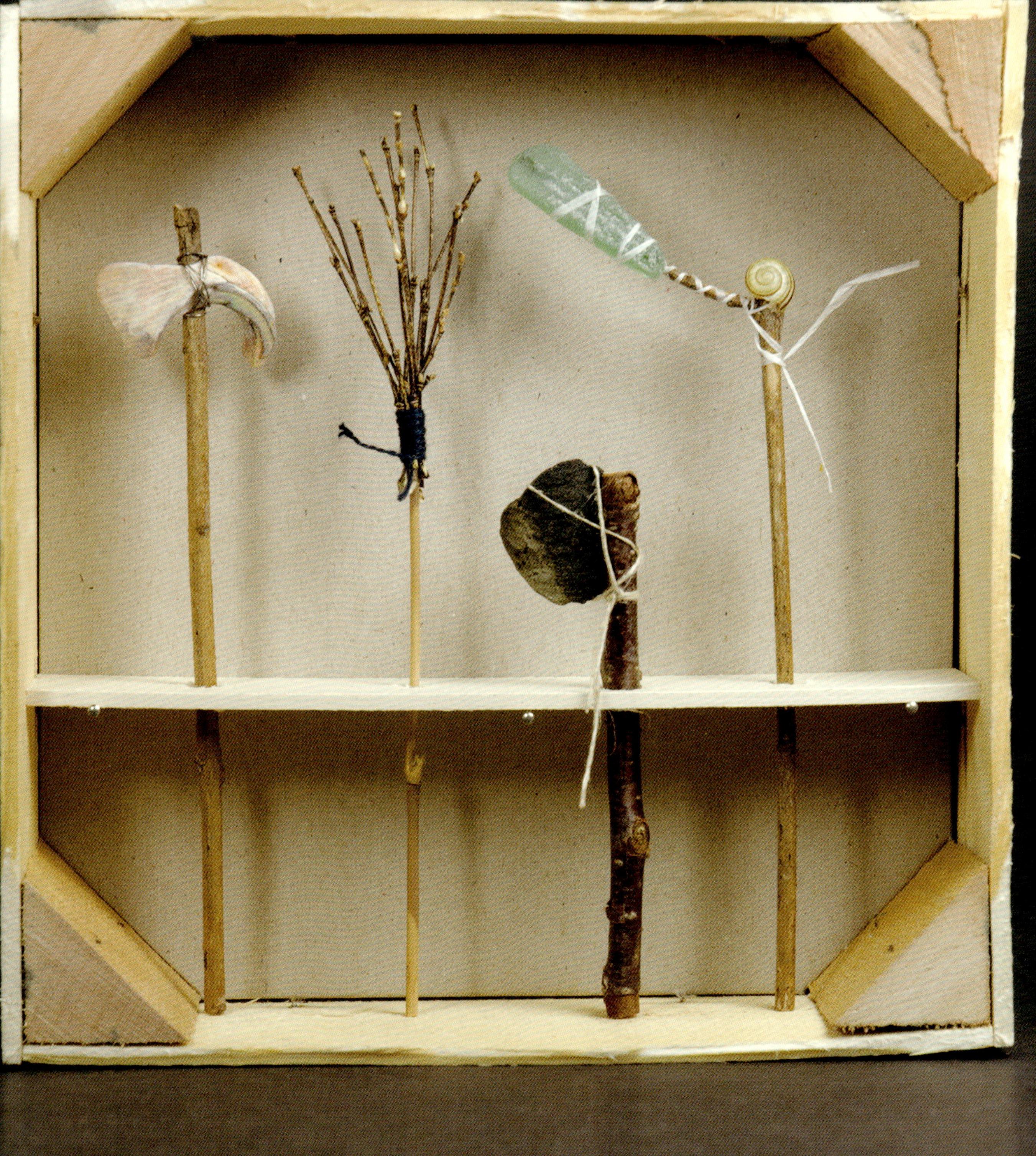

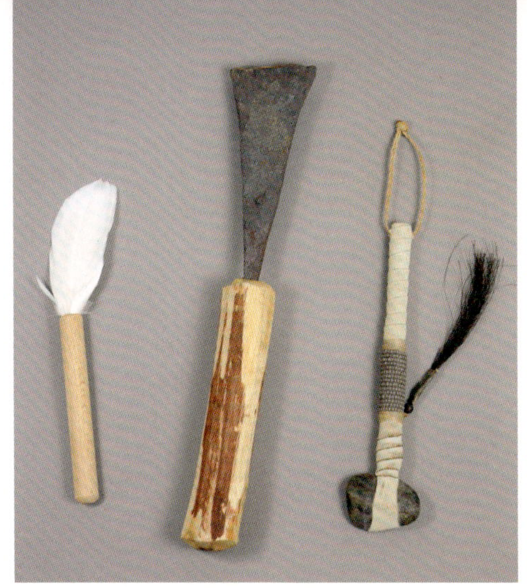

Convert a Small Fruit Crate to Hold Small Tools

Materials + Tools

Small fruit crate

Small saw

Wire cutter and side cutter

Ruler, cutter, and cutting mat

Awl or paper drill

Pins or thin nails, 50 mm long

Scissors

Foam board

Paper for the back panel

Masking tape or washi tape

You can find rough, stackable fruit crates filled with clementines at the supermarket around Christmas time. Otherwise you can sometimes find empty ones at the weekly farmers market (and maybe get them for free after making a big purchase). First shorten the square corner wood pieces to the height of the frame. You can do this with a small household saw and—in keeping with the character of the box—it is by no means necessary that the sawn edge is of carpenter quality.

Then use a pair of wire cutters to bend over the protruding metal clamps from the inside and use the side cutter to snip them off close to the wood, so that you can insert the rear panel later without damaging it.

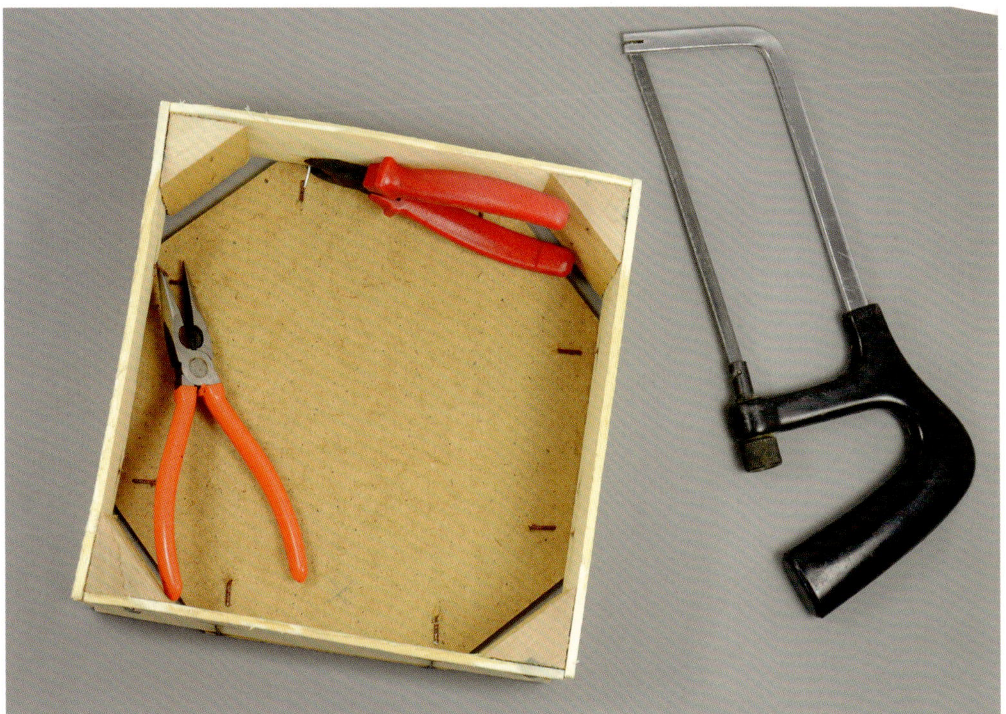

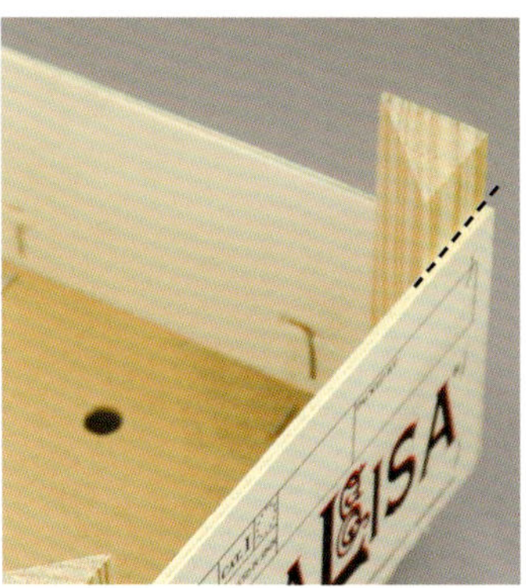

◀ *8″ × 8″ × 2½″*

Since it is hard to measure the size of the back panel from inside, place the foam board on the back of the box, mark where the top comes with a cross, and draw where the slanted sections come exactly with a pencil. Cut off the corners with a cutter and make sure to insert the foam board with the cross toward the back panel (= with the underside, which was on the top on the back side). Every fruit crate is irregular in some way; otherwise the foam board wouldn't fit properly at the corners.

Despite the slanted corners, you can cover the back panel by folding paper over it, instead of covering it moist. To do this, cut the cover paper at the corner points, fold closely around the edges, and fasten firmly to the back with masking tape or washi tape. Use a leftover piece of paperboard to hold the miniature tools; trim the length to exactly match the (inner) width of the box, and make it about 1/3" narrower than the box depth. Use the awl or paper drill to bore the holes through which the tool handles are inserted.

The piece of paperboard fastened between the side panels can be additionally fixed in place by using long pins inserted underneath through the rear panel (see figure on page 78).

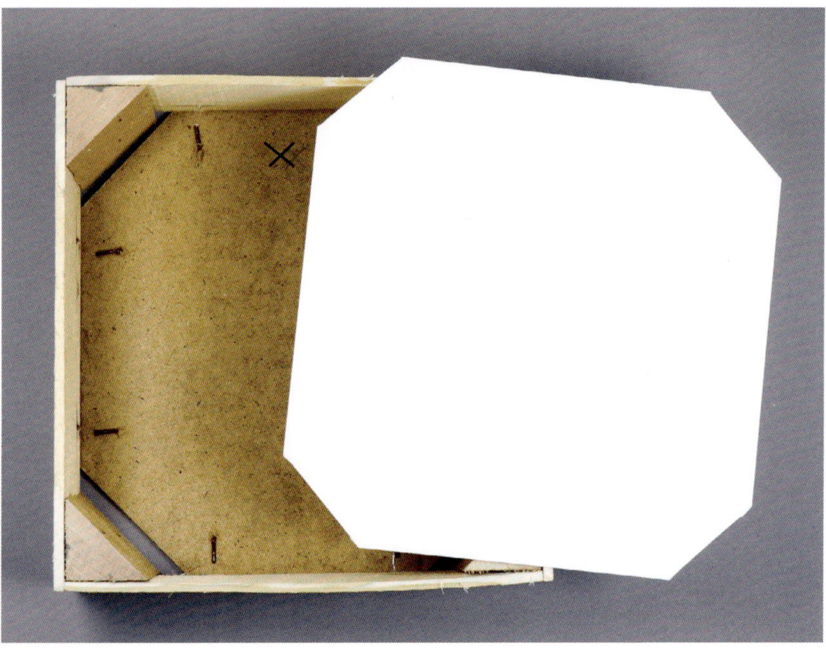

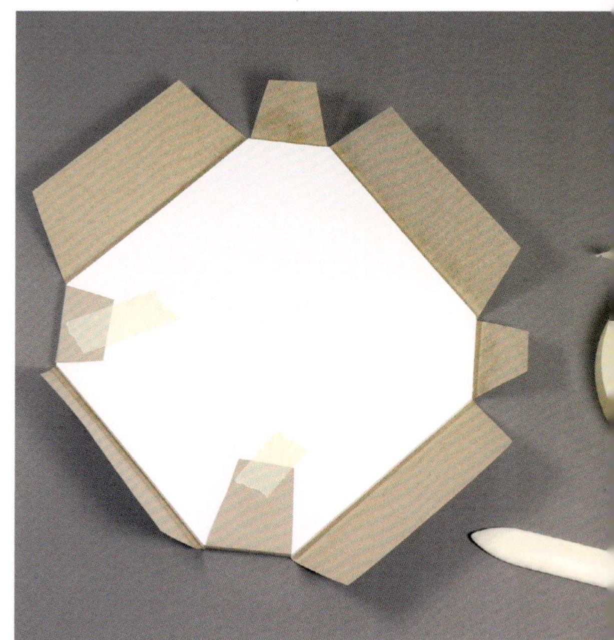

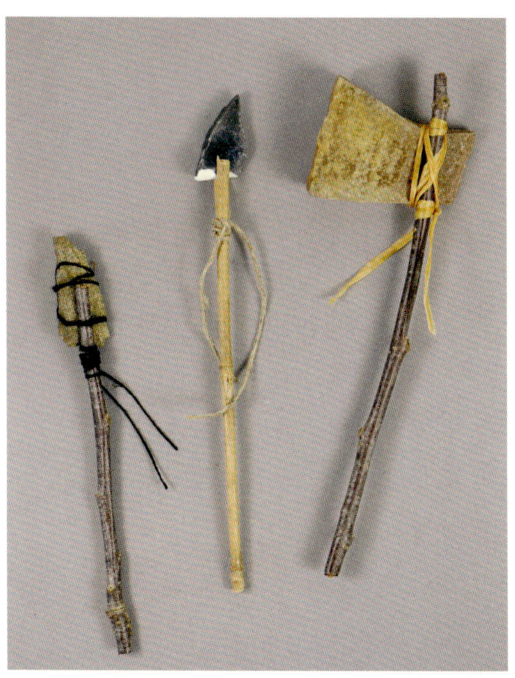

I love all kinds of tools. For me, these are things that work for a lifetime in my hands without ever becoming worthless, because they haven't been updated. When traveling, I often find strange, unknown pieces in markets or in old-fashioned household item stores (see figure on page 79). And in ethnological museums you can admire all kinds of strange tools in glass cases.

Admiration encourages inspiration—and it is a great pleasure to invent your own, imaginatively archaic tools with the help of finds from nature or from junk. These then work very well in the rough box and, inside it, don't seem useless at all.

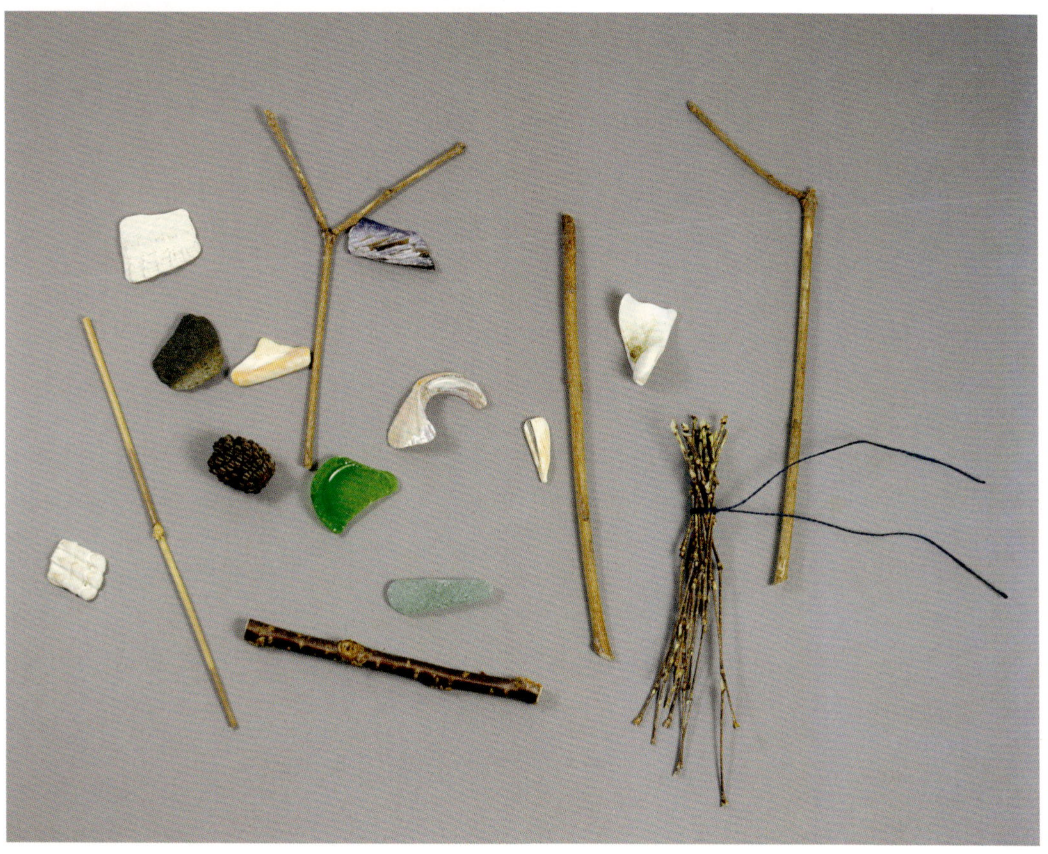

Materials for Self-Invented Tools

Bamboo twigs, twigs from pruning, driftwood . . .

. . . and almost anything that can be tied fast or clamped in a slot:

Flat stones, seed pods, old bits of iron (nuts, washers, etc.), flattened crown corks, or wire champagne cork cages, shells and shell pieces, beach glass, small bones, feathers, beads, porcelain pieces, ethnic or costume jewelry, etc.
To fasten them in: waxed shoemaker's thread, thin wire, linen yarn, thin paper yarn, dental floss drawn through beeswax . . .

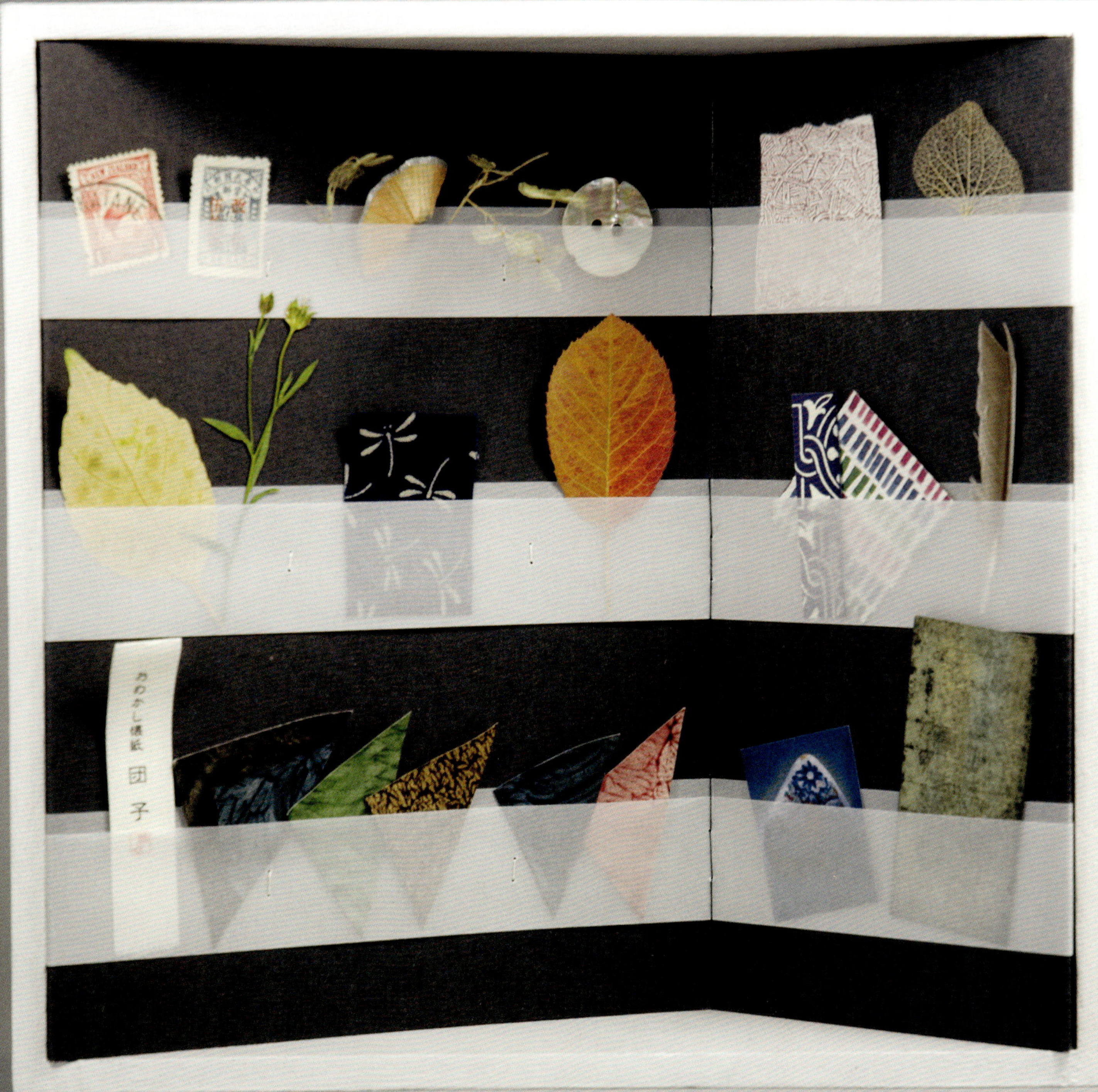
団子

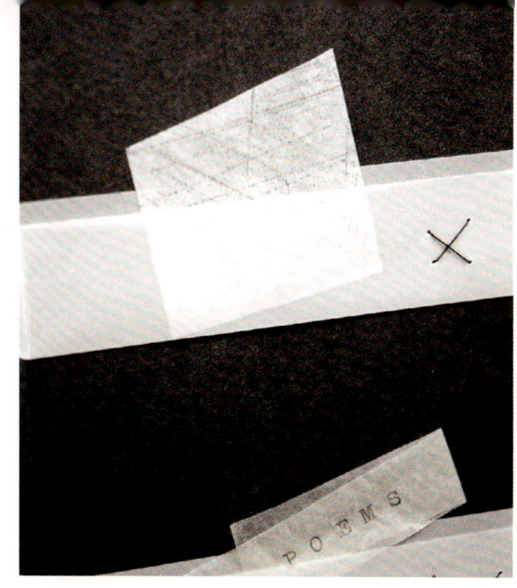

Inserted Strips for Delicate Collections

The second half of the decorative box sawn in half (see page 68) now provides a restrained background for delicate collections displayed on translucent insert strips, similar to a stamp album.

First, underneath the frame fasten a piece of plywood that you have had cut to size at a home improvement store using white glue to make a bottom, and weigh it down while drying. That should be sufficient, since there is no tensile force on the bottom when it is used as a back panel.

Then trim a strip of dark, thin cardboard to the height (inner dimension) of the box, 1 mm smaller than measured, so that nothing gets stuck. At the right edge of the strip, measure the inner depth (here: 2¹/₃"), make a groove by using the bone folder [1], and fold over backward. Make a mark on the back panel of the box at about one-third of the width [2] and measure the distance to the side upper edges from there.

Materials + Tools

Decorative box

Ruler, drawing triangle, cutter, and cutting mat

Bone folder

Awl for pricking holes

Dark, firm construction paper or thin cardboard, 150–200 gsm, maximum length twice as long as the box width, with the grain direction parallel to the short side

Tracing paper

Needle and thread

Masking tape or washi tape, double-sided adhesive tape, and white glue

1

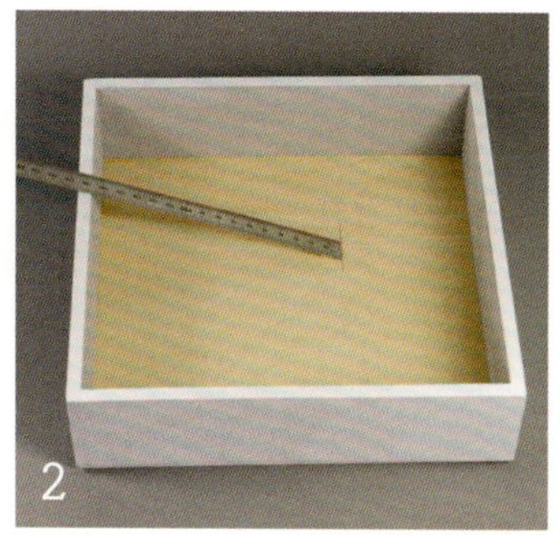
2

◀ *9½" × 9" × 2½"*

Fold the strip twice from the folded-over right edge on the basis of the measured distances, and cut off the excess length (left) back to $2^1/_3$" (= box depth) [3].

When inserted horizontally from above, the strip now has to go into the box at a long slant from the left and then steeply up to the right again. Then cut several strips of tracing paper (with the grain direction parallel to the long side). The strips should be at least $^3/_4$" longer than the width of the asymmetrical insert. Fold the strips lengthwise—almost in the middle—so that the back half protrudes by a few millimeters. Then insert at a slant so that the tracing-paper strips protrude on both sides. Transfer the vertical, middle fold of the cardboard strip to the tracing paper strips and prick several holes into the fold. Next fix the insert strips in place with vertical stitches while using the triangle to monitor that they are exactly horizontal when sewn in. (Stitching is more flexible than gluing, and glue remains visible under tracing paper.) Insert the slanted piece into the box and fold over the insert tabs to the left and right so that they are only slightly taut and the ends with the side panels disappear into the box.

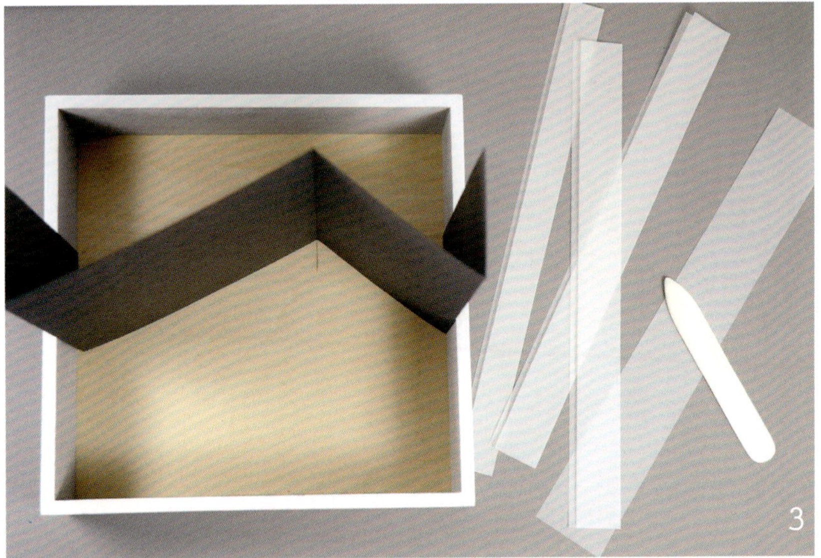
3

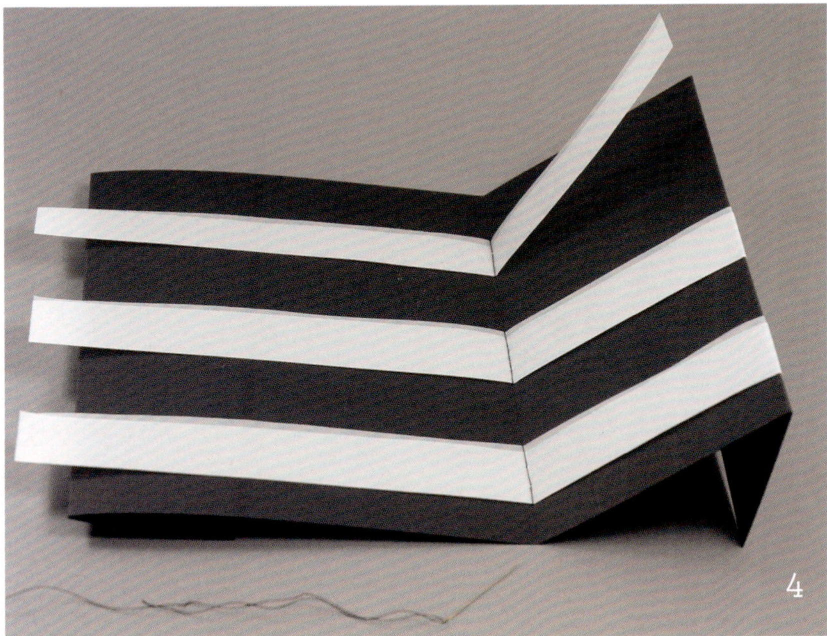
4

If nothing bulges out, the strips can be fastened to the side panels with masking tape or washi tape [4]. If the insert strips do not lie completely flat, you can fasten them additionally to the long slanting side using small stitches (see page 83). Then fill with flat treasures and attach the back mountain fold and side panels to the inside of the box with double-sided adhesive tape.

Alternative design:

Fill the insert strips only very sparingly with what was left lying next to the cutting machine as waste, yielding an elegant monochrome overall image. ▶

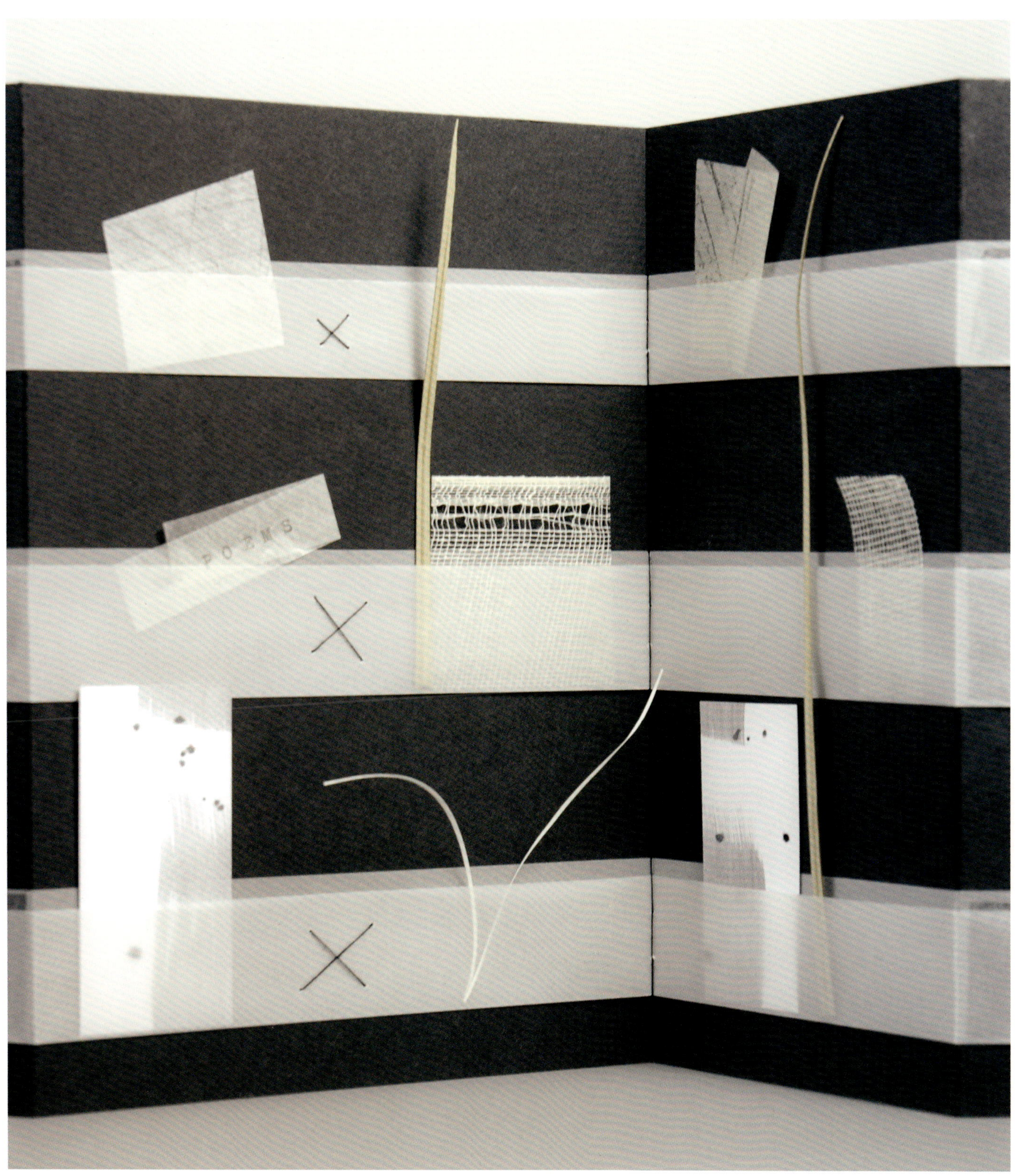
POEMS

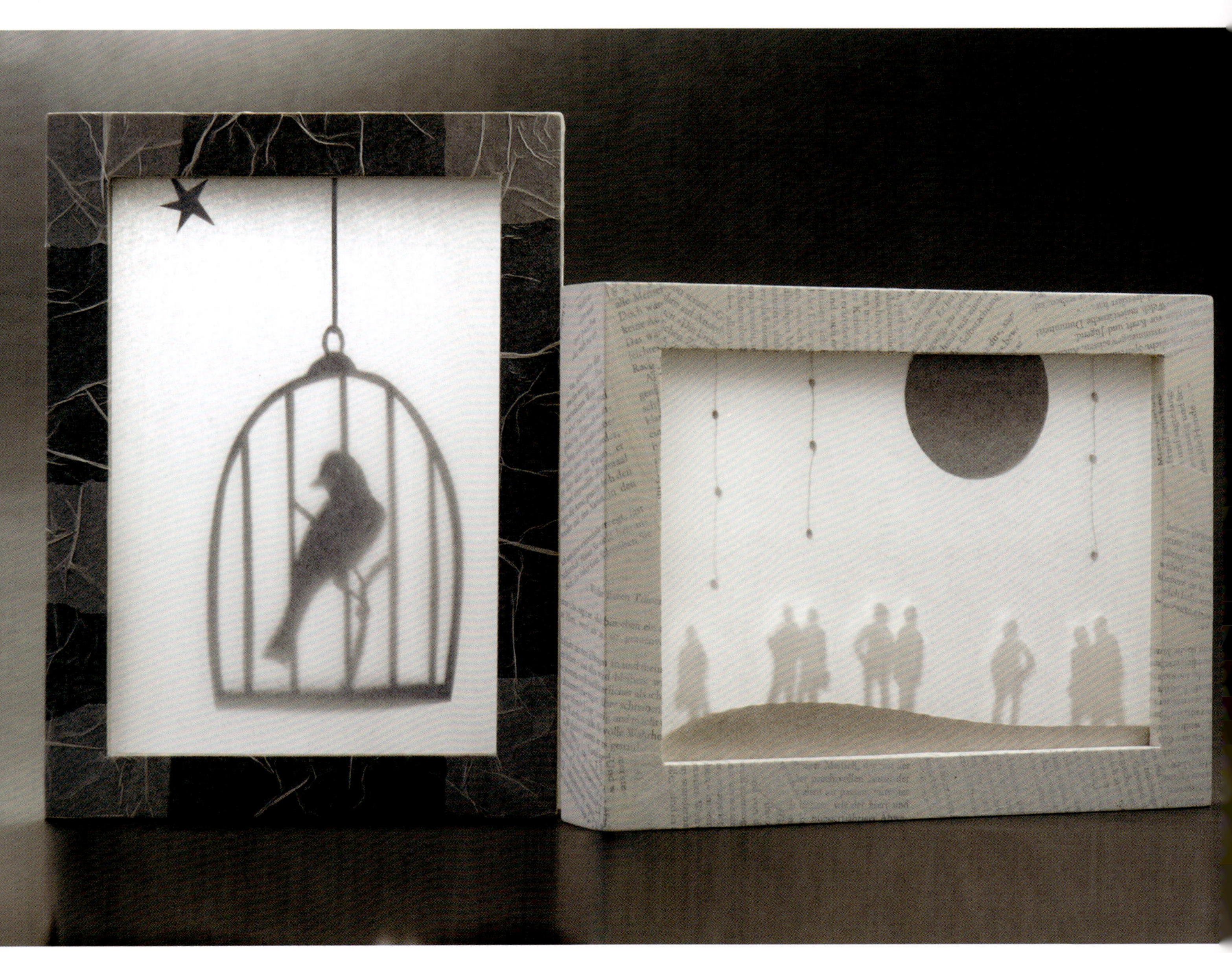

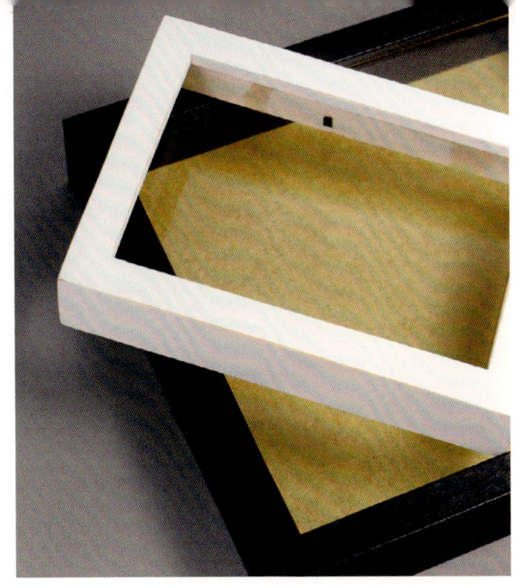

Translucent Boxes as Shadow Dioramas

You can create a very special kind of box by converting inexpensive picture frames from a photo supply store.

The translucent front makes the contents visible as a silhouette and thus creates an effect similar to that of a shadow theater.

First, free boxes of their sterile appearance due to industrial manufacturing. Paste a layer of torn tissue paper pieces to the black lacquered frame; these become translucent as they dry and yield an interesting structure through the overlays.

Cover the white frame with torn pages from books (if possible, use thin pages from classic editions or dictionaries) or snippets of newspaper. After drying, paint over these with very dilute white acrylic paint to lightly "fog" the text.

Materials + Tools

Simple photo picture frames (without the glass pane)

Ruler, cutter, scalpel, and cutting mat

Paste and brush

White acrylic paint and brush

White glue or double-sided adhesive tape

Translucent sandwich wrap paper

Dark, smooth construction paper for paper cuttings

Remnant of corrugated cardboard

Tissue paper

Thread and beads

Model figures from an architecture supplier

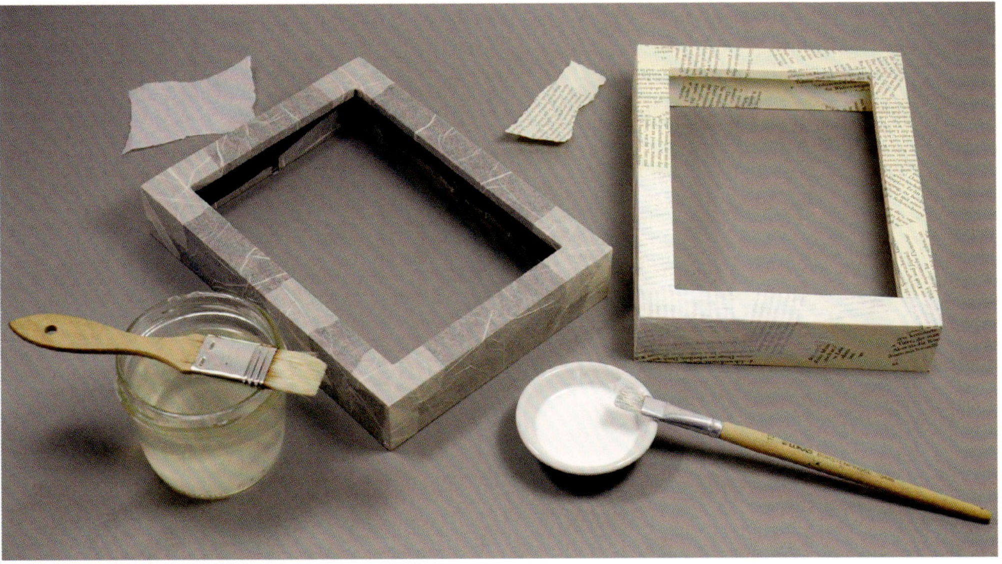

◀ *8″ × 6″ × 1½″ / 6″ × 8″ × 1½″*

Use white glue to attach a piece of translucent sandwich wrap paper, cut to fit, directly to the back of the front frame slats—already covered and let dry. When doing this, make absolutely sure that the paper is lightly and evenly taut and does not sag into folds, because it will become the "screen" for the shadow diorama. After making a preliminary sketch (or an enlarged photocopy from this book), use a silhouette knife or scalpel to make a paper cutting that fits into the frame picture cutout.

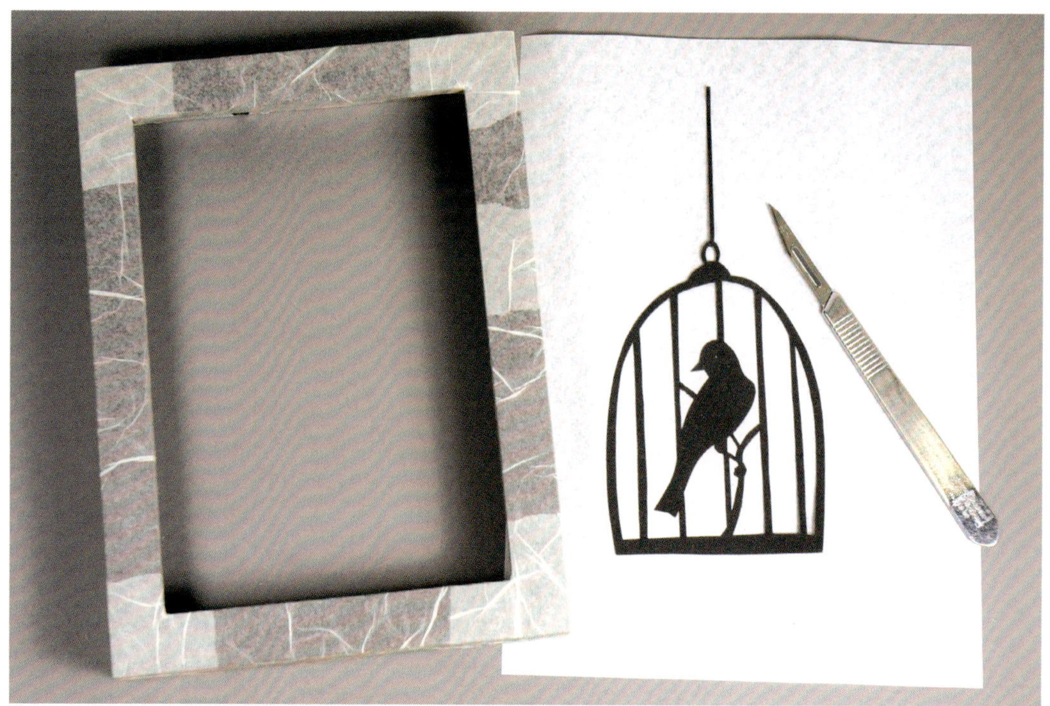

To make the terrain shape as shown in the white box, cut a thick piece of waste corrugated cardboard from a packing box to match the (inner) width of the frame, insert it from behind, and mark how high the curve of the terrain should appear in the picture cutout. Cut along the curve with the cutter. Insert the model figures into the "honeycomb" you can see from above. If the honeycomb is too big, you can use some white glue to keep the figures from sinking in too far. Glue the terrain shape onto the frame from the back on top of the sandwich wrap paper.

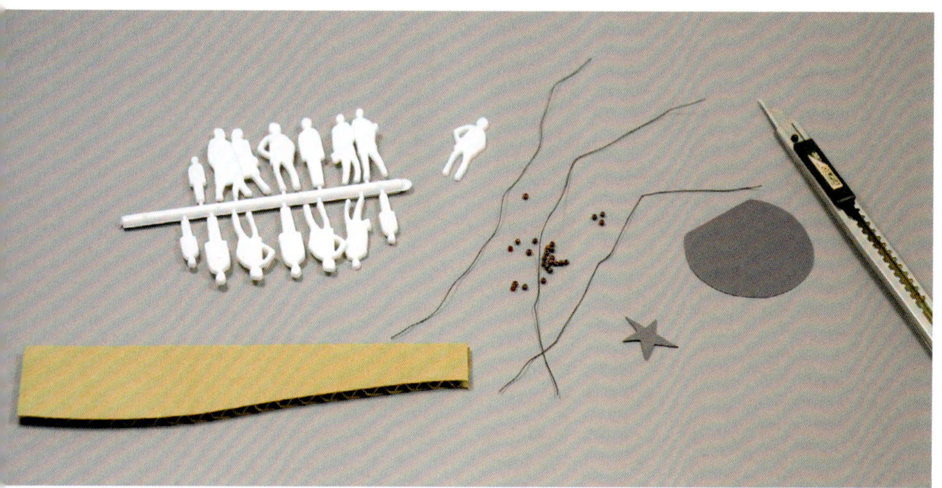

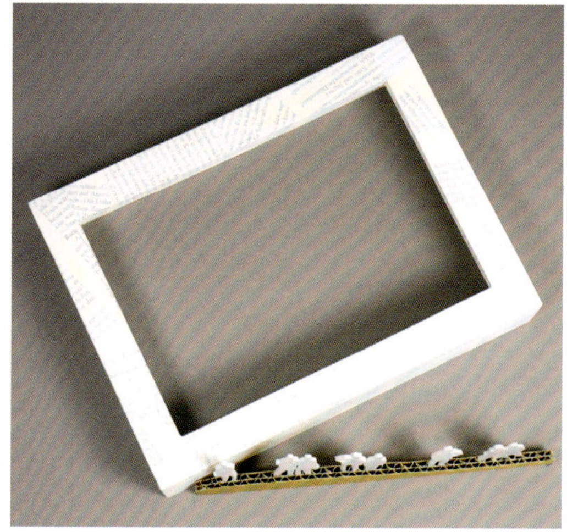

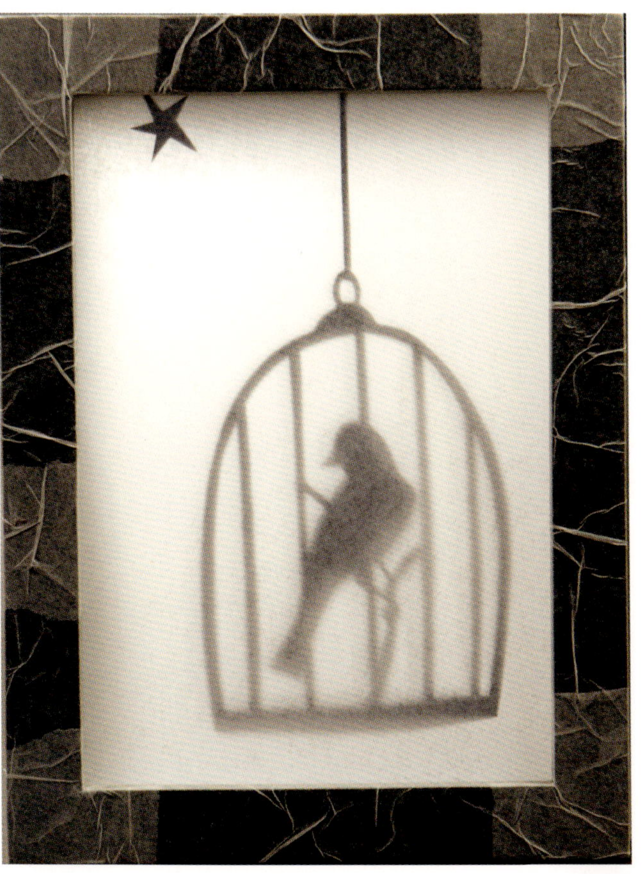

The bird in a cage was given an irregularly cut star for a companion. If the star is glued right behind the front edge of the frame it appears darker, while the bird (about 2 mm farther back) is fastened into the frame from above, thus creating a slightly blurry effect and appearing to be farther away.

Tip:
You can also create a glazed shadow box from a picture frame by gluing a made-to-size paperboard box (see page 109) to the frame from the back.

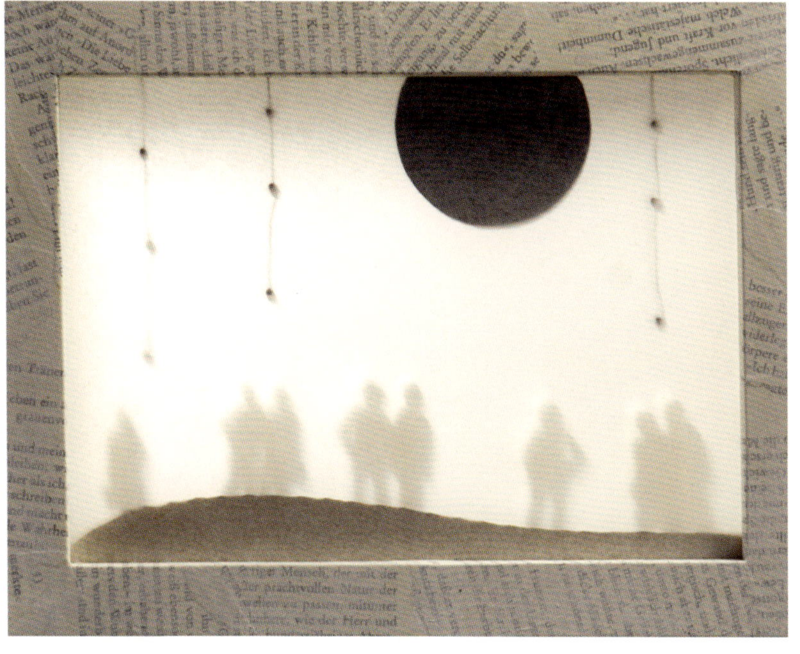

Here again, you can clearly recognize the effect of the differing distances from the sandwich wrap paper "screen." The moon is—like the star above—glued directly behind the front edge of the frame, just like the curved terrain. As a result, these two image elements appear darker and closer.

The figures were inserted into the corrugated cardboard at a little distance from the "screen." The beads knotted on threads lie on another level and contribute to the three-dimensional impression.

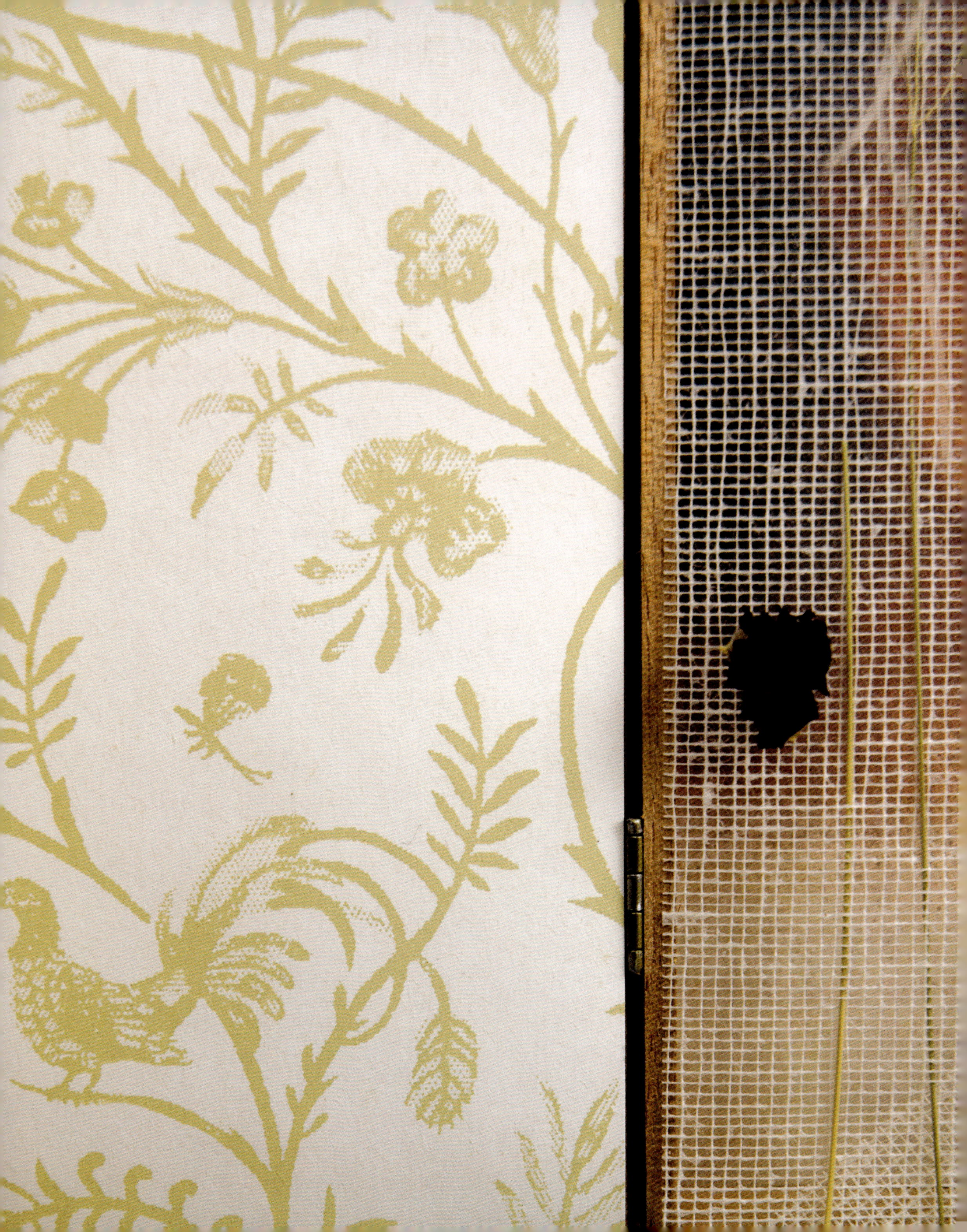

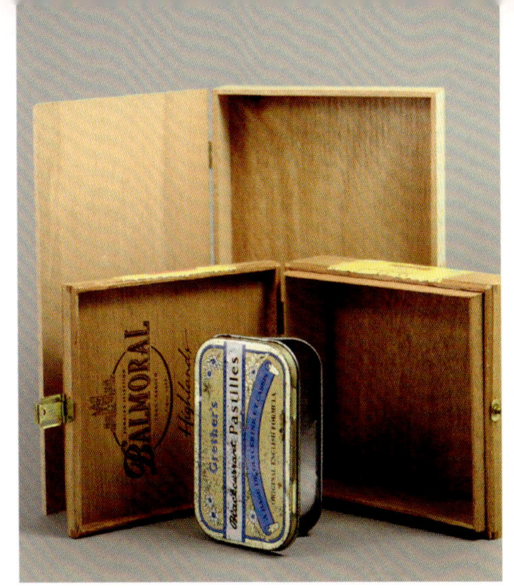

4 Double Boxes and Miniatures That Flip Open

Another way to play with the world of boxes is to use cigar boxes with a hinged lid that flips open, or various kinds of chocolate, wine, and other wooden gift boxes. Small metal candy tins can also be made into miniature boxes.

The "double page spread" that emerges—as in a book—from the open box inspires new design ideas.

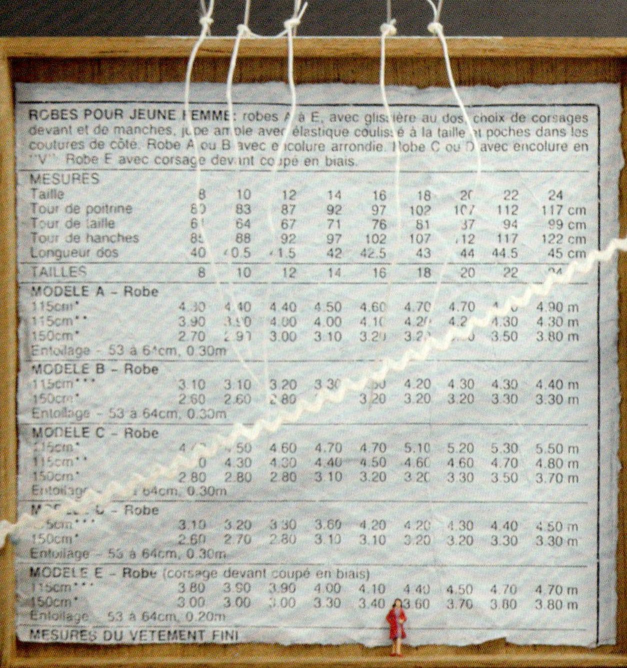
ROBES POUR JEUNE FEMME
MESURES
Taille
Tour de poitrine
Tour de taille
Tour de hanches
Longueur dos
TAILLES
MODELE A – Robe
MODELE B – Robe
MODELE C – Robe
MODELE E – Robe (corsage devant coupé en biais)
MESURES DU VETEMENT FINI

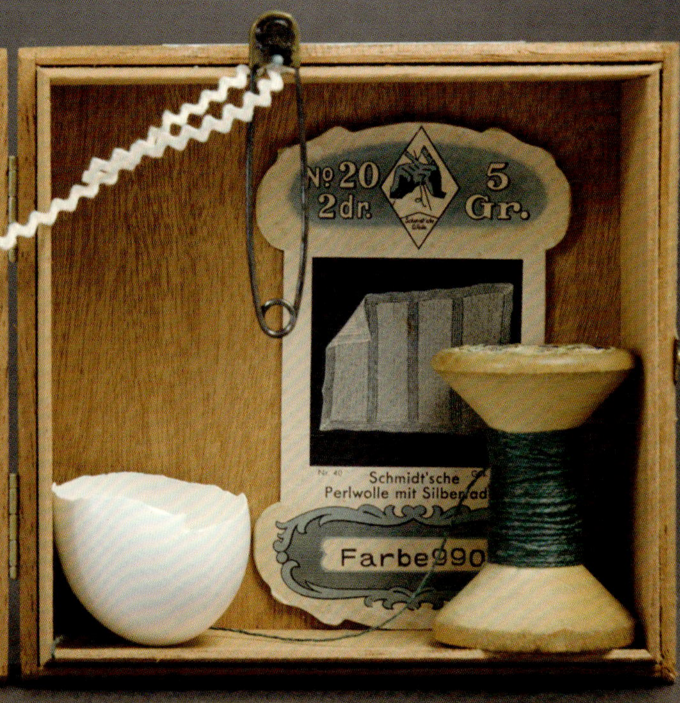
No 20
2dr.
5
Gr.
Schmidt'sche
Farbe 990

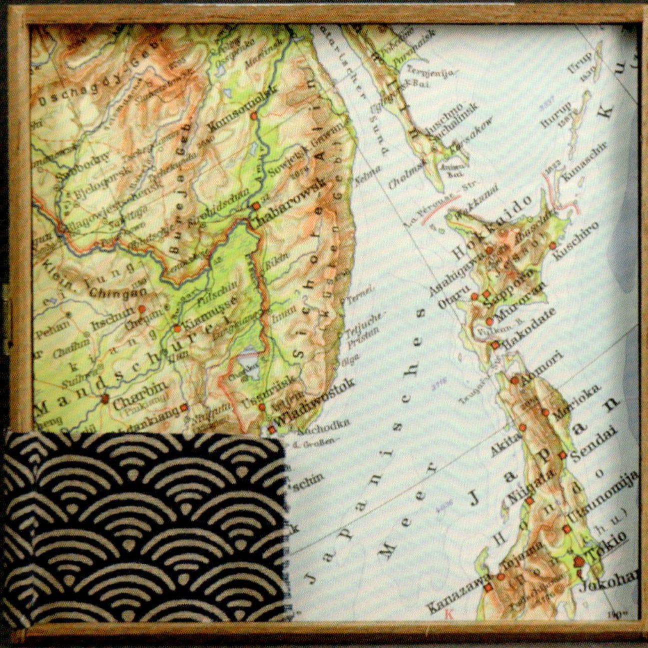
Hokkaido
Sapporo
Hakodate
Chabarowsk
Wladiwostok
Charbin
Sendai
Tokio

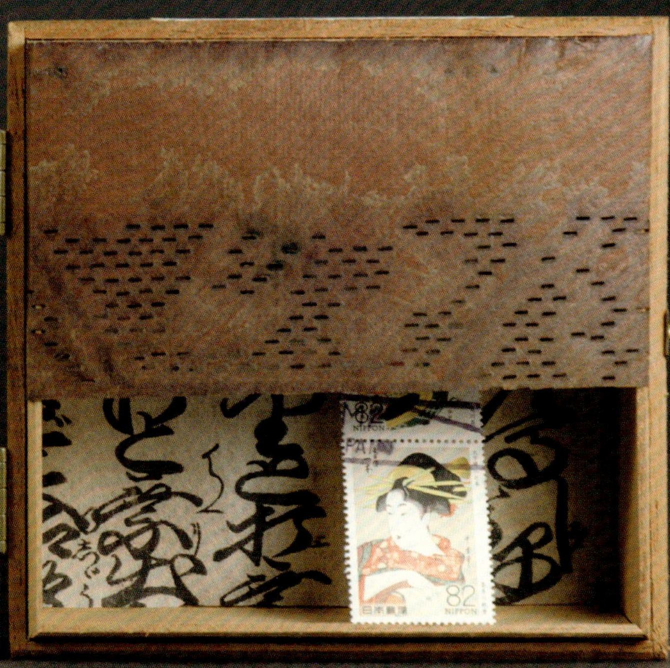
82
NIPPON

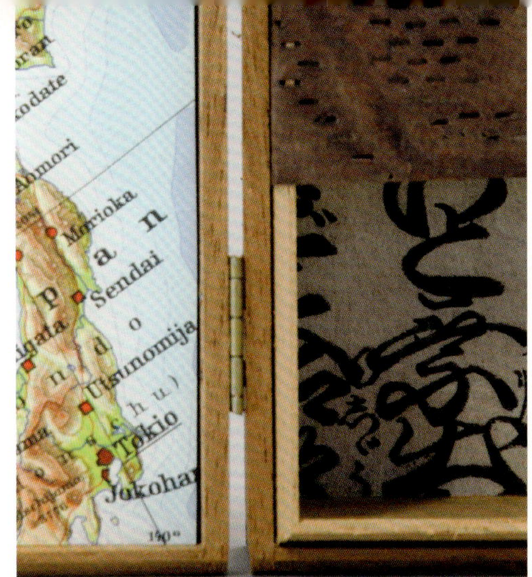

A Cigar Box Displays the World of Thread or the Far East . . .

Cigar boxes are classics among boxes with hinged lids. Even if the pleasant tobacco fragrance has faded away after many years, they still have a special smell due to the woods used to make them. Therefore, I find it hard to give these boxes a neutral priming, especially if they have inscriptions that "stimulate your wanderlust."

In the upper box I have collected leftovers from an old sewing box. It is easy to insert needles into the soft plywood. The delicate blue-green eggshell already matches the color of the old sewing thread; the size chart was rubbed with crayons, then crumpled and torn.

The same box (*below*) can also house mementos of Japan: a section from an old school atlas, a swatch of cloth with a classic Japanese pattern, a sheet of brushwork for the back panel, and a piece of stencil paper used for printing fabric as the screen hanging in the front, beneath which a casually tilted postage stamp peers out.

Materials + Tools

Small cigar box

Ruler, cutter, and cutting mat

Paste and brush

White glue or double-sided adhesive tape

Colored pencil and a cotton ball if needed

Collectibles from an old sewing box, such as pins, zigzag tape, yarn cards, safety pins, a measurement chart for cutting, a wooden bobbin . . .

Also: model train figures, possibly eggshells or collectibles such as on a Japanese theme here: the "Far East" section of a school atlas, fabric swatches with a Japanese pattern, Japanese stamps, a piece of old stencil paper, old paper with brush writing . . .

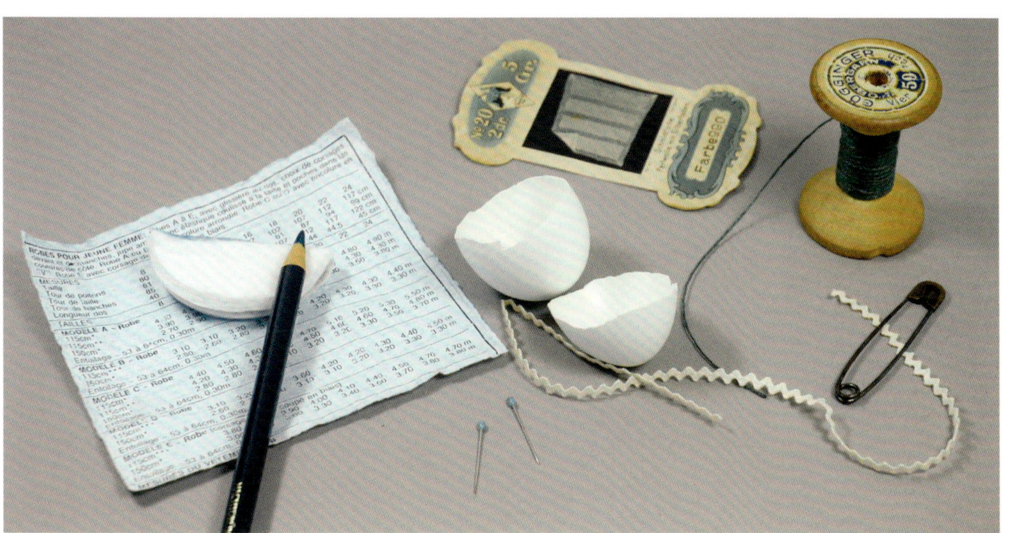

◀ *4¾" × 5" × ⅓" / 4¾" × 5" × 1½"*

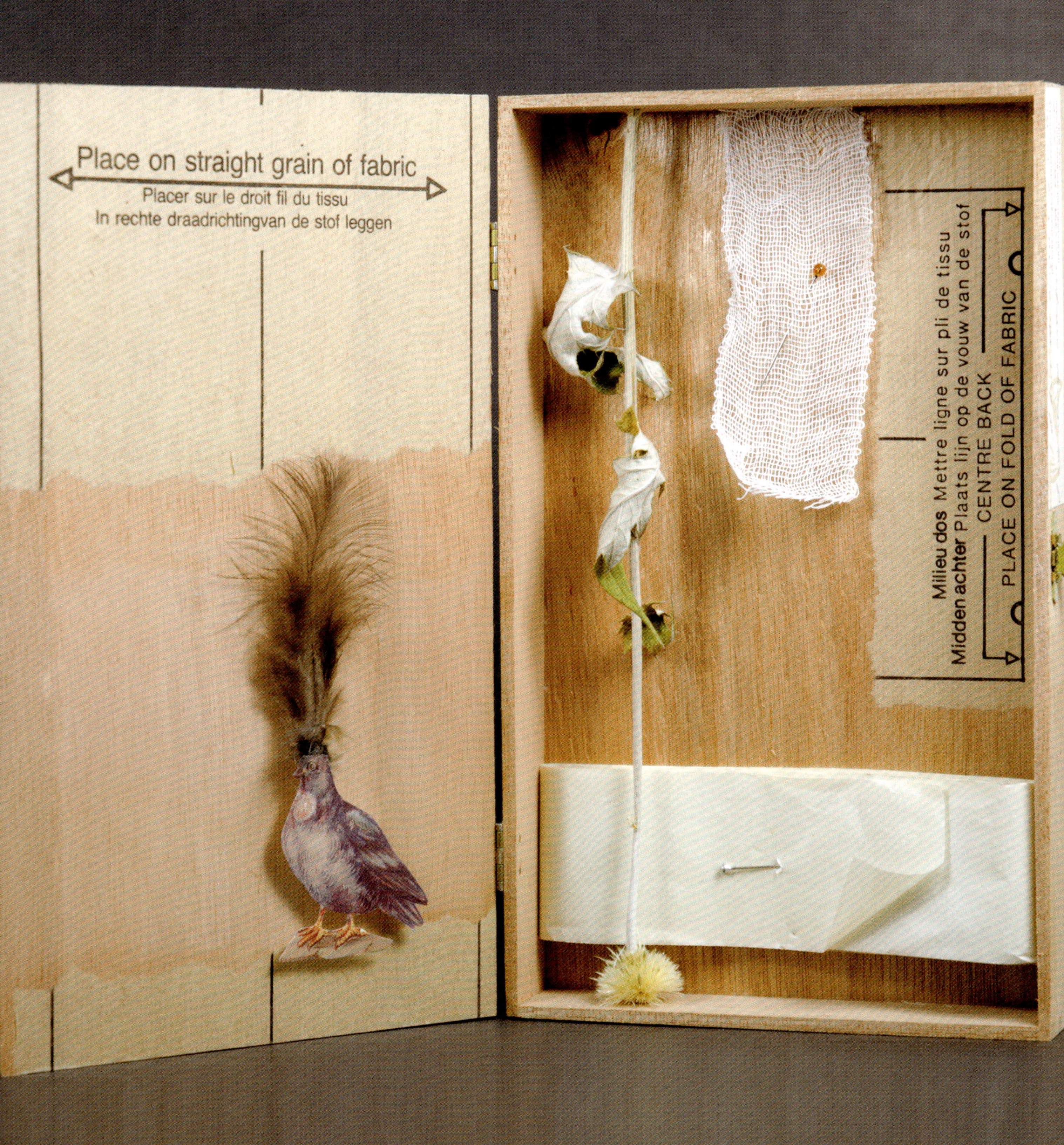
Place on straight grain of fabric
Placer sur le droit fil du tissu
In rechte draadrichtingvan de stof leggen
Milieu dos Mettre ligne sur pli de tissu
Midden achter Plaats lijn op de vouw van de stof
CENTRE BACK
PLACE ON FOLD OF FABRIC

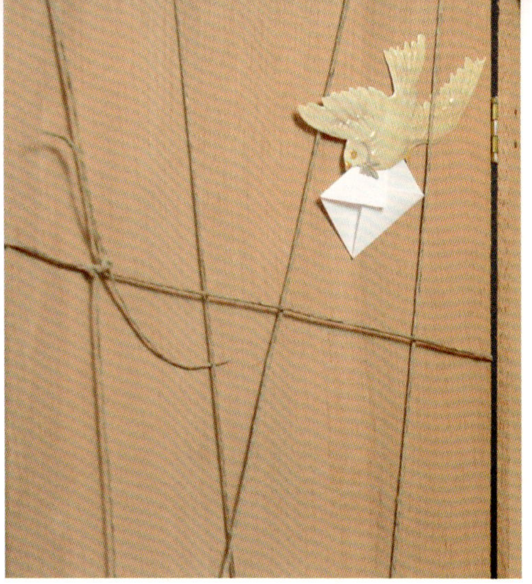

A Cigar Box Displays Cutting Patterns or Signs of Wanderlust . . .

The rough, unpainted wood of the cigar box with its fibers feels like paper and fabric. In this project, you smoothly wallpaper torn pieces of old sewing patterns onto the box. But you can also consciously paper them on in folds (see page 27). It is important to know that the thin plywood (just like paperboard) reacts strongly to moisture. Therefore, use a brush to apply a little water or paste on the reverse side each time so that nothing warps as it dries.

A glossy print of a bird—crowned with a real feather and with a foam board spacer on the back—adorns the flat lid, which is not recessed. At right (*in the bottom*) old pins, a dried thistle, wound-up paper tape, and a piece of mull are simply wedged in or lightly glued on. All the elements should be arranged so that you can still close the box lid.

Materials + Tools

Cigar box with flat lid

Ruler, cutter, and cutting mat

Paste and brush

White glue or double-sided adhesive tape

Pieces of old sewing patterns, newspaper clippings, old wallpaper

Glossy pictures of birds

Feathers

Thin string, gauze

Remnant piece of foam board

Finds such as dried thistle, old pins, a band of mull cloth, paper tape, dried grasses, leaves and flowers, stones, a rusty piece of iron . . .

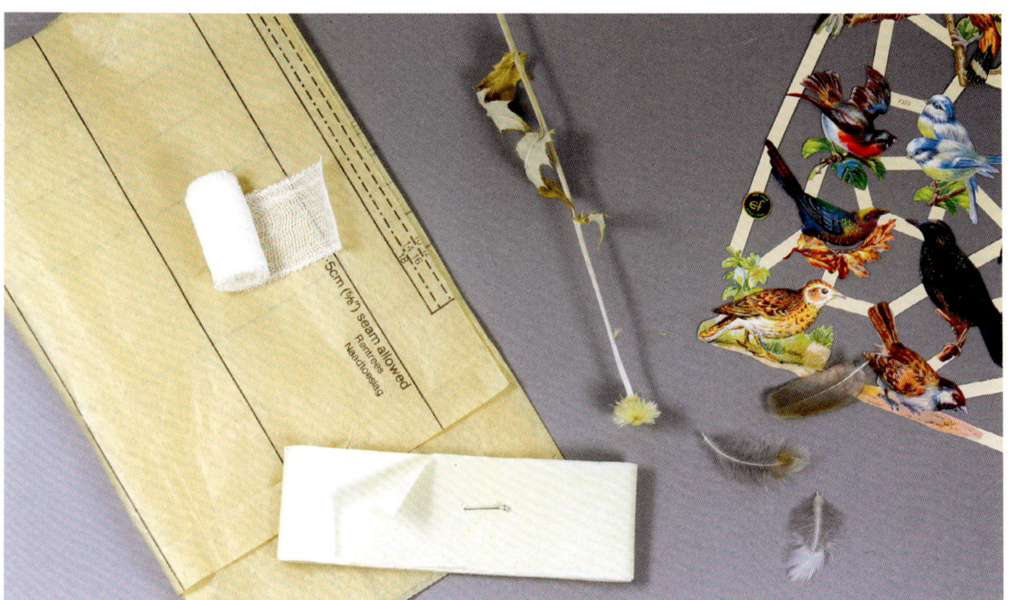

◀ *8″ × 5″ × 1¼″*

Alternative design:

Using gauze—a stiff, coarsely woven fabric used in bookbinding (mull) or in print graphics (wiping gauze for etchings)—allows you to play with textile elements more. Since the box is intended to remain permanently open, you can cover the flat lid with old wallpaper. An image on absorbent newsprint paper is wallpapered on the bottom to make the background.

Trim a narrow strip of gauze so that it is wide enough to cover half of the face on the newsprint image. The length of the gauze strip should correspond to the height of the box, plus its depth and a few extra inches. Trim a second piece of gauze so that it fits taut in the shape of a triangle over the lower right corner and can be glued firmly to the back panel. Carefully pull delicate blades of grass through it before attaching the long strip; to do this, the gauze should not be pulled taut yet. Then also wind the strip tightly (vertically) around the box and fasten it to the back panel. Afterward, you can insert small dried flower buds into the gauze triangle; for these short stems it is no longer necessary that the gauze be kept pliable.

Then a random text excerpt from a newspaper, only loosely glued on, gives the box another enigmatic meaning.

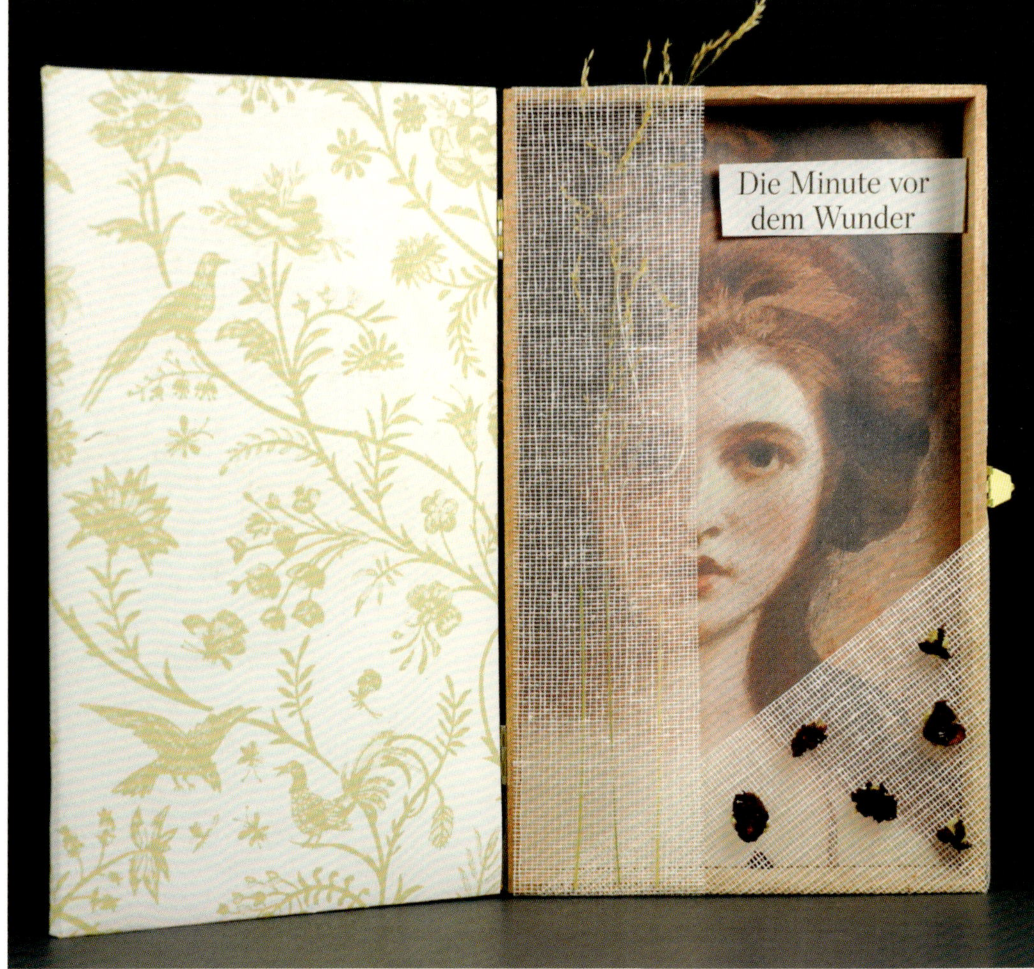

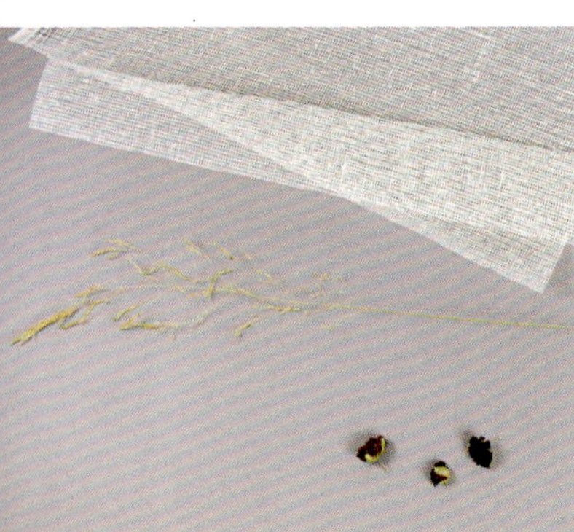

Alternative design:

The same box can also be given a very sturdy and rustic appearance by using an old map, thin hemp cord, a stone, and a dried and pressed oak leaf.

The wanderlust theme finds its expression in a glossy print of a woman driving a 1930s convertible and in a compass from the toy store. By wrapping the flat lid with hemp cord you create not only a graphic pattern, but also a way to insert the glossy picture. The back panel is papered with the back of the hiking map, whose uniform lettering works well to create a peaceful background. The compass and stone rest on the bottom, and the half oak leaf is glued to the edge of the box on the side. A rusty old piece of iron, suspended on hemp cord from an (also rusty) tack, creates an important eye-catcher in the airspace.

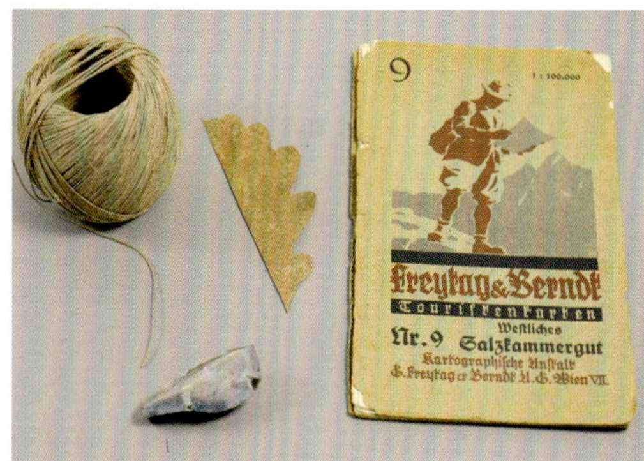

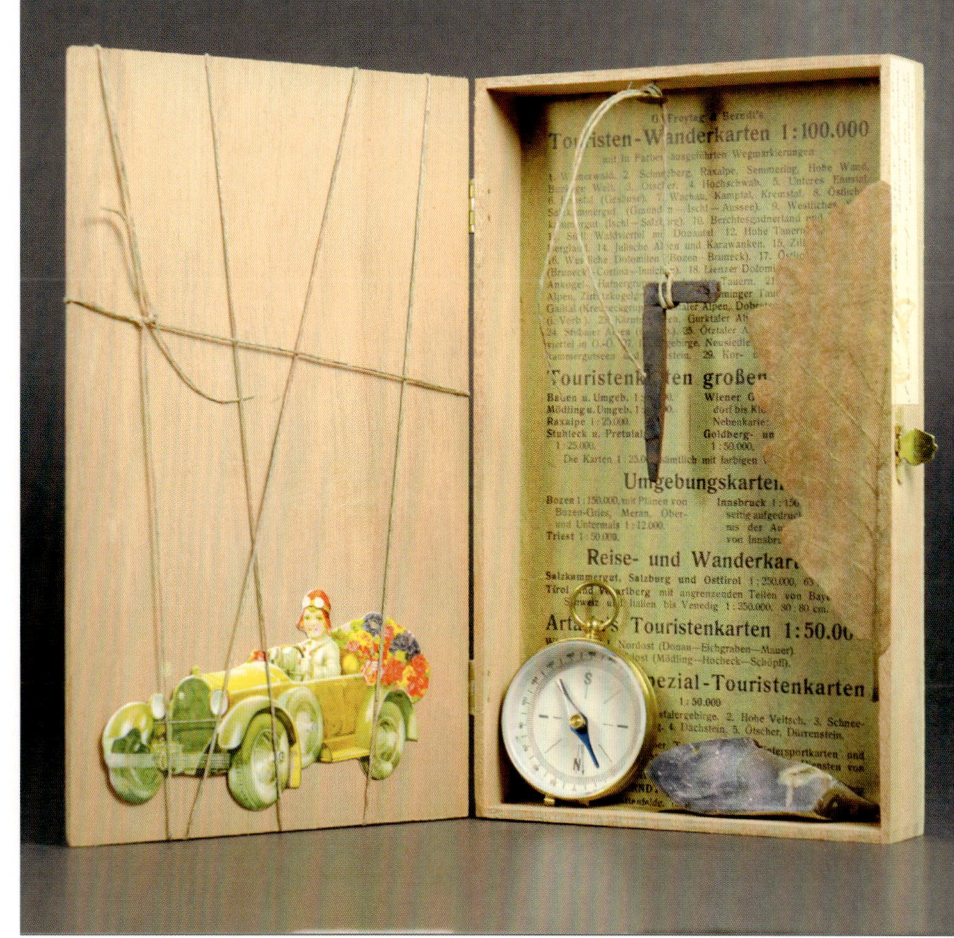

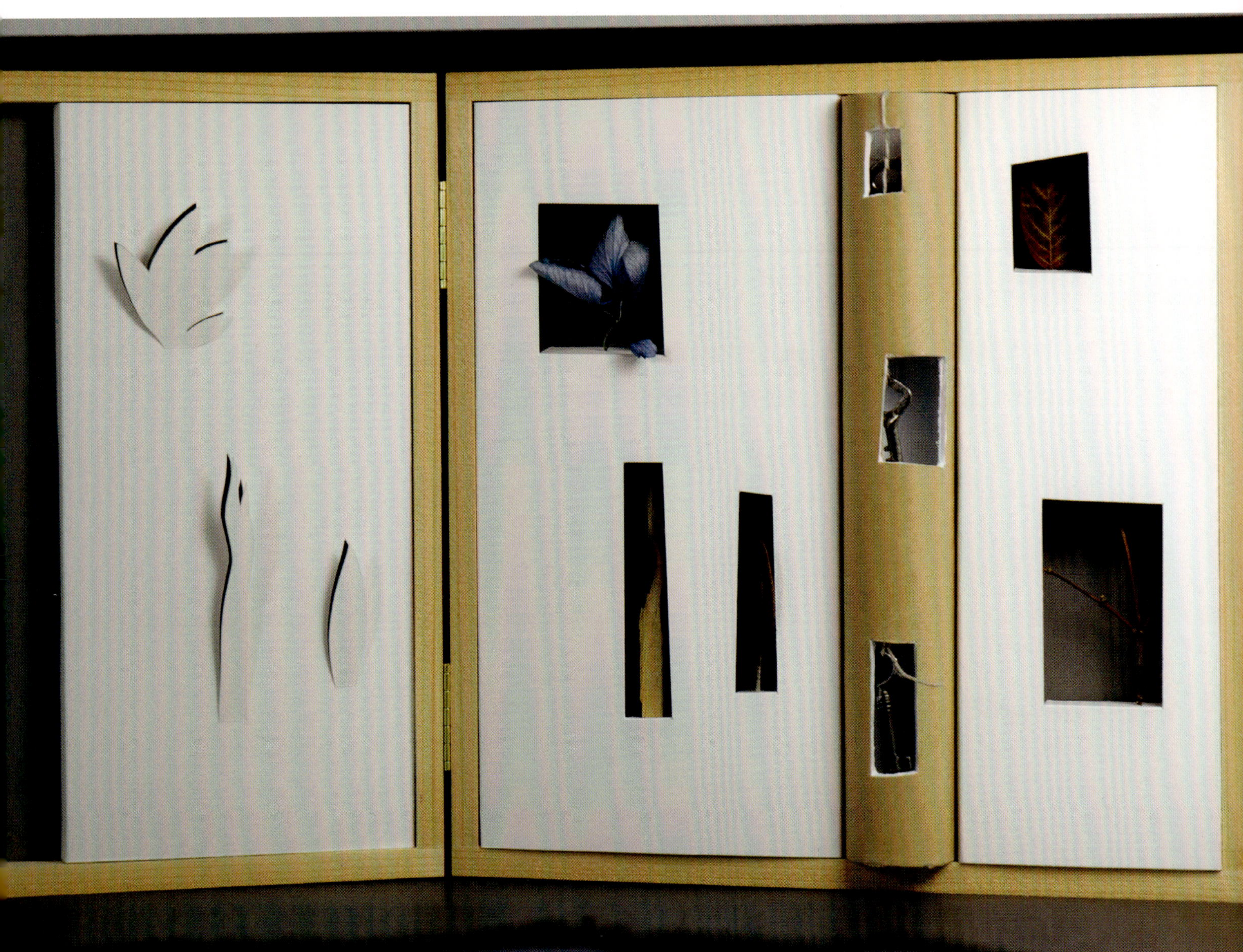

Wooden Box Flat on Both Sides with Divisions and Insights

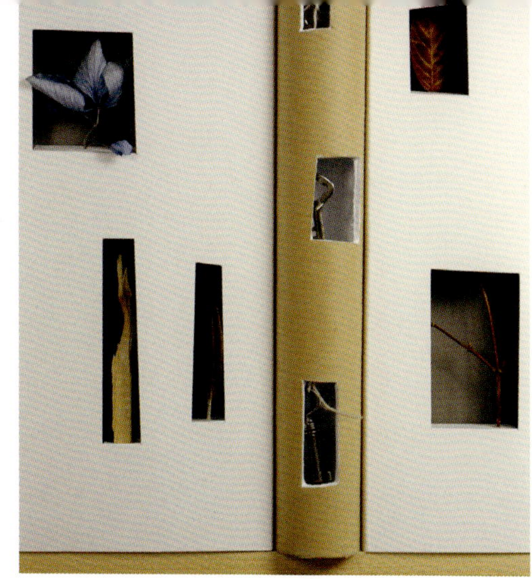

Materials + Tools

Large, flat wooden box

Ruler, cutter, and cutting mat

Awl, bone folder

Wooden stick or knitting needle for pressing on the glued places

Gesso, acrylic paint, and a brush

White glue and double-sided adhesive tape

Sturdy cardboard tube, diameter (here) at most 1³⁄₁₆"

Small piece of sandpaper

White cardboard, about 150–200 gsm

Remnant piece of foam board as long as the box height

Twine or thin cord

Finds such as dried blossoms, a pressed leaf miniature twig sculpture, small old keys, a miniature waste wood sculpture . . .

This square, wooden box is relatively large, but the lid is only 1/2" deep and the bottom is just 3/4" deep. To make it possible to fill in the two box halves well, it is a good idea to divide it up.

The eye-catcher among the divisions is a sturdy cardboard tube with a diameter that cannot exceed the total box depth. The natural tone of the cardboard tube works well with the wooden frame of the box. The box back panels are painted a warm shade of gray to create a contrasting color background. (Hint: Some gesso mixed with a very small amount of acrylic paint yields beautiful, chalk-like effects.)

Cut or saw off the cardboard tube at exactly the height of the box (inner dimension) and sand the edges smooth. Then put the cardboard tube into the deeper side of the box (*at right*) and determine the lateral intervals (here: 2 3/4" to the right of the cardboard tube; to its left, it will then be 4 1/2"). Trim the white cardboard likewise to the box height; here the grain direction should run parallel to the height (along the hinge edge).

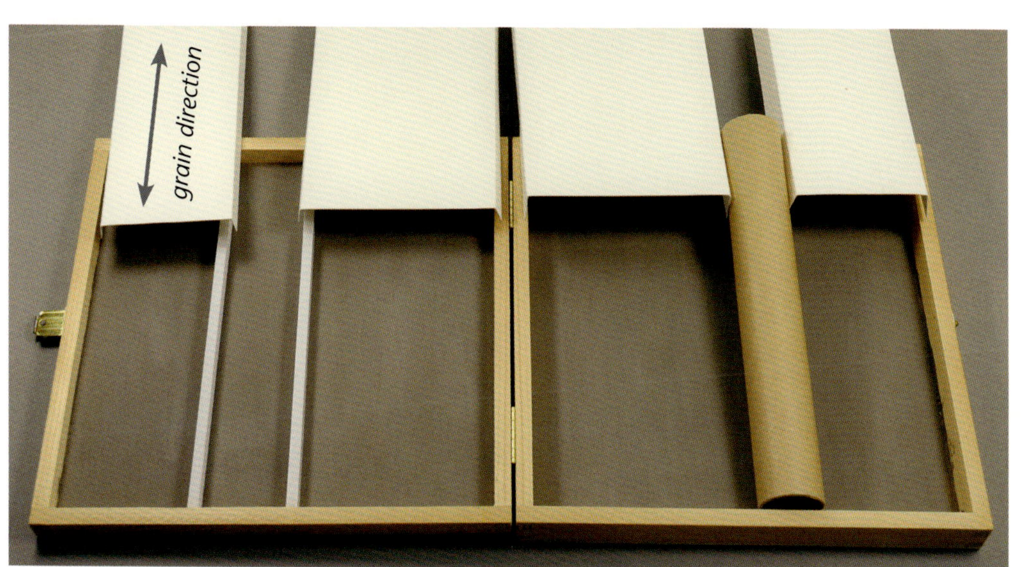

◀ *9" × 9" × ½" / 9" × 9" × ¾"*

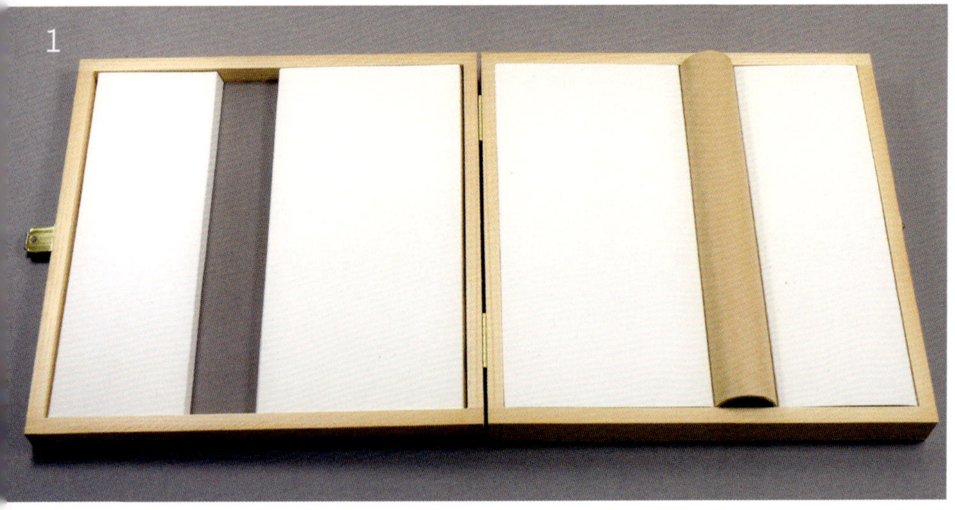

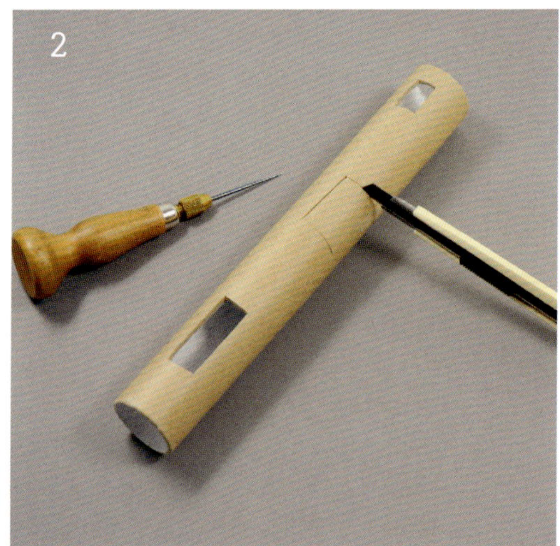

Now cut off four strips of cardboard, once to the width of the narrow interval plus $\frac{3}{4}$" x $\frac{3}{4}$" depth (here: $2\frac{3}{4}$" + $1\frac{1}{2}$" = $4\frac{1}{4}$") and once to this width plus $\frac{3}{4}$" x $\frac{1}{3}$" depth (i.e., to $3\frac{1}{2}$") for the lid. Use the same process to make the wider interval.

When you have cut all four strips to size, fold them over at an interval of $\frac{1}{3}$" or respectively $\frac{3}{4}$" from the long edge, so that they fit exactly into the lid or bottom and flush with the box frame [1]. This creates an empty space inside the lid that corresponds to the space needed to accommodate the cardboard tube when you close the box. Cut out irregular "windows" in the cardboard tube [2], sand their edges, and, if necessary, highlight them using a coat of white paint.

Make window-like cutouts in the cardboard strips for the deeper box; these look most beautiful when they are cut freehand as a contrast to the right-angled box—prick in the corner points beforehand as a guide. You can try out the divisions and size by using template shapes made of (darker) waste paper and then transfer the corner points [3]. Cut the "windows" out only at the top and sides. Fold the lower edge over to the back. Then, at an interval matching

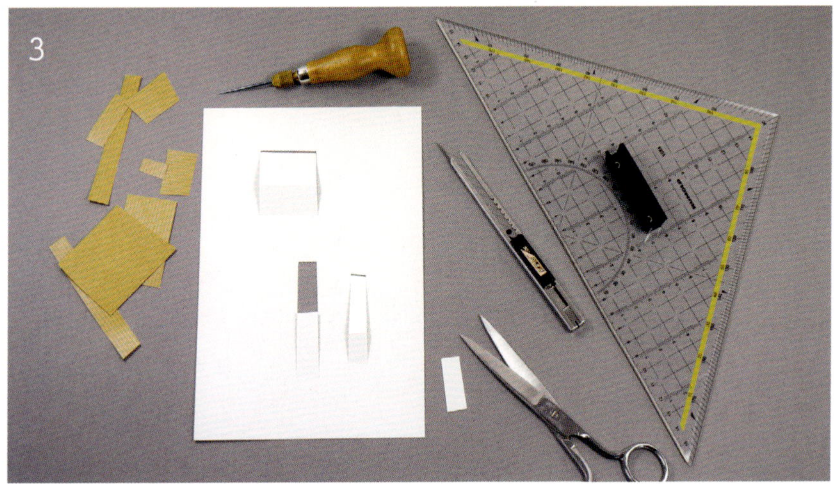

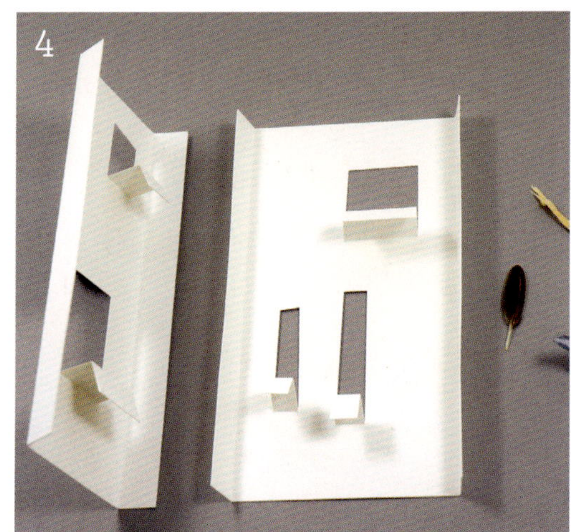

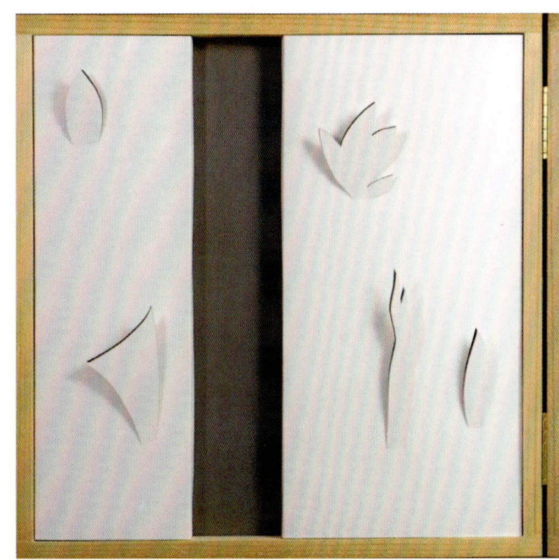

the depth of the box part for which the strip is intended (here: $^{3}/_{4}$"), fold it over again downward [4]. This "podium" then becomes the pedestal for exhibiting the small, lightweight objects displayed in the "windows." You can insert anything with a pointed end into prepunched holes or cutouts as a way to fasten them on the pedestals. Things with a horizontal base are taped on using double-sided adhesive tape.

Later, when you install the cardboard strips, attach the folded-down surfaces to the back panel by using wood glue or double-sided adhesive tape. The flatter box (the lid) contains the side strips in a mirrored sequence. Here it is a good idea to represent the objects displayed in the "windows" as paper cuttings.

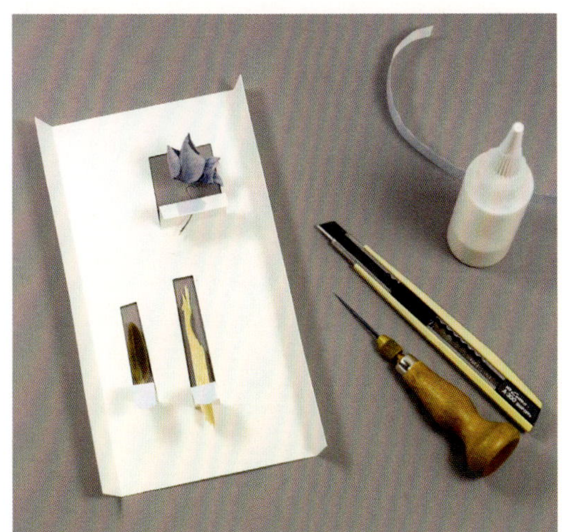

To make the paper cuttings, likewise just cut along the top and side, but not the bottom edge. Bend the paper cutting slightly forward there, so that it forms shadows and creates a 3-D effect. In the lid, attach the side pieces to the box edge with wood glue or double-sided adhesive tape.

Strips of foam board ($^{1}/_{3}$" wide) glued upright at the side of the empty space form a support for the inner edge of the cardboard, so that the cardboard does not sag (see figure on page 99, *bottom*).

In the deeper box, the side pieces are glued to the edge of the box on the outside. Now unfold the two inner edges once again, so that the small folded-over surfaces of the "podium" can be glued to the back panel. Depending on how deep the box you have available is, using a wooden stick or a knitting needle can be helpful when pressing the pieces down.

Images that you have attached to the back side of the tube might be made visible through the "windows" in the cardboard tube or, as here, objects that hang down tied to a thread at the top.

Finally, insert the tube and glue the side pieces to it firmly.

The charm of this presentation lies in its suggestions and fragments. Not everything is apparent.

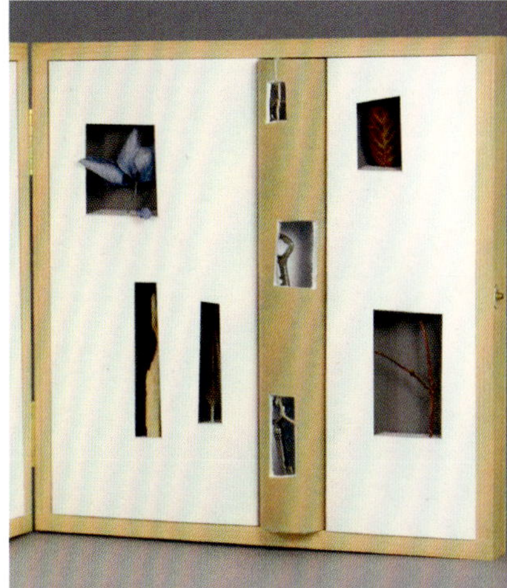

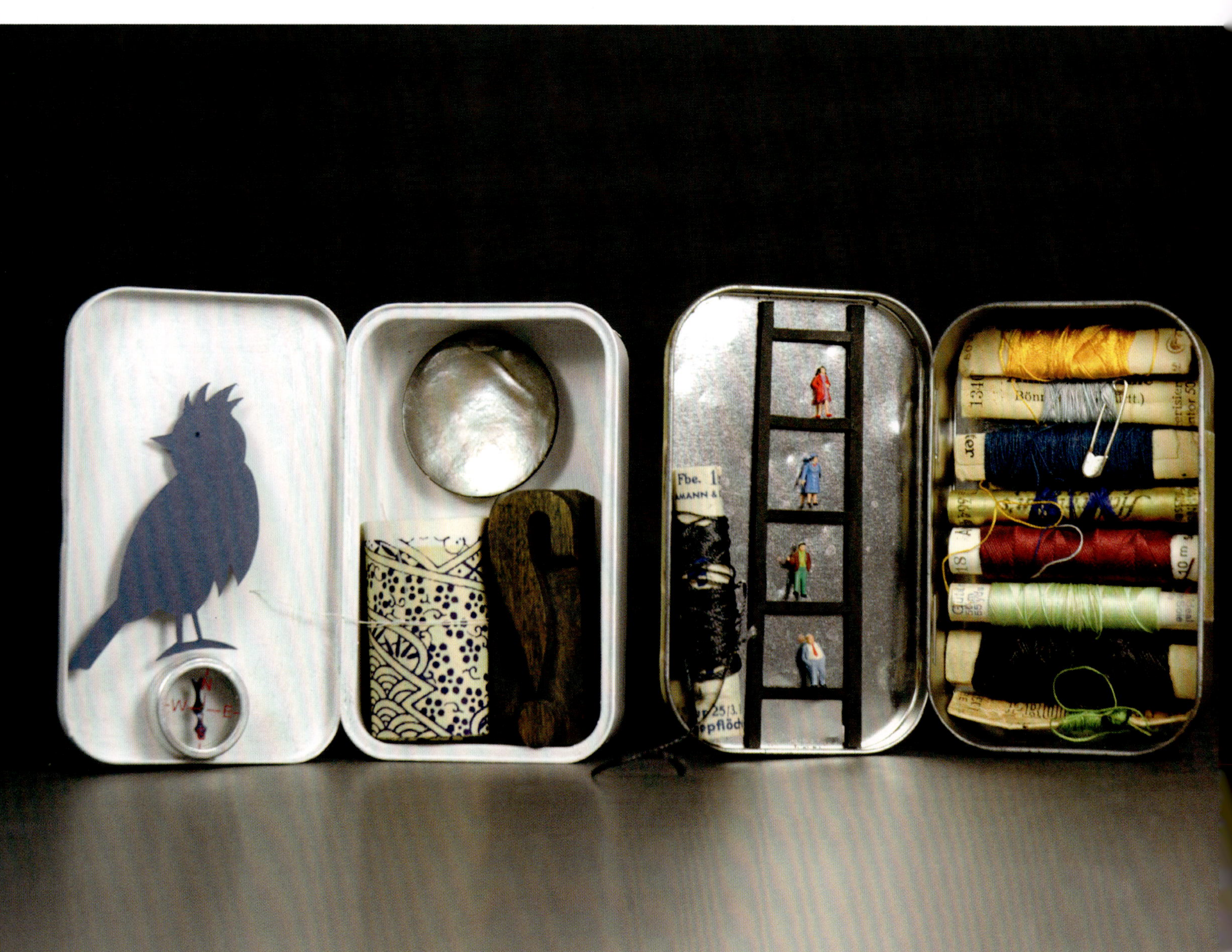

Metal Candy Tins Containing Miniature Worlds

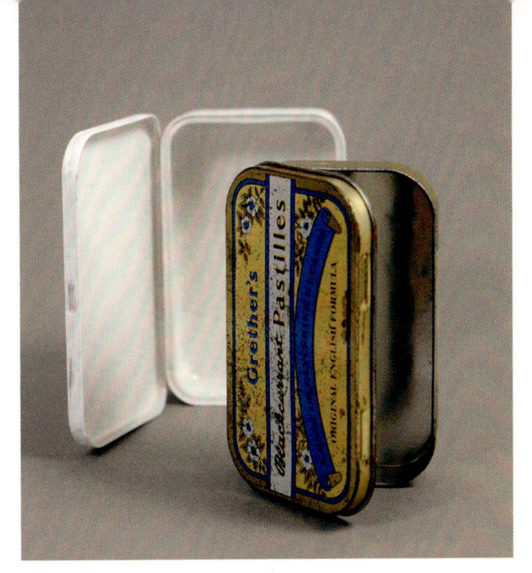

You can conjure up your very own little box world using metal tins. Old candy or peppermint tins work especially well. Metal tins that don't have an attractive printed cover can be given a neutral appearance with white acrylic paint. At the same time, there are also unprinted metal tins available in various shapes and sizes from your art supplies store.

These miniature worlds fill up quickly. You can play with how huge some things suddenly appear in small containers, and in contrast to this, add in tiny things like the model train figures, who seem—on their little ladder made of black cardboard—to be in no way afraid of the oversized spools of thread.

Since metal tins do not have an absorbent surface, the only way to fasten the objects inside is to use double-sided adhesive tape. It is possible to wallpaper the back panel using paste, as long as no tractive force will be exerted.

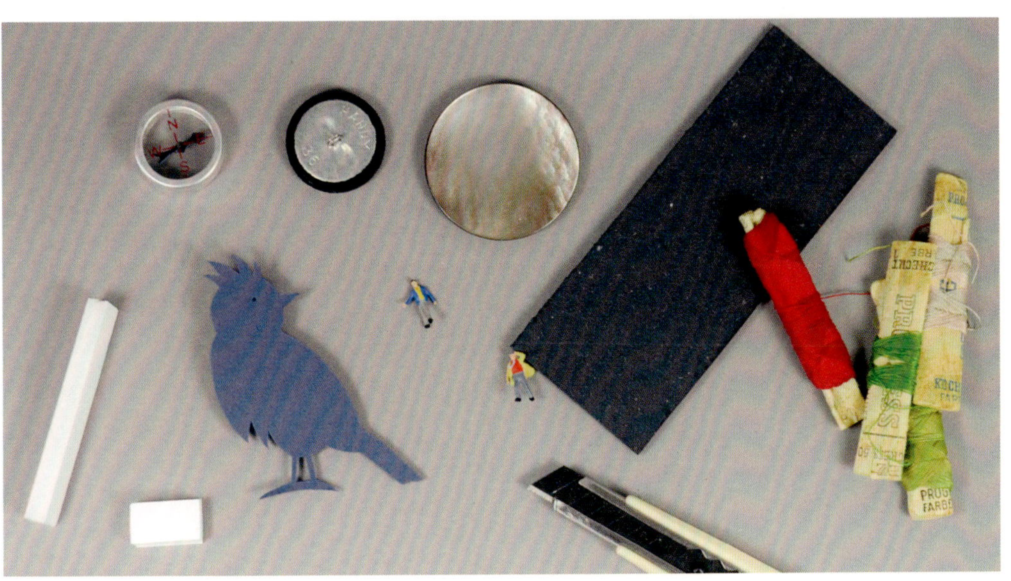

Materials + Tools

Metal candy tin

Ruler, cutter, and cutting mat

Acrylic paint and brush

Double-sided adhesive tape

Smooth construction paper for paper cuttings

Remnants of foam board for a spacer

Remnants of black or brown paperboard

Collectibles such as a long remnant of special gift wrap paper rolled up and tied with thread, wooden letters, a compass, a large mother-of-pearl button . . .

or

old buttonhole thread spools, model train figures . . .

4″ × 2⅓″ × ¼″ / 4″ × 2⅓″ × ¾″

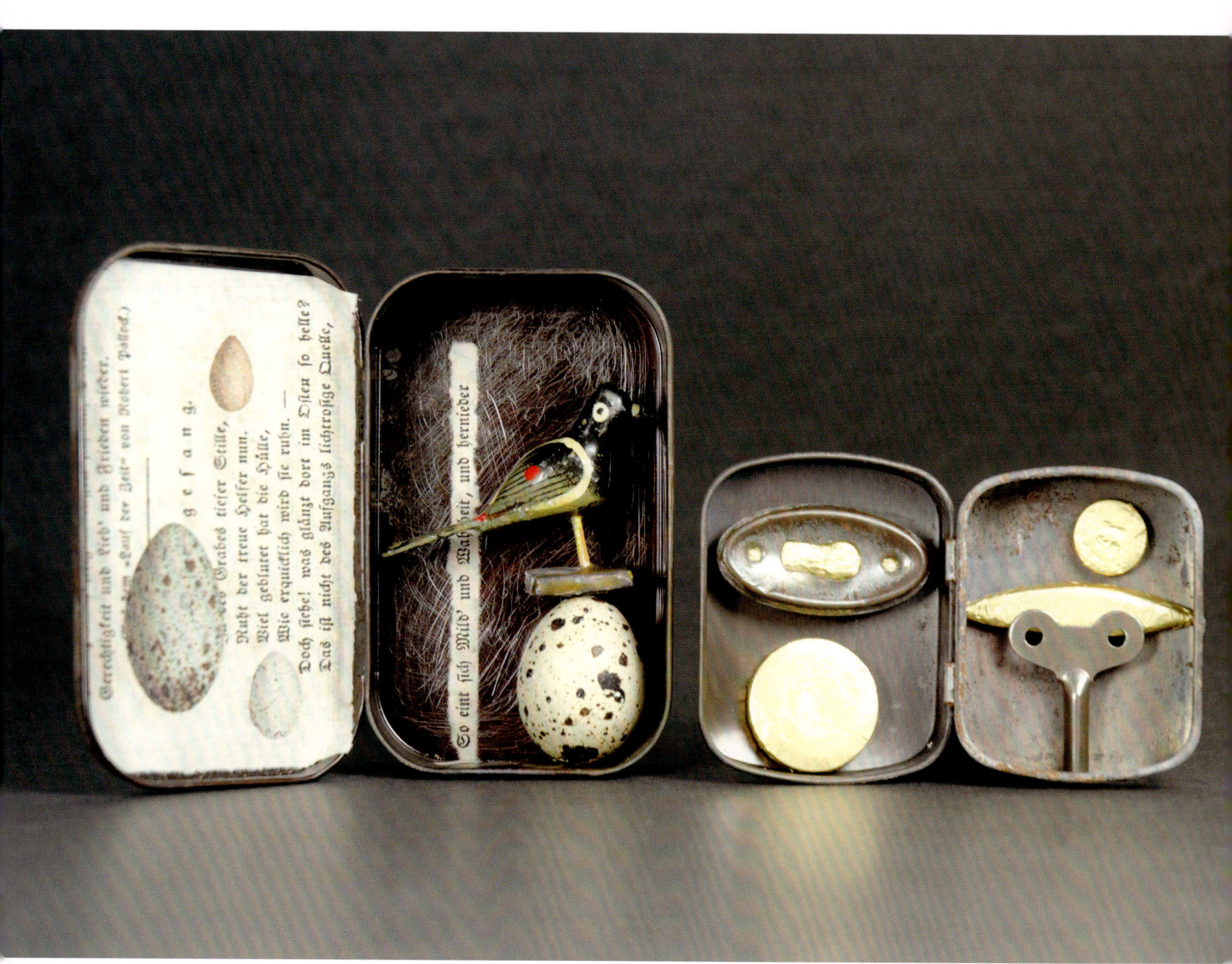
Gerechtigkeit und Lieb' und Frieden wieder.
„Lauf der Zeit“ von Robert Pollock.)
g e s a n g.
Grabes tiefer Stille,
Ruht der treue Helfer nun.
Viel geblutet hat die Hülle,
Wie erquicklich wird sie ruhn. —
Doch siehe! was glänzt dort im Osten so helle?
Das ist nicht des Aufgangs lichtrosige Quelle,
So eint sich Mild' und Wahrheit, und hernieder

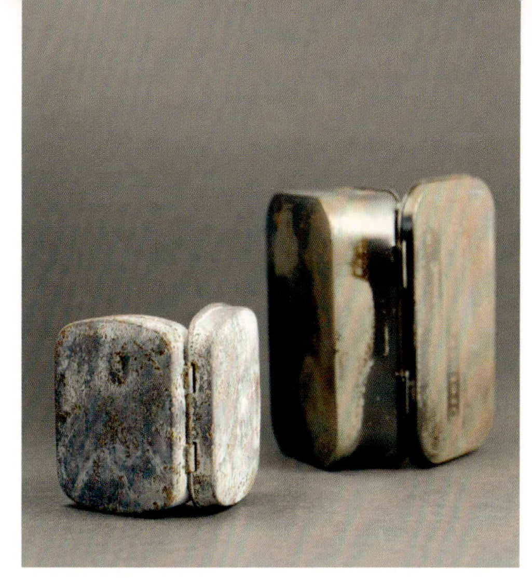

Metal Tins Given an Archaic Patina by Fire

A completely different look is achieved by sanding the smooth, glossy tins a little and tossing them into a fire. After about ten minutes, they have taken on a wonderfully shabby patina that can inspire new ideas. The larger tin was evenly blackened on the inside and was therefore sandpapered again. A wooden bird and a quail egg are combined with a piece of a page from an antiquarian book that was wallpapered inside the lid of the tin. The connection is created by pasted-on pictures of bird eggs.

Besides, the box material itself becomes a theme. The small tin offers hardly any space for objects, so you have to make do with very little: A small winding key and an old cupboard keyhole cover capture the metallic theme. The other pieces only give the impression that they are made of metal. Buttons and a cutout piece of paperboard are wrapped tightly with thin, gold-colored foil from a chocolate wrapper and are attached to the back panel with double-sided adhesive tape. Just like creating frottage with coins and a pencil, this wrapping technique using a chocolate wrapper is reminiscent of childhood—and is still effective.

Materials + Tools

Big and small candy tins

Cutter and a cutting mat

Paste and brush

Sandpaper

Double-sided adhesive tape

Remnants of thick paperboard

Thin, gold-colored foil, buttons

Collectibles such as winding keys, pages from old books, a quail egg and bird figurine, images of bird eggs . . .

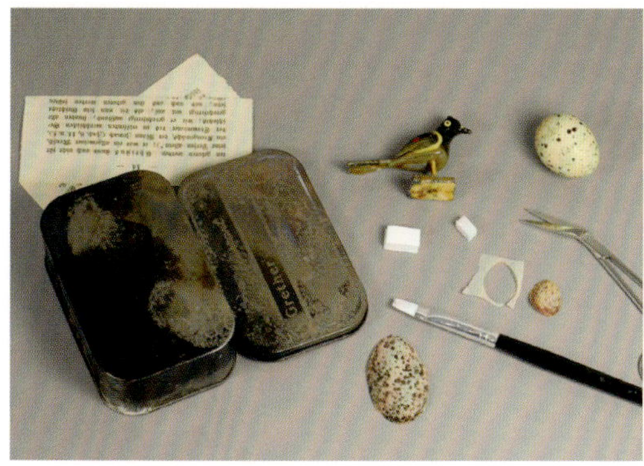

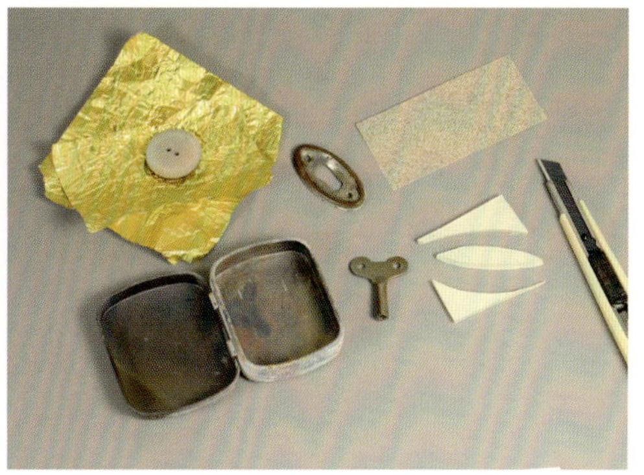

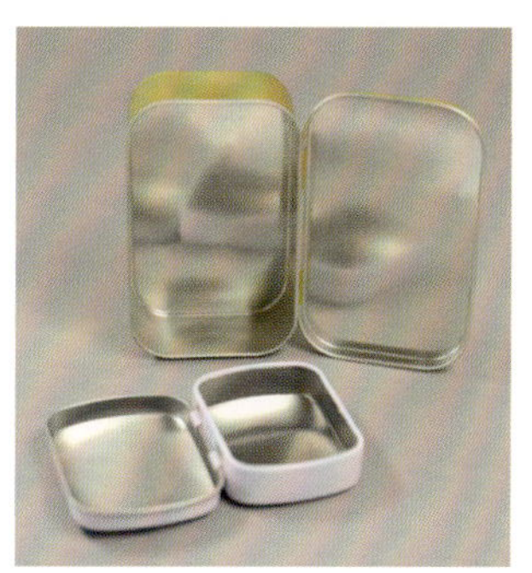

◀ *3½" × 2⅓" × ¼"–1" / 2⅓" × 2" × ⅓"–½"*

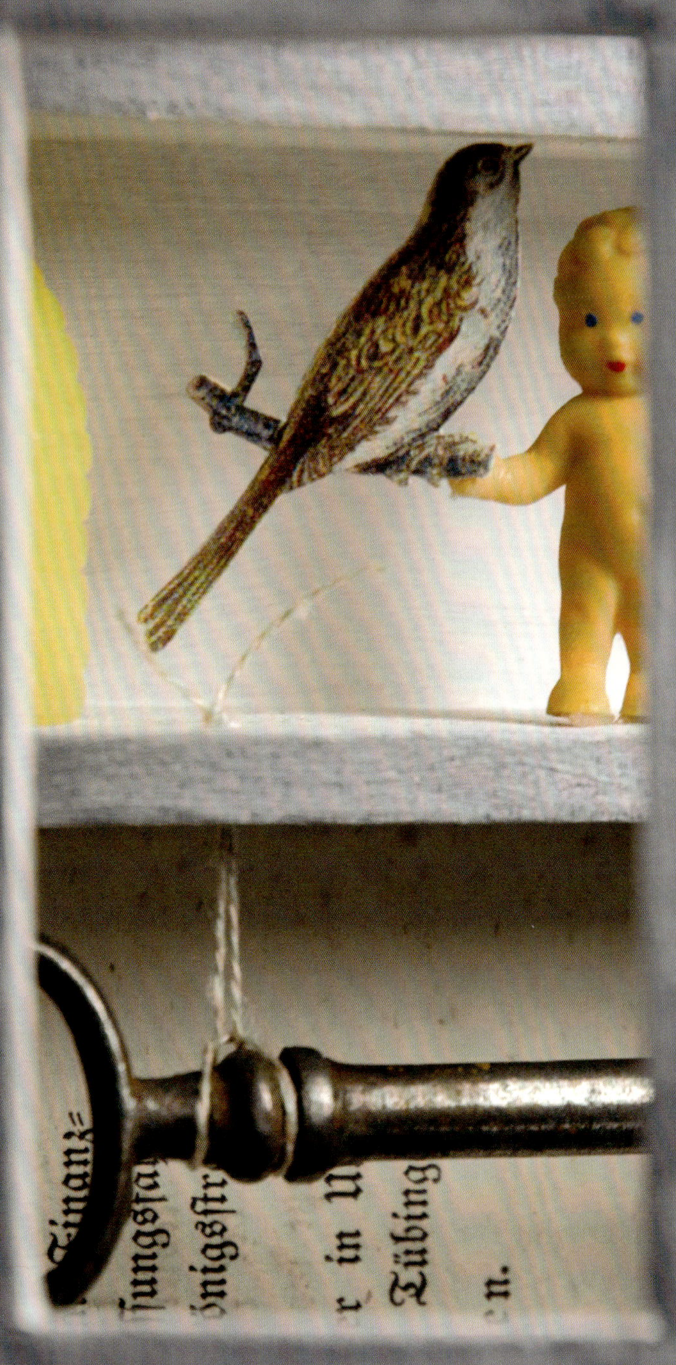

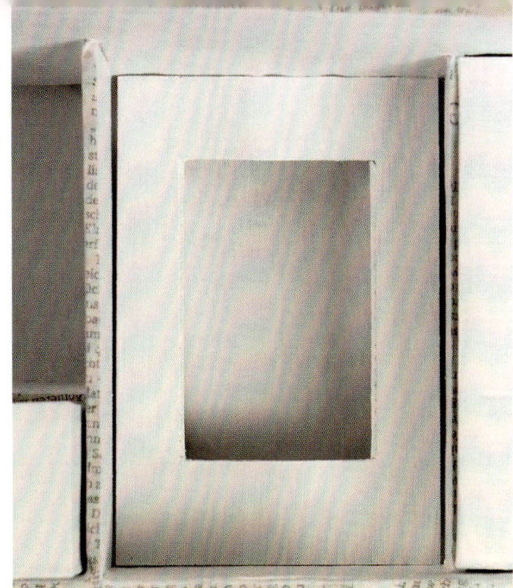

5 Build the Housing Yourself

Making a box yourself allows you to apply your own ideas, so that your personal collections, mementos, or aspirations can be adequately accommodated. Since a house represents the epitome of "protected space" and the selection of ready-made rectangular boxes is already very large, this chapter will present the way to construct only house designs.

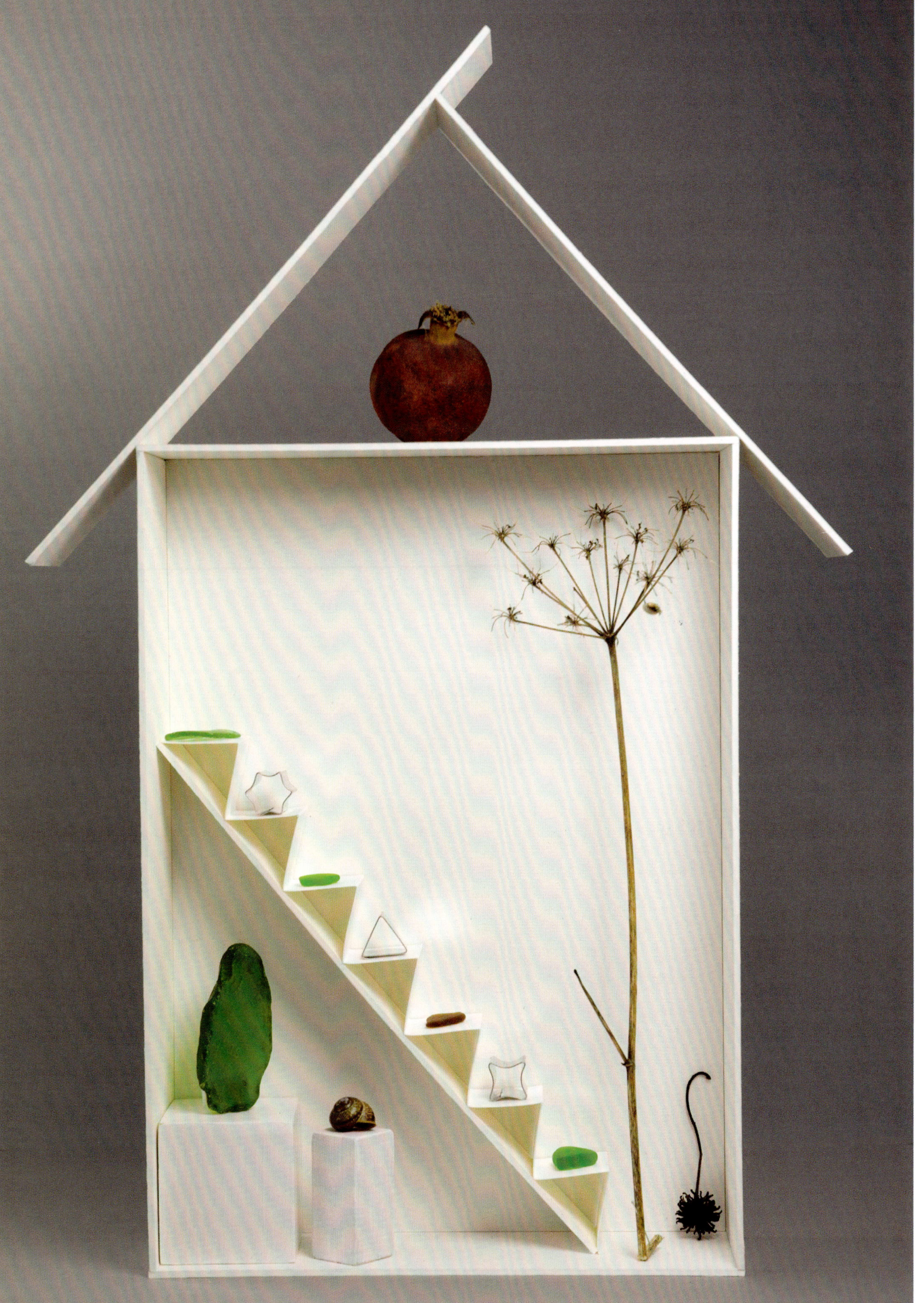

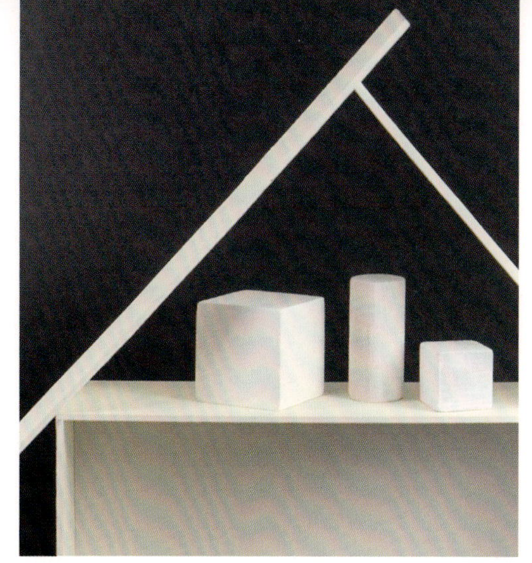

Minimalist Construction Made of Picture Mat Board

Very elegant, minimalist boxes in a house design can be constructed using white mat board. You can often find remnant pieces of mat board (including larger ones) at a reasonable price. Since everything is visible, you have to work cleanly and accurately here—in contrast to the project that follows.

First, cut out a back panel, four side panels, and two sloping roof pieces, using a cutter (for dimensions, see the drawing on the following page). The dimensions refer to a template for paperboard that is 2.5 mm thick. You will need only 3 mm thick quality for larger objects, to make sure that the construction is sufficiently stable.

After cutting out the pieces, glue the side panels to the back panel with white glue, flush to the side edges. To make the glued edges neat and strong, you can also tape white paper-packing tape around the edges along the rear side. The asymmetrical roof consists of two paperboard strips of different sizes. The best way to determine the apex is to place the strips on the cutting mat along a horizontal line as the bottom edge and find a vertical line as the center point. Draw a line with a pencil just where the second, shorter paperboard strip meets the apex, and apply some white glue there.

Materials + Tools

White mat board, 2.5–3 mm thick

Remnant piece of white cardboard with the grain direction parallel to the short side

Ruler, cutter, and cutting mat

Acrylic paint and brush

White glue, gummed paper-packaging tape

Wooden blocks

Collectibles such as beach glass, dried parts of plants, snail shells, miniature cookie cutters . . .

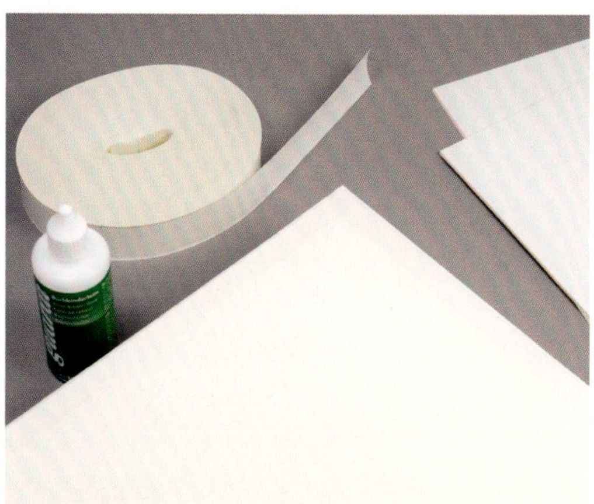

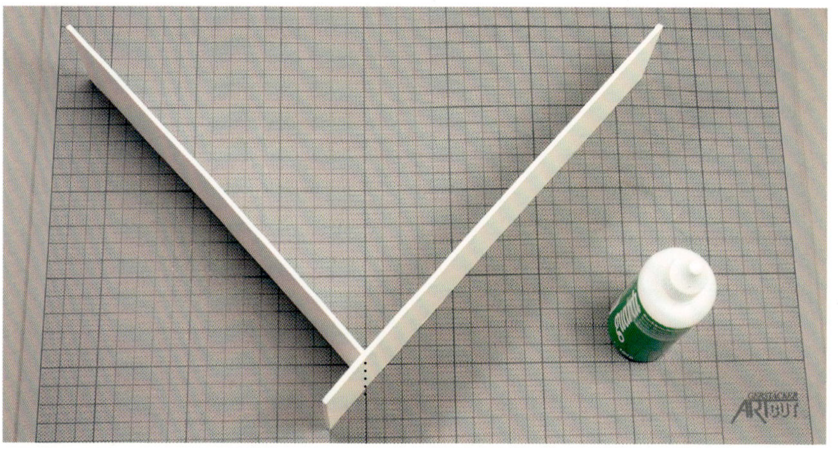

Hold the roof gable on firmly until the glue has adhered to it, then apply white glue likewise to the two upper-side edges of the house construction and place the roof in the middle on top. Hold firmly until everything is dry and is solidly connected.

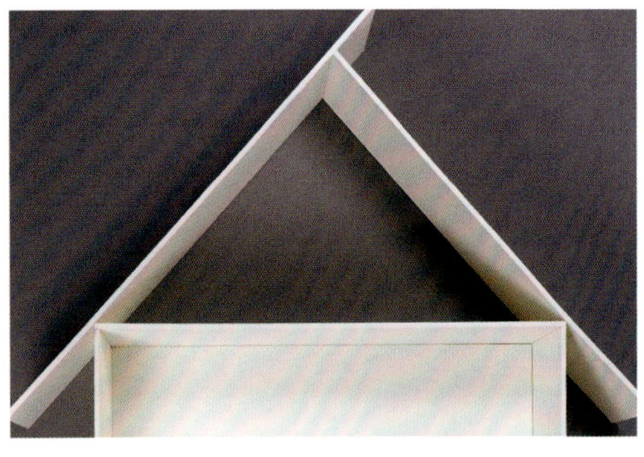

For the staircase, trim a remnant of the mat board to 1$\frac{1}{2}$" wide and about 11$\frac{3}{4}$" long. Then cut off a piece of white, thinner cardboard (about 150–200 gsm) to 19$\frac{3}{4}$" cm long and, with the grain direction along the short side, trim it to 1$\frac{1}{2}$" wide. Fold this (as described on page 20) into a 16-sided zigzag fold.

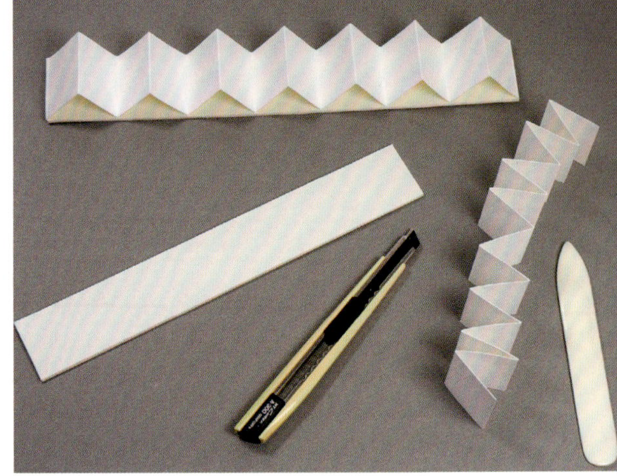

You can easily see from the drawing which parts have the same measurements and therefore can be cut out together to save space. Any minor unevenness or ridges can be smoothed away with fine sandpaper. Cutting by hand is definitely easier on the material; using a paper cutter often tears the bottom edge of the cut piece in an ugly way.

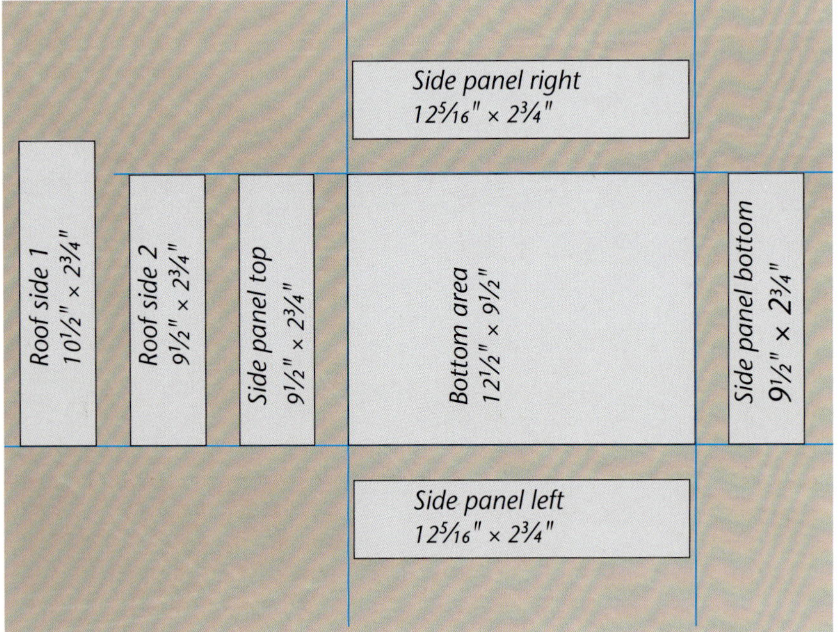

Since the staircase is intended to occupy only about two-thirds of the height of the house construction, cut off two sides of the zigzag fold so that it has only 14 sides (= 7 steps). Now pull these steps apart and arrange them at 90° angles on the paperboard strip. Mark the end of the zigzag and trim the paperboard strip to fit it exactly. Using white glue on the backs of the folds, fasten the stairs to the paperboard and glue them (at an angle) into the house so that the steps are level. The miniature objects are presented on these small surfaces and on the wooden blocks, which are painted white.

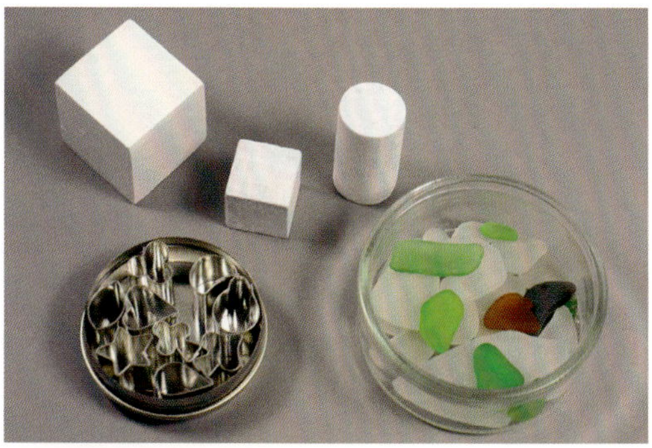

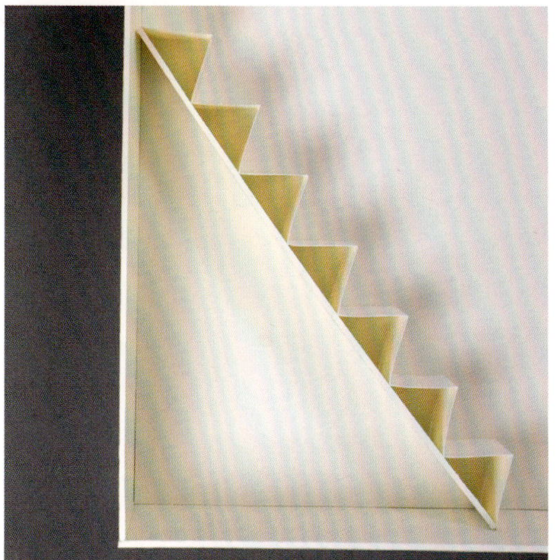

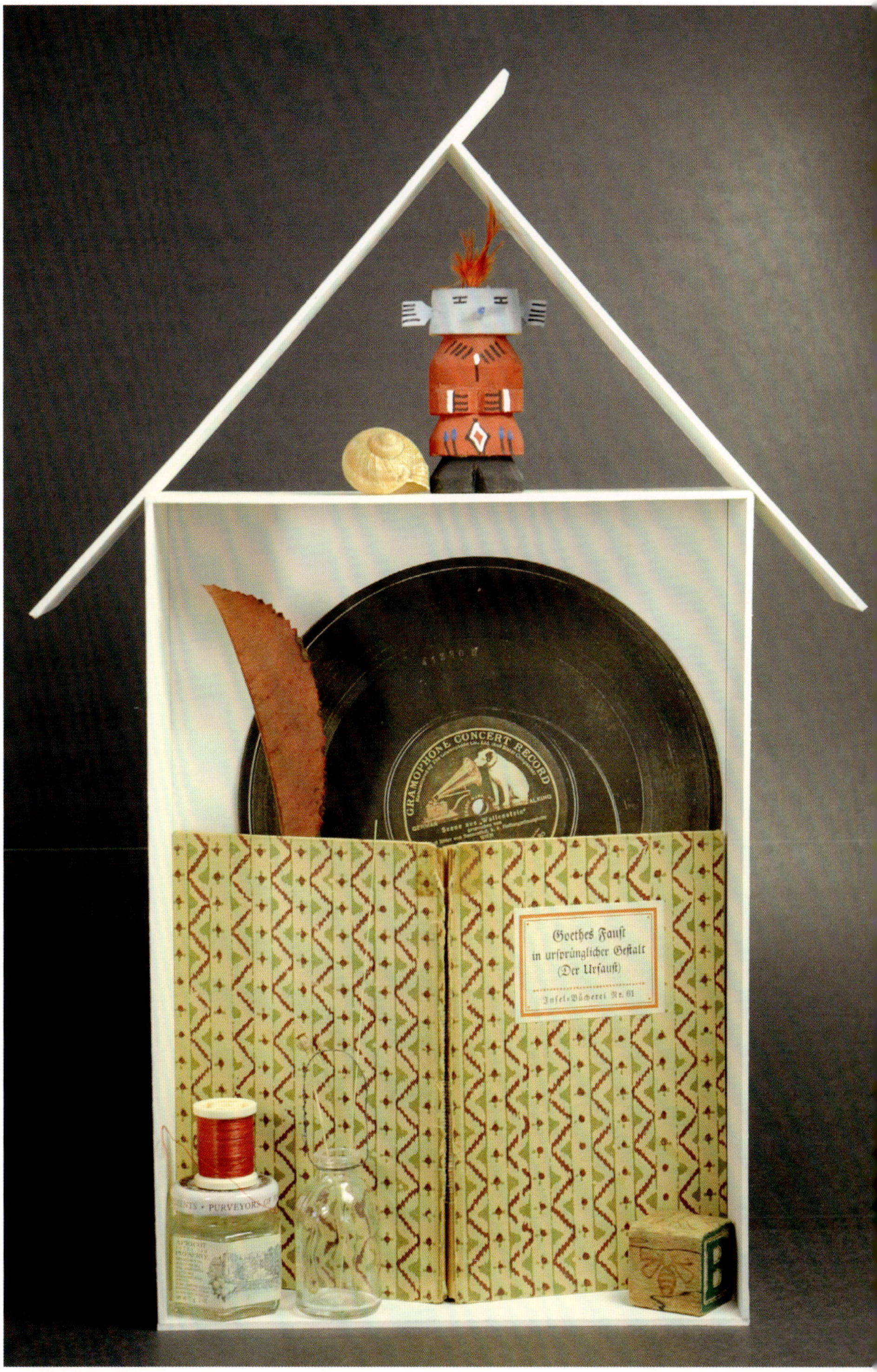

Alternative design:

The same house displays a completely different world when it contains an open book with a dried leaf as a bookmark and the printed record label as the background. But it still has a neutral, elegant atmosphere.

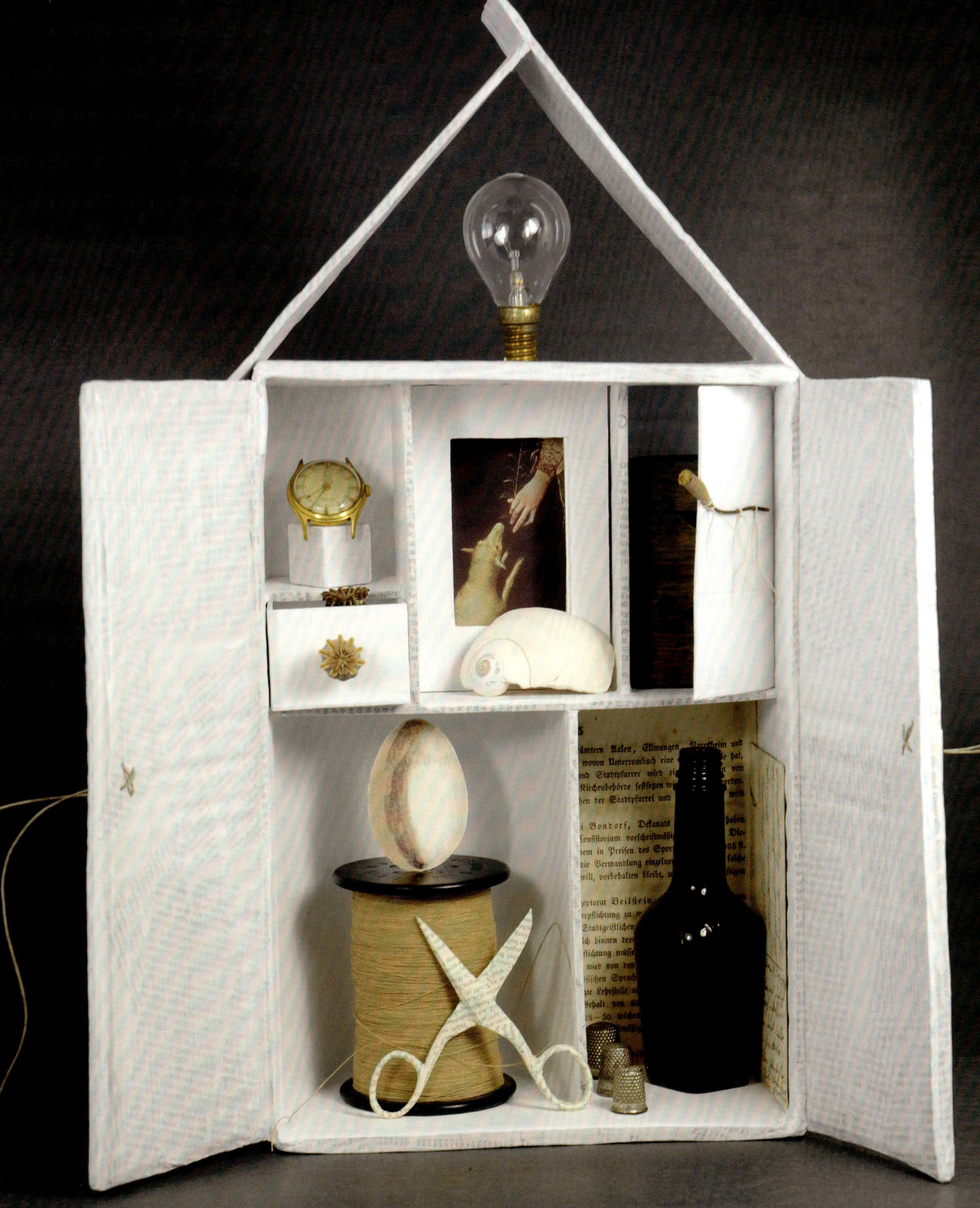
ämtern Aalen, Ellwangen
wovon Unterrombach eine
und Stadtpfarrer wird
Kirchenbehörde festsetzen
hen der Stadtpfarrei und
Bondorf, Dekanats
Konsistorium vorschriftmäßi
nem in Preisen des
die Verwandlung
will, vorbehalten bleibt,
zeptorat Beilstein
Stadtgeistlichen
ich binnen
wird von
Gehalt von
28—30

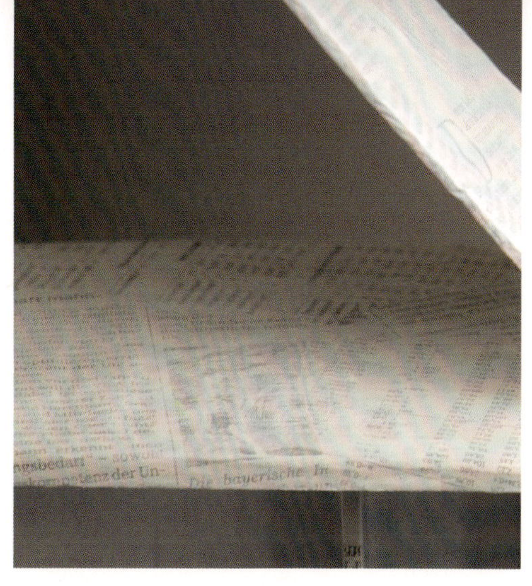

Build It Yourself from a Corrugated Cardboard Shipping Carton

Materials + Tools

Shipping carton made of at least 4 mm thick corrugated cardboard with a bottom area of about 12" × 8" and also remnants of thin corrugated cardboard

Ruler, cutter, scissors, cutting mat

White gesso, acrylic paint, and a brush

White glue and paste

Masking tape or washi tape

Newsprint or thin printing paper from old books

Thin package twine of hemp, coarse linen twine

Collectibles such as a small lightbulb, dried poppy seed pods, pieces of shell, a page from an old book, an old postcard, thimbles, old yarn spool, images, an old wristwatch . . .or not very nice things that are given a brand new look when covered with inscribed newsprint or thin printing paper

In contrast to the previous project, where it was necessary to work with greater, bookbinding-like precision, you can get started on converting this simple used shipping carton, using freehand. "A bit crooked and lopsided" is definitely welcome as the stylistic device here.

First, remove any remaining labels from the carton. Then check that the closure flaps on the short sides, when folded inward, reach all the way to the carton back panel. If they are too short, cut off the flaps at the edge and cut out two inserts to double the wall thickness from the remnant pieces. If the closure flaps reach to the back panel, cut off the flaps at the edge likewise, turn them, and glue them back on with white glue, with the inner edge outward. If you just turn them over, the edge will be too narrow.

Now tape over all the connecting pieces, any scratches, and, above all, any open (corrugated cardboard) edges, using high-quality masking tape or washi tape. Then trim two corrugated cardboard remnants to use for the roof (see drawing and dimensions on the following page) and two narrow side panels for the doors. You should first cut the pieces of cardboard for dividing up the interior to size when you can check the dimensions on the finished, covered, and painted construction.

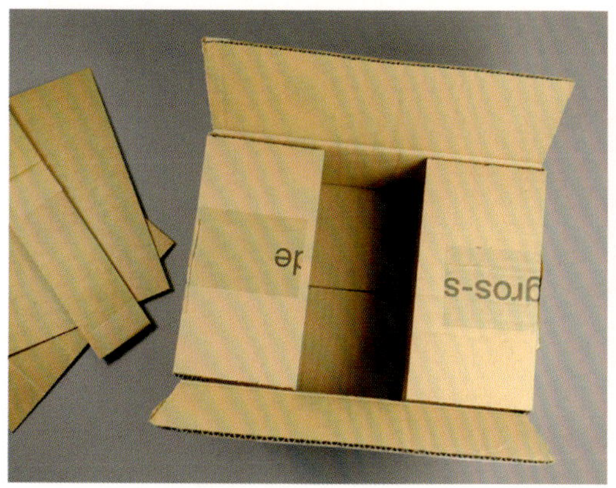

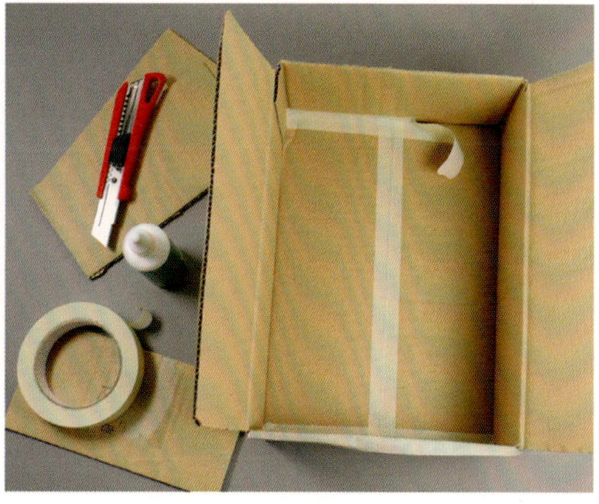

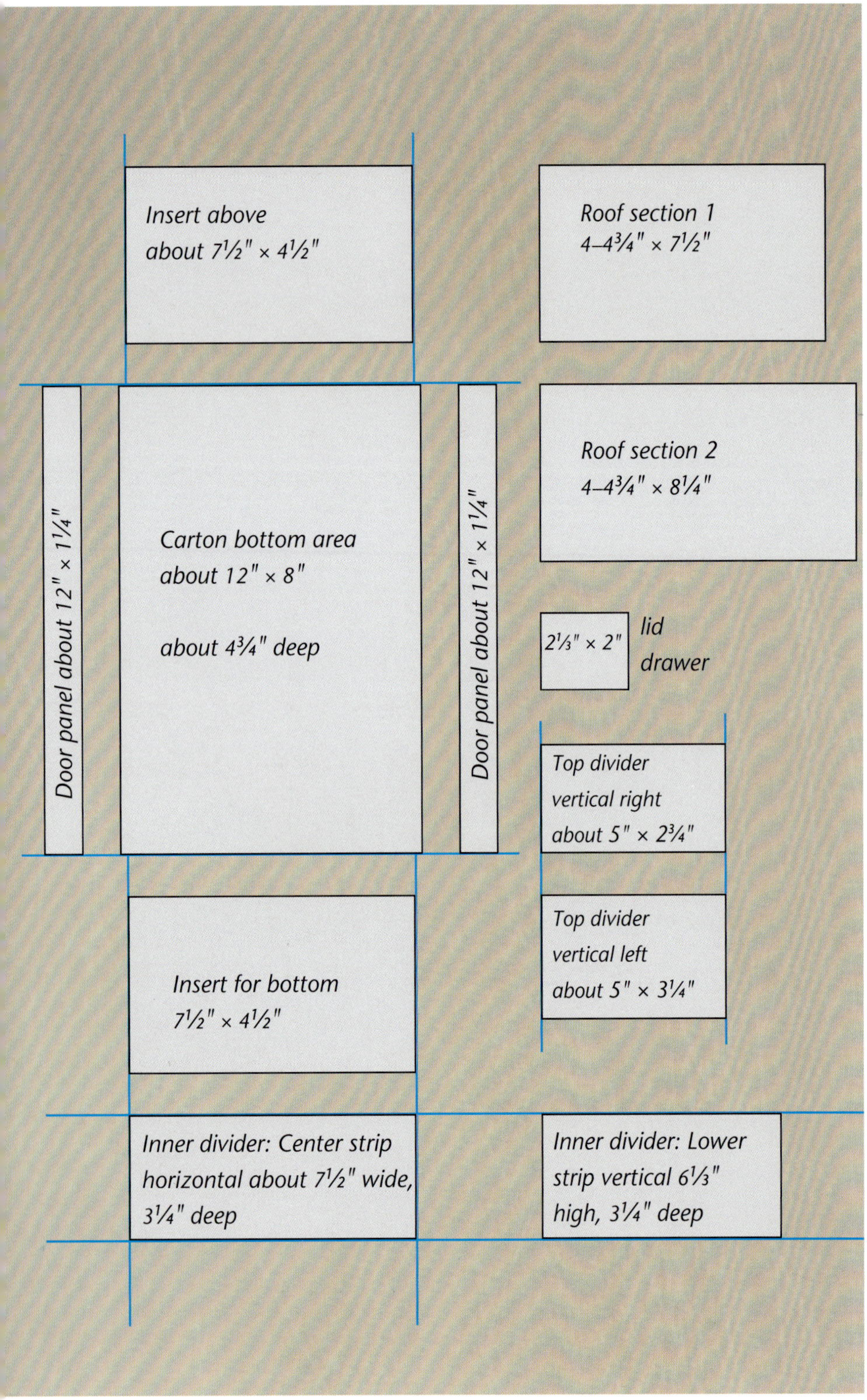

Insert above
about 7½" × 4½"

Roof section 1
4–4¾" × 7½"

Door panel about 12" × 1¼"

Carton bottom area
about 12" × 8"

about 4¾" deep

Door panel about 12" × 1¼"

Roof section 2
4–4¾" × 8¼"

2⅓" × 2" *lid drawer*

Top divider
vertical right
about 5" × 2¾"

Top divider
vertical left
about 5" × 3¼"

Insert for bottom
7½" × 4½"

Inner divider: Center strip horizontal about 7½" wide, 3¼" deep

Inner divider: Lower strip vertical 6⅓" high, 3¼" deep

In the drawing, all parts made of thicker corrugated cardboard are indicated with dimensions; the small parts, such as the drawer, door, and picture frame, must be measured on the finished construction. In addition, using thinner corrugated cardboard is recommended for these insert elements.

The two pieces for the roof (like the side panels for the doors) should be cut from thicker corrugated cardboard approximately as thick as the carton. One piece for the asymmetrical roof is 3/4" longer than the other; the width can correspond to the carton's depth. A somewhat narrower roof (as in the model), which still has some airspace to the front, is more elegant and easier to decorate.

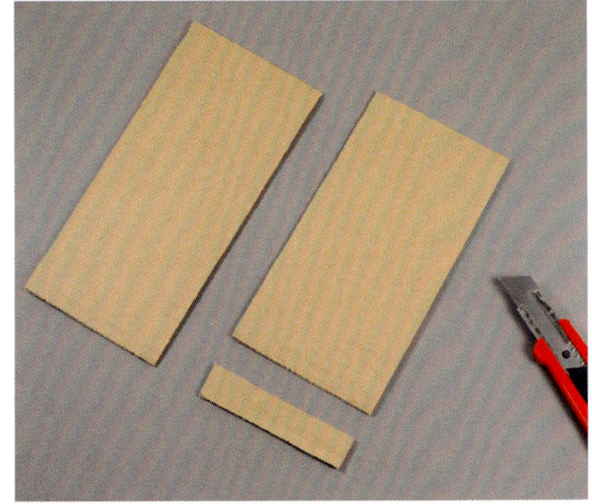

When you have covered all the open edges with masking tape and mended any tears likewise with masking tape, you can glue on the side panels of the doors, using white glue.

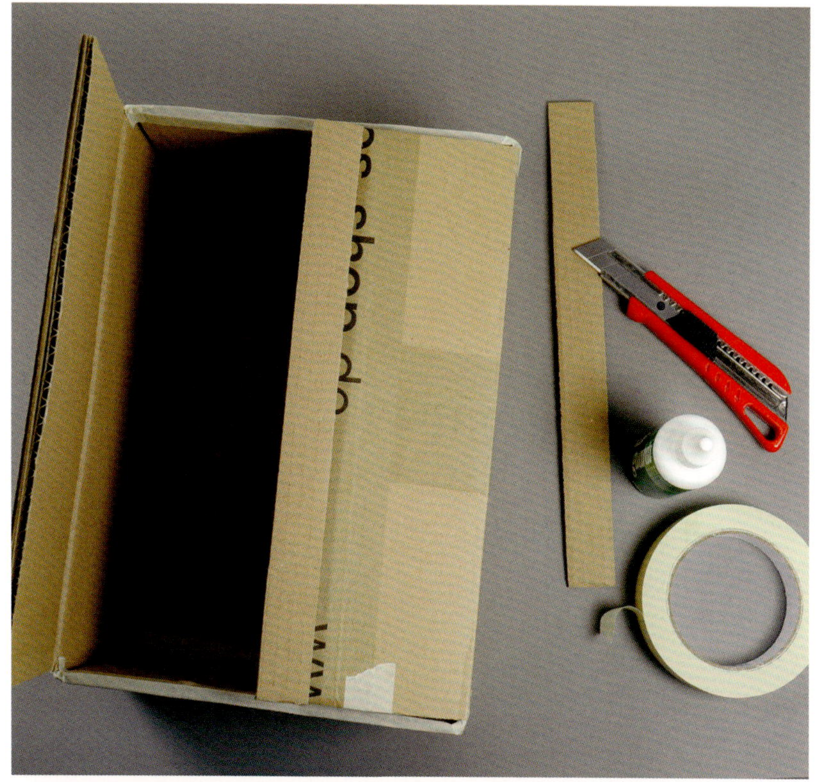

Now cover the entire carton—with the doors—with paper on the inside and outside. To do this, tear newsprint or book pages from old thin-print editions into irregular pieces, brush with paste, apply them to the carton so they overlap, and brush smooth from on top, using a brush with a light coat of paste. At the same time, hold the paper taut over the edges and press down well. Let dry thoroughly overnight.

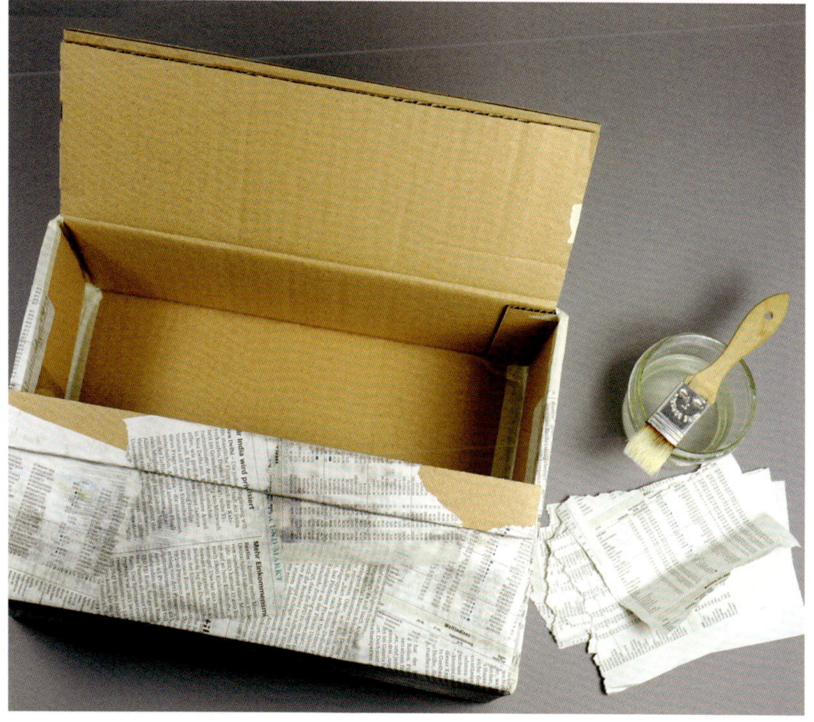

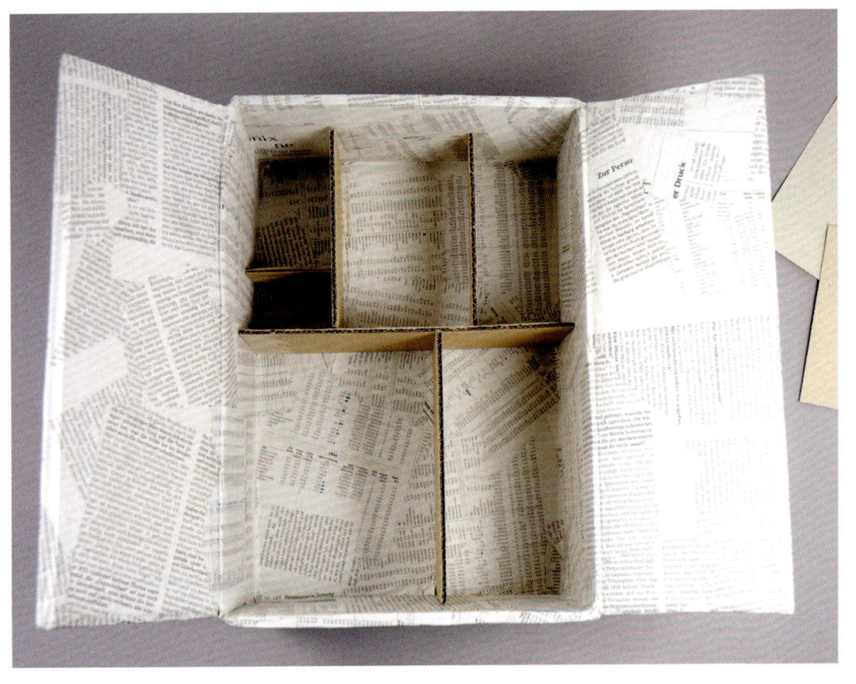

Then put the inner dividers into the already covered box. Before cutting them out, insert the pieces of cardboard you intend to use for the dividers into the carton to check whether the partition panel of the specified size actually fits in the carton, which has certainly warped slightly due to the water-containing paste.

The partitions should be fitted so tightly that they sit firmly even without using glue. Fasten them in, using white glue, and then measure what size the top right door should be and how high the rounded bottom left wall should be.

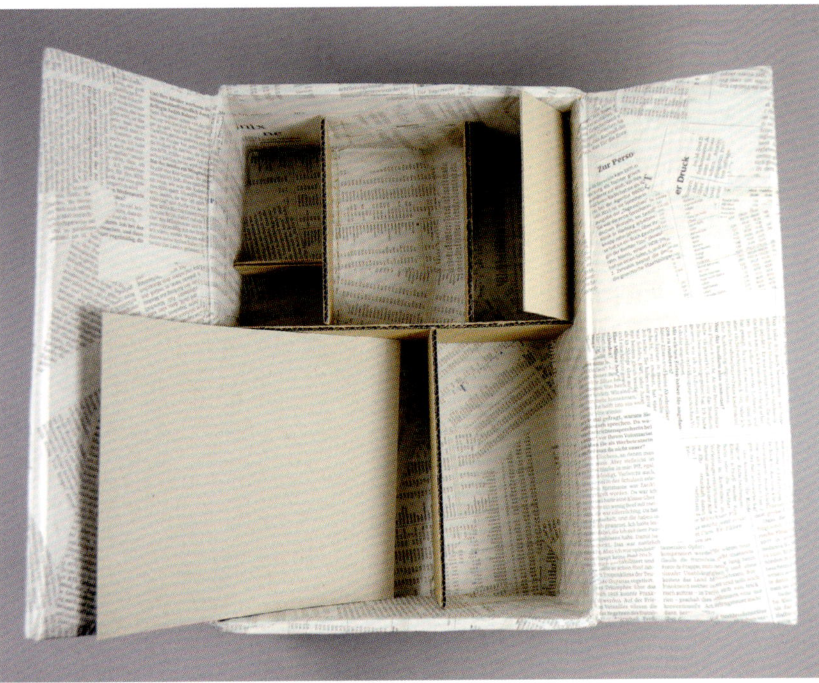

The door can be cut out of thinner corrugated cardboard; you will need some flexible cardboard for the rounded wall. Cut the cardboard to the height of the corner, then insert the piece so that it is bent from the right edge to the back panel, and mark where it should be cut off at the end of the left side.

Lay the two pieces for the roof on the cutting mat—as done for the previous project—to find the apex.

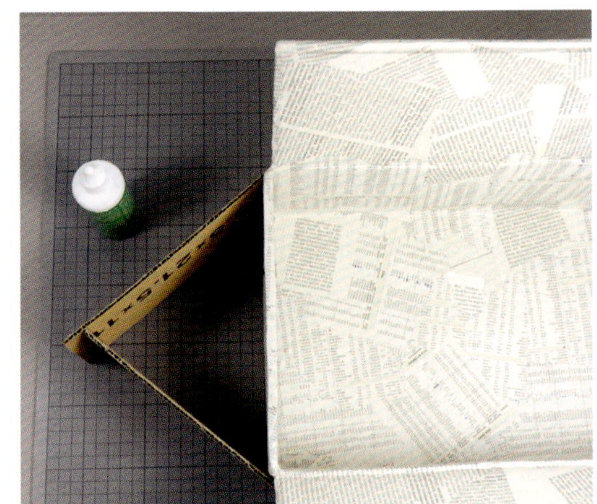

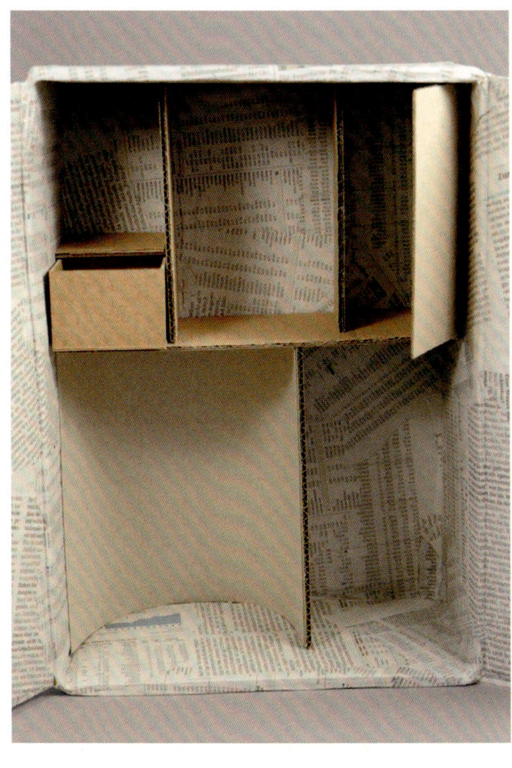

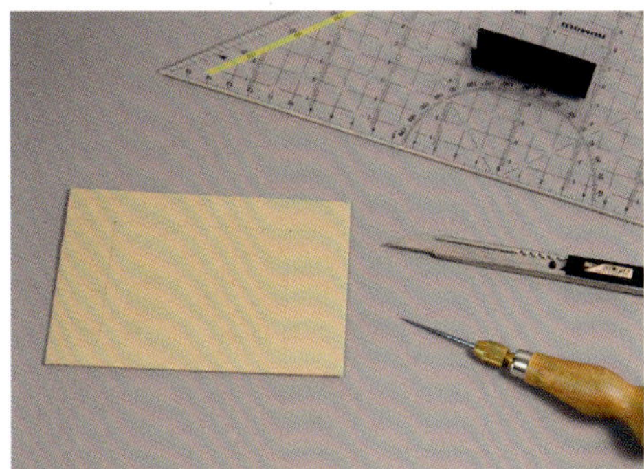

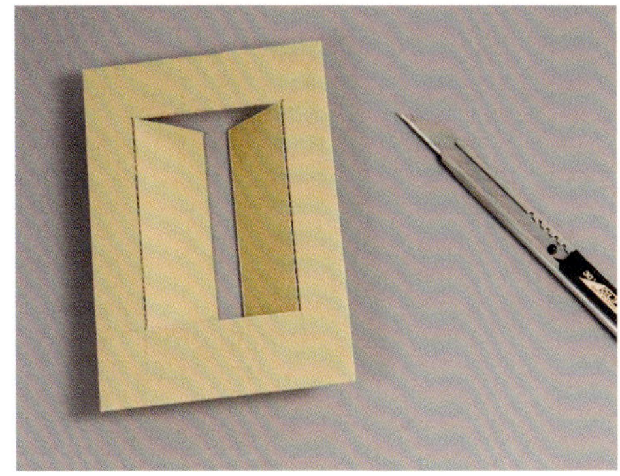

You can determine the dimensions of the door, the drawer, and the picture frame on the basis of the partitions fastened in with white glue.

Make the drawer as you made the construction in the previous project (see page 109, *bottom right*).

The picture frame is cut at the top, at the bottom, and along the middle. The sides are scored only so that the side panels can be folded back as spacers.

After gluing it together at the apex, cover the roof with pieces of paper. Cover over the front open edges of the partitions in the interior by pasting on pieces of paper.

Then prime the entire interior space—except for the front "writing edges" of the partitions—with gesso. The fittings (door, drawer, and picture frame) are also primed with gesso.

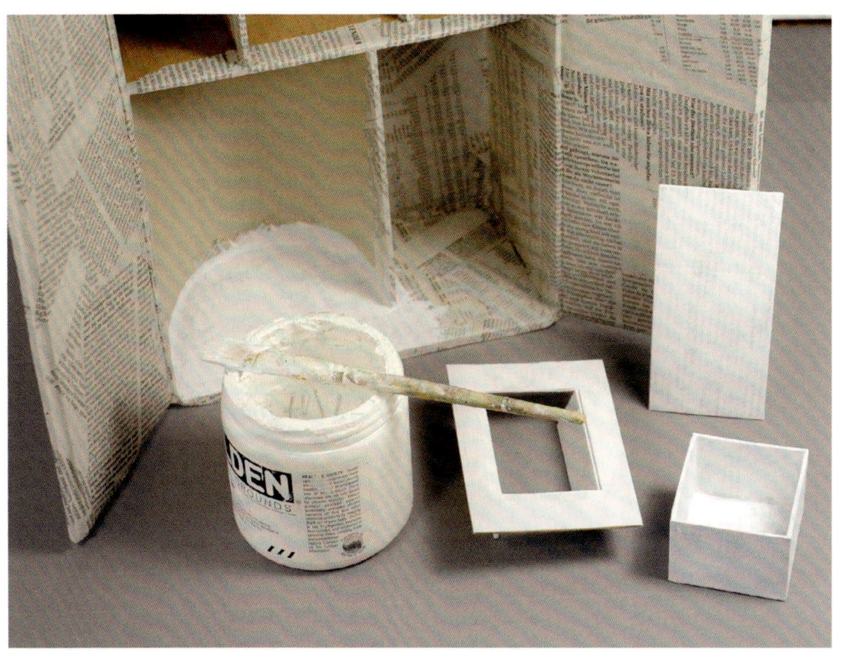

After the interior has been primed with gesso, paint over all the surfaces that have been covered with (writing) paper, using very diluted white acrylic paint. This protects the covering and lets the writing fade into the background.

Finally, after letting them dry for two to three hours, paint the gesso-primed areas with undiluted white acrylic paint, which makes them less susceptible to getting dirty.

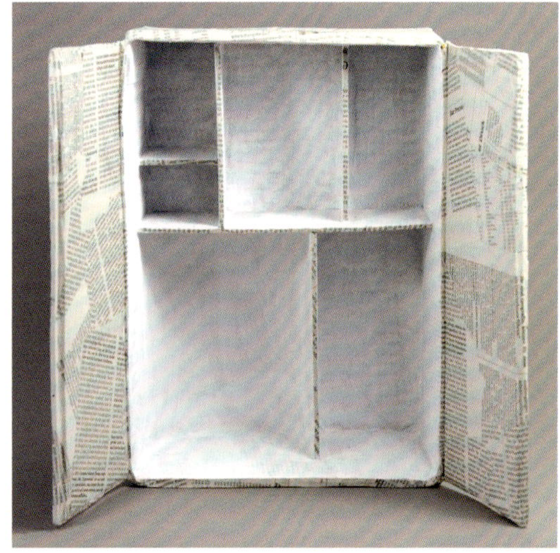

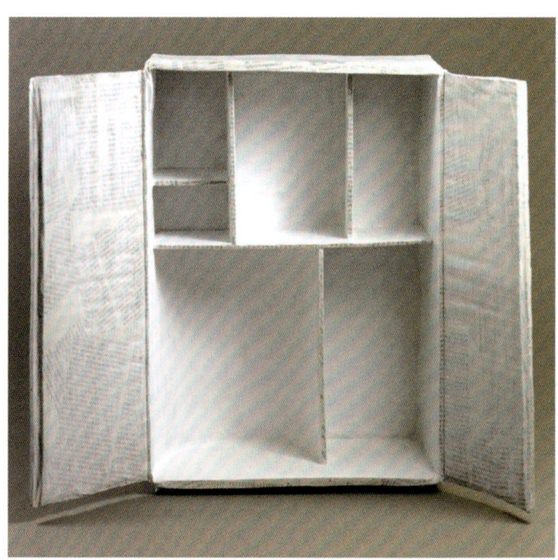

Half insert the finished drawer and give it a handle (a button, a piece of bamboo, a roll of paperboard ...). This will let you close it if desired, but it is more attractive to present it always slightly open.

It is not necessary to fasten on the picture frame. If it sits firmly, as soon as the folded-back side panels touch the back panel, that will be sufficient. This is also practical in case you want to change the image on the back.

The small door can be attached perpendicular to the side wall from inside with a strip of washi tape. If it is made of thicker material, you can even give it "hinges" by sticking a pin into the door from both above and below through the ceiling and floor. (Attention: This must be done before the roof is attached!)

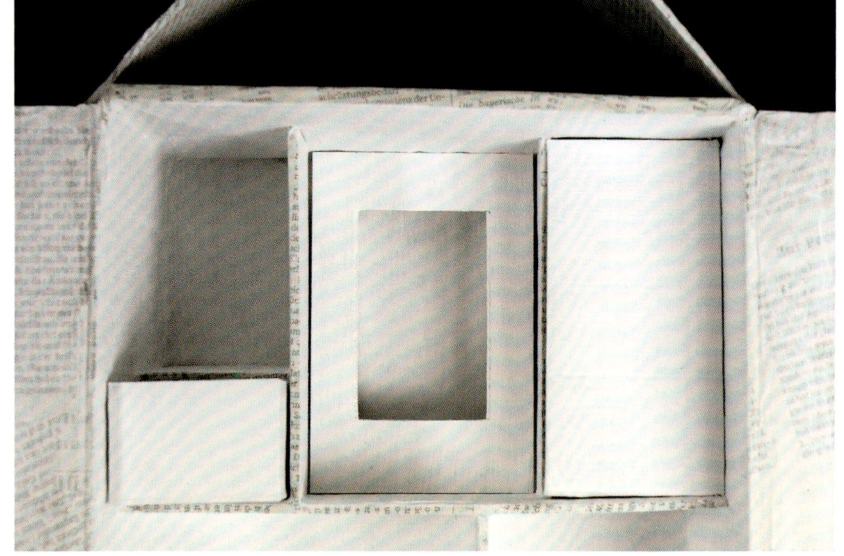

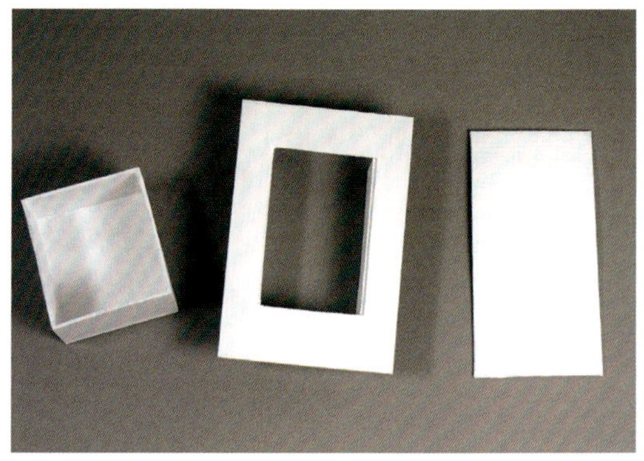

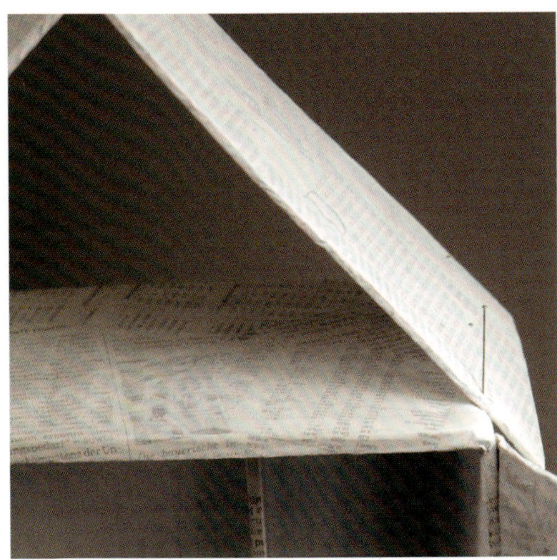

Finally, use white glue to fasten the roof to the edges of the carton. To reinforce it here, you can also stick some pins through the roof into the side panel.

It is easy to push needles or awls through the soft materials used in this house. Thus, you can sew a "door handle" made of a dried poppy seed pod onto the small door, and a lock made of hemp cord onto the large door, as can be seen in the figure on page 112.

It is even possible to imagine a little house completely sewn together.

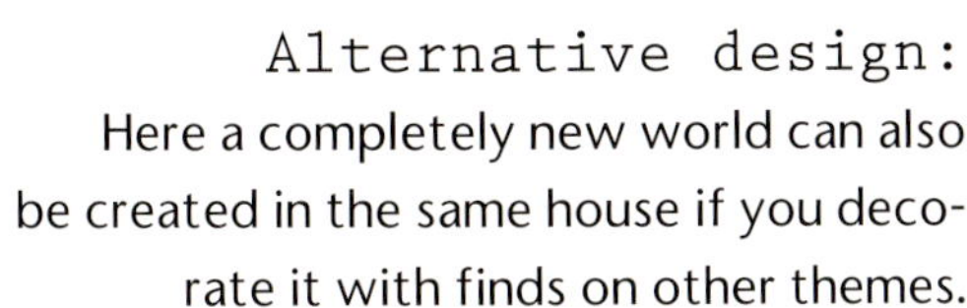

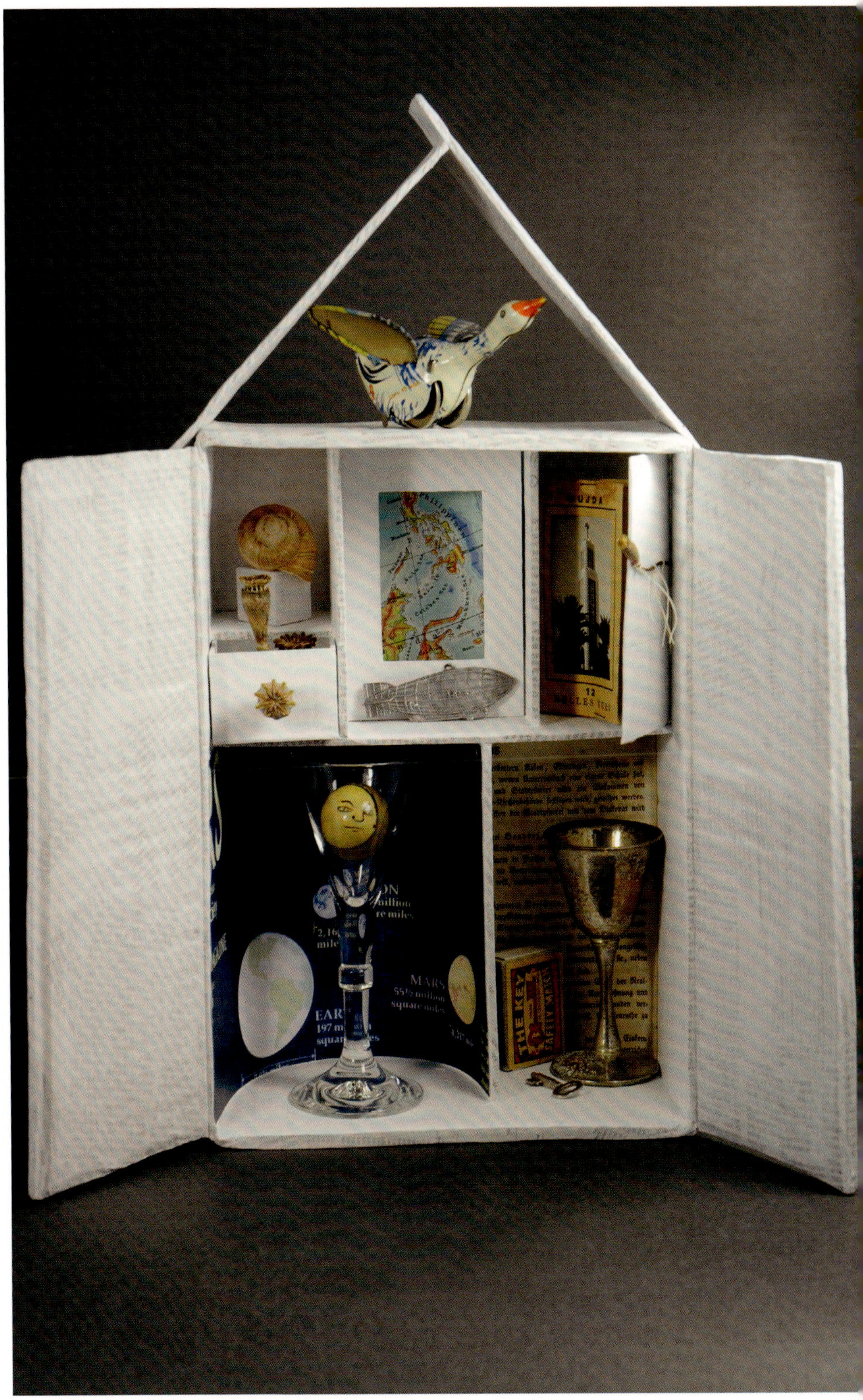

Alternative design:
Here a completely new world can also be created in the same house if you decorate it with finds on other themes.

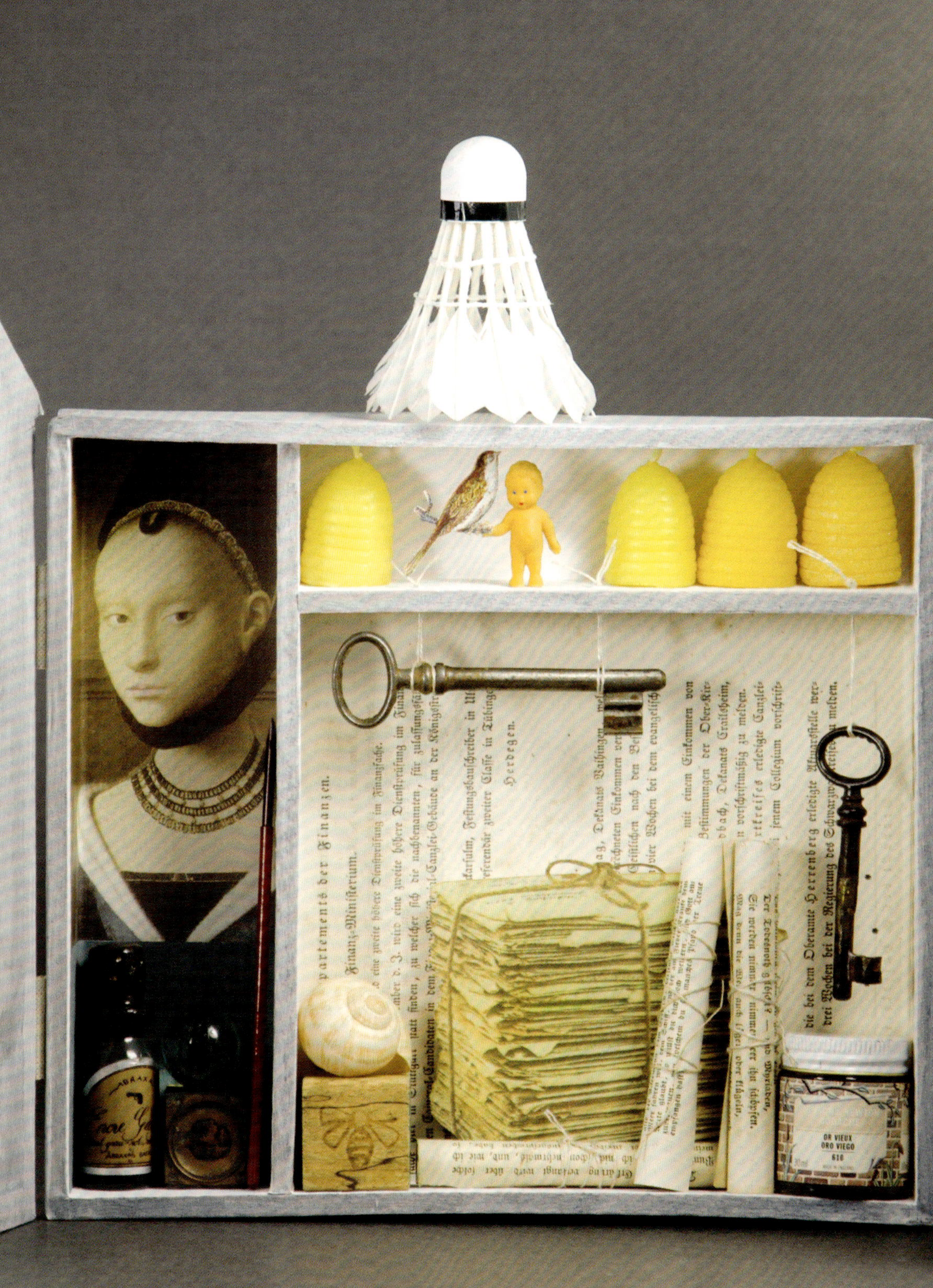

Finanz-Ministerium.
Herdegen.
OR VIEUX
ORO VIEGO
610

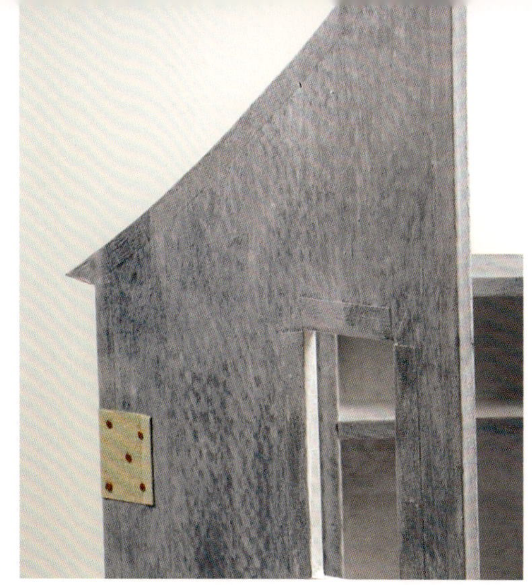

Make It Yourself from Good-as-New Corrugated Cardboard

Thick, multi-ply corrugated board in a smooth, clean condition is a material that works very well for making a more ambitious house.

Here the doors are used to give the house a sham gable, behind which you can hide more small apartments (which get narrower as you go upward), depending on your requirements. Very tall, narrow houses of this kind are especially interesting, but they do not fit that well into the current book format. The construction manual on the following page can be easily converted into a vertical or portrait format. Cut out the pieces for the basic shape neatly, using a large, sharp cutter and keeping the blade extended according to the thickness of the material. It is easy to measure the rectangular elements. (It will be necessary to enlarge the drawing on a photocopier. Then pricking the corner points through the photocopy will be enough to be able to cut straight edges.) You can trace the curved gable on the cardboard or cut it out directly through the copy laid on top.

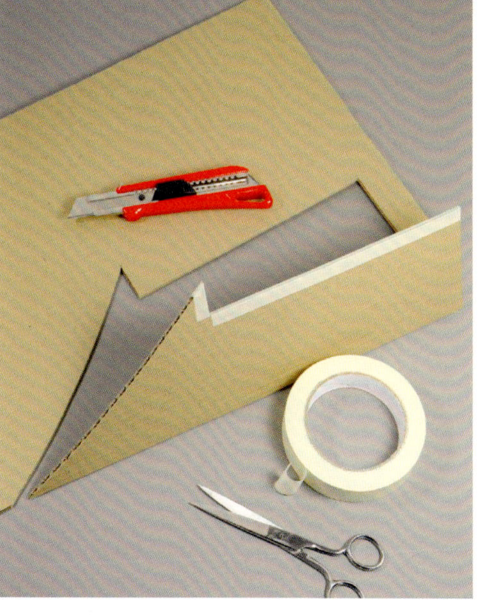

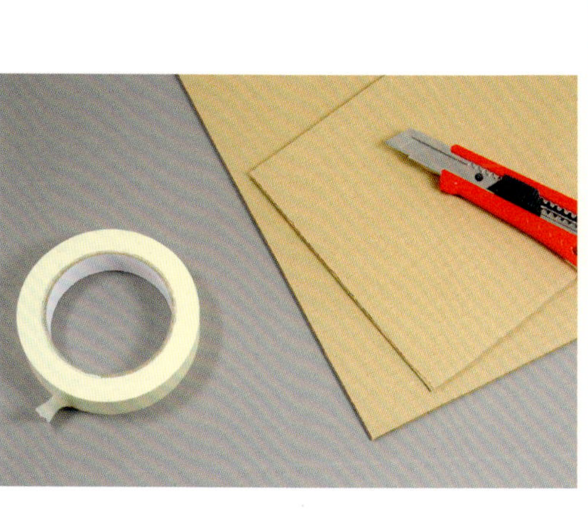

Materials + Tools

Large pieces of thick corrugated cardboard at least 5 mm thick (not bent; use clean parts of the side pieces of large shipping or furniture cartons)

Ruler, cutter, scissors, and cutting mat

White glue; paste if needed

Gesso and brush

India ink or water-based wood stain or acrylic paint

Washi tape or high-quality masking tape, at least 20 mm wide

Collectibles such as old keys, old book pages, a shuttlecock, snail shells, illustrations from art books, a sealed ink bottle, small beehive-shaped candles, miniature dolls, glass marbles . . .

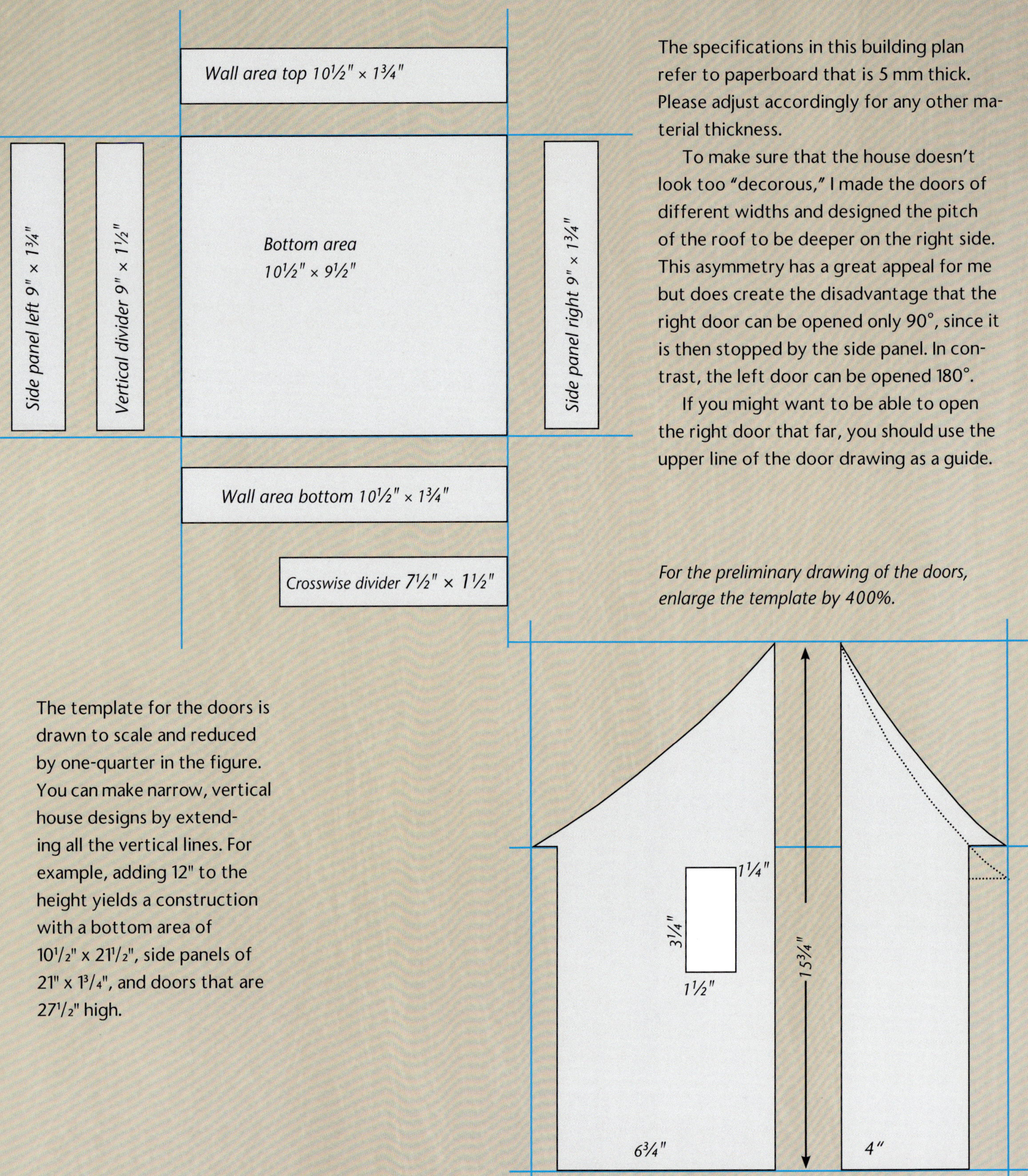

The specifications in this building plan refer to paperboard that is 5 mm thick. Please adjust accordingly for any other material thickness.

To make sure that the house doesn't look too "decorous," I made the doors of different widths and designed the pitch of the roof to be deeper on the right side. This asymmetry has a great appeal for me but does create the disadvantage that the right door can be opened only 90°, since it is then stopped by the side panel. In contrast, the left door can be opened 180°.

If you might want to be able to open the right door that far, you should use the upper line of the door drawing as a guide.

For the preliminary drawing of the doors, enlarge the template by 400%.

The template for the doors is drawn to scale and reduced by one-quarter in the figure. You can make narrow, vertical house designs by extending all the vertical lines. For example, adding 12" to the height yields a construction with a bottom area of 10½" x 21½", side panels of 21" x 1¾", and doors that are 27½" high.

After cutting them out, glue the side panels to the back panel, using white glue as usual—flush with the side edges.

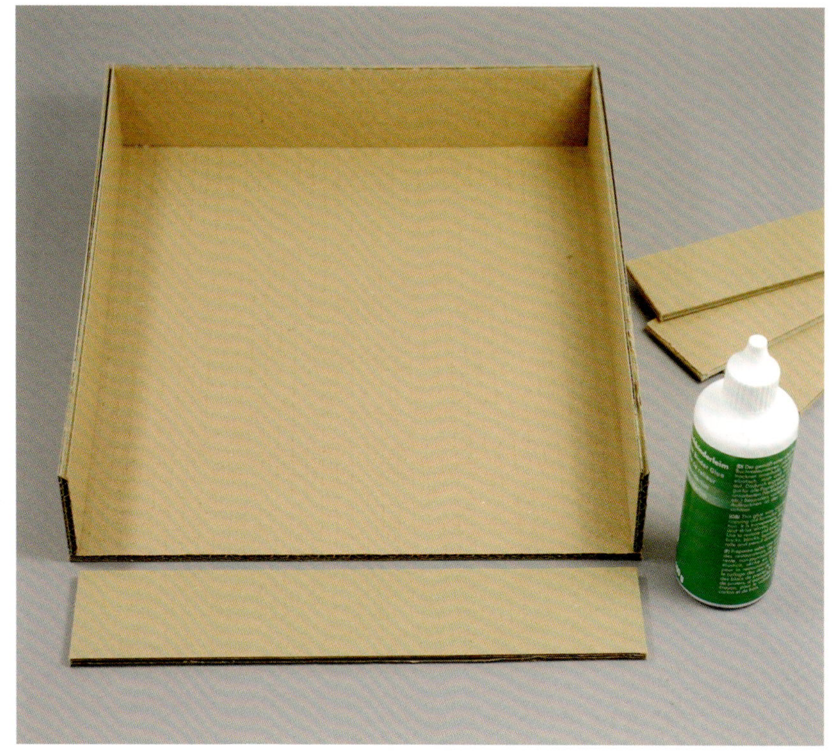

After that, you will have to tape over the open edges of the corrugated cardboard again. Do this by using high-quality masking tape, washi tape, or (for those who are experienced) gummed paper-packaging tape. Apply the band of tape as smoothly and tautly as possible around the edges and press on hard.

All open edges should be covered so that nothing will weaken. Therefore, apply the tape on the upper edge of the corners right up to the next edge and use scissors to make a small, slightly slanted cut on the inner side. This lets you press the tape into the corner and still cover the small part of the corner that you would not reach from the next side.

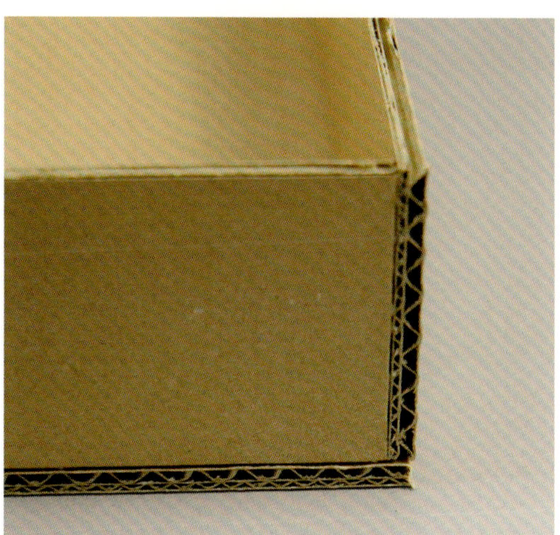

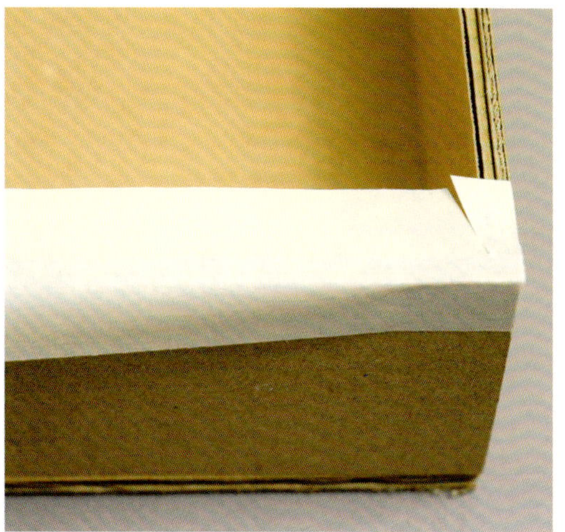

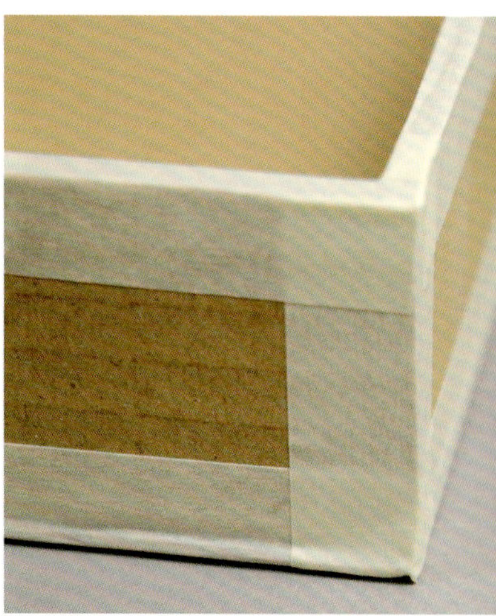

If you have cut out everything neatly, the partition panels for dividing the interior should now fit into the finished construction without any problem, and you will be able to attach them using white glue. Use masking tape to tape over their open edges, as well as those on the doors. Be aware, especially on the doors, that the edge of the adhesive tape will remain subtly visible later. Therefore, work carefully, apply the tape as evenly as possible, and don't just tear it off, but cut it off evenly. Then prime everything with gesso.

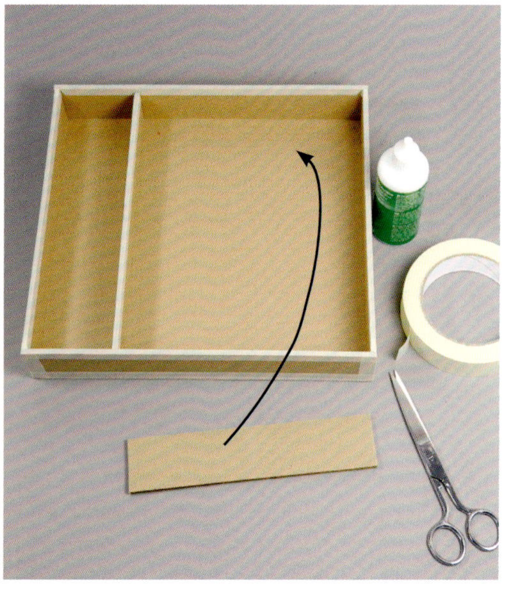

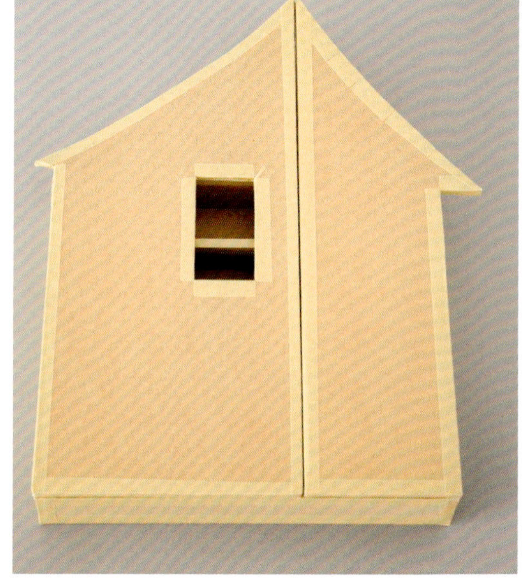

Any possible little wrinkles that might occur due to the moisture on the adhesive tape usually smooth out when dry. Here it is also worthwhile to apply a second coat of paint (after at least two to three hours of drying time); then the interiors will be a nice opaque white. After the second drying time, give the outer sides, the doors, and the edges of the partitions (inside) a coating of glaze (here: silver gray) of heav-

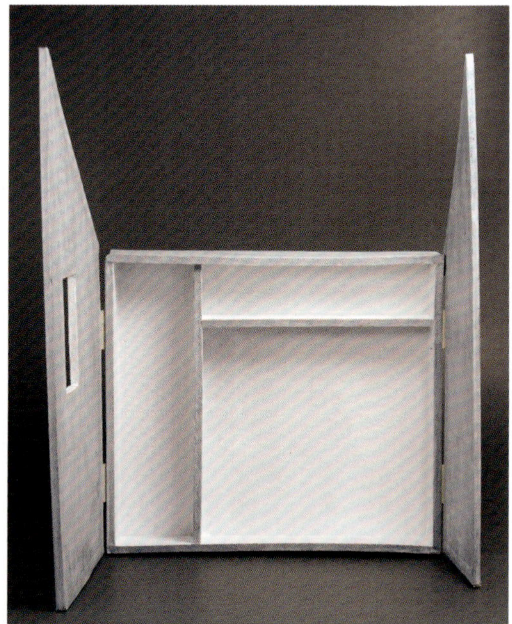

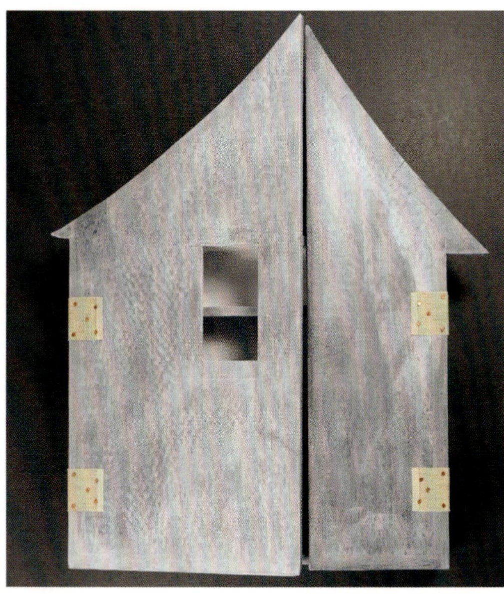

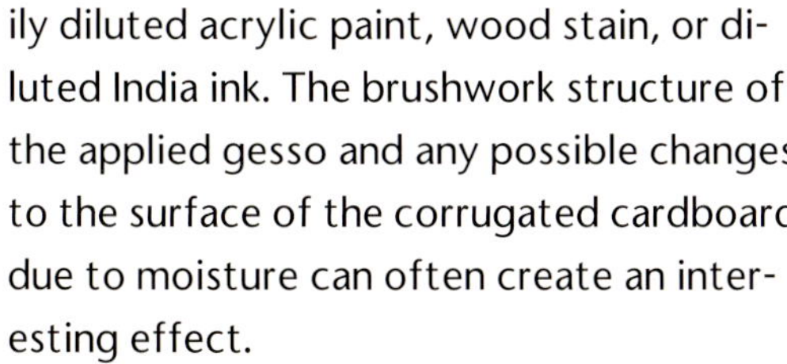

ily diluted acrylic paint, wood stain, or diluted India ink. The brushwork structure of the applied gesso and any possible changes to the surface of the corrugated cardboard due to moisture can often create an interesting effect.

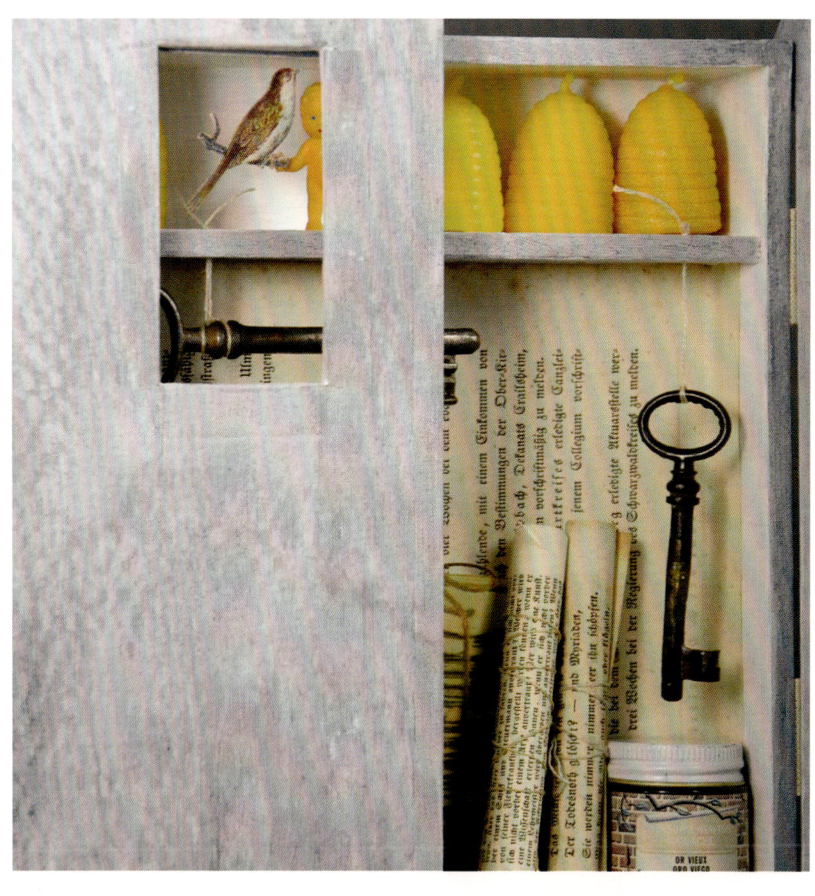

Finally, attach the doors: either in a very simple way (as shown in the template), using sturdy textile tape, which is glued on from the outside with white glue [A] and is held additionally with small decorative nails. Or by a proper hinge [B], which is recommended if the doors are to be moved frequently. To do this, glue two strips of textile tape to the edge of the door with white glue, halfway narrowly offset at top and bottom [1], then fold over and fasten firmly to the construction both outside and inside [2].

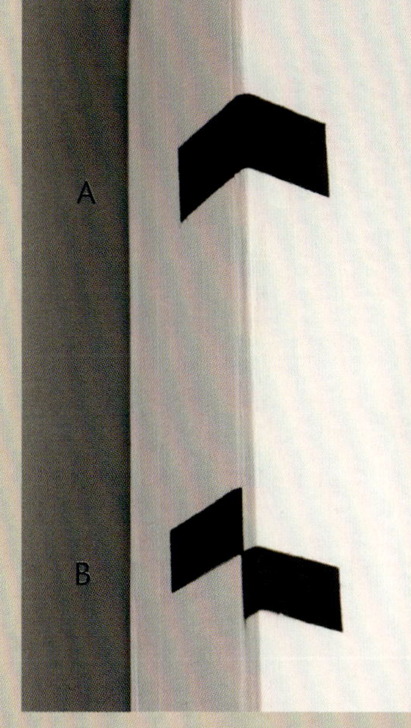

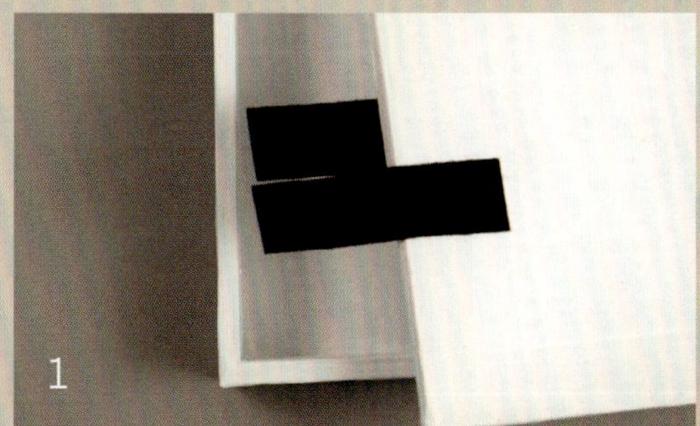

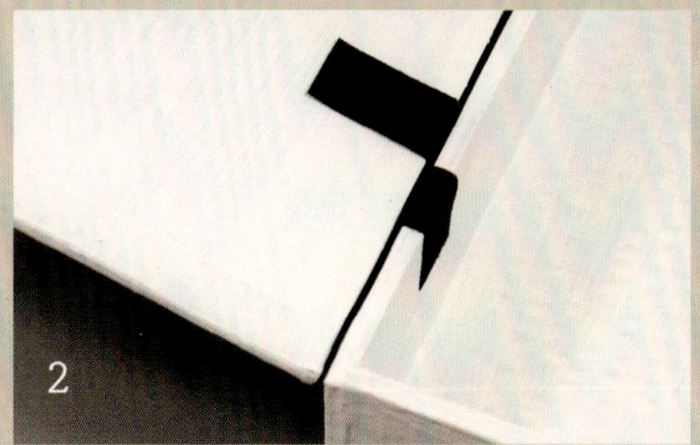

GALLERY

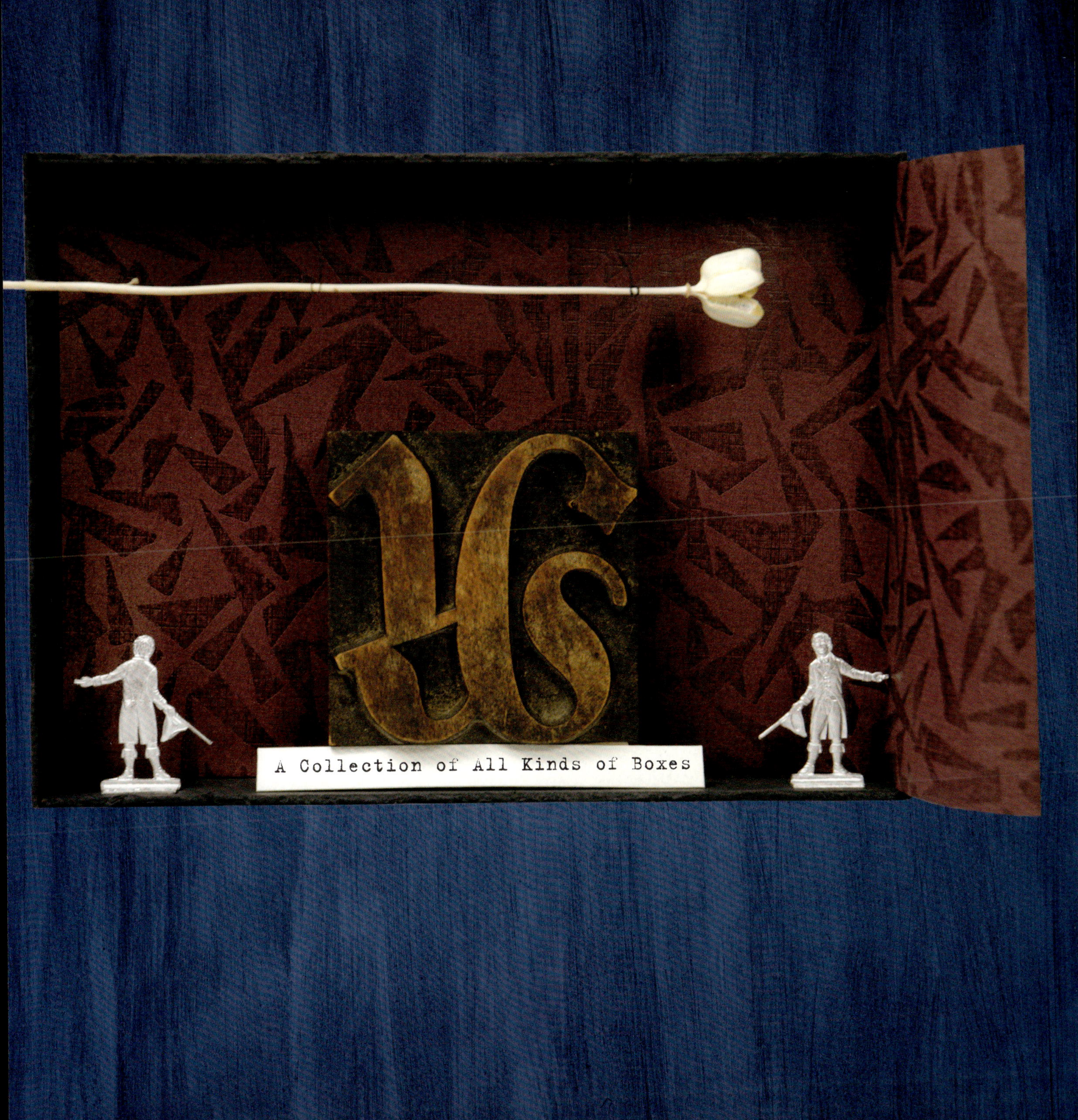
A Collection of All Kinds of Boxes

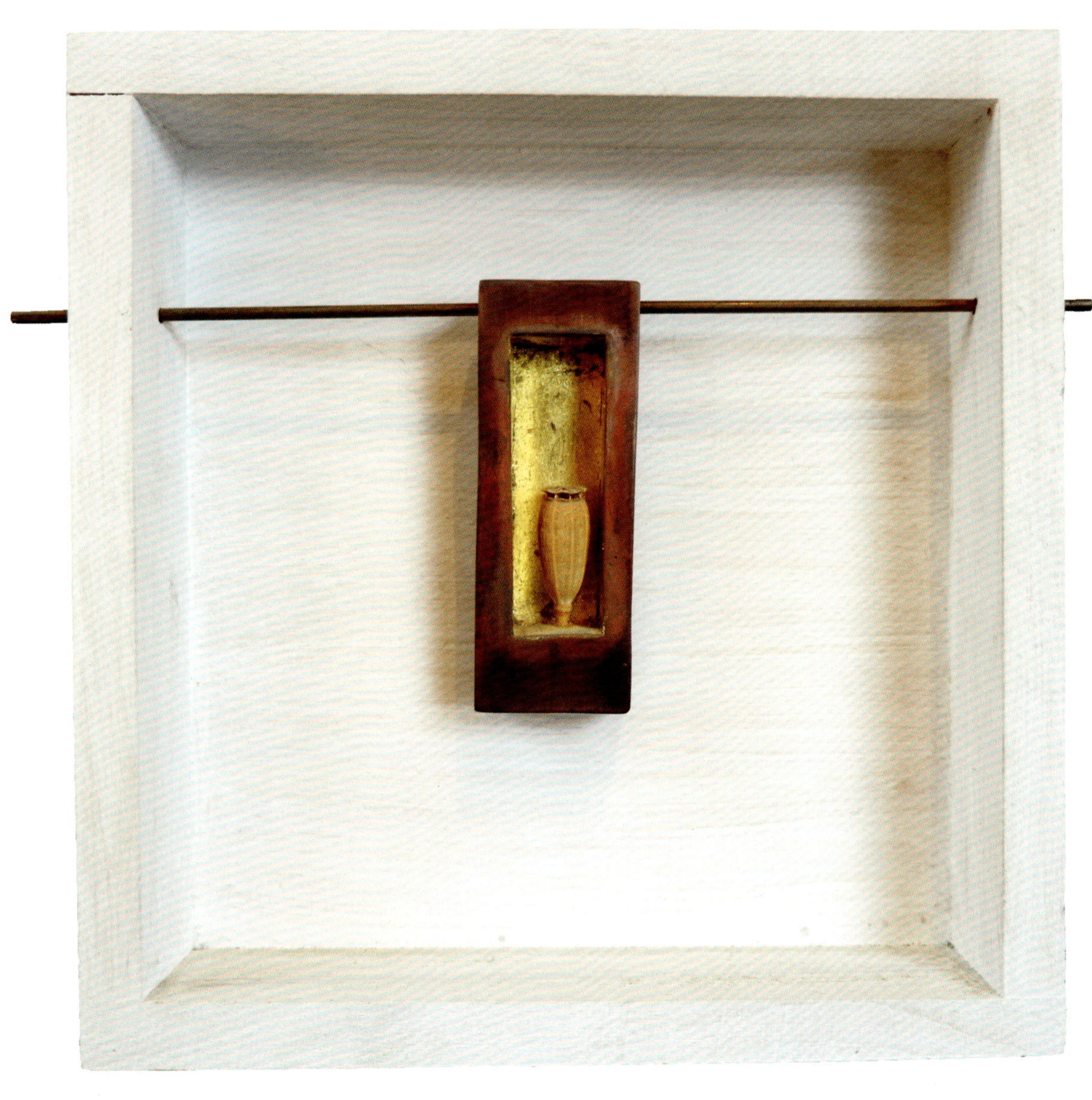

Uli Seitz-Sperling · *Pendant in a Box* · 15 × 15 × 3 cm · Copper, poppy seed pod, gold leaf

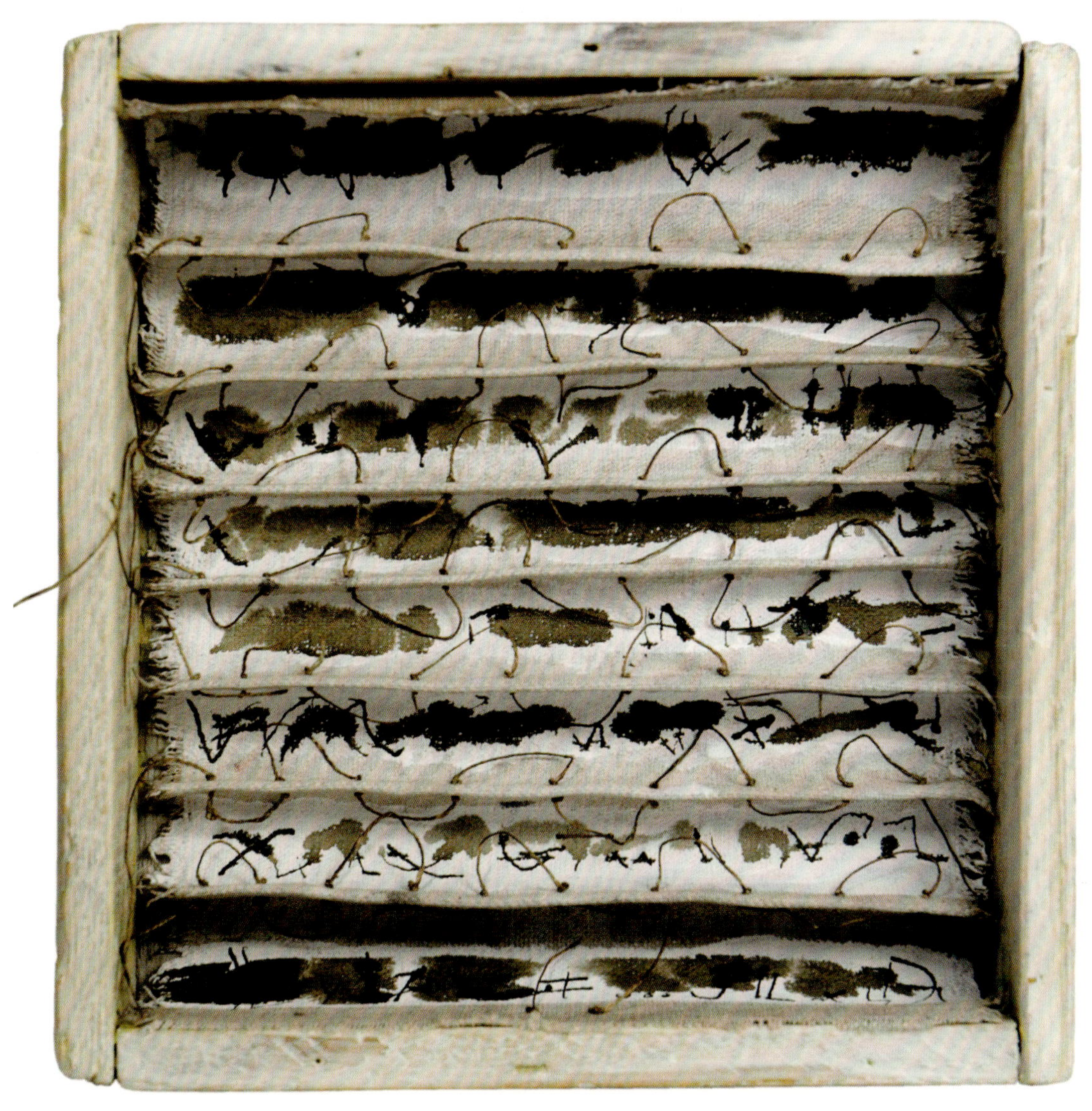

Barbara Sackermann · *Wants to Grow* · 16.5 × 16.5 × 4 cm · Old linen, black-walnut ink, thread

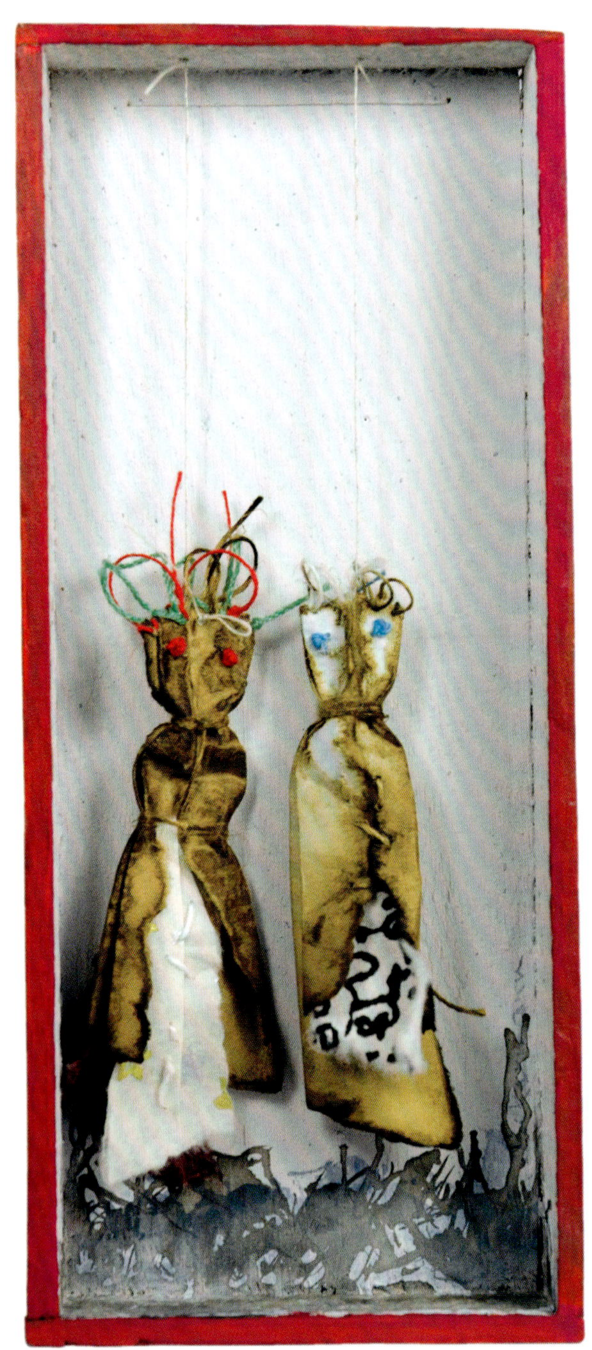

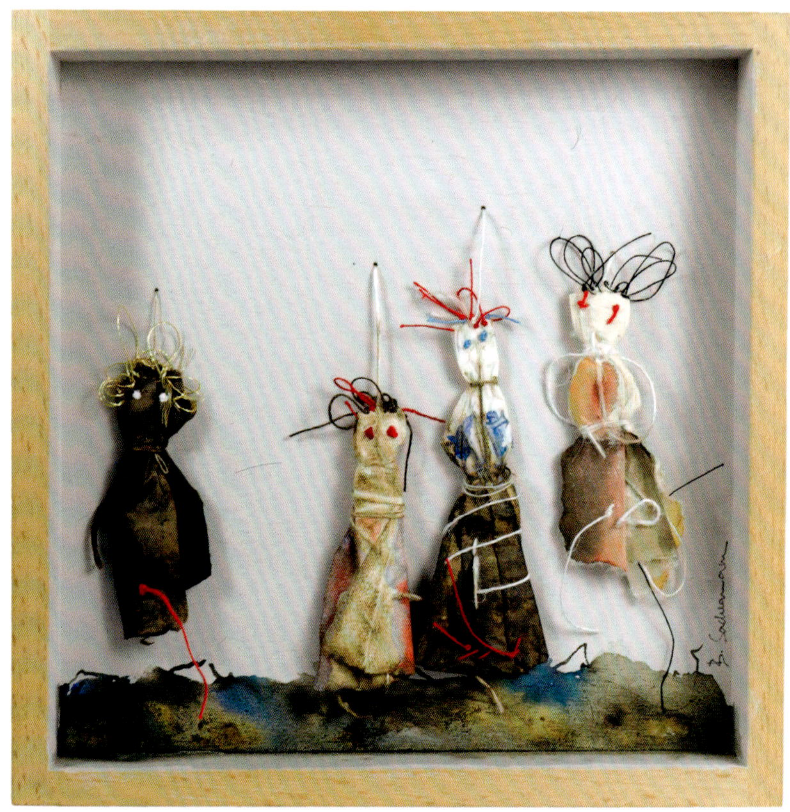

Barbara Sackermann · *Two Beings* · 19 × 8.5 × 2 cm
With a Black Sheep · 15 × 15 × 3 cm · Paper, black-walnut ink, thread

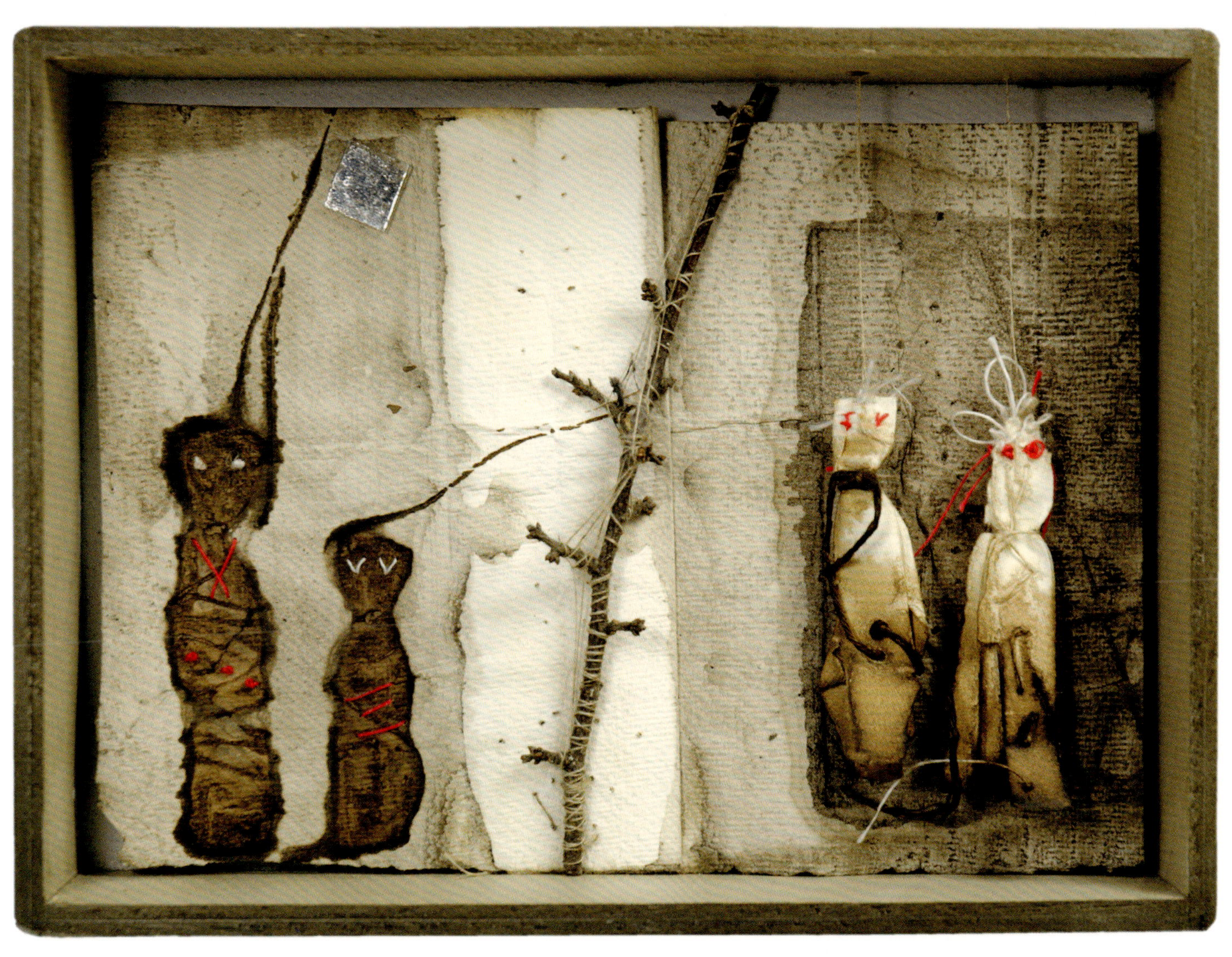

Barbara Sackermann · *Light with Shadow* · 18.5 × 25.5 × 6.5 cm · Paper, black-walnut ink, thread

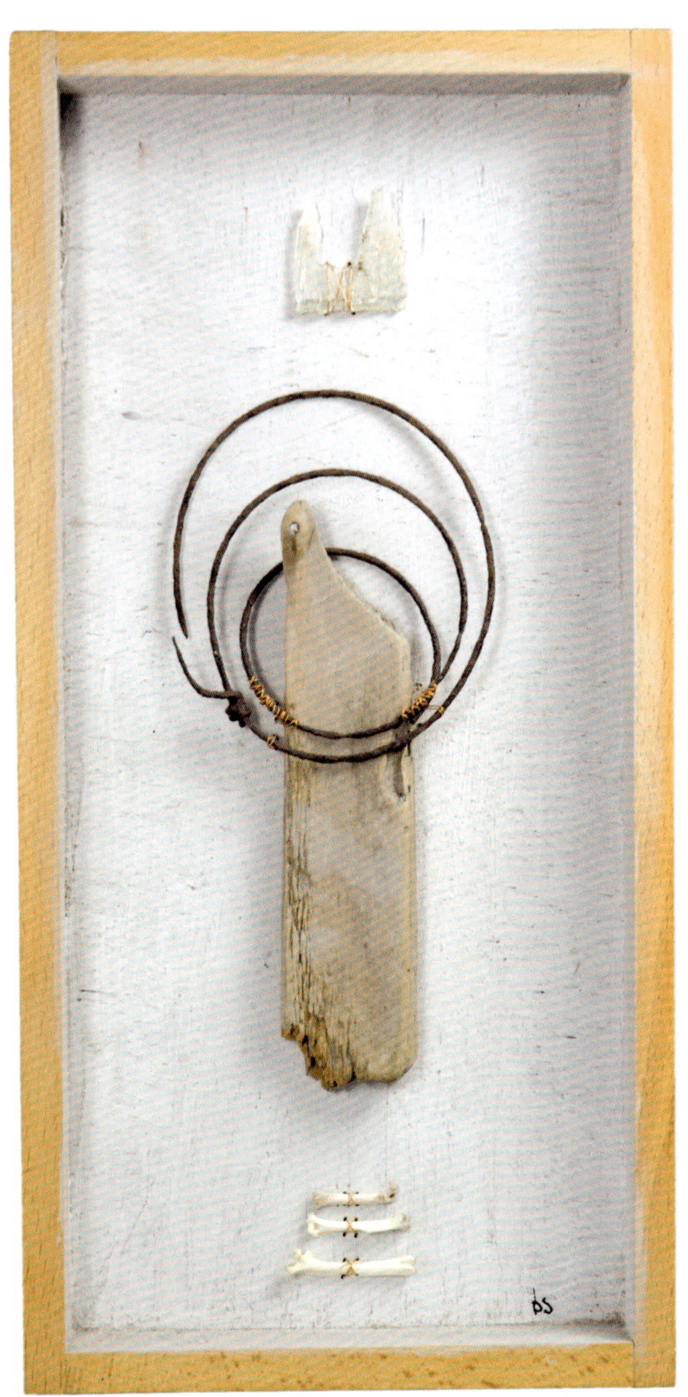
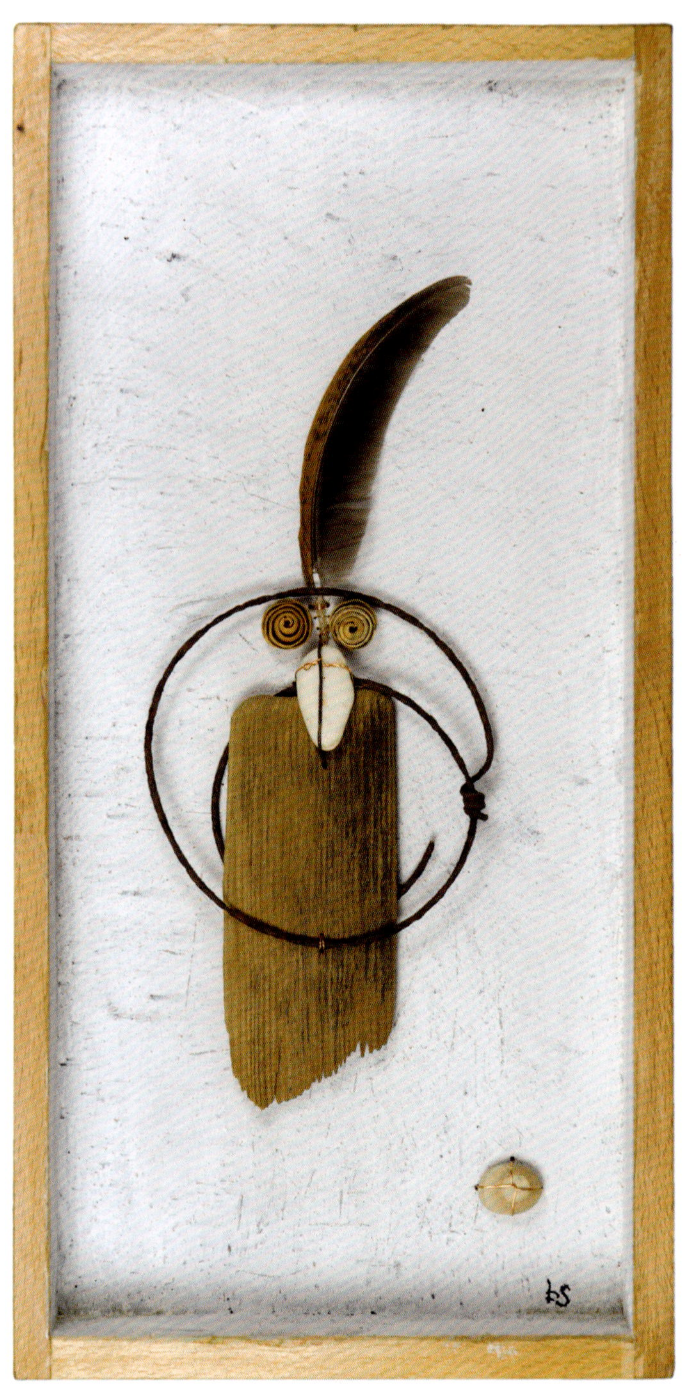

Barbara Sackermann · *The Mouse King* | *The Watchwoman* · each 30 × 15 × 3 cm · Finds

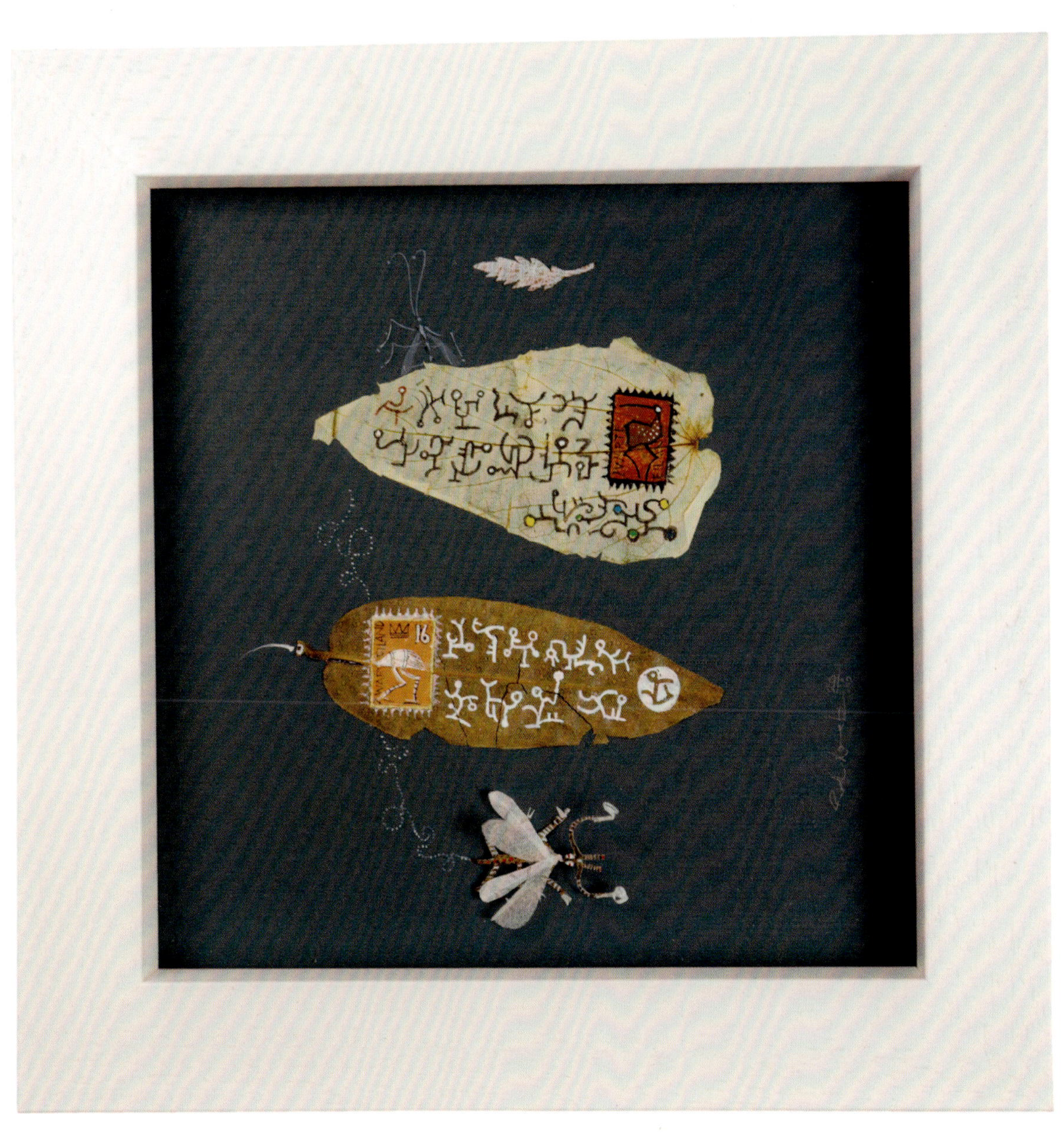

Rolf Lock · *Insectoglyph* · 24.5 × 24.5 × 4.5 cm · Pressed leaves, paper, India ink

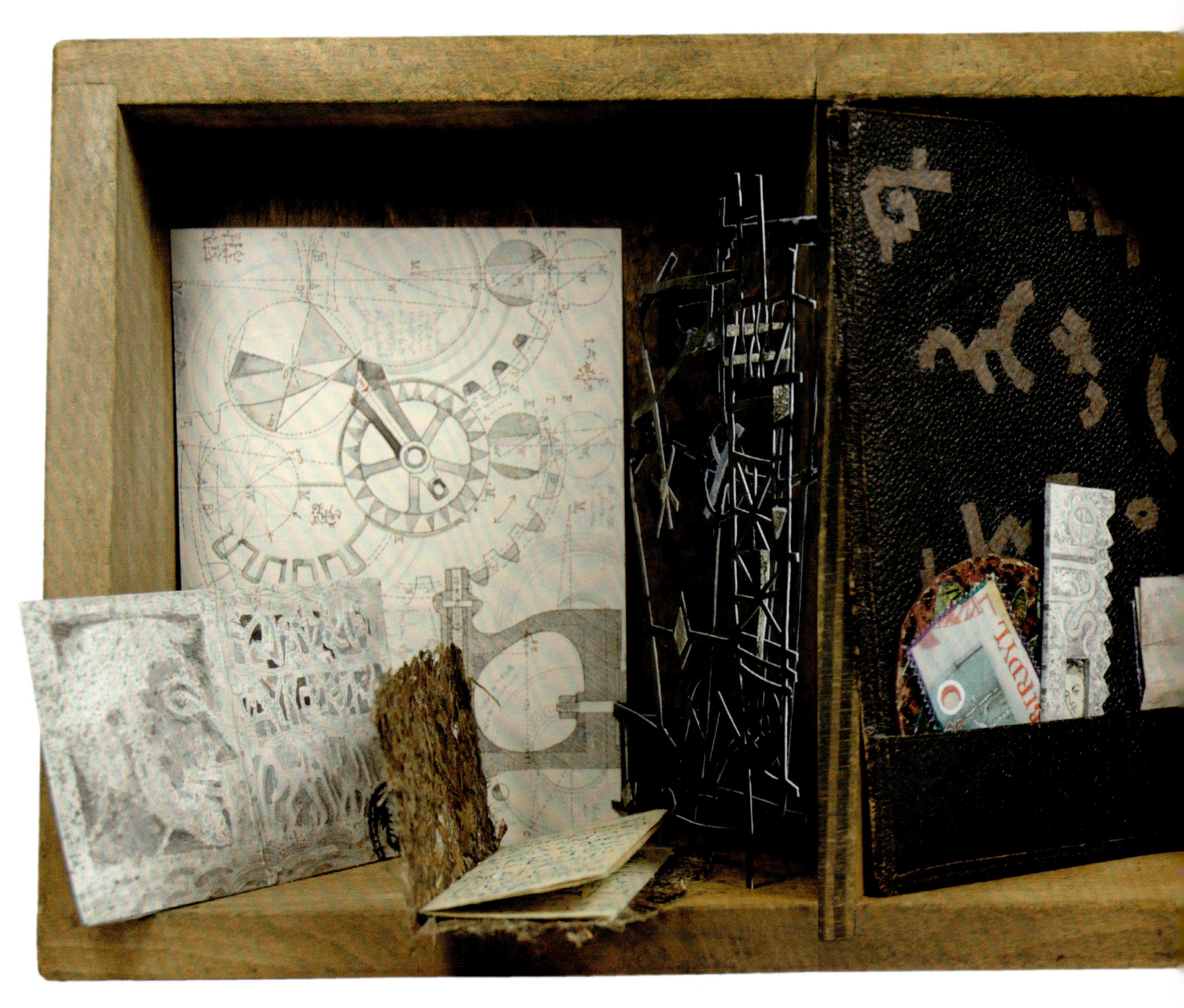

Rolf Lock · *Identity* · 20 × 52 × 11 cm

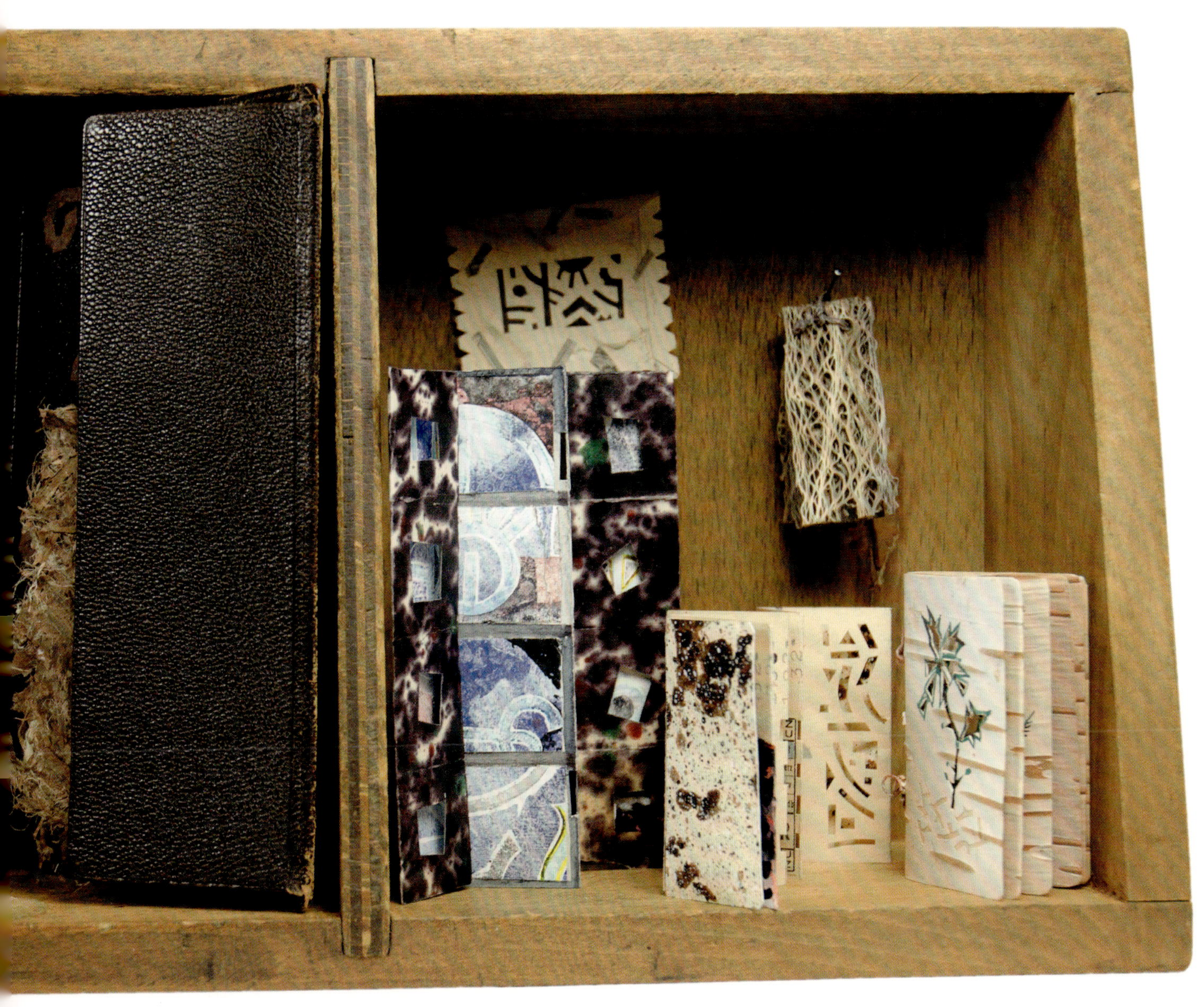

Old billfold, paper, birch bark, and other natural materials · Drawing, calligraphy, paper cutting

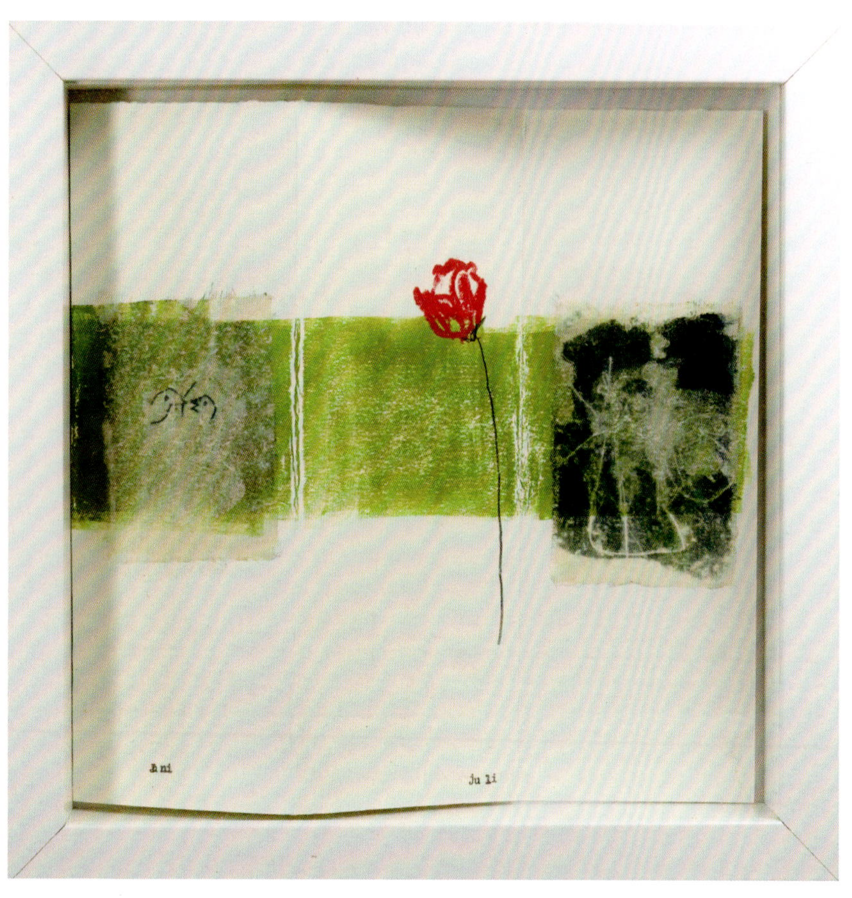

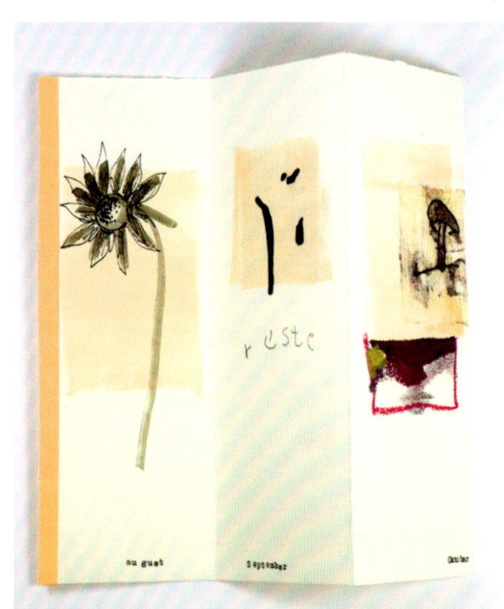

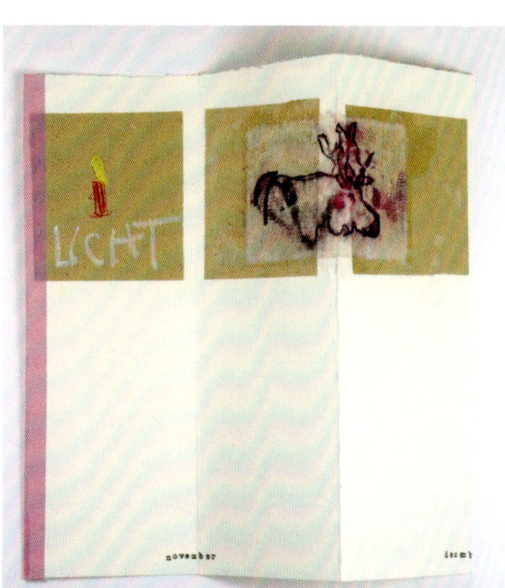

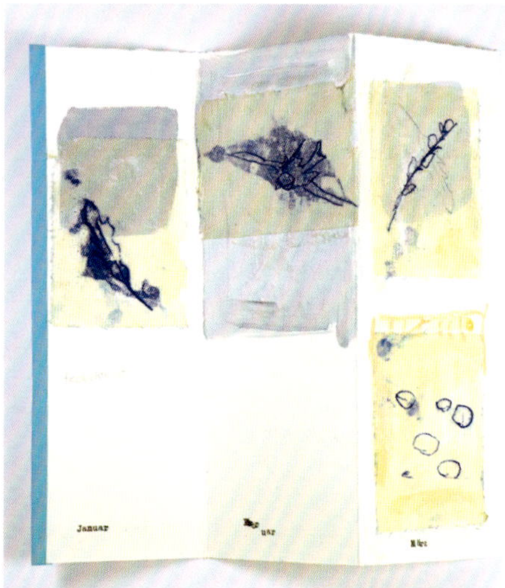

Simone Schäffer · *Yearly Companion* · Four leporello pages in 25 × 25 cm large box (to be exchanged)
Monotype, wax, collage, pencil

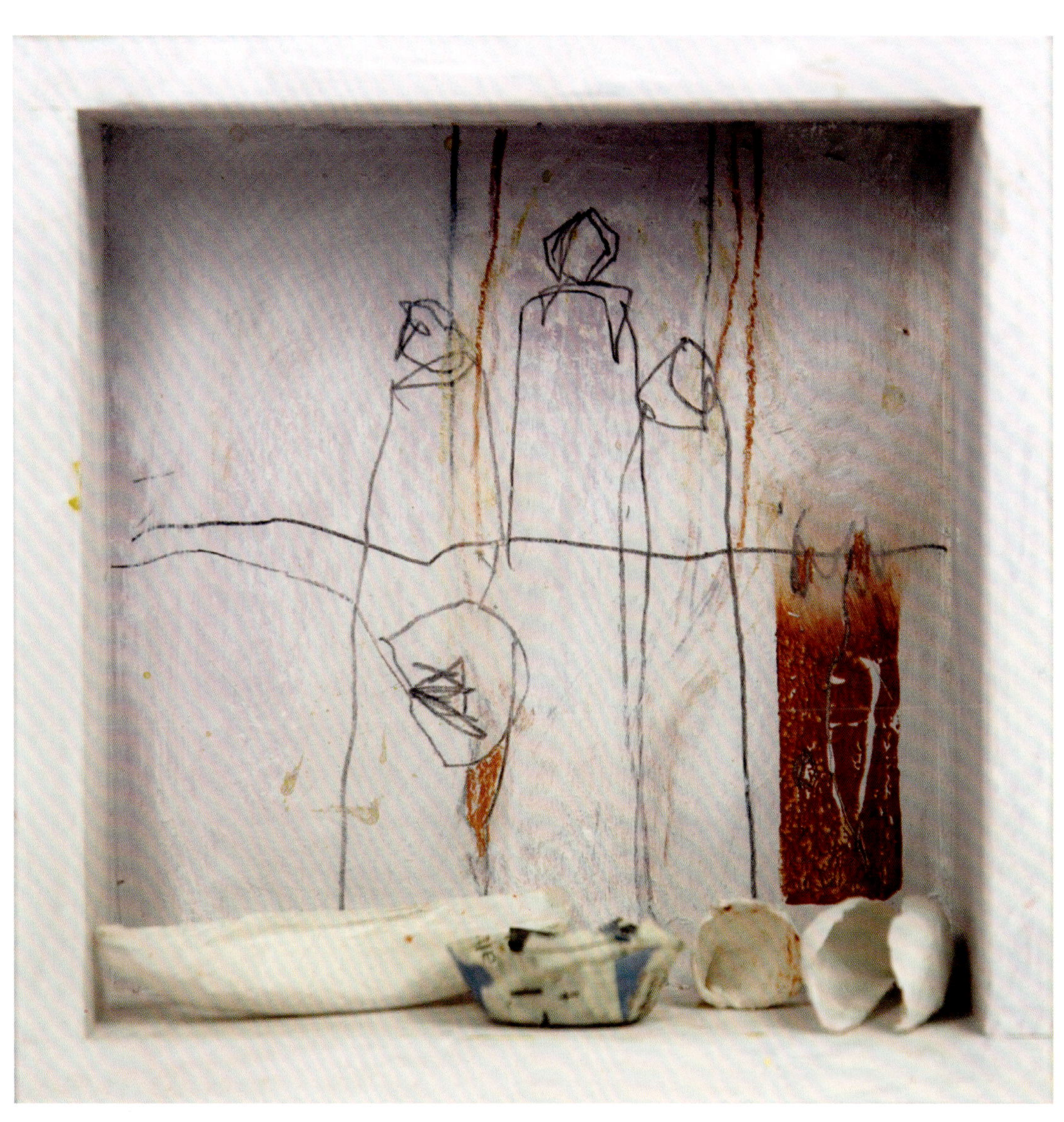

Simone Schäffer · *Unfold* · 15 × 15 × 9 cm · Pencil, acrylic, laminated paper

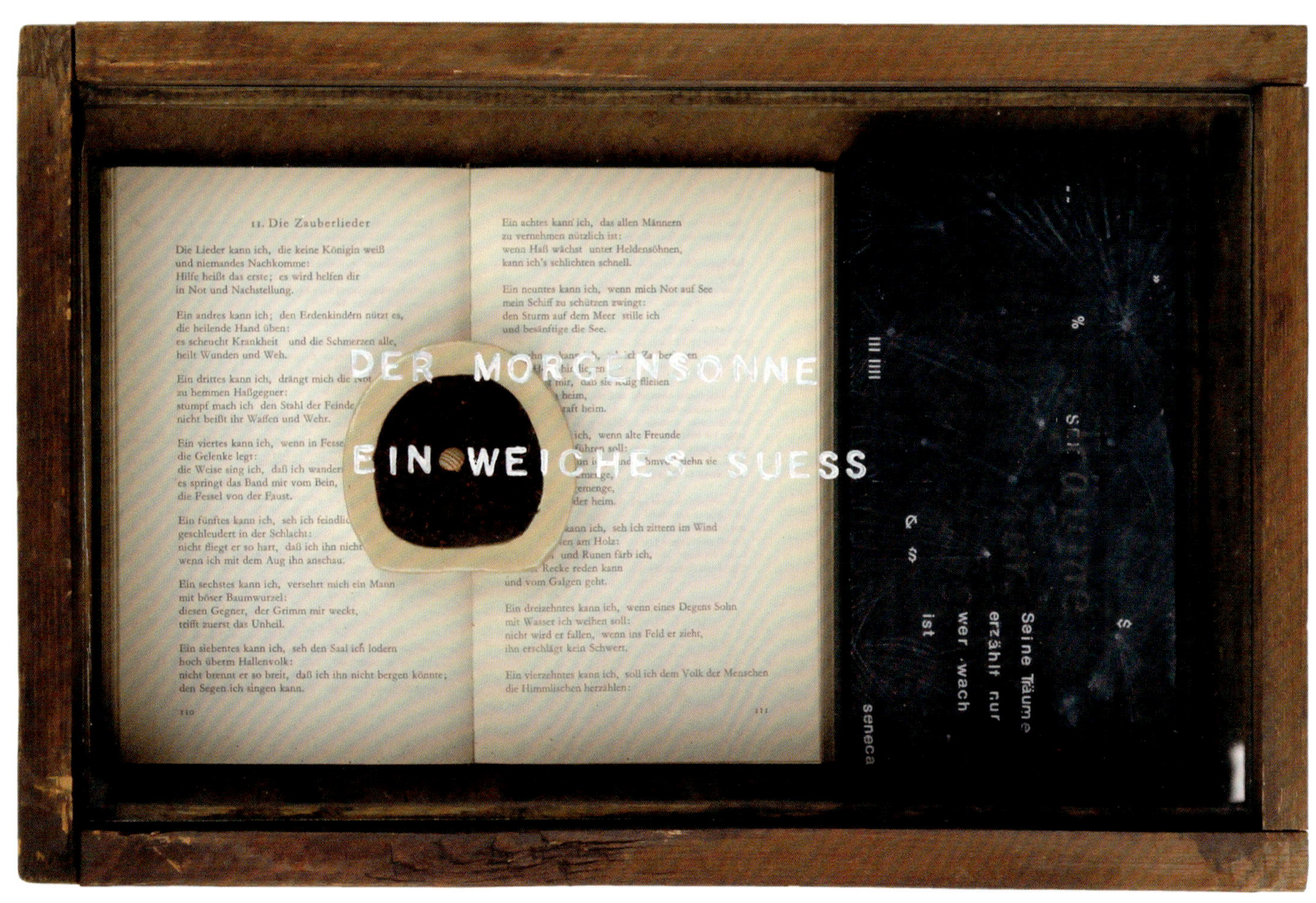

Setsuko Fukushima · *Recollection* · 25 × 35 × 10 cm · Wood, paper, ceramics

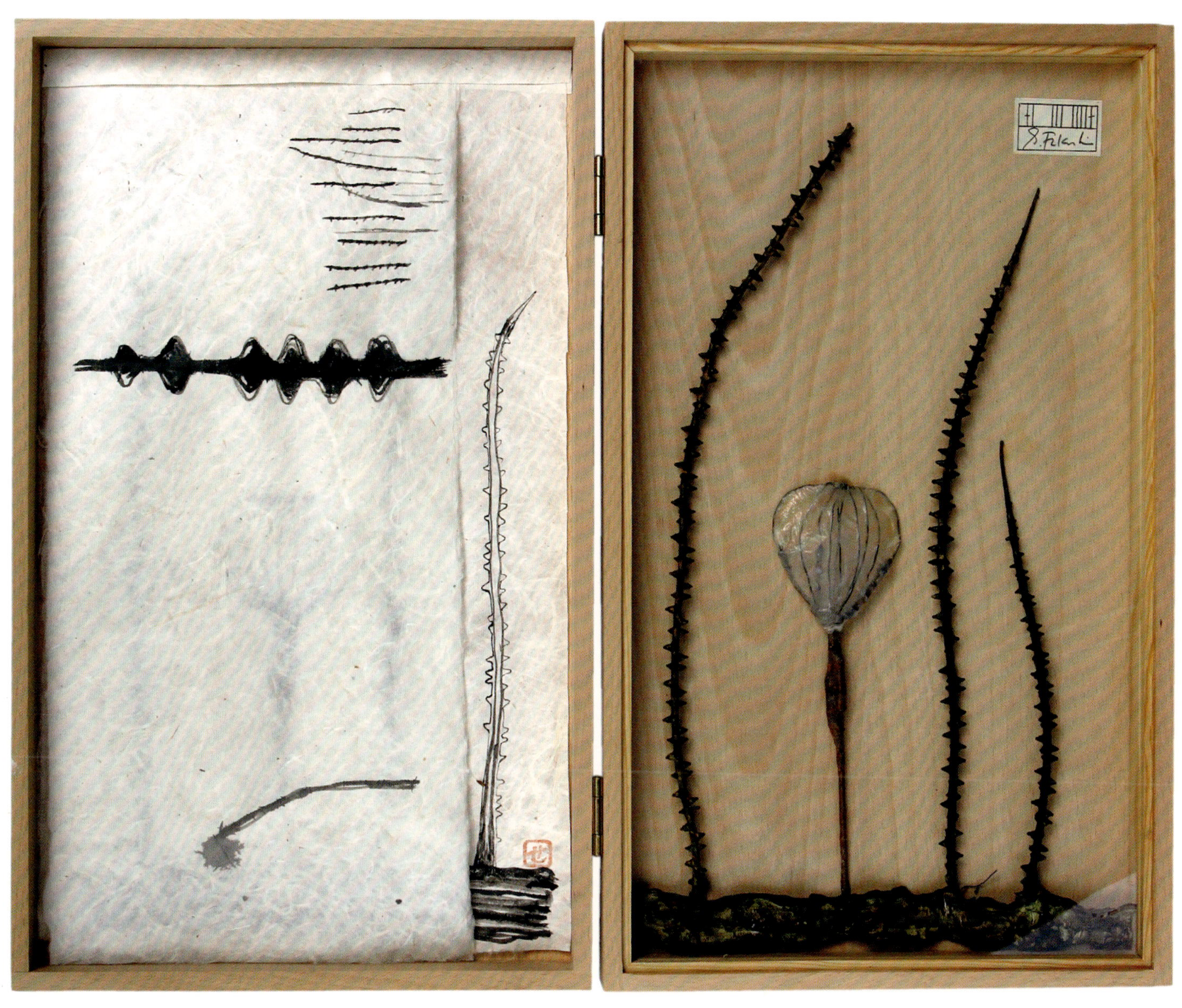

Setsuko Fukushima · *Alternative Botany* · 45 × 50 × 5 cm ·
Wood, paper, plastic, glass

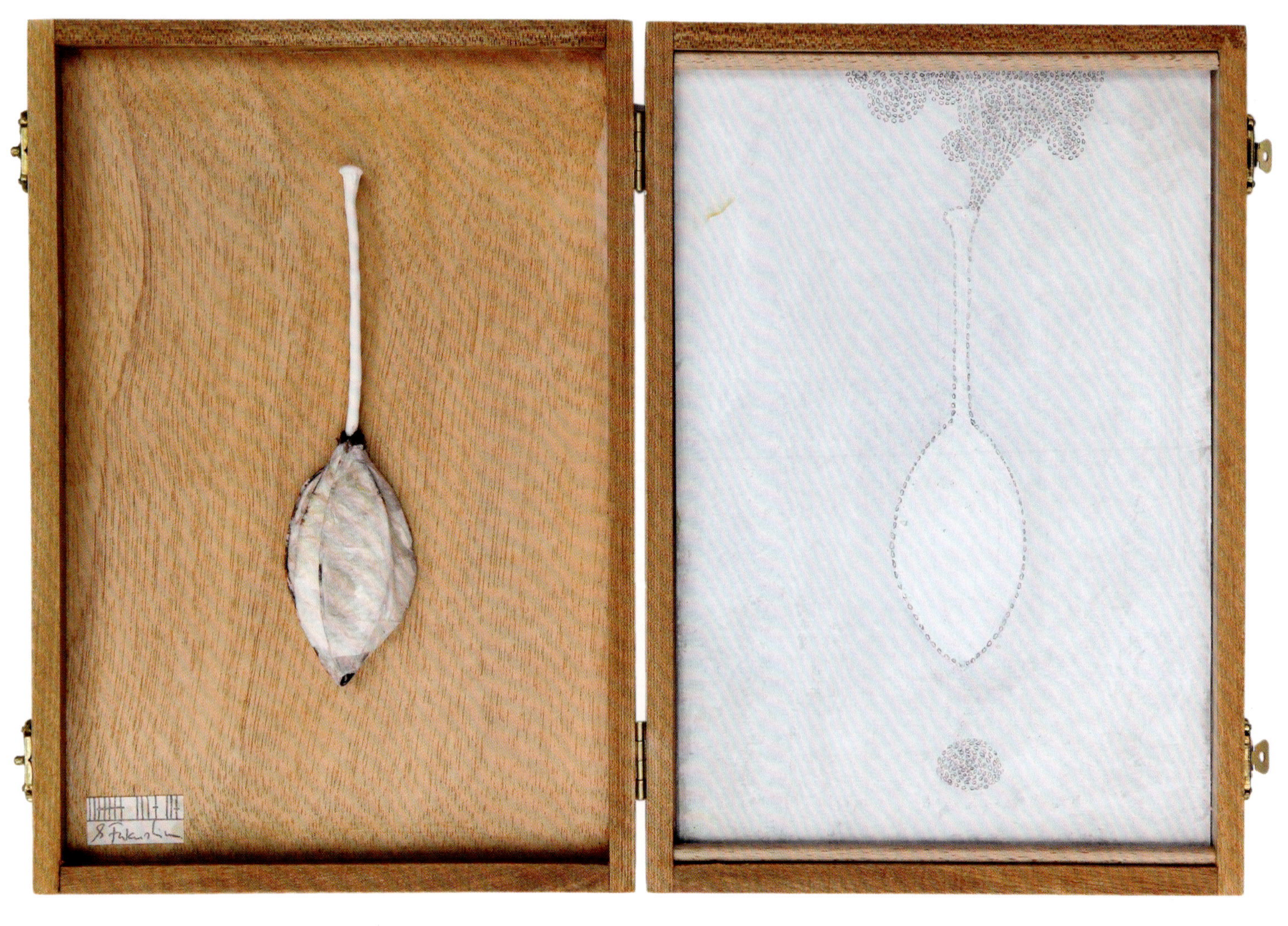

Setsuko Fukushima · *Alternative Botany* · 28 × 40 × 3 cm · Wood, plastic, paper

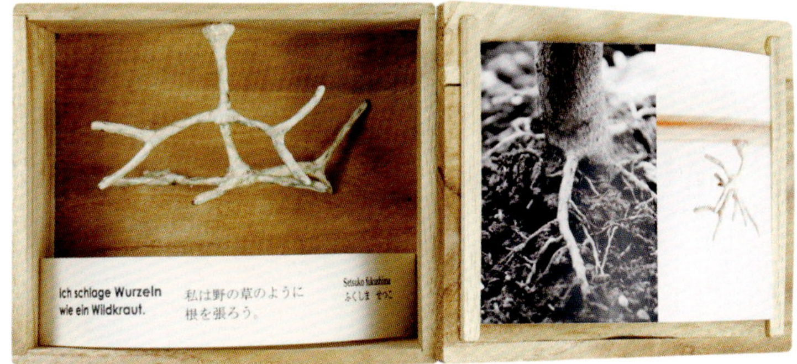

Setsuko Fukushima · *Alternative Botany* · 11.5 × 19 × 5 cm · Wood, paper

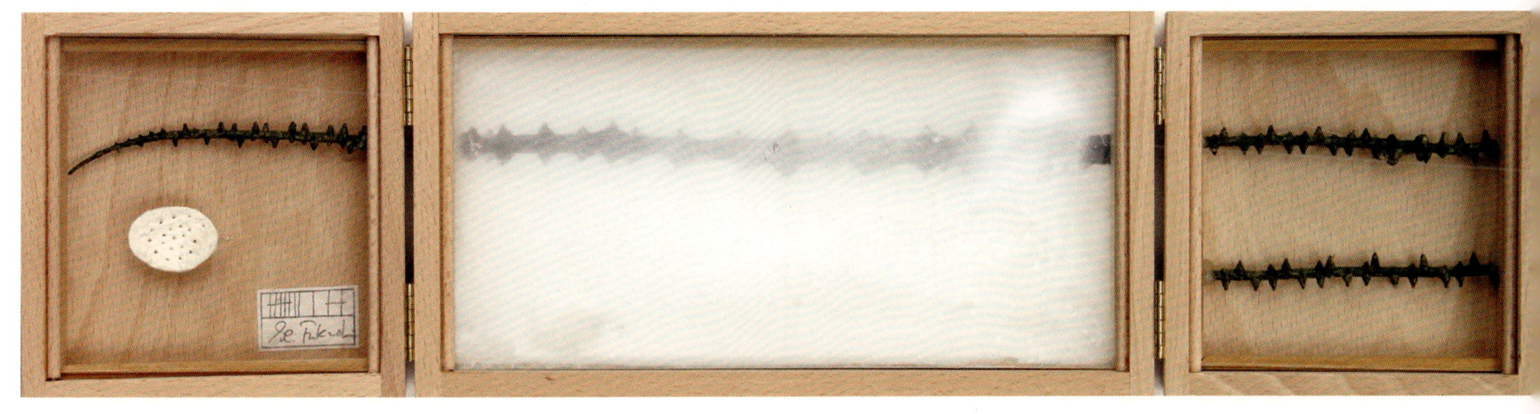

Setsuko Fukushima · *Alternative Botany* · 14 × 48 × 3 cm · Wood, plastic, glass, metal

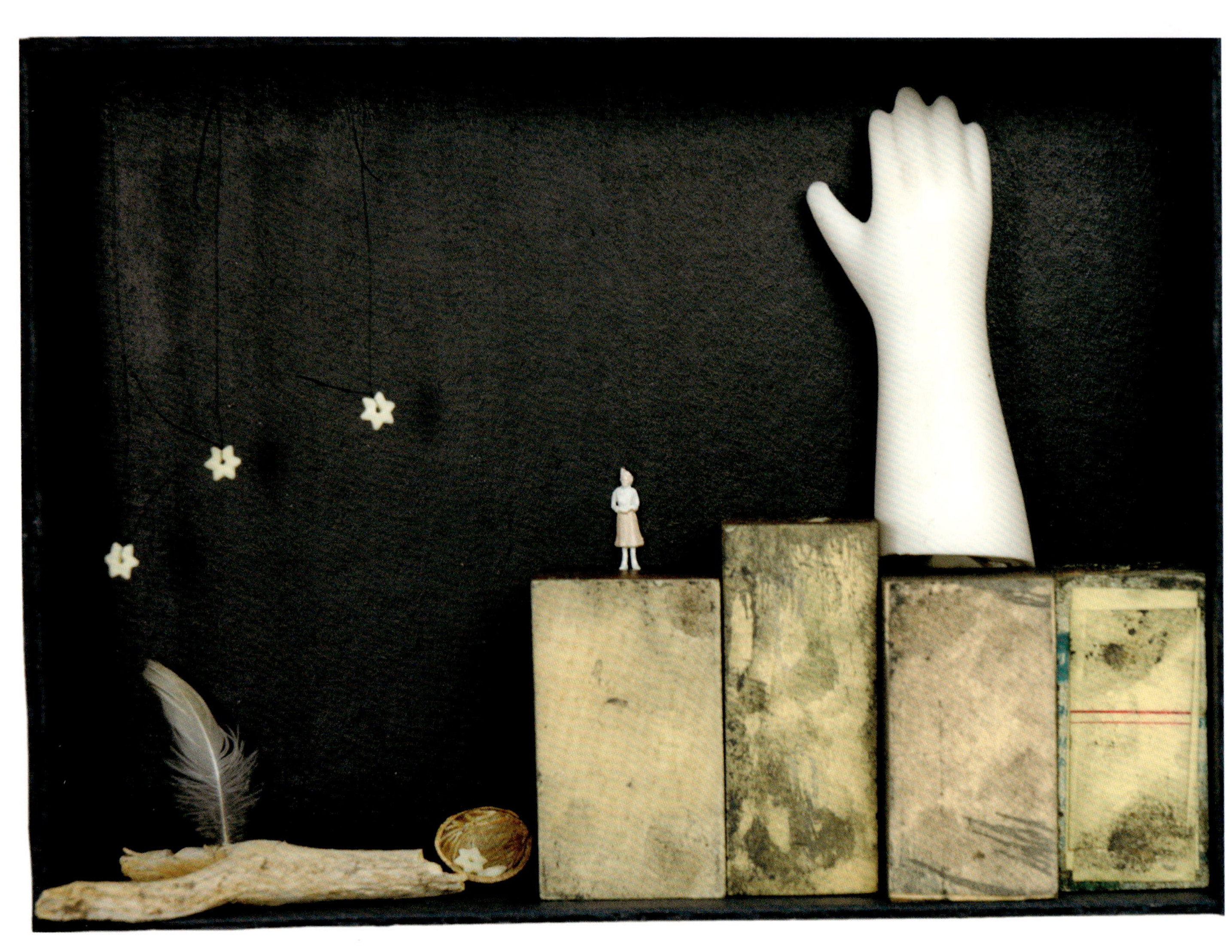

Marlis Maehrle · *Star Money Fairytale* · 15 × 20 × 4 cm · Black paperboard, finds, model train figures

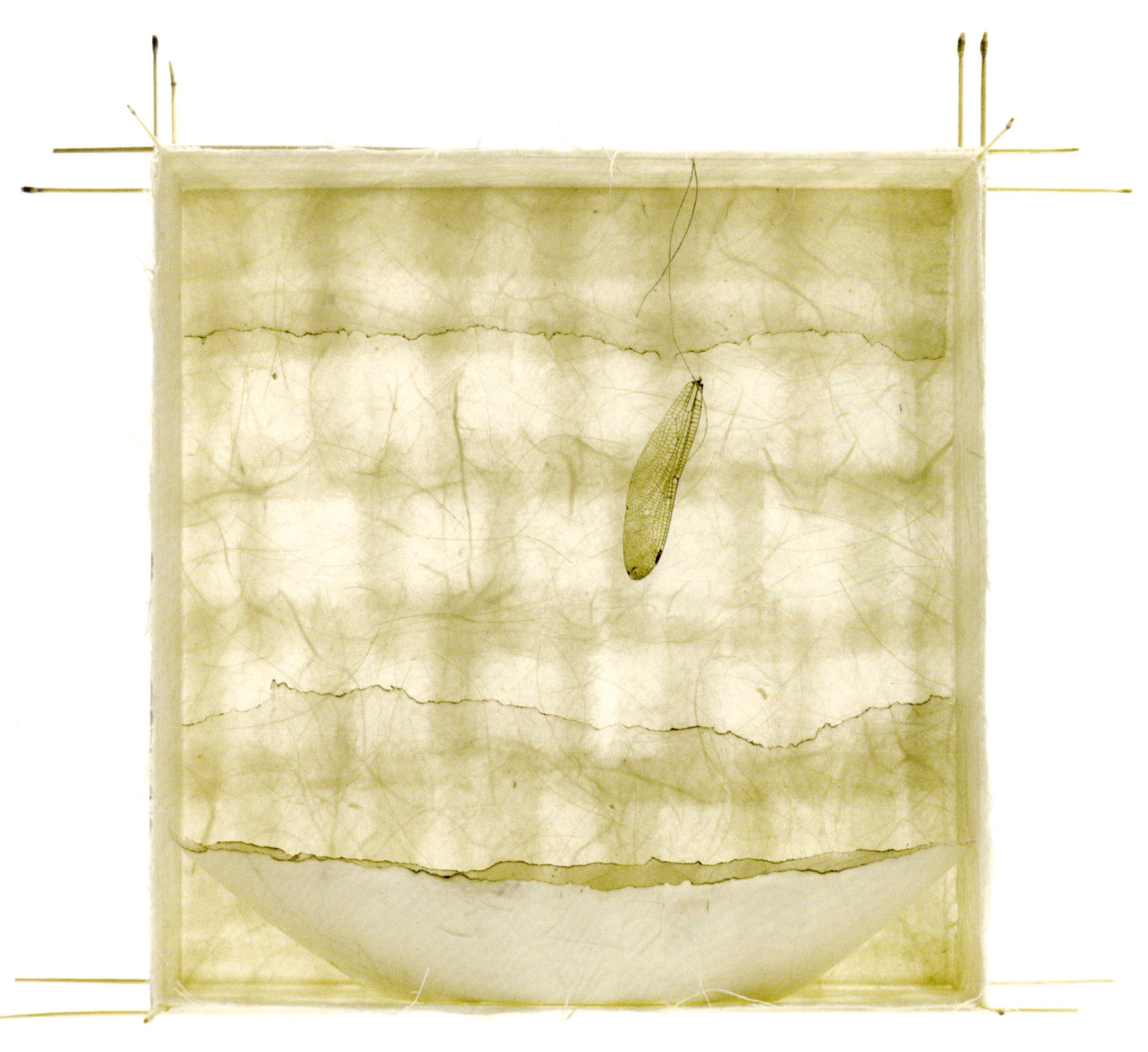

Marlis Maehrle · *Blade of Grass Series 1: Fire lines + Boat in the light* · 20 × 20 × 5 cm
translucent paper, blades of grass, dragonfly wing

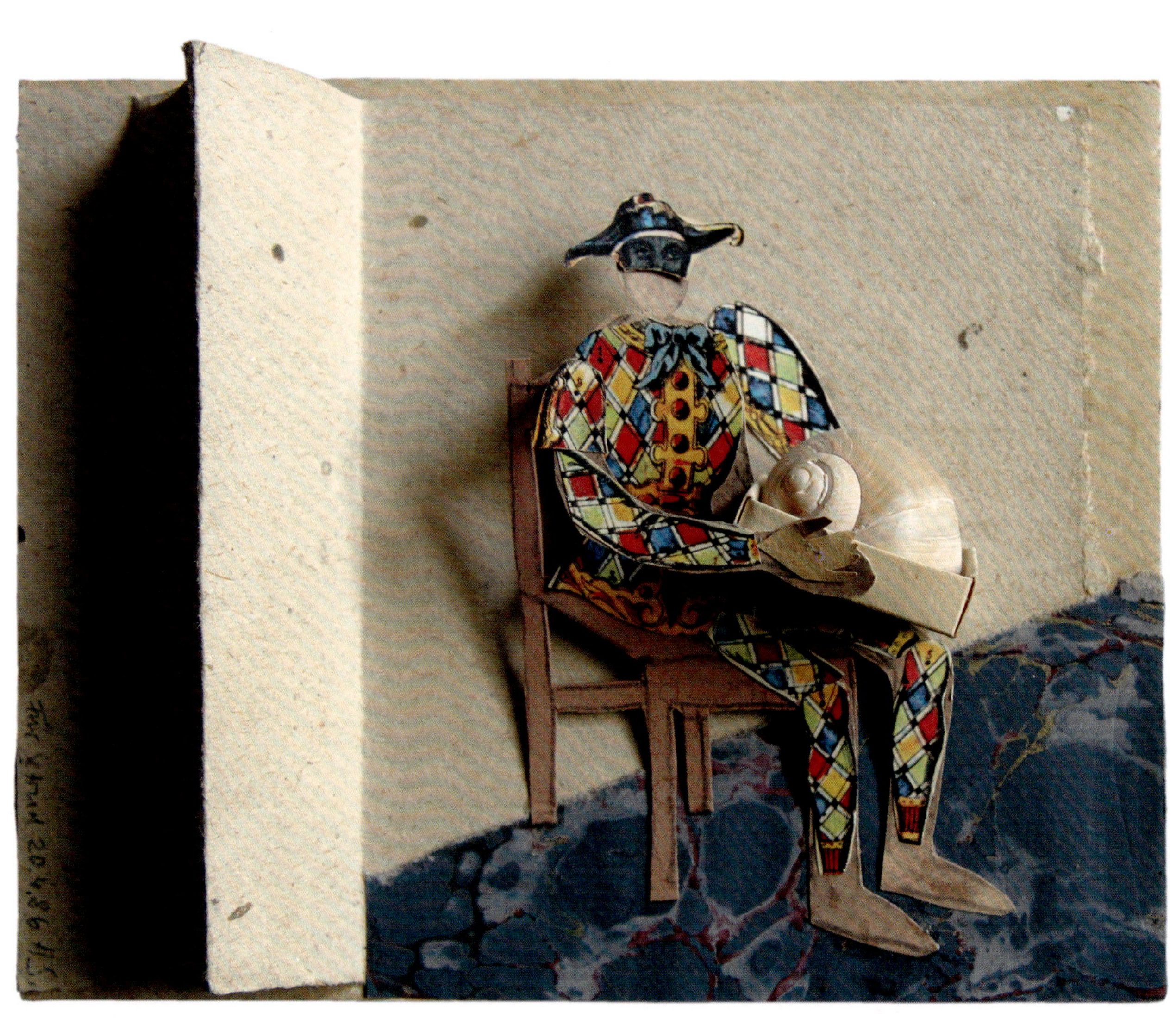

Heribert Schulmeyer · *Harlequin* · 14 × 12 × 3 cm · Paper, matchbox, snail shell

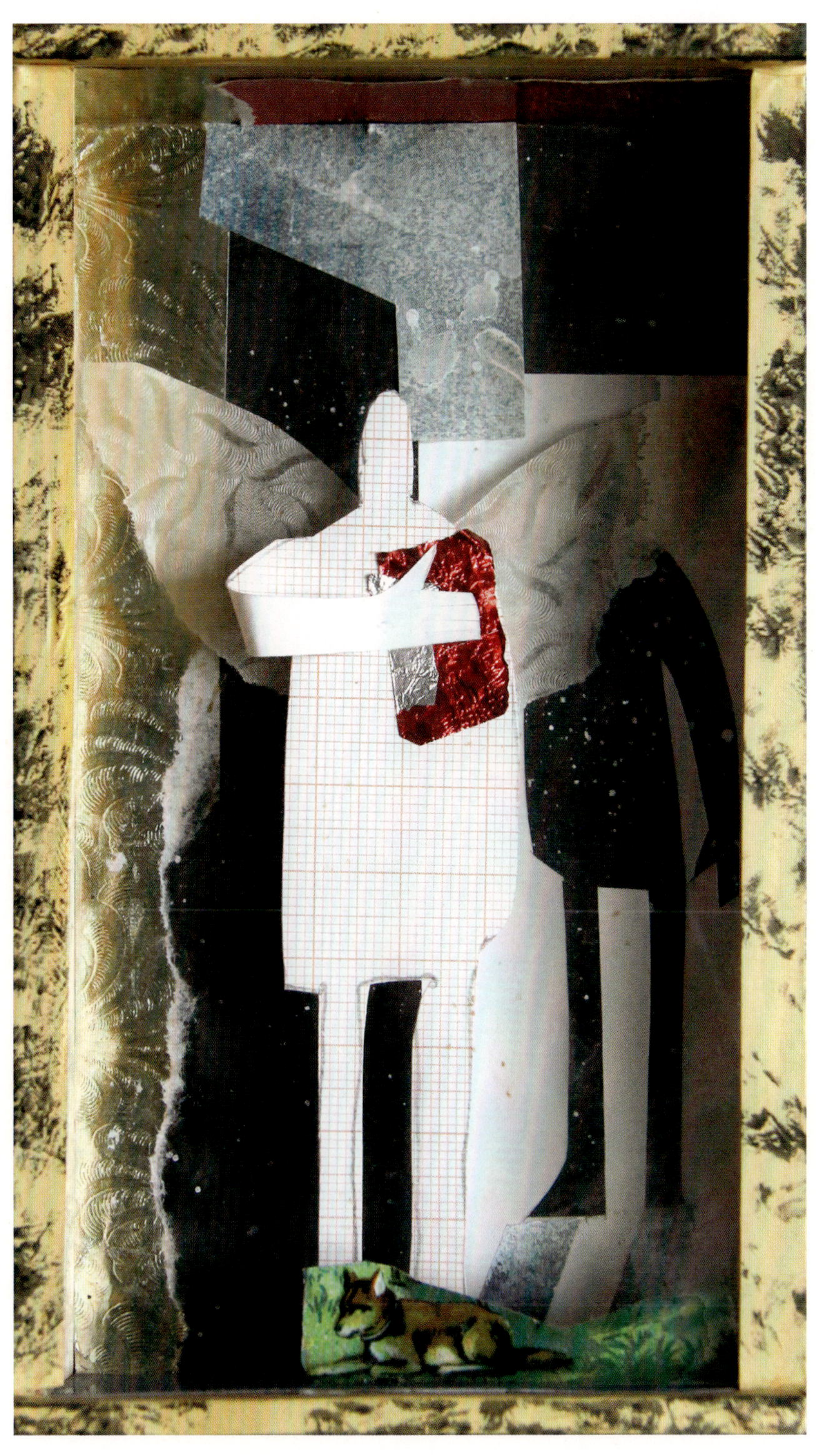

Heribert Schulmeyer · *My Darling* · 20 × 12 × 3 cm · Paper finds, aluminum foil

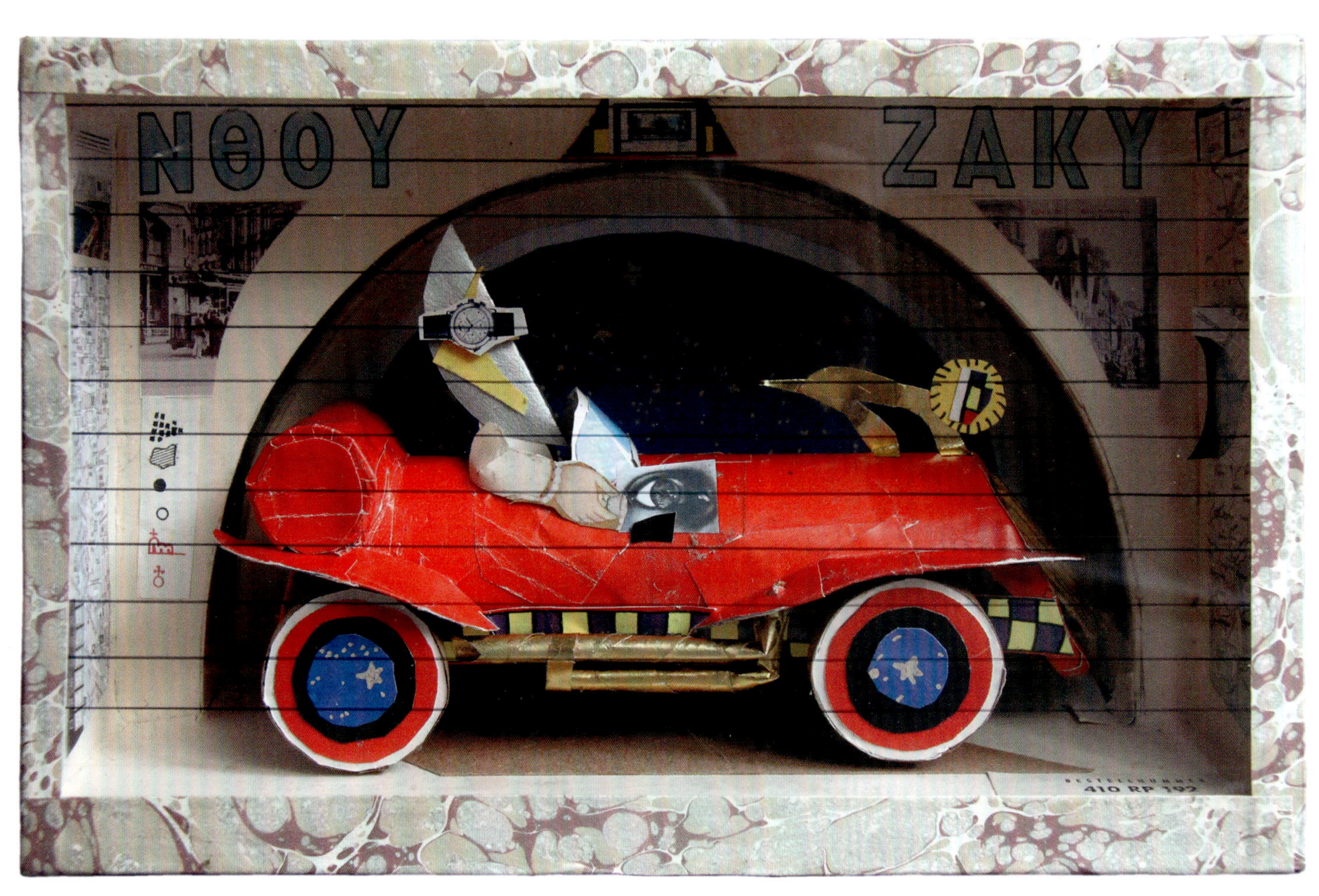

Heribert Schulmeyer · *Moon Car* · 12 × 19 × 6 cm · Paperboard, colored paper, finds

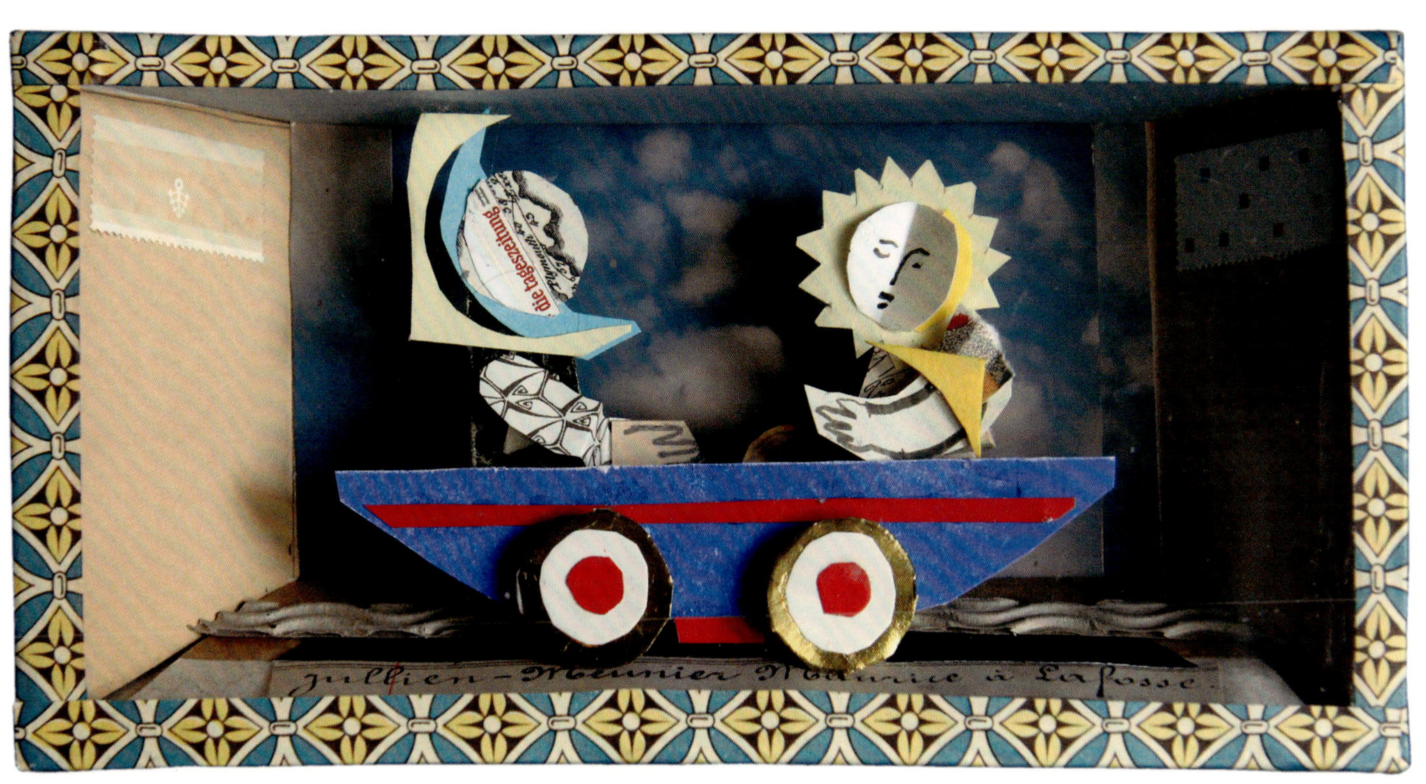

Heribert Schulmeyer · *Sister Sun & Brother Moon* · 10 × 19 × 10 cm · Paperboard, colored paper, paper finds

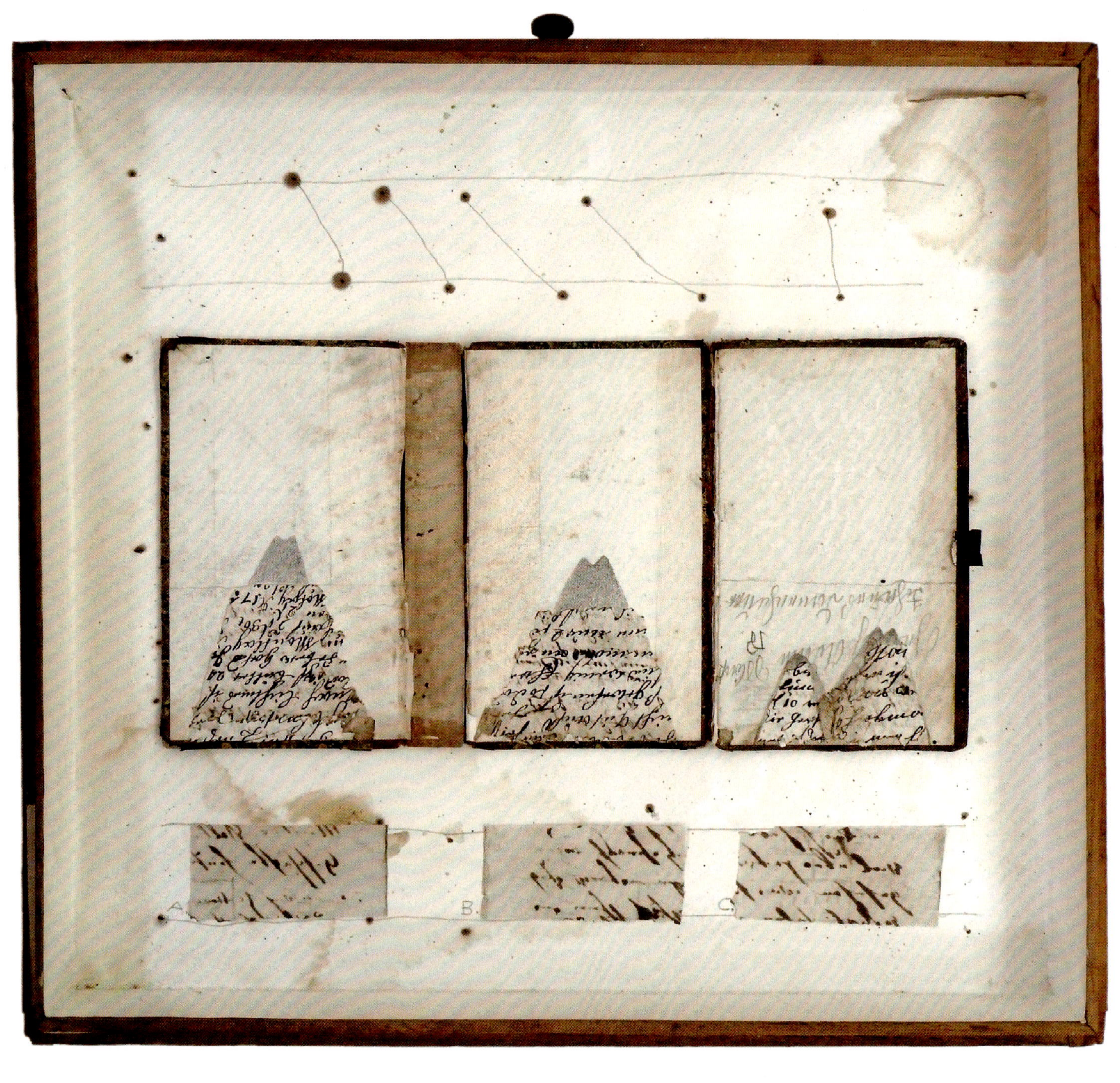

Peter Schlack · *Untitled* · 39.5 × 44 × 6.5 cm · Old book covers, sheets of writing paper, pencil drawings

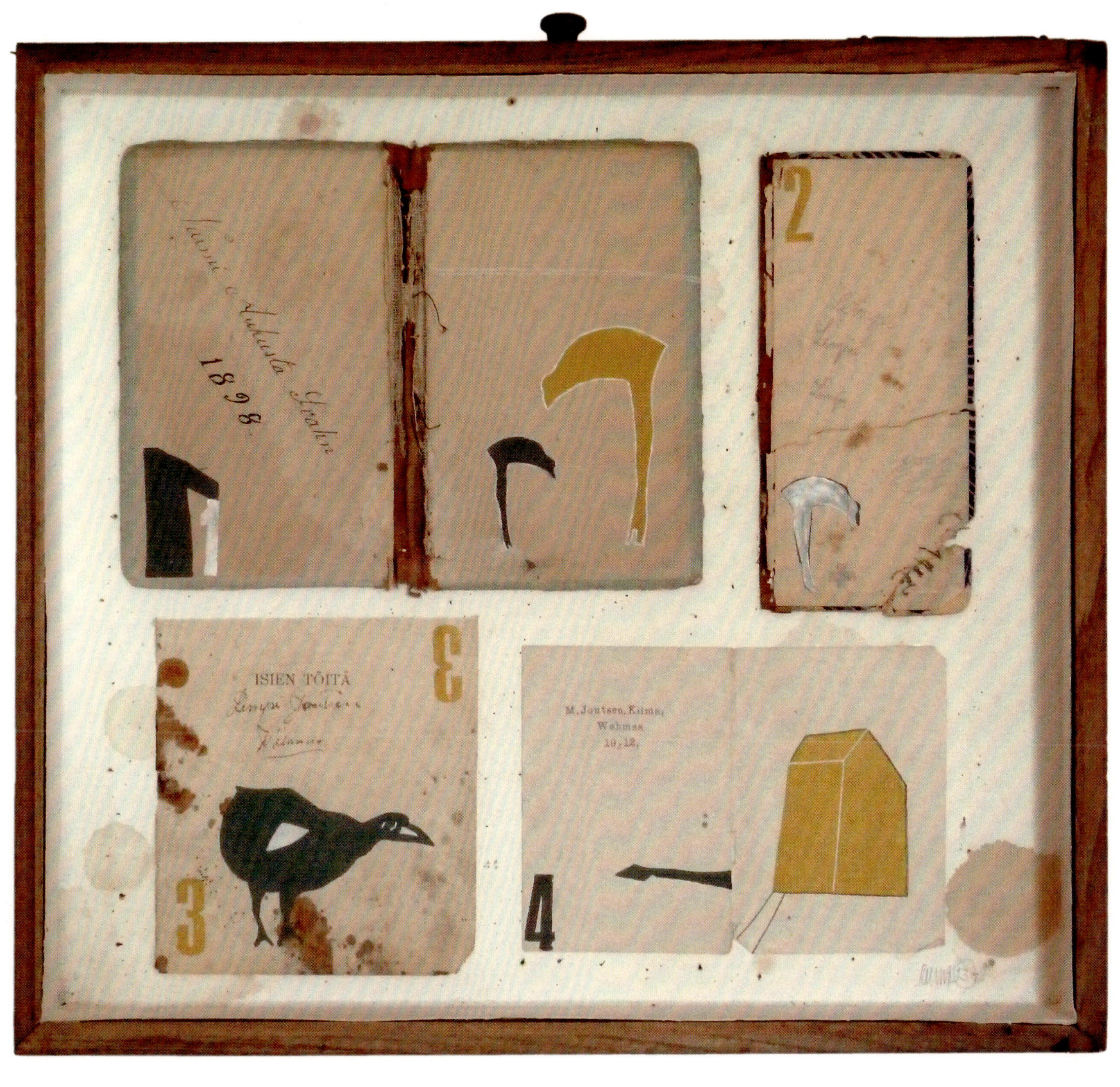

Peter Schlack · *Untitled* · 39.5 × 44 × 6.5 cm · Linoprints on book covers and old papers

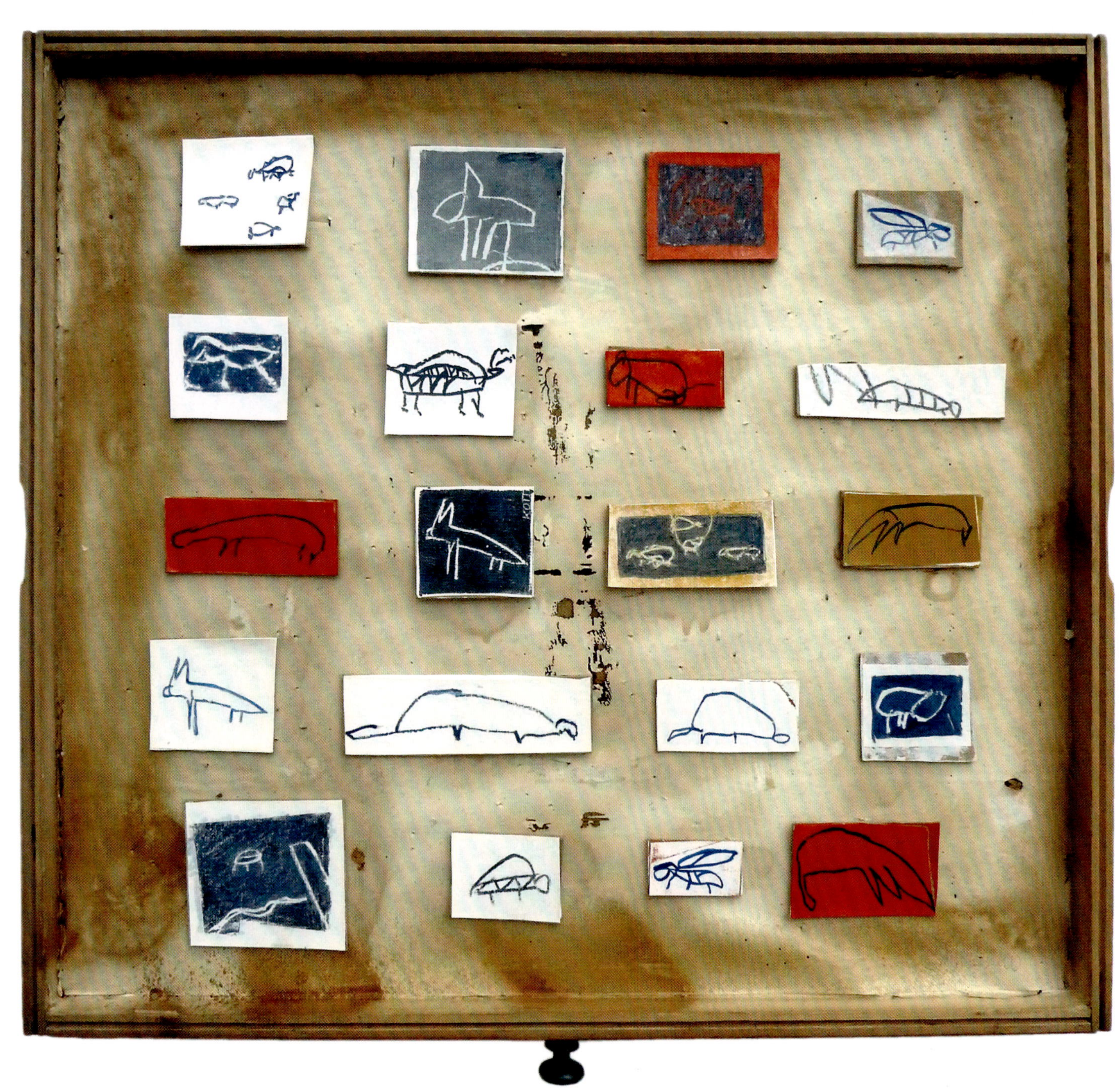

Peter Schlack · *Menagerie* · 40 × 45 × 6 cm · Transfer prints

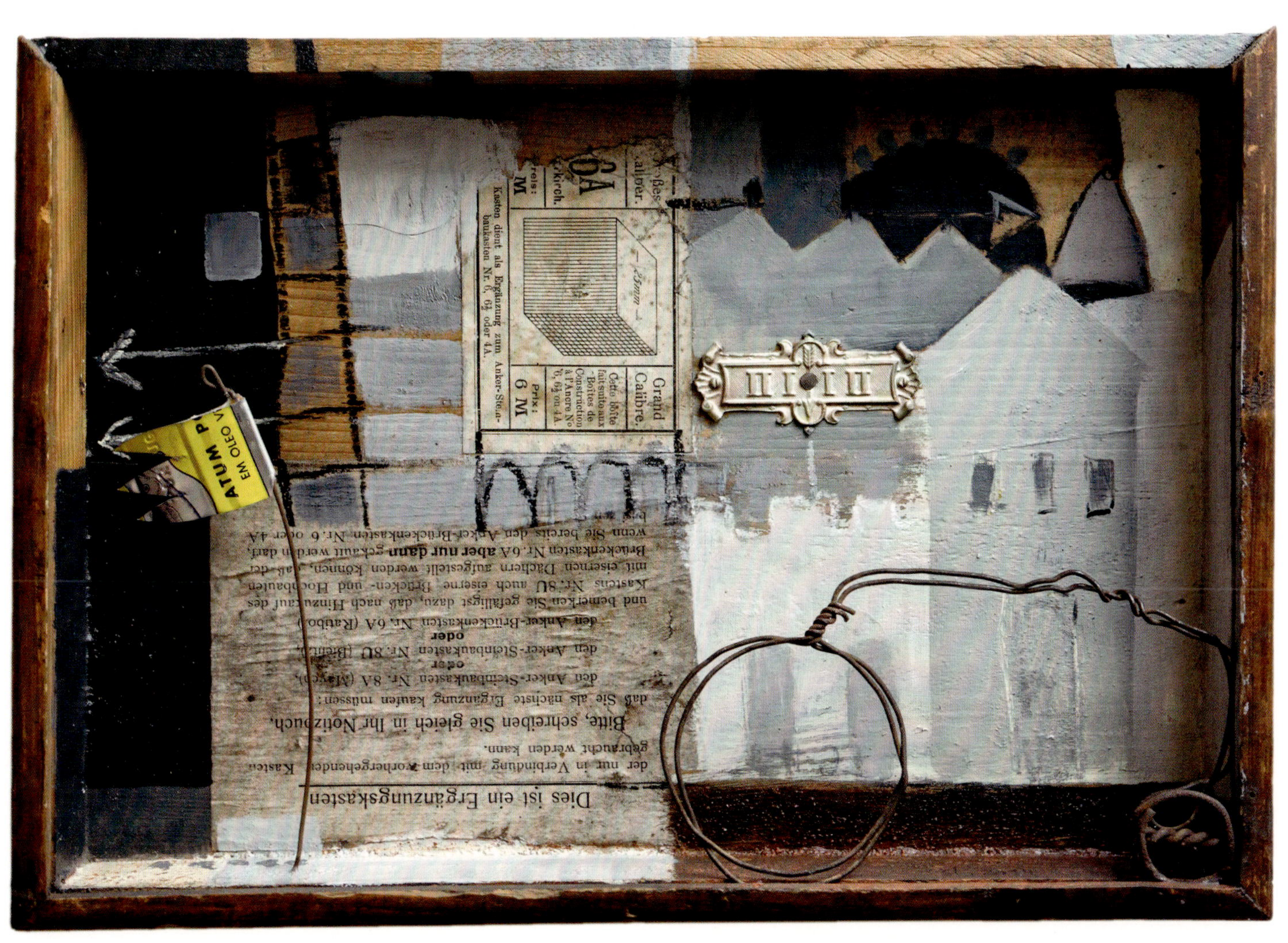

Annemarie Steiner · *City* · 22.5 × 33 × 4 cm · Painted wooden box, paper, wire and metal finds

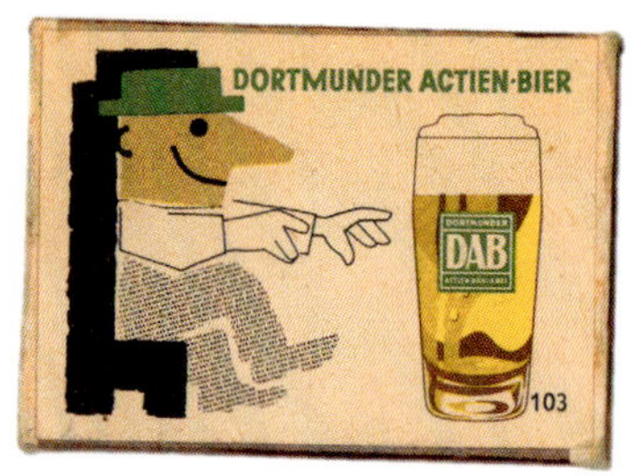

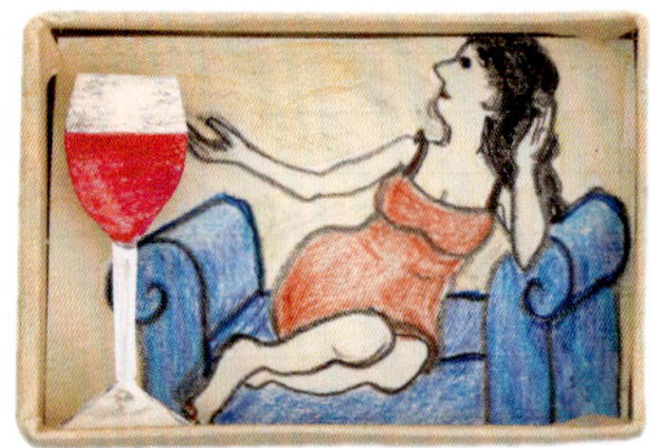

Beer + Wine · each 3.6 × 5.2 × 1.3 cm

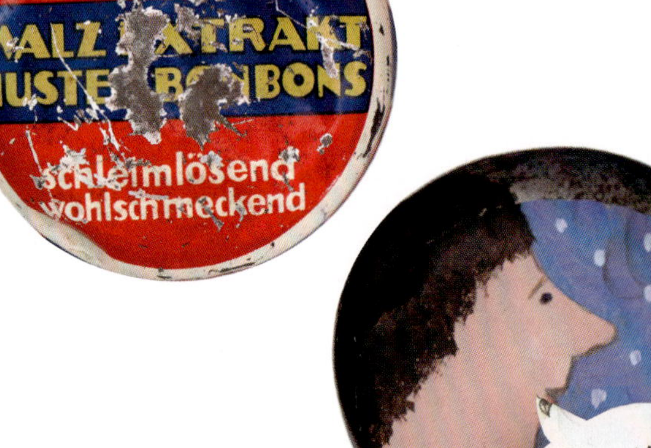

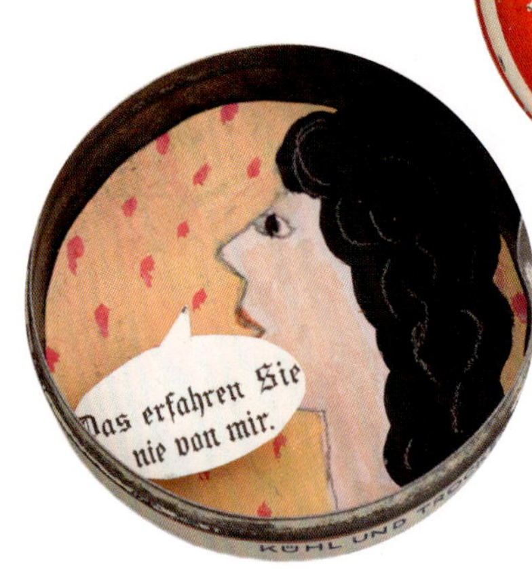

Dialogue · Diameter 6.5 cm · Candy tin (front and back)

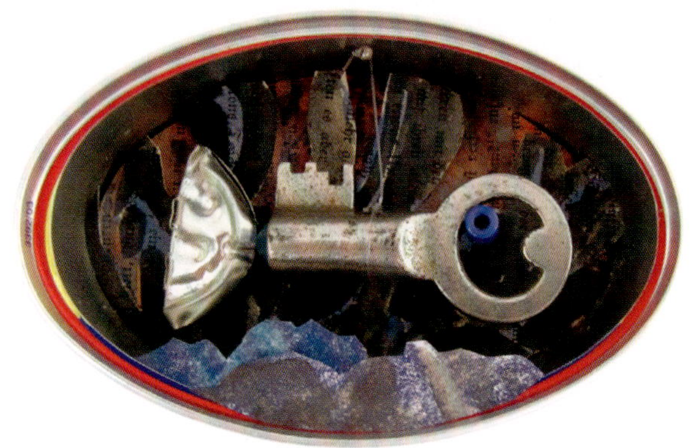

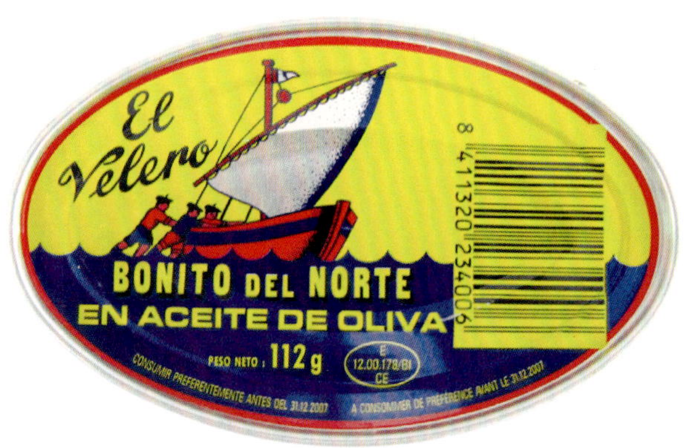

Annemarie Steiner · *Canned Fish, Species-Appropriate* · 7 × 11 × 3 cm · Fish can, key, paper

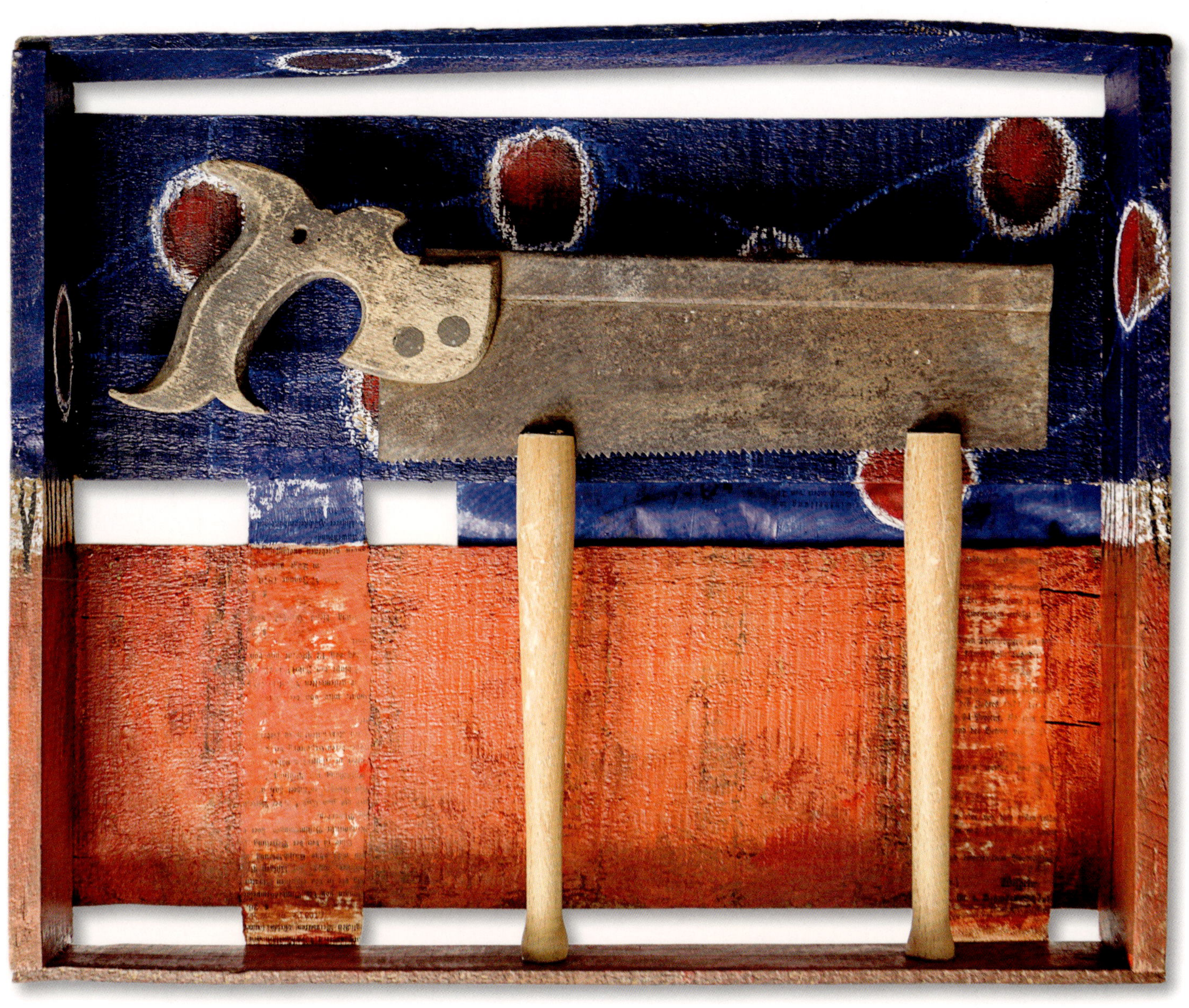

Annemarie Steiner · *Saw Animal, Reading* · 35 × 44 × 6 cm · Painted wooden box, saw, wood finds

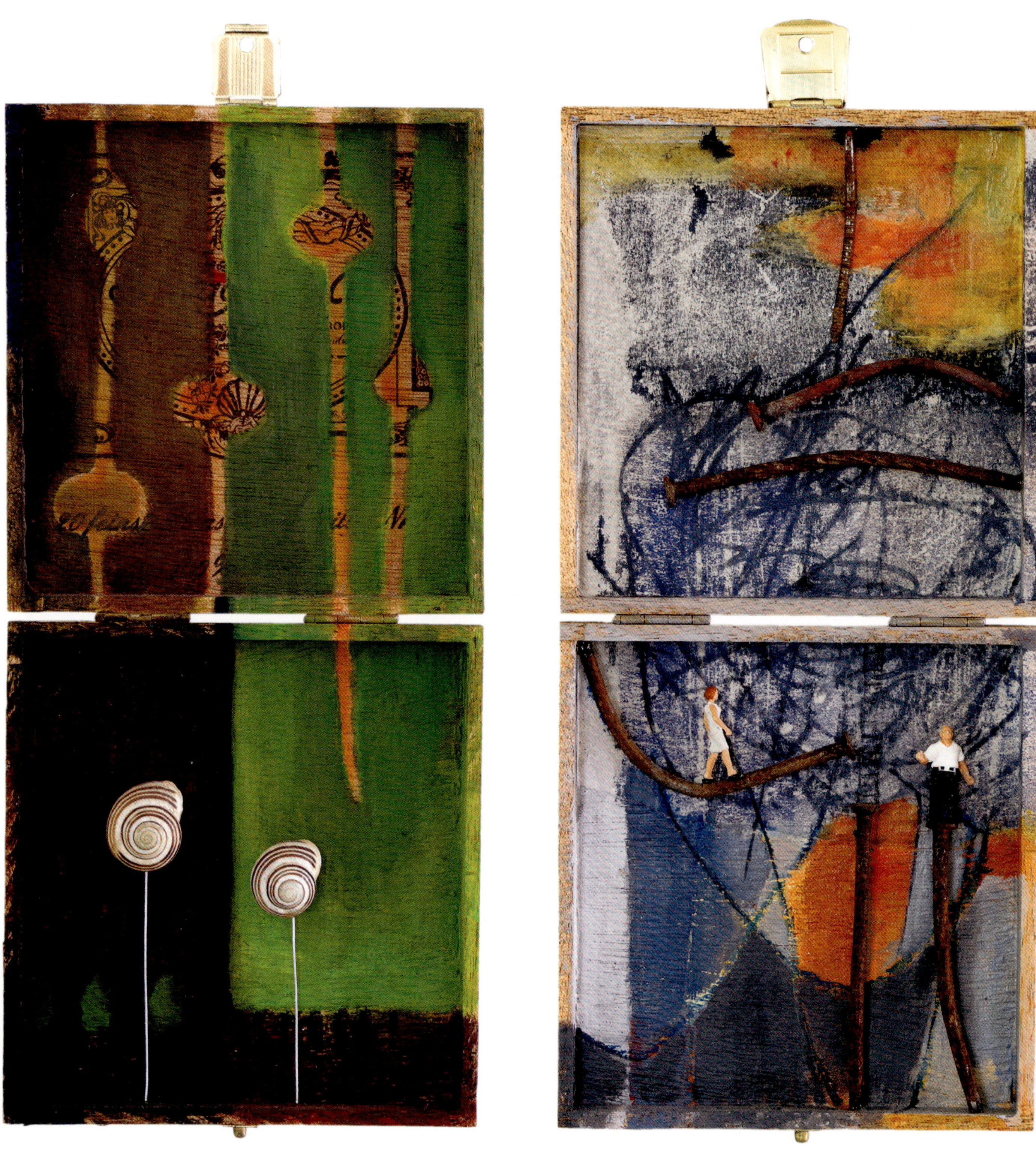

Annemarie Steiner · *Untitled* · 21 × 10 × 1 cm · Painted cigar box, snail shells
Detours · 21 × 10 × 1 cm · Painted cigar box, model figures, nails

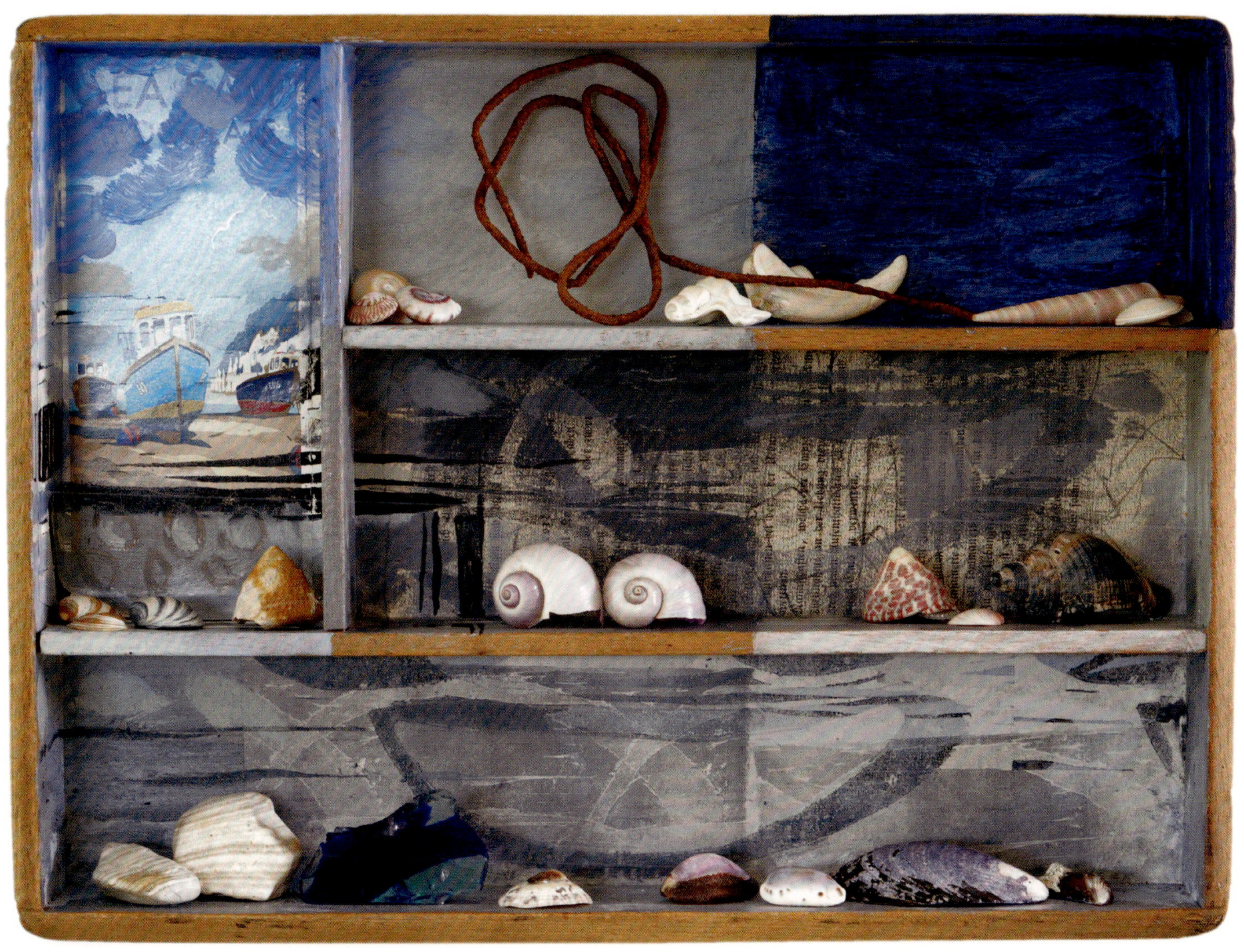

Annemarie Steiner · *Flotsam and Jetsam* · 23.5 × 33 × 5 cm Painted wooden box (mixed media and paper finds) for variable vacation memories

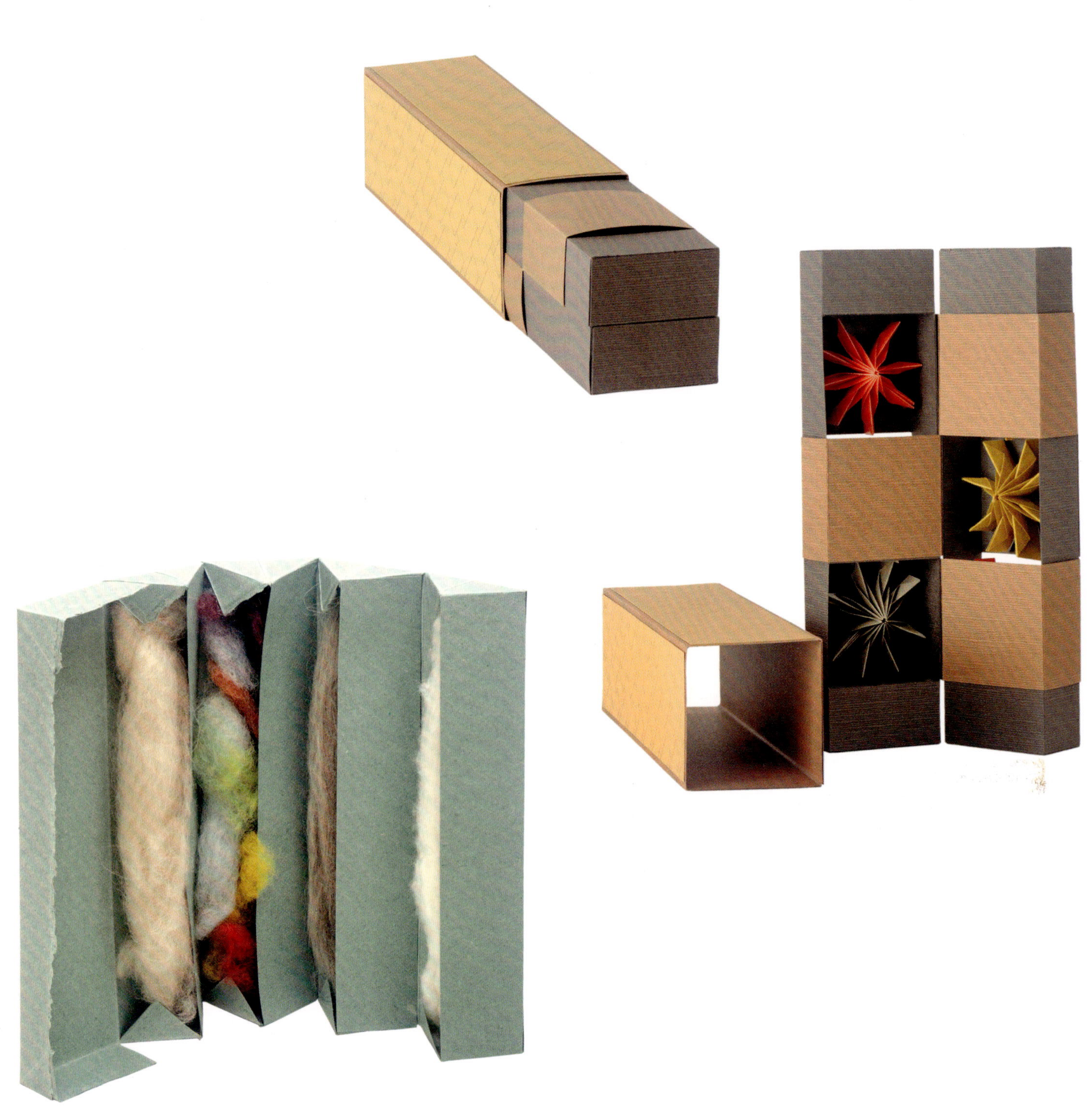

Hedi Kyle · *Star Box* · 25 × 6.5 × 6.5 cm | *Cabinet of Curiosities with Slipcase* · 20 × 10.5 × 2.5 cm · Paper

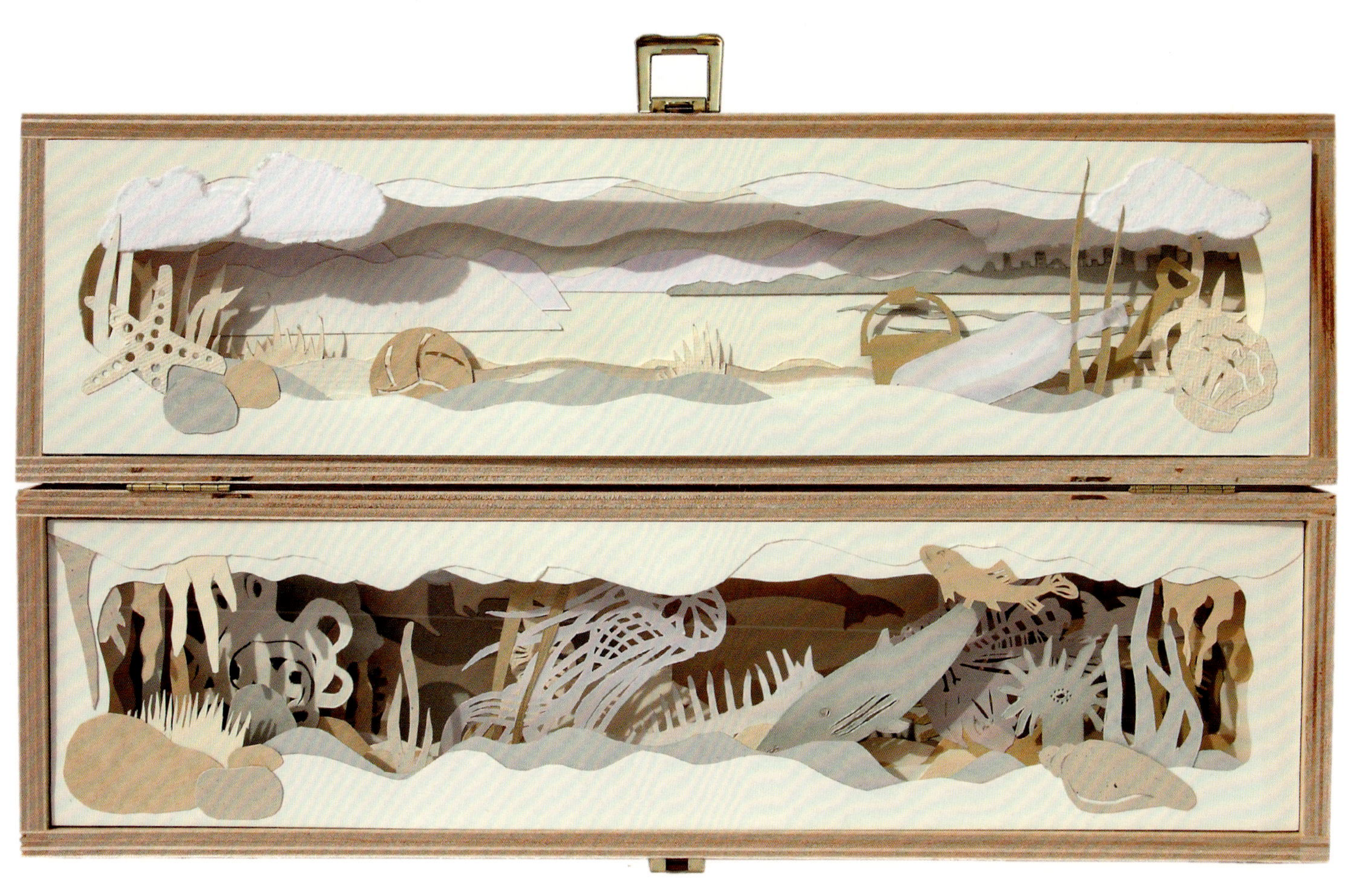

Dagmar Reiche · *Bottle Mailing Box* · 21 × 38.5 cm (open) · Collapsible cut-paper diorama in wine box

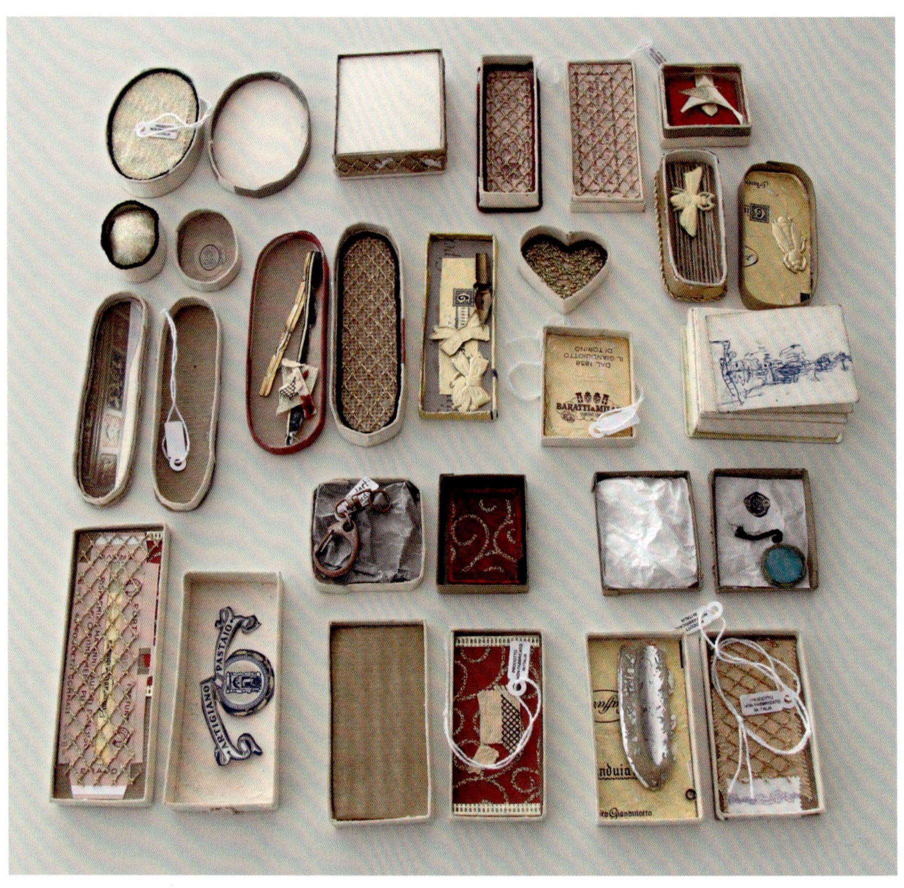

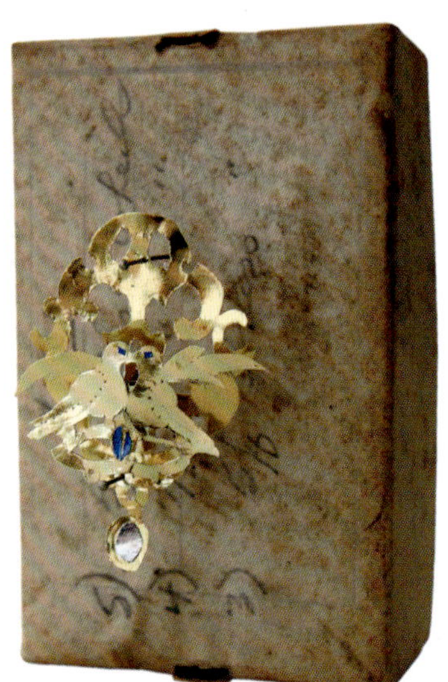

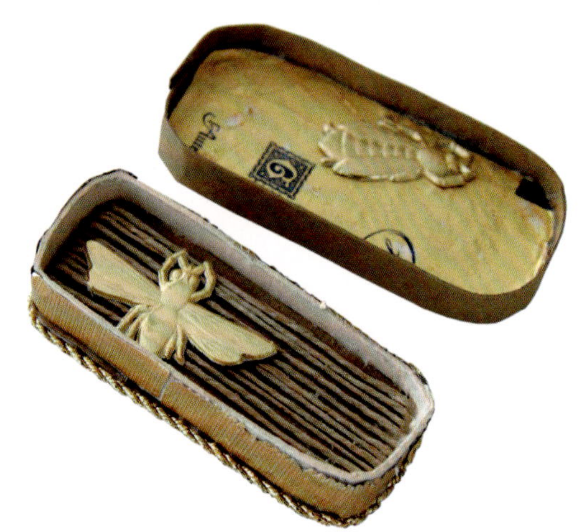

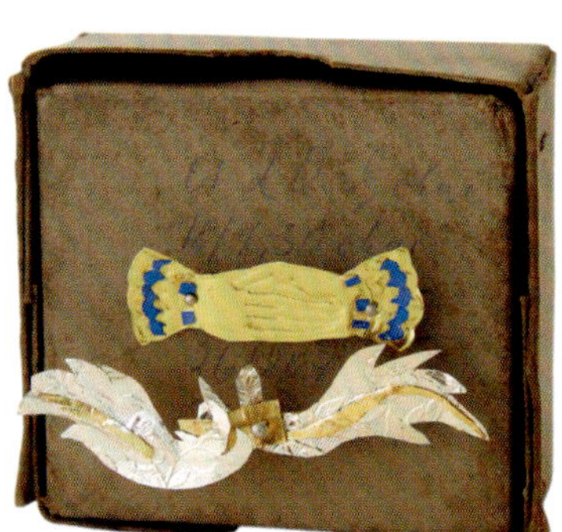

Barbara Räderscheidt · *Venetian Jewelry Collection* · 10 × 7 × 3 cm | each 2 × 6.5 × 2 cm | 6 × 7 × 3 cm
Paper, cardboard, gray paperboard, various small pieces

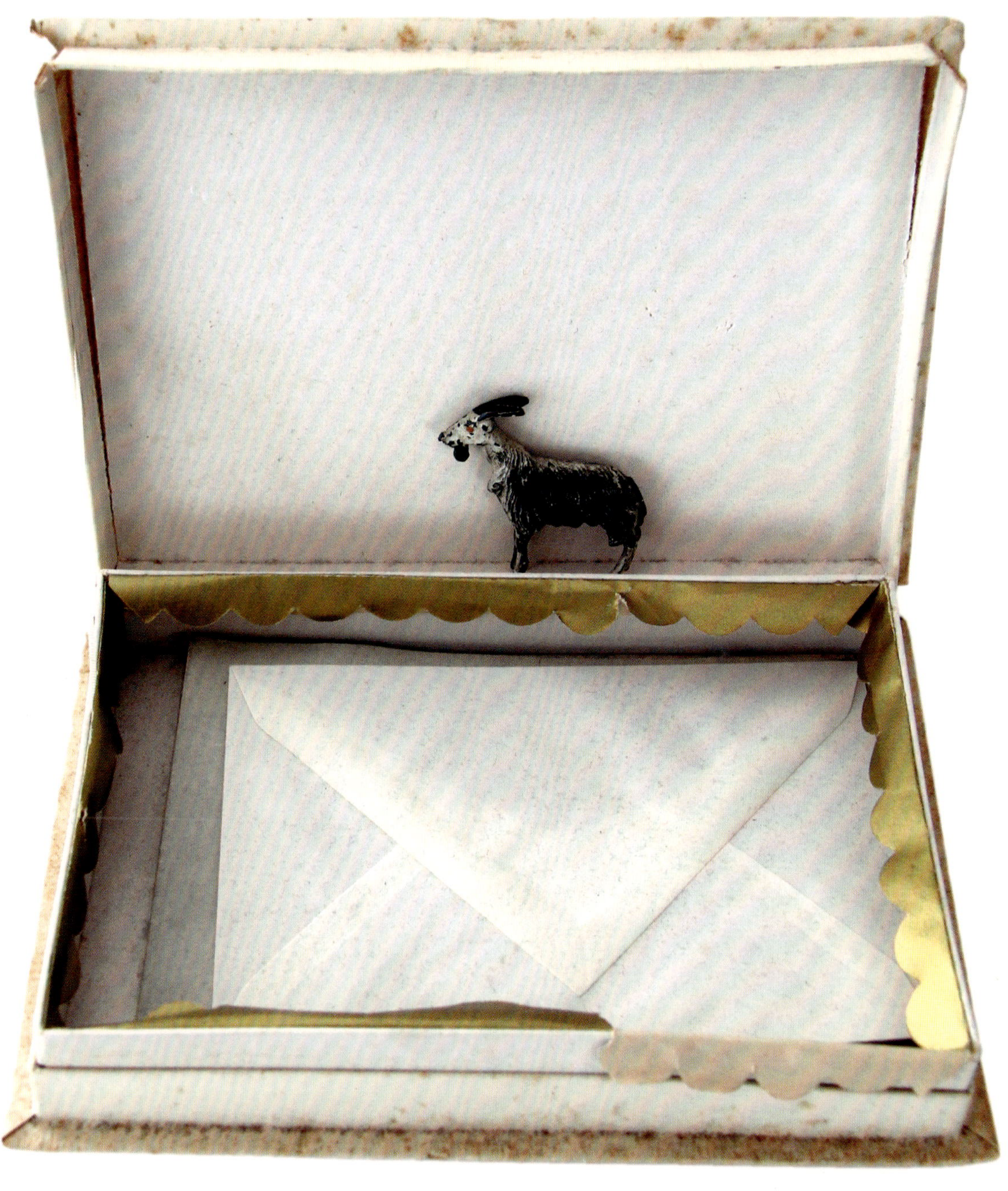

Barbara Räderscheidt · *Confidential and Obsolete* · 19 × 12 × 2.5 cm (flipped open)
Gray paperboard, gold paper, envelope, finds

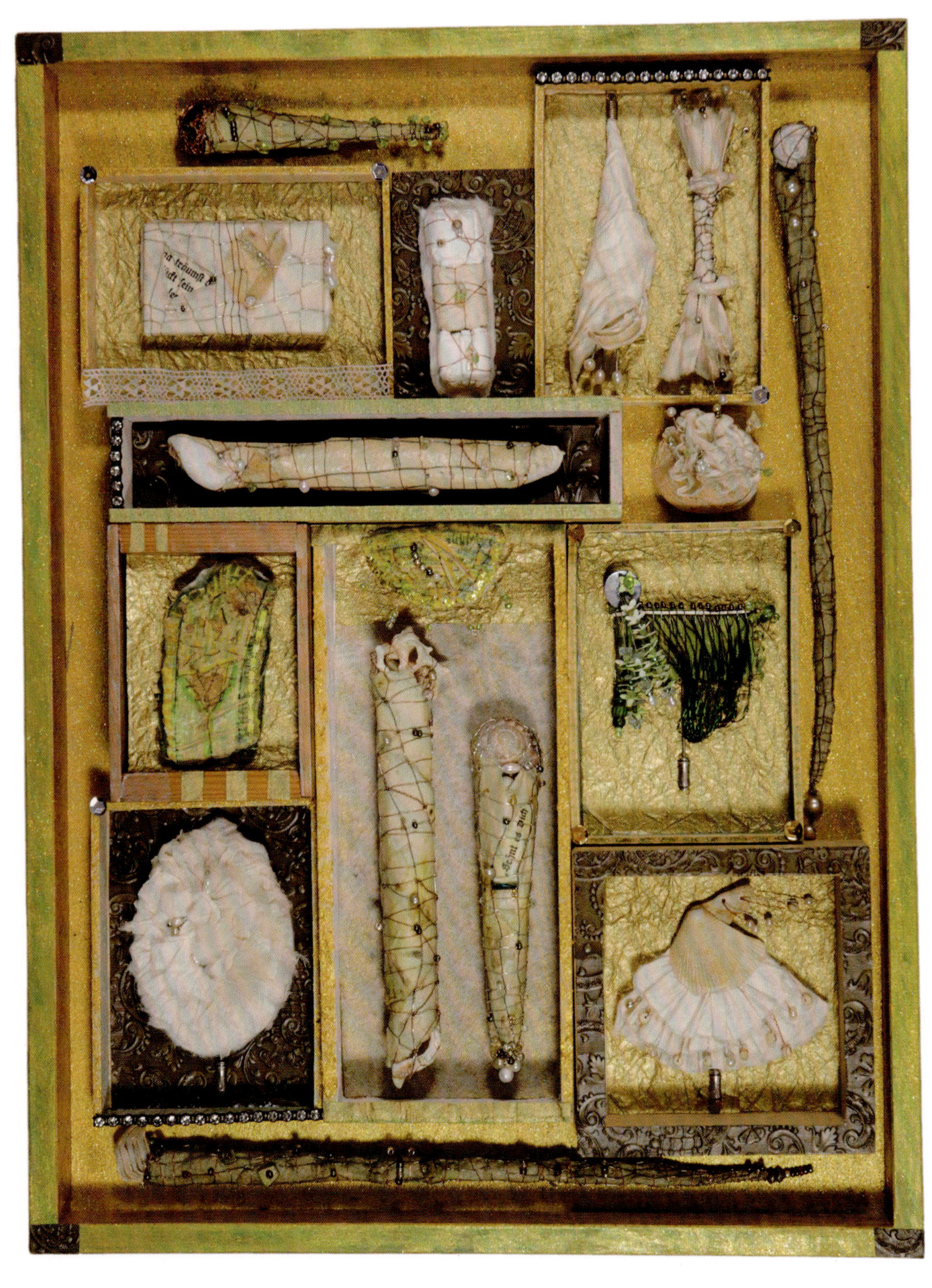

Sabine Ammann · *Cabinet of Curiosities Jewelry* · 39.5 × 30 × 3 cm Small wooden box, painted and collaged, conserved jewelry made of paper, wire, natural materials

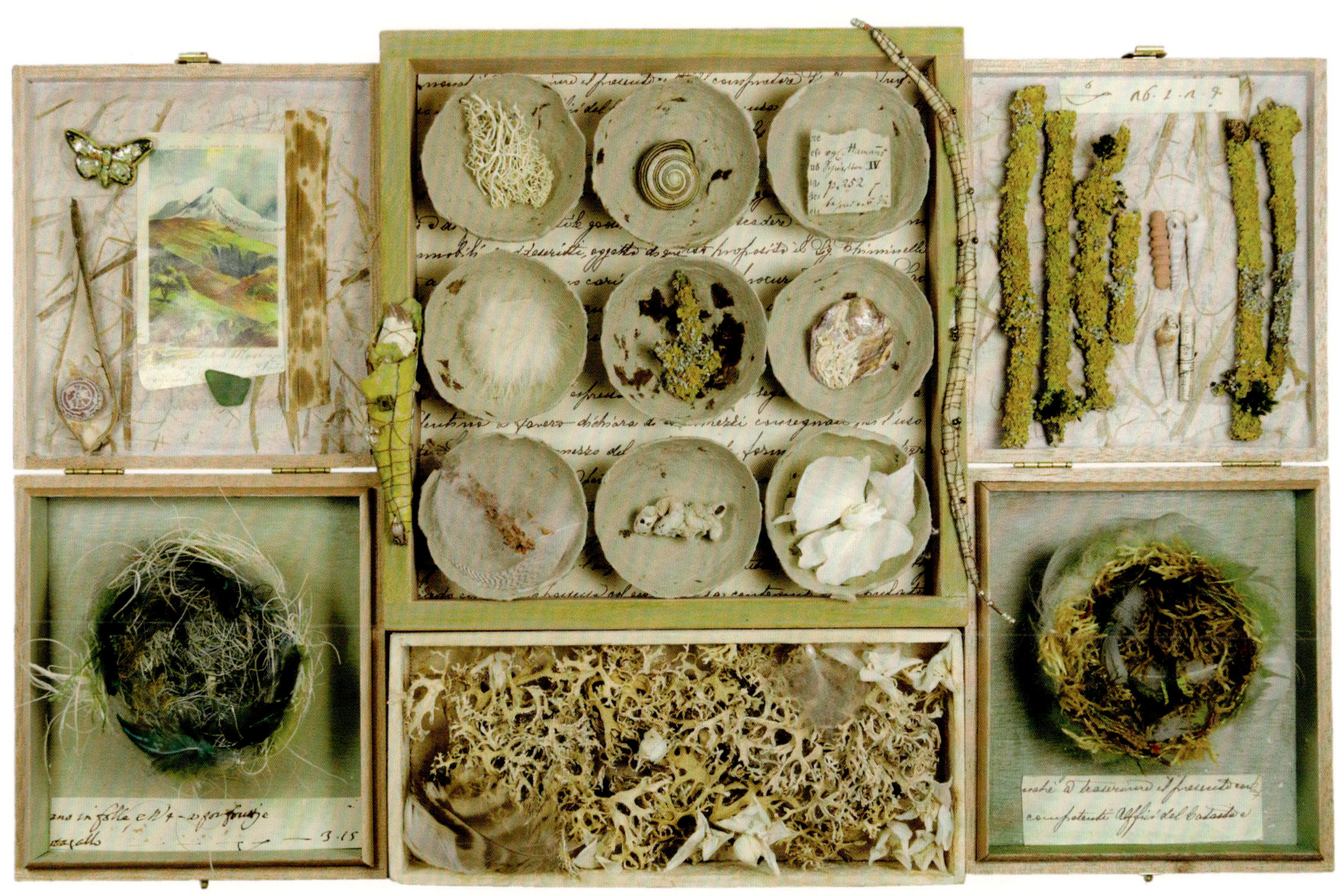

Sabine Ammann · *Nest-Box Expedition* · 28 × 45.5 × 4 cm · Cigar boxes and other wooden boxes, paper bowls, finds from nature, grass paper, fragments of writing, paper ornaments, handmade nests of yarn, wool, hemp, textiles, cotton wool, feathers

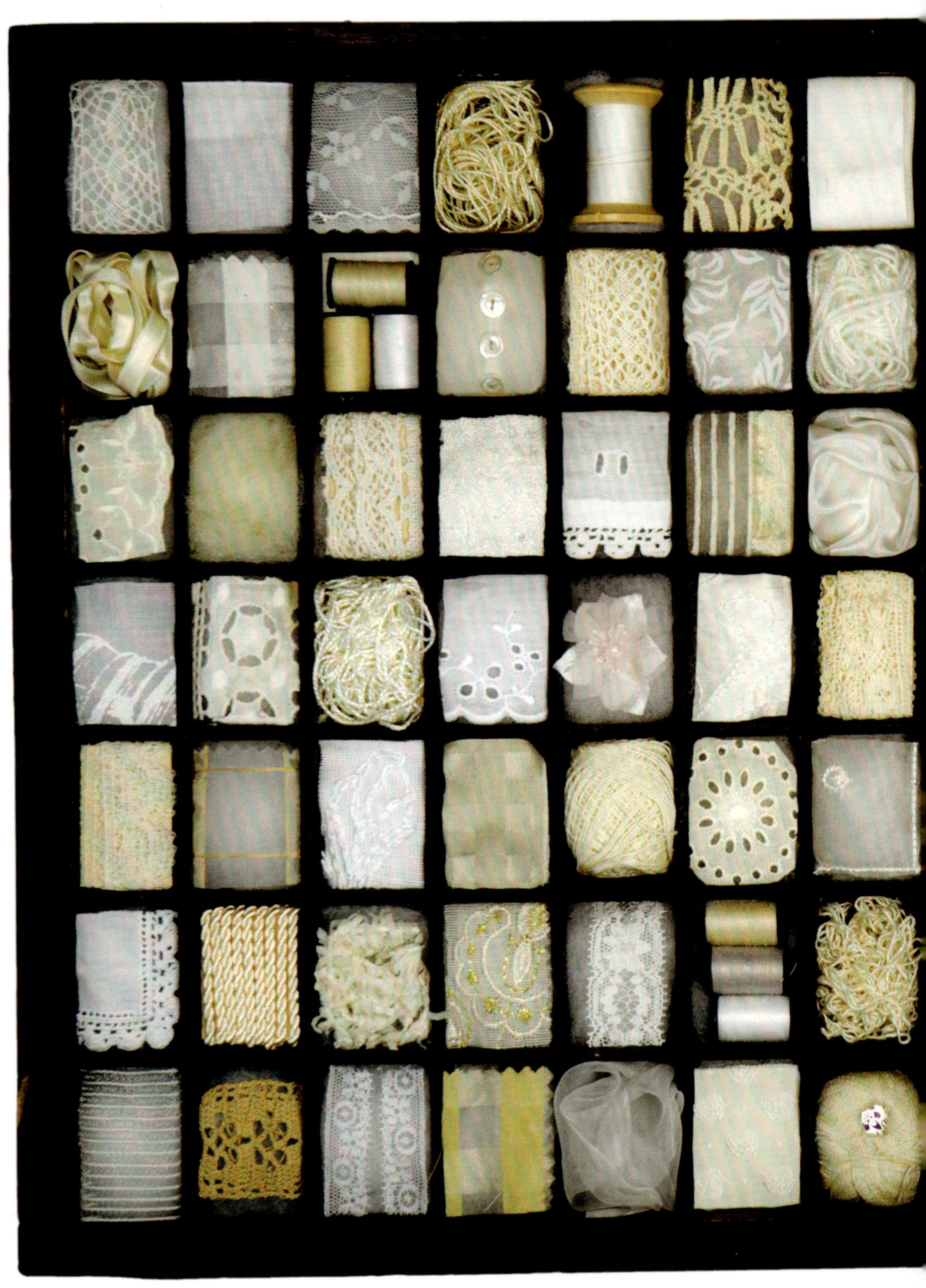

Sabine Ammann

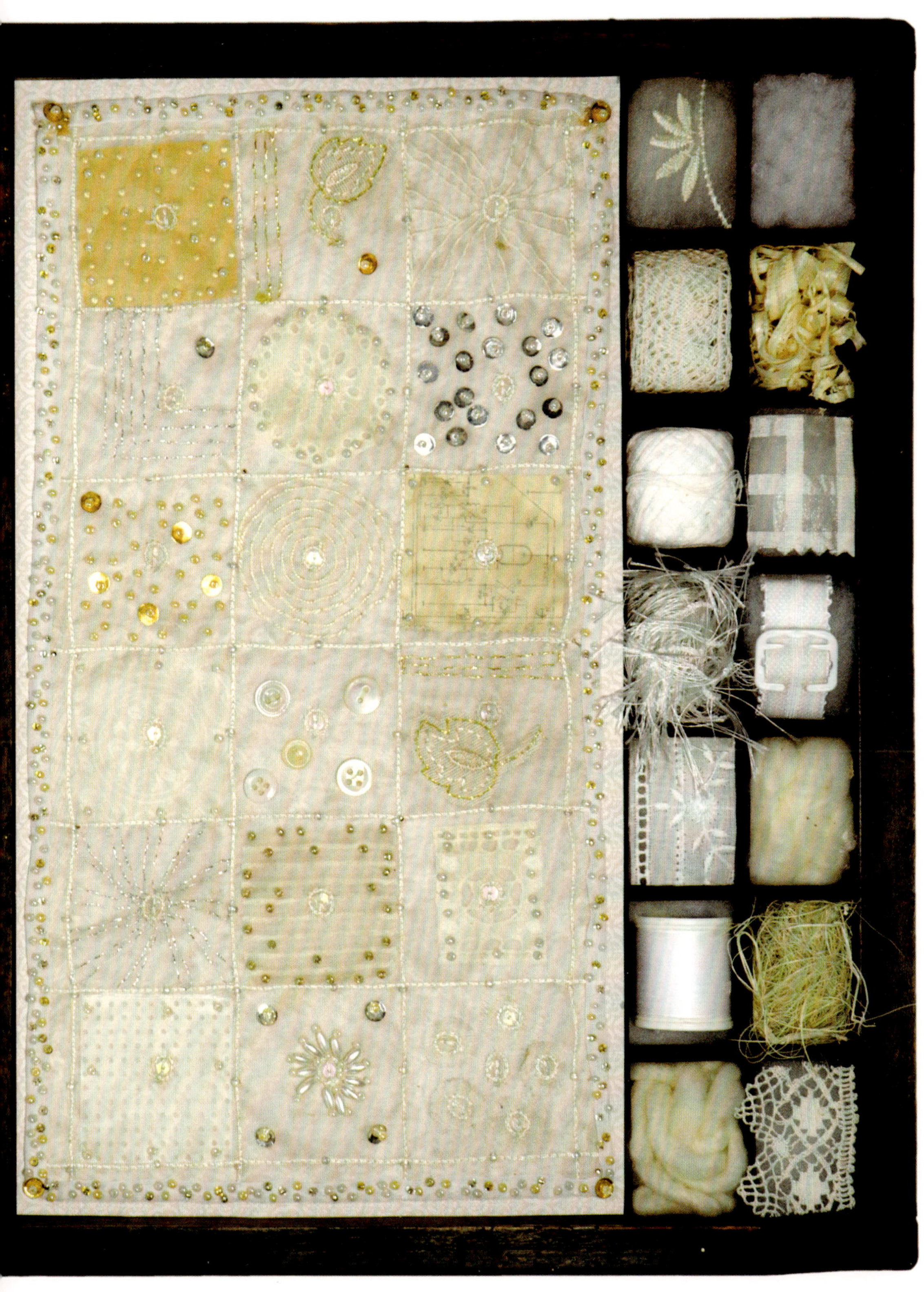

Cloth Samples Case
35.5 × 54.5 × 3 cm
Old type case, hand embroidery, collection of textile materials

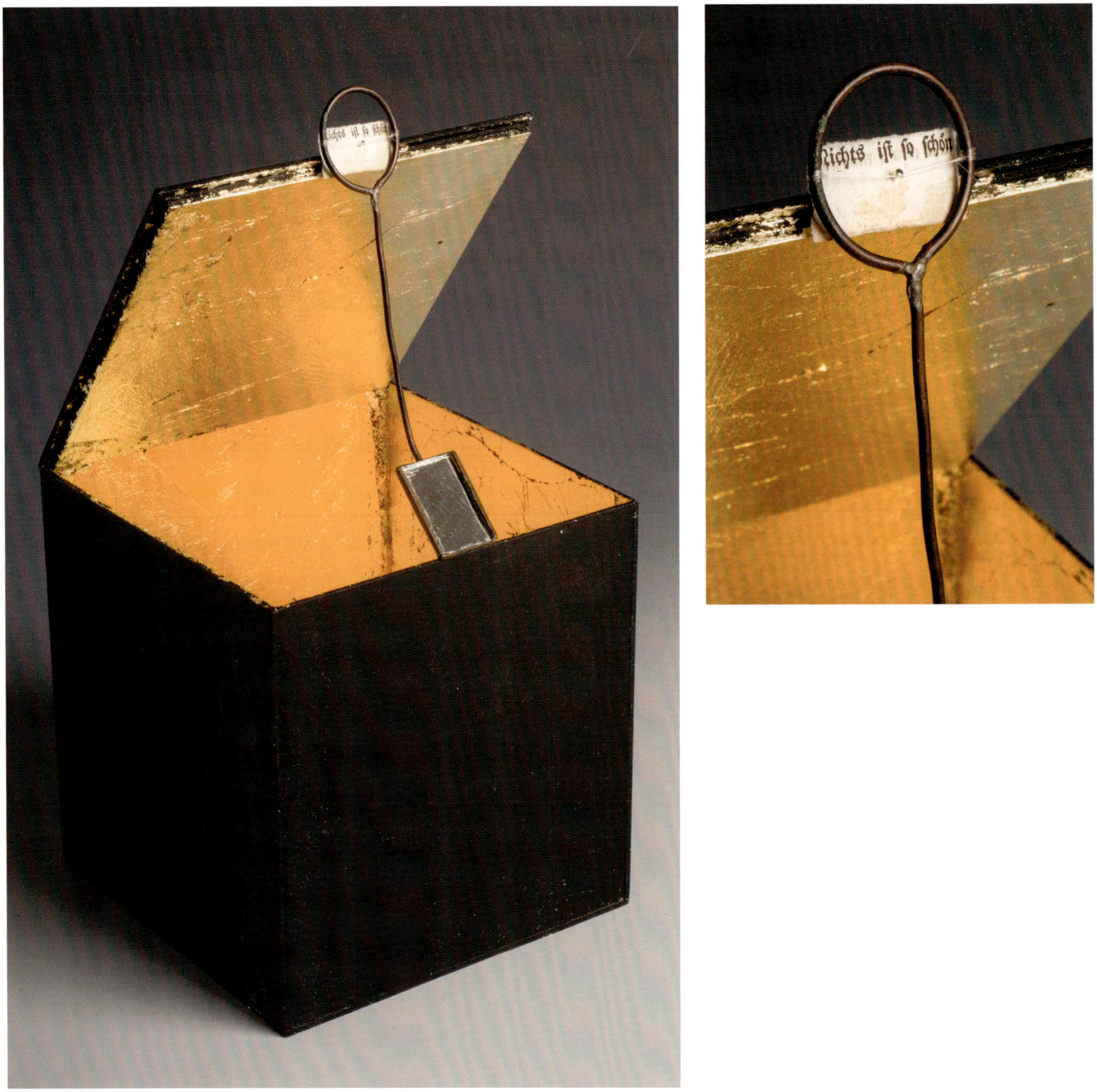

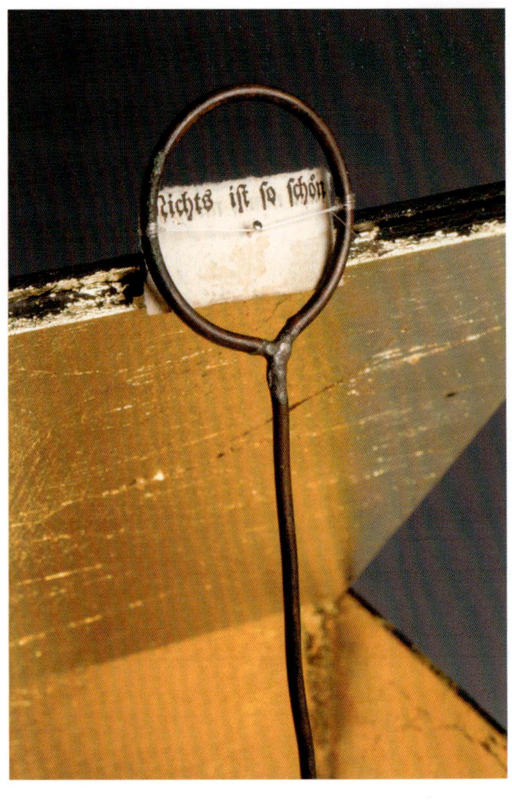

Marí Emily Bohley · *Nothing is so beautiful* · 15 × 15 × 15 cm · Object with mirror and gold leaf

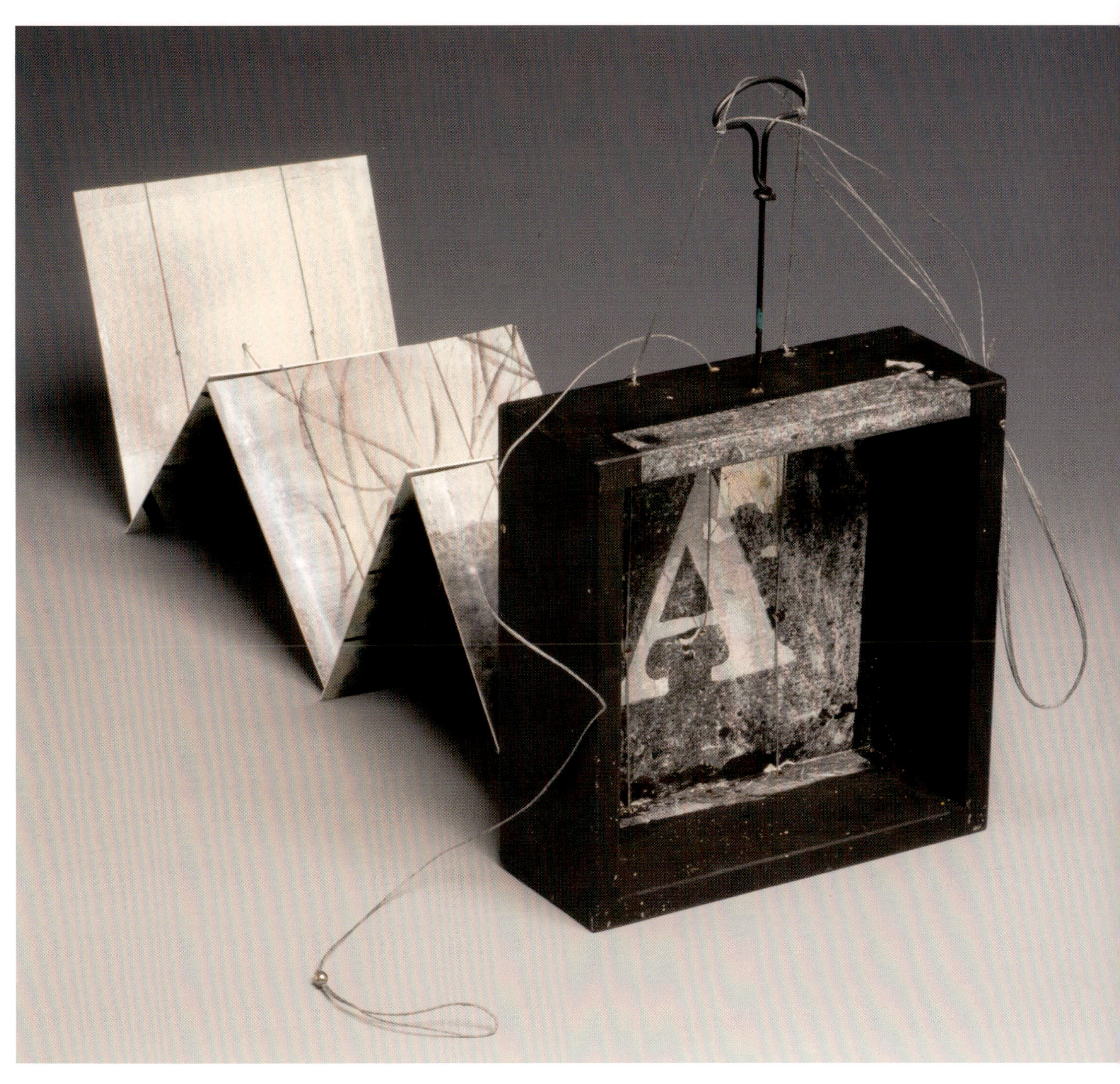

Marí Emily Bohley · *If you say A, you must also say B* · 15 × 15 cm · Book object with collage

Artist Biographies and Box Philosophies

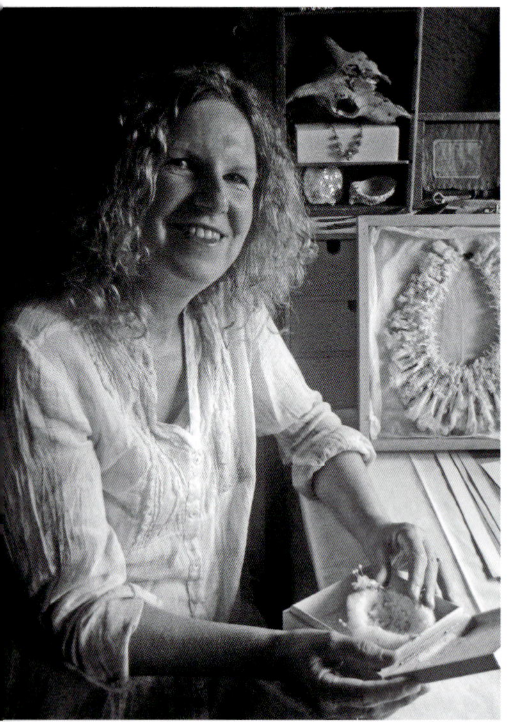

Sabine Ammann

Born in 1960, raised in Thuringia, and a diploma in art education. In addition to professional activities and family, time and again she worked on her own handcrafted projects, which soon led from ceramics to paper and textiles. Her paper jewelry has been displayed in exhibitions in Germany and Austria.

She lives in a wild and creative garden paradise in Naheland (Rhineland-Palatinate).

"In my boxes, I have the wonderful opportunity to bring two loves together: the happiness of working with my hands in a sensual way and the passion for collecting valuable things of no value and conserving them.

"Every box project means a dwelling for my 'creatures.' These can be pieces of jewelry made of paper or textile mixed-media objects, which I join together with finds from nature or small treasures from my stock of collectibles. This often yields poetic stories that always also tell about the conservation and appreciation of both things, as well as of craftsmanship skills. I use boxes and cases of all kinds, often combined together. The selection is always based on the unique paper or textile items I have made which I would like to imbed in a protective refuge while including the other ingredients.

"At the same time it is important for me to bring balance and calm into this work, which corresponds to my inner harmony and quiet way of working. My studio is in a wild garden kingdom, and my work is unthinkable without a close connection to nature and inspiration from it. But also emotions that are reminiscent of travel memories or dream images."

Marí Emily Bohley

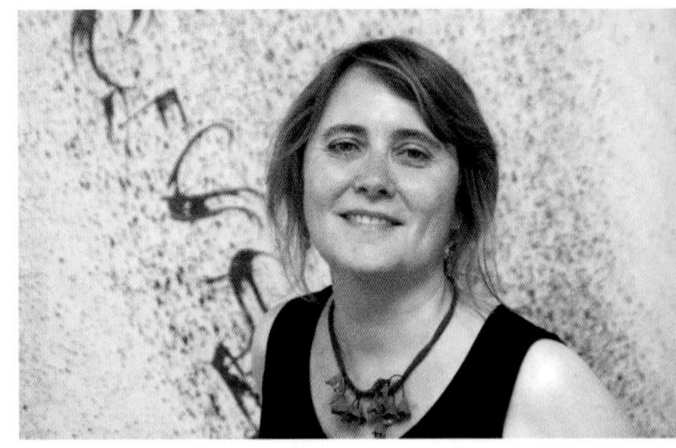

Born in 1973, the daughter of a Czech father and a German mother, she grew up in Halle an der Saale. At an early age she wanted to become a bookbinder, but 1989 brought new possibilities with its awakening of freedom.

After traveling through Morocco, Nepal, Tibet, and South America, she studied philosophy, art history, and social education before returning to bookbinding. From 1996 to 1999, she studied at the Roehampton Institute London; in 2000, she opened Blue Child studio and store gallery in Dresden. Calligraphy and bookbinding are combined in her own unique way in her works and artistic activity throughout Europe.

www.mari-emily-bohley.de

"I like to combine traditional with newly devised techniques. At best, I find myself in a river of inspiration that carries me forward. This leads to new ideas and results that are often surprising for myself. Artisanal perfection is only the foundation, not the goal.

"A work interests me only if it contains something hidden—a history, experience, or mood that can be experienced through the style, material, and white space. If the result tells of feelings and yet preserves its secret, then I feel the work is successful. In the work shown here, 'Nothing is so beautiful,' I am playing with the potential to refer the glance in the mirror to yourself, or to connect it with the glitter of the gold. The work 'If you say A, you must also say B' is the implementation of a glib sentence, to which a certain gravity can also adhere."

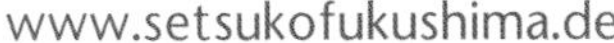

www.setsukofukushima.de

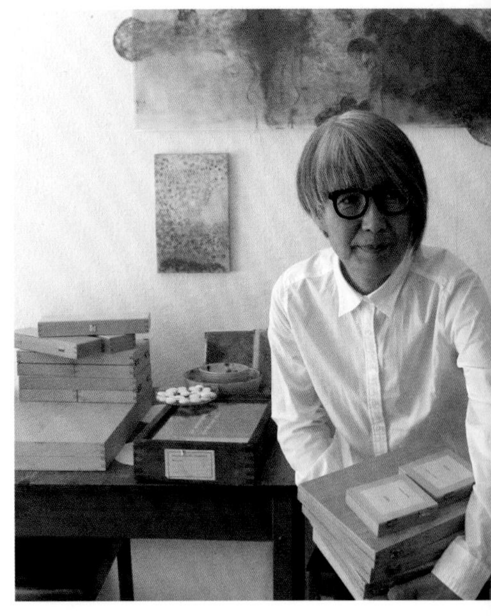

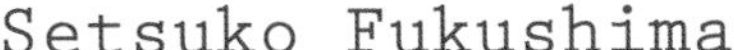

Setsuko Fukushima

Born in Japan. Studied fine arts / oil painting in Tokyo (Musashino Art College). Has been living in Germany since 1983. Numerous exhibitions at home and abroad and works in public ownership.

"My works are preparations with which I preserve what I encounter.
They are a kind of laboratory experiment through which I get on to things myself.

As a child, I created my 'world' in paper boxes.

Even then I was a collector. Stones, wood, seed pods, earth . . .

Yes, I even saved earth from my grandfather's garden in a small wooden box and experienced a surprise when I opened it later. Collecting and observing were my important daily employment—and things have remained that way ever since . . ."

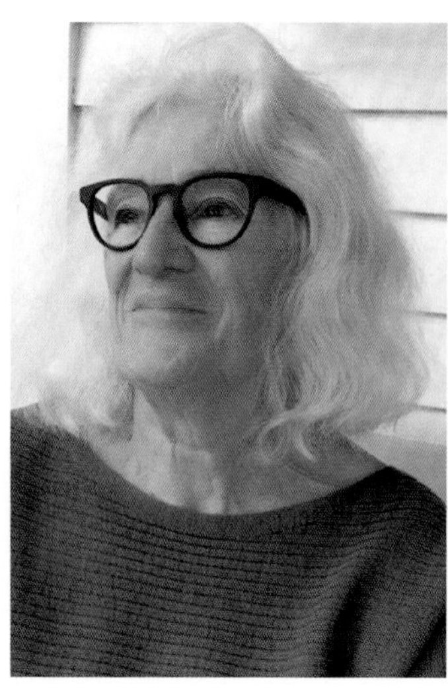

Hedi Kyle

Born in Berlin and studied at the Werkkunstschule [College of Applied Arts] in Wiesbaden. After a long stay in Greece, she immigrated to the United States and worked first as a graphic artist before concentrating on the conservation of old books.

In dealing with historical book structures, she discovered her interest in developing other new and contemporary forms. She also researched unusual materials and techniques, which she has been consistently teaching in her workshops for forty years. Today, Hedi Kyle lives in the Catskill Mountains, New York. Her small, offbeat studio is a perfect place for continuing to experiment, for folding, and for figuring out whatever you can do with paper.

"Boxes, tins, cartons, and similar containers play an important role for me. Bought readymade or recycled, they are sitting everywhere on my shelves. There they safeguard a hodgepodge of materials just waiting to be rediscovered and used. Remodeled or made myself, many of my containers already announce their contents from their exteriors. They have the effect of a kind of front yard or vestibule, making you curious about what's in there before you get to see anything. Signals of different kinds, which of course should also provoke surprises: contrary to expectations, something completely different is revealed when you open it. The whole thing is a spectrum of strange objects or collections of valuable but also worthless things. It's always an exciting moment when I experiment with them and develop new versions.

"The 'Wunderkabinett' ['Cabinet of Curiosities'] pictured here works like a flexagon, or a Jacob's ladder. If you turn the two connected boxes in the opposite direction five different views are revealed in sequence. Three of them are the side panels, while two views each present three openings with six different displays. A matchbox slipcase holds the two closed boxes together.

"The 'Star Box' is so named because it forms a four-pointed star when it is opened and closed. There used to be velvet-lined wooden folding boxes that were part of the equipment of an old sewing machine. They were used to hold additional parts. Such a box was the inspiration for my 'Star Box.' When closed, the four compartments form a square held together by the cover."

Rolf Lock

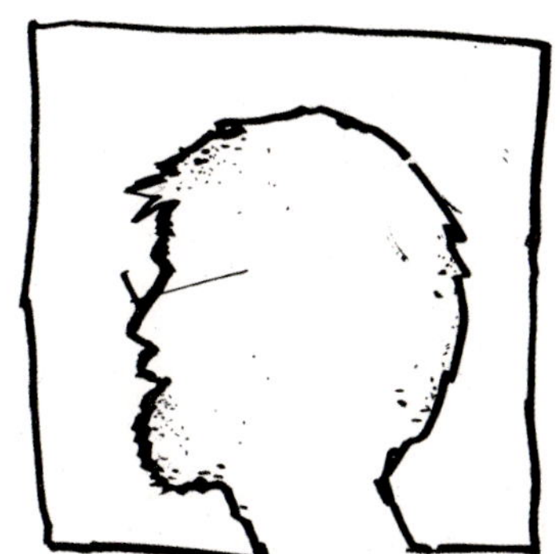

Before 1993, he was a script lithographer, draftsman, and object designer—after 1993, a book artist with a penchant for calligraphy, quirky nonsense literature, and beautiful, crazy books—with and without letters.

"In the box ...

When the box opens, it provides insights into other worlds.

Perhaps amusing or mysterious; there are many possible adjectives.

In any case, things live here in the midst of a world that is protected all around.

These things may belong to imaginary collections or they are part—concealed and puzzling—of a world theater.

To be able to work in the small artistically in an unlimited variety; that is what creates the appeal of this medium."

Barbara Räderscheidt

Studied art, English, and pedagogy. Studio in Cologne; since 1987, exhibitions and paper theater with the "Kölner Kästchentreffen" ["Cologne Box Gathering"] artists' group. Exhibitions of her own artistic works since 1990.

In 1997 she curated her first museum exhibition, and since 1998 she has been working closely with Daniel Spoerri. She is president of his Italian foundation "Hic Terminus Haeret—Il Giardino di Daniel Spoerri" ["Here is the end of all things—the garden of Daniel Spoerri"] and has been managing the Spoerri exhibition house in Hadersdorf am Kamp (Lower Austria) since 2010.

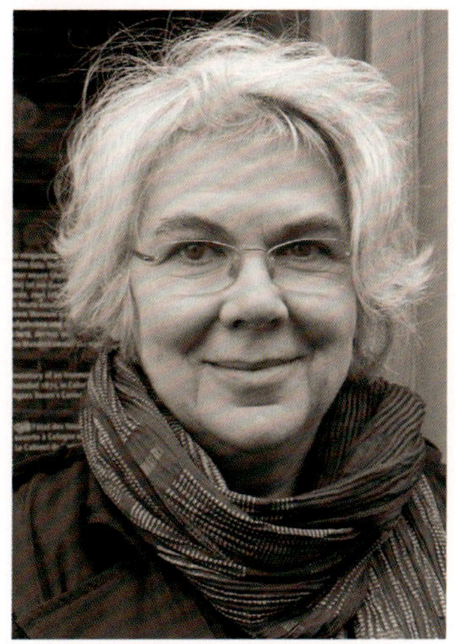

"'You will always find something to put inside,' an object artist friend remarked. In my work, case and box finds are often the impetus for an object; sometimes they become one.

"For the example shown, I had seen a stall with old pieces of jewelry at a flea market in Venice. The old jewelry cases for rings, brooches, earrings, and bracelets were more interesting than the jewelry, carefully marked with tiny labels. I tried to reconstruct the abundance of forms and stories in that I made small cases of paperboard and paper (while in Venice on a grant). At first I thought of putting jewelry in them, but that was superfluous."

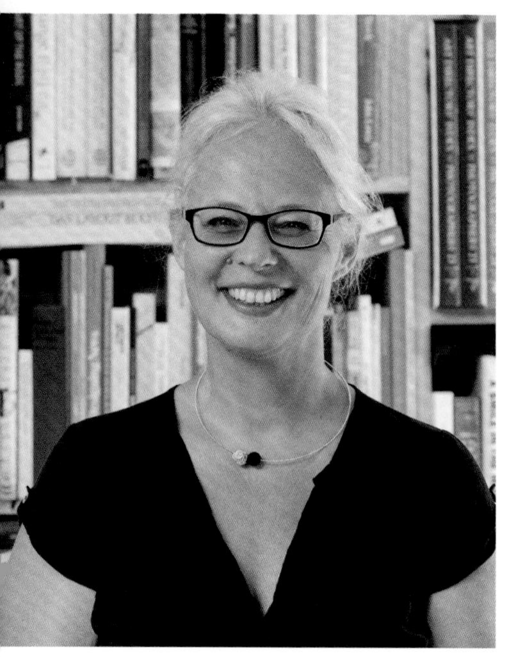

www.designreiche.de
www.kunstreiche.de

Dagmar Reiche

Studied medicine and worked as a physician in England and Germany; subsequently trained and worked as a lecturer at a medical publisher; freelance since 2004. Part-time intermedia studies; in 2012, completed her MA in arts and design, then founded "designreiche" (graphic design, book design, illustration, and paper art).

"The love for boxes—out of the box.

"See the bigger picture. Think beyond the box. Broaden your horizons. All this is only possible if you move out into space.

"I love working with paper: Folding it, constructing pop-ups, developing paper mechanics, layering collages. To pierce it, to glue and to print it, to inscribe it, to paint and to tear it. Enhancements that use the space and let paper sparkle even more, that surprise and enchant you. Paper likes to work with other materials, with wood and cloth as close relatives, with thread and wire, or with totally different things.

"Despite computers, what I do is predominantly analog. Only when I use the space do I understand things. I have to grasp them to comprehend them, to penetrate them. And what is a carton, a box, a crate? A room in miniature format: Limitations so you are able to perceive potentials. Frames for windows or doors, the permeable membranes between interior and exterior. Or also walls that are inside and outside at the same time. Stereotyped thinking? No, not necessarily. Boxes are there so that you can step out of them, pass borders, 'Raum um Raum [zu] durchschreiten' (Hermann Hesse) ['we should stride from space to space']. Only those who think creatively, thus 'outside the box,' can fill the hearts of others with their art."

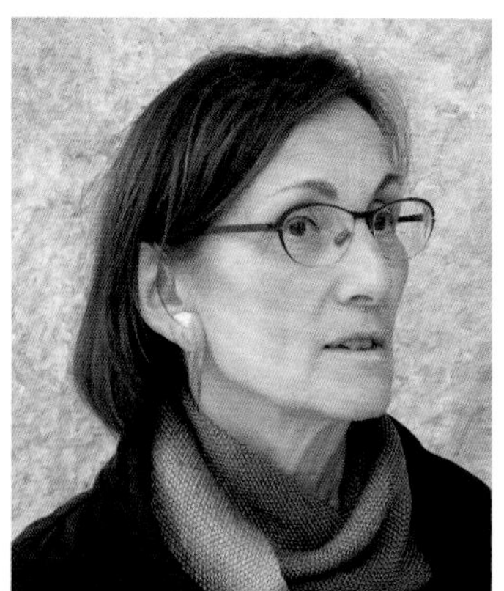

Barbara Sackermann

Born in 1945 in Lörrach. Trained as a goldsmith—master craftsman examination—and has her own workshop in Stuttgart. Devoted to archeology and art.

"For me as a goldsmith and collector, boxes are a familiar necessity. They provide valuable and, for me, an important protection and shell. From that which is useful, I have found an affinity: I collect boxes. Boxes with histories that connect with my own stories. Boxes preserve memories, give meaning to everyday life, and give space to strange beings. They awaken curiosity, encourage looking, and open your eyes to what is hidden. They surprise the child with play and poetry."

Simone Schäffer

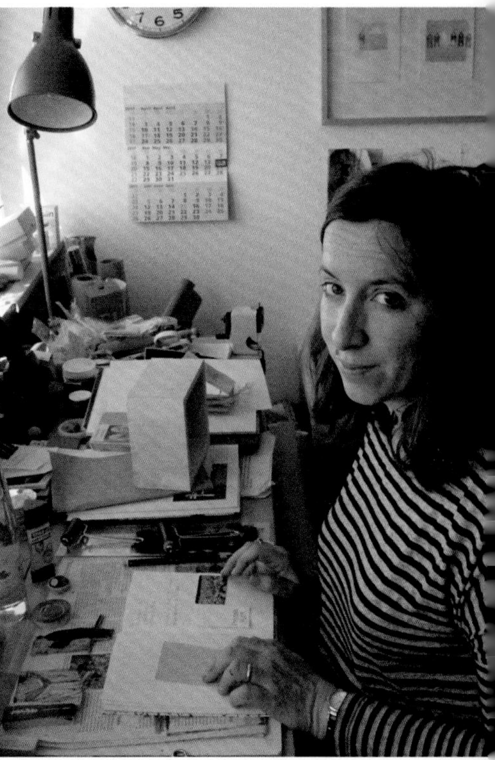

Born in 1973 in Ruit auf den Fildern. Interested in paper since childhood; loves and collects paper. Drawing, pasting, creating, sewing, mixing colors, printing, and collecting. Studied art therapy and is a member of the KüFi (Künstler der Fildern [Artists of the Filder Plain]).

"Homage to the small scale—I work in small scale—and always have. At first maybe unconsciously . . .

"While studying I was also supposed to paint in large scale. The teachers thought that otherwise I would restrict myself too much; that I should have more trust in myself; they thought the large format would be a kind of liberation for me.

"At the time, there was actually a large acrylic painting that did not mean that much to me, and the instructors were happy with this.

"Thereafter, I was able to return into small space. A box is a treasure chest full of precious little things, an interstice for thoughts and seasons, living space for finds, and a shelter for gems and words. It's like the container of an essence: compact—concentrated—protected."

Peter Schlack

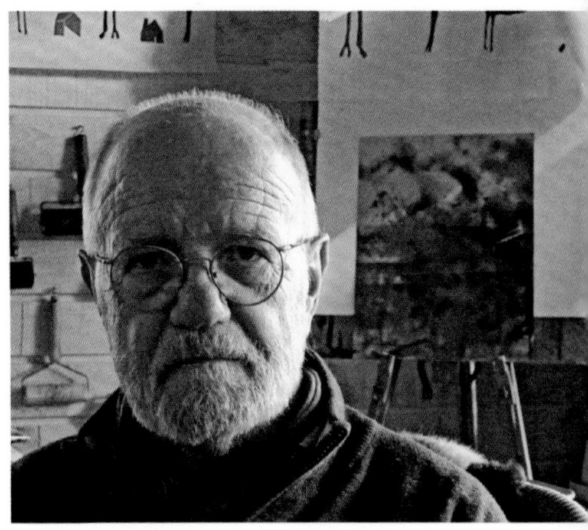

Born in Stuttgart in 1943 and grew up there. Apprenticeship as a lithographer. Studied social work. Since 1970, an active artist, painter, and writer.

Since 1975, he has had exhibitions in southern Germany, Finland, Norway, and Liechtenstein.

At the same time he founded a publishing house, with publications of poems and short prose in the Swabian dialect.

"I don't make my boxes myself; I find them at flea markets. They should not be new but rather have a history. That maybe has something to do with beetles or butterflies. Boxes in which important, strange, and whimsical things were kept. I integrate my printed or painted finds in them: old book covers, pages from a Finnish milk booklet, or book pages on which a child practiced writing his name. Traces that have survived marked with my symbols—images and legacies."

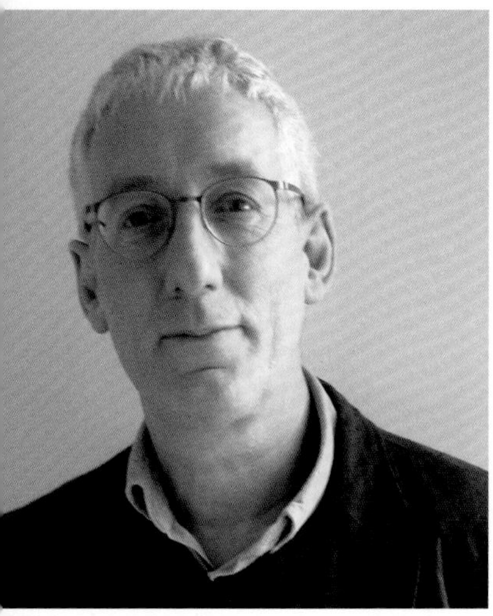

Heribert Schulmeyer

Born in 1954, completed his Abitur [secondary school final examinations] and studied art in Cologne. Since graduating he has been working as a freelance illustrator. First in advertising, then for "Sendung mit der Maus" ["Broadcast with the Mouse"] at the WDR (Westdeutscher Rundfunk [West German Broadcasting]), and then for many German publishers of children's books.
Cofounder of the "Kölner Kästchentreffen" ["Cologne Box Gathering"], an association of object makers and paper theater players.

"I can do almost anything with paper. I remember an early sense of achievement when, as a nine-year-old, I used gray paperboard and a whole tube of Uhu glue to painstakingly glue together my first double-decker.

"As an adult, I'm interested in narrative boxes that recall staged spaces, theatrical situations—cuttings from life.

"Also I like to use paper to imitate other materials, such as tin toys or spaceships. The playful narrative context is important for me. And the Uhu tube."

Uli Seitz-Sperling

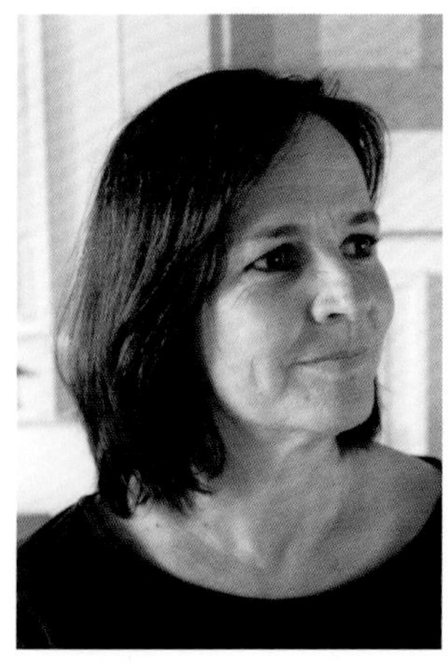

Born in 1958 in Stuttgart. Studied interior design, then had a professional focus on furniture design. A jewelry designer since 1987, initially using model-building materials such as wood, acrylic, and brass. After taking courses on goldsmithing, she also began working with precious metals in combination with the widest variety of "finds" and gemstones.

In 2000 she founded "formidabel," a small shop with a workshop in Stuttgart-Vaihingen.

"Small finds, which may be inconspicuous for some, mean a lot to me. To enhance and look after these, I came to the idea of framing them in miniature copper boxes (soldered as hollow objects).

"The warm, mottled copper adapts well to the small treasures from nature. Originally intended as a necklace pendant, the copper box suspended in the shadow box frame is presented in a protected space."

Annemarie Steiner

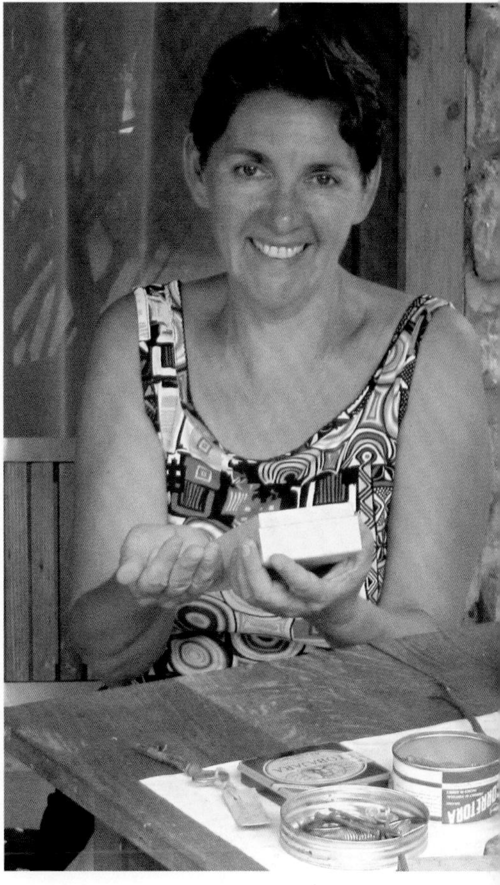

Is a graduate art therapist (FH) (Fachhochschule [University of Applied Sciences]); she lives and works in the Stuttgart area.
In addition to her work as a lecturer at a technical school for social education, she realizes ideas and projects as an artist and author.

Cartons, crates, and boxes. . .
"preserve, frame, and order things in a wonderfully soothing and beautiful way. Almost every little crate and each carton is an incentive for me to hoard them. Indeed, in every one of them there is an inkling, a promise of some possibly wondrous content. Just the very idea of what could be protected, wrapped, and hidden inside is enough to find the box beautiful in itself and to keep it. Already as a child I had this love for cartons and boxes.

"First there was a large, disused drawer under my child's bed which I filled with all kinds of stuff and in which I arranged and preserved my treasures—in smaller boxes. Later came the type case, in which I displayed and showed many small treasures, knickknacks, and kitsch next to each other in changeable positions."

And today?

"I still own some of my first boxes, drawers, and cartons—more have been added to them. Some of them I work on, paint, fill, and change. They become (three-dimensional) images or frame small scenes. Neither the boxes nor the materials that I worked on inside them were bought specially. Everything is 'found somehow.' I bring these old and newer, more or less used finds that have accumulated over time into new aesthetic contexts by using simple tools. It often takes a lot of time to organize the individual objects and snippets, to juxtapose them, to reject ideas to seek and to consider new ones.

"I do not work on all the boxes; some I need to hold all the old nails and screws, the wood scraps and wires, snail shells, buttons, and cutlery . . .Painting and printing inks as well as paper (remnants) complete my material pool. I am fascinated by the flexible and above all spatial possibilities that come from painting for designing boxes. Depending on size, shape, and depth, different elements can be accommodated and arranged. If a crate is lopsided and battered, it requires a different approach than a perfectly symmetrical carton. If it is torn through, perhaps has a lid, or if it is printed, then these features each inspire other designs. Thus, there is a new suggestion and challenge in every crate, every tin, in every carton, and every box."

www.annemariesteiner.de

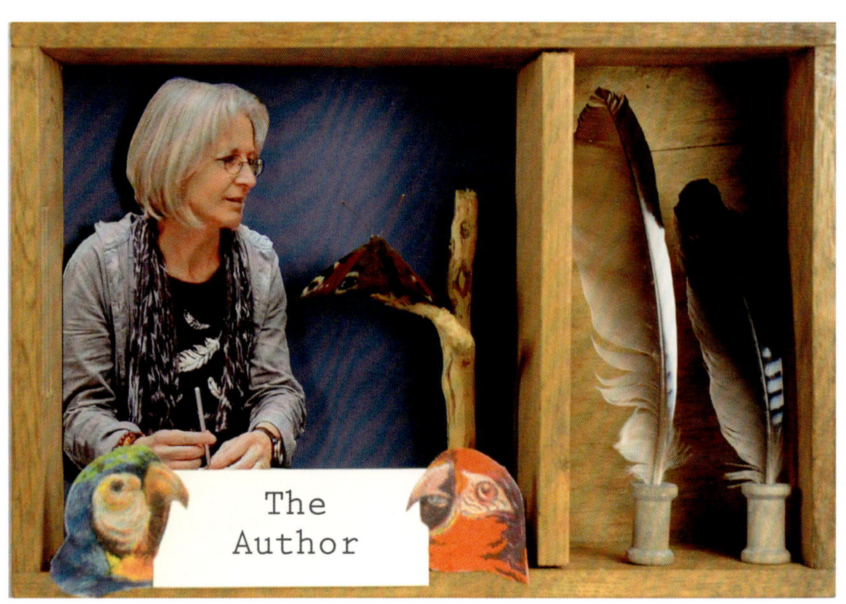

Marlis Maehrle

Marlis Maehrle loves paper, books, and all things handmade. She works as a freelance book designer and has been teaching paper- and book-crafting courses in the US and Germany for more than two decades. Her work has been featured in *Uppercase* and *500 Paper Objects*. She served as artist in residence at the Mino Paper Village in Japan and is a member of the International Association of Hand Papermakers and Paper Artists (IAPMA). For Maehrle, as a collector and finder, boxes are important components of her Archive of Wondrous Things.

www.papierzeichen.de/?lang=en

Literature & Inspiration

Diane Waldman
Joseph Cornell—Master of Dreams
Abrams, New York 2002

Exhibition catalog:
Joseph Cornell—Fernweh [Wanderlust]
Kunsthistorisches Museum Vienna, 2016

English edition
(since the German is already out of print):
Joseph Cornell—Wanderlust
Royal Academy of Arts London, 2015

Octavio Paz, Marie José Paz
Figuren und Variationen [Figures and Variations]
Insel Verlag, 2005

Literary collecting dreams:

Charles Simic
Medici Groschengrab—Die Kunst des Joseph Cornell [Medici Slot Machine—the Art of Joseph Cornell]
Carl Hanser Verlag, 1999

Fréderic Clement
Die Wunderboutique [The Boutique of Wonders]
Carl Hanser Verlag, 1997

The charm and horror of historical scientific collections:

Senckenberg Gesellschaft [Senckenberg Society]
Senckenbergs verborgene Schätze—Über das Sammeln und Forschen [Senckenberg's Hidden Treasures—on Collecting and Research]
Schweizerbart'sche Verlagsbuchhandlung [publisher's bookstore], 2015

Mat Fournier
Bauen wie die Biene, fliegen wie der Vogel [Build like the Bees, Fly like the Birds]
Haupt Verlag, 2016

The wonderful book for women who want to saw their own boxes:
Antje Rittermann
Einfach Holz [Simply Wood]
Haupt Verlag, 2015

An artistic new version:
Die Xylothek von Marion Gülzow [The Xylotheque of Marion Gülzow]
www.xylothek.de

The original:
Die Schildbachsche Holzbibliothek (1771–1799)
Naturkundemuseum im Ottoneum [The Schildbach Xylotheque Natural History Museum in the Ottoneum]
Steinweg 2, D-34117 Kassel
www.naturkundemuseum-kassel [kassel natural history museum].de/wissenschaft/sammlungen/gefaesspflanzen/schildbach/index.php [science/collections/vascular plants/schildbach]

Photo credits:
Ronald Ammann, p. 166 • Setsuko Fukushima, pp. 138–141 • Takashi Fukushima, p. 167 bottom
Marcus Kazmeier, p. 171 top • Marlis Maehrle, pp. 2–127, 129–137, 142–143, 160–163, 170 bottom, 174
Barbara Räderscheidt, pp. 144–147, 158–159, 172 top • Dagmar Reiche, p. 157 • Susanne Mölle, p. 170 top
Peter Schlack, pp. 148–150, 171 bottom. • Philline Schlick, p. 167 top • Uli Seitz–Sperling, p. 128
Uwe Sperling, p. 172 bottom • Annemarie Steiner, p. 151, 173 • Paul Warchol, p. 156 • Ulla Warchol, p. 168
Eusebius Wirdeier, p. 169 bottom • Gerhard Wöhr, pp. 152–155 • www.zwoacht.de/Michael Kretzschmar, pp. 164–165

Originally published as *Art in a Box* by Haupt Verlag © 2018 Haupt Bern
Translated from the German by Simulingua, Inc.

Library of Congress Control Number: 2019936103

Book design by Marlis Maehrle
Production Design by Jack Chappell
Edited by Ian Robertson

Type set in Prestige Elite/Trixie text/Stone Sans
ISBN: 978-0-7643-5841-8
Printed in China

Published by Schiffer Publishing, Ltd.
4880 Lower Valley Road
Atglen, PA 19310
Phone: (610) 593-1777; Fax: (610) 593-2002
E-mail: Info@schifferbooks.com
Web: www.schifferbooks.com